WEBSTER'S
NEW WORLD
DICTIONARY
OF MATHEMATICS

WEBSTER'S NEW WORLD DICTIONARY OF MATHEMATICS

by William Karush

Webster's New World
New York

First Webster's New World Printing 1989

   Webster's New World

Simon & Schuster, Inc.
One Gulf + Western Plaza
New York, NY 10023

DISTRIBUTED BY PRENTICE HALL TRADE

Manufactured in the United States of America

1 2 3 4 5 6 7 8 9 10

ISBN 0-13-192667-5

Library of Congress Cataloging-in-Publication Data

Karush, William.
     Webster's new world dictionary of mathematics / by William Karush
 : Oscar Tarcov, general editor.
          p.   cm.
     Rev. ed. of: The crescent dictionary of mathematics. 1962
     Bibliography: p.
     ISBN 0-13-192667-5
     1. Mathematics--Dictionaries.   I. Tarcov, Oscar.   II. Karush,
William.   Crescent dictionary of mathmetics.   III.   Title.
QA5.K27 1989
510' .3--dc20   89-5759
                                                                          CIP

CONTENTS

INTRODUCTION TO REVISED EDITION

This book, titled *Webster's New World Dictionary of Mathematics,* is a new version of the *Crescent Dictionary of Mathematics,* and presents an up-to-date, all-inclusive reference tool for the general reader who is not a specialist in mathematics and for the student and teacher of high school and college mathematics. A number of changes have been made in the original version.

Important mathematical advances have occurred since the original publication, and those of interest to the general reader have been incorporated. Among these are the solution of the four-color problem and the resolution of the continuum hypothesis. Another modernization involves the updating of terms and definitions related to the field of computers, where growth and change have been so extensive.

The list of outside references has been updated and considerably extended. Many excellent books have been added, especially books on biographies of mathematicians, general mathematics, and history of mathematics. References in these categories appear under the dictionary entry *Mathematics*, with subheadings *biography*, *general*, *history*. References to a biography also appear under the dictionary entry where the name of the mathematician concerned occurs in the discussion of the entry.

The intended audience for the dictionary remains unchanged—a spectrum covering the general reader with a curiosity about mathematics, the non-specialist in mathematics whose professional interests touch upon mathematics, and the students and teachers of high school and college mathematics. The over 1400 entries of the dictionary have been selected and treated with these users in mind, and the books in the list of outside references have been chosen for being specifically directed toward this audience. An aim of the dictionary continues to be to attempt to engage the user in a further exploration of a mathematical idea beyond an initial inquiry as to the definition of a term. This is done by discussing the term to a certain depth in the dictionary proper, by cross-referencing to other terms in the dictionary, and by giving reference to outside readings. It is hoped that this will help lead the user of the dictionary toward an enrichment of the user's mathematical understanding.

William Karush

INTRODUCTION

The subject matter of the 1422 entries in this dictionary covers two general categories. First, a detailed treatment is provided of the following standard high school and college mathematics material: arithmetic; elementary, intermediate, and college algebra; plane and solid geometry; plane and spherical trigonometry; plane and solid analytic geometry; differential and integral calculus. Second, a wide selection of items is provided from more advanced mathematics, including the following fields: logic and fundamental concepts; theory of equations, theory of numbers, and modern higher algebra; advanced calculus; geometry and topology; probability and statistics; recent areas such as computer sciences, information theory, operations research, and so on.

The explanations of entries range from brief definitions of a few lines to expository discussions of various lengths. Several goals motivated the treatment. The dictionary was to satisfy the immediate technical needs of the user. Mathematics was to be presented as a unified, ever-growing, and stimulating body of knowledge. The reader who was a nonspecialist in mathematics was to be served in advanced mathematics and in new fields (such as computer sciences) that were significant for the future. In terms of its broader objectives, the present book may be viewed as an outline or compendium of mathematical ideas correlated with a large collection of specialized items. There are concern and activity in the educational field with regard to revitalizing and modernizing scientific training and creating a better understanding of science; it is hoped that this volume will contribute to these aims in mathematics.

The dictionary is intended for several audiences. First, it is designed to meet the educational needs of the participants in high school and college mathematics—the student and the teacher. It serves as a convenient summary of the concepts, formulas, and techniques studied in courses; beyond this, it may be used as an avenue for the student to step into fresh realms of mathematical ideas. The dictionary is also intended for many professional workers in behavioral and social sciences, biological and physical sciences, and engineering; it aims to satisfy both their needs in techniques of mathematics as well as their interest in advanced concepts and recent developments. Finally, it should serve the general reader with an intellectual interest in mathematics.

Several practices were adopted to make the dictionary as useful as possible for the intended class of readers. Specific formulas are given for solving problems, and examples and diagrams are called upon frequently for clarification. Attention is confined largely to terms and definitions that are in common use and that are pertinent for the reader. An attempt is made to reduce to a minimum the need to use cross references to find a given term. Related information is often introduced to stimulate interest; this, for example, may be of a historical nature or it may connect the given term to other terms. With regard to the question of technical rigor, the following view was adopted: in the case of an entry for which a formal definition meeting the requirements of the professional mathematician was judged as being too technical, a balance was attempted between mathematical precision and an informal description meaningful to the reader; when it seemed helpful, both an informal and a formal description were given.

Various reference works were helpful in the preparation of this dictionary. Especially useful were the following two: (1) *The Development of Mathematics,* by Eric T. Bell, 2nd edition, McGraw-Hill, New York, 1945; (2) *Mathematics Dictionary,* edited by Glenn James and Robert C. James, 2nd edition, D. Van Nostrand Co., Princeton, New Jersey, 1959.

The author is happy to express his gratitude to his generous colleagues, Dr. Richard E. Bellman and Dr. Mario L. Juncosa, for their comments and advice in the writing of this book. He also wishes to thank Professor H. S. MacDonald Coxeter for his suggestions on a number of entries, and Professor Kenneth O. May for his general remarks on an initial version of the manuscript. His gratitude is extended to Mr. Oscar Tarcov, General Editor of the Crescent Dictionaries, and Miss Lee Deadrick of The Macmillan Company for the opportunity to write one of the dictionaries in this series, and for their solicitous cooperation in many matters connected with the publication of this book. Thanks are also expressed to the many others who in their individual ways helped to create whatever qualities this work may possess.

William Karush

A GUIDE TO THE USE
OF THE DICTIONARY

All entries have been entered in strict alphabetical order.

Boldface type has been used throughout for all words and terms for which definitions are included. The cross references are planned to facilitate fuller exploration of a subject beyond an initial, specific question. Therefore, in addition to main entries, all cross references appear in boldface; a cross reference may either be designated as such, or it may occur as a word or phrase in a definition.

Italics have been used to emphasize certain words and phrases within the body of the definition.

Synonyms are indicated by the abbreviation (syn.)

References for further reading are indicated at the end of certain entries by the abbreviation (Ref.) together with the appropriate number as listed in the List of References beginning on page 293.

WEBSTER'S
NEW WORLD
DICTIONARY
OF MATHEMATICS

Abacus (Syn.: Counting Board) A device of ancient origin used for recording numbers and calculating. It has had several forms during its history, but the most familiar one is a frame with several parallel rods and individual counters that are free to slide along the rods. One rod is for the units place, the next for the tens place, and so on; in carrying out a calculation the counters are moved back and forth on the rods. The abacus was widely used in Europe by merchants up to the latter half of the thirteenth century, when it began to yield to the superior arithmetic of the Hindu-Arab decimal number system. Ref. [29, 42, 48].

Abscissa The first, or horizontal coordinate, x, of a pair (x, y) of **Cartesian coordinates in the plane**. The second, y, is the *ordinate*.

Absolute Convergence An infinite series $a_1 + a_2 + a_3 + \cdots$ *converges absolutely* in case the series

$$|a_1| + |a_2| + |a_3| + \cdots$$

of absolute values converges. Absolute convergence implies (ordinary) convergence of the given series. An example of an absolutely convergent series is:

$$1 - \tfrac{1}{2} + (\tfrac{1}{2})^2 - (\tfrac{1}{2})^3 + \cdots$$

(the series of absolute values, $1 + \tfrac{1}{2} + (\tfrac{1}{2})^2 + (\tfrac{1}{2})^3 + \cdots$, is a convergent geometric series). See **Conditional convergence**.

Absolute Inequality See **Unconditional inequality** (syn.).

Absolute Maximum (Minimum) Of a function, the largest (smallest) value. See **Function of real variable**.

Absolute Number See **Constant** (syn.).

Absolute Value (Syn.: Numerical value) The absolute value of a number, geometrically, is its distance from the zero point on an ordinary number scale (regardless of direction). For example, the absolute value of 4 is 4, of -5 is 5, and of 0 is 0. The

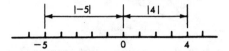

absolute value of a is denoted by $|a|$; for example,

$$|4| = 4, \; |-5| = 5, \; |0| = 0.$$

See **Linear coordinates**.

A formal definition of $|a|$ is: if a is positive or zero, then $|a| = a$; if a is negative, then $|a| = -a$. For example, $|-4| = -(-4)$, or 4.

The following properties of absolute value are important:

(1) $|a| \geq 0$;
(2) $|a \cdot b| = |a| \cdot |b|$;
(3) $|a + b| \leq |a| + |b|$.

As an example, verifying these, let $a = -2$ and $b = 7$; by (2), $|-14| = |-2| \cdot |7|$, or $14 = 2 \cdot 7$; by (3), $|(-2) + 7| \leq |-2| + |7|$, or $5 \leq 2 + 7$.

Absolute Value of Complex Number (Syn.: Magnitude; Modulus) For a **complex number** $a + bi$, the absolute value is the (real) number $\sqrt{a^2 + b^2}$; it is the distance of the complex number from the origin, when the complex number is represented as the point with rectangular coordinates (a, b). For example, the absolute value of $-2 + 3i$ equals $\sqrt{4 + 9}$, or $\sqrt{13}$. The absolute value is denoted by $|a + bi|$. The following properties are important:

(1) $|a + bi| \geq 0$;
(2) $|(a + bi)(c + di)|$
$\quad = |a + bi| \cdot |c + di|$;
(3) $|(a + bi) + (c + di)|$
$\quad \leq |a + bi| + |c + di|$

1

(this last expresses the "triangle inequality," namely, that the length of

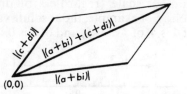

a side of a triangle is not greater than the sum of the lengths of the other two sides).

Absolute Value of Vector   The length of a **vector V**; it is often denoted by $|\mathbf{V}|$.

Abstract Mathematics   Mathematics as knowledge apart from its meaning in terms of physical or concrete experience. Such experience may guide the development of a mathematical theory, and it may provide a helpful way to think about mathematical concepts; however, the conclusions of an abstract theory are expressed and deduced by logical means which are independent of "real" or "specific" interpretation. For example, it may be helpful to regard a *number* as a physical quantity, but the theory of real numbers can be developed as a deductive theory which requires no reference to this, or any other, specific meaning.   See **Axiomatics**, **Deductive theory**, **Mathematical system**, **Mathematics**.   Ref. [148].

Abstract Space   In general, a formal mathematical system of a geometric-like nature. It is a **deductive theory** whose undefined terms and axioms, typically, "abstract" the features common to several more specific, or more familiar, systems; the latter serve as *models* of the abstract system.   See **Hilbert space**, **Metric space**, **Vector space**.   Ref. [41].

Abundant Number (Syn.: Redundant number)   See **Perfect number**.

Acceleration   The rate of change of **velocity** with respect to time t. If the motion of a particle in the plane is given by $x = x(t), y = y(t)$, then the second derivatives $(d^2x)/(dt^2)$, $(d^2y)/(dt^2)$ give the components a_x, a_y of the acceleration along the x-axis and y-axis, respectively. The absolute magnitude of the acceleration is $\sqrt{a_x{}^2 + a_y{}^2}$; this equals the second derivative $(d^2s)/(dt^2)$ (where $s(t)$ is distance along the curve from a fixed point), except possibly for sign.

Accuracy   Of an **approximate number**, a numerical measure of its closeness to the true value for which it stands. For example, 3.1416 is commonly used as an approximate value of π; it is said to be *accurate*, or correct, to four decimal places, meaning that the true value of π lies between 3.14155 and 3.14165. A decimal approximation, when all its digits are *significant*, is correct to the last decimal place shown, and the **error** is then no more than $\frac{1}{2}$ the unit of the last place.

Accuracy of Table   The accuracy of the numerical entries in a table, such as a table of common logarithms or of the values of a trigonometric function. Nearly all entries in such tables are approximate, because the true functional values are typically unending decimals.   See **Table of function**.

Acute Angle   An **angle** of numerical measure less than 90 degrees.

Acute Triangle   A **triangle** with each of its angles an acute angle.

Addend   Any one of the individual constants of an expressed sum of constants. For example, in $2 + 3 + 5$, the addends are 2, 3, and 5.

Addition   Addition of numbers is one of the fundamental operations of arithmetic. The result of combining two numbers a and b by addition is the *sum* of the numbers, and is denoted by $a + b$ (the symbol "$+$" was introduced about 1500). The sum of two whole numbers, say 3 and 5, is interpreted as the number of objects in the collection obtained by putting together a collection of 3 objects and a collection of 5 other objects. As the concept of number is extended to negative numbers, rational numbers (fractions), and, finally, the full set of real numbers, the meaning of addition is similarly extended. The rules of arithmetic provide ways of carrying out addition of numbers in various forms. **Algebraic addition**, for example, shows how to add signed numbers.   See **Common denominator**, **Transfinite number**.

Addition of numbers is a binary operation—it combines two things (numbers), to produce a single thing. This operation has certain basic properties. One is the existence of the particular number 0 which leaves any number a unchanged under addition; that is, $a + 0 = a$ (0 is called the "identity element" of addition). Another property is that addition is associative; that is $(a + b) + c = a + (b + c)$. Also, addition is commutative; that is, $a + b = b + a$. The associative and commutative properties account, for example, for the fact that a sum of any number of terms can be checked by adding in the reverse order. Such general properties and others that account for certain aspects of the behavior of numbers, are treated in higher algebra in the study of the **field**.

Addition Formulas (trigonometry) Formulas which express a trigonometric function of the sum (or difference) of two angles in terms of the functions of the individual angles.

The most commonly used are the following:

$$\sin(A + B) = \sin A \cos B + \cos A \sin B$$
$$\sin(A - B) = \sin A \cos B - \cos A \sin B$$
$$\cos(A + B) = \cos A \cos B - \cos A \sin B$$
$$\cos(A - B) = \cos A \cos B + \sin A \sin B$$
$$\tan(A + B) = \frac{\tan A + \tan B}{1 - \tan A \tan B}$$
$$\tan(A - B) = \frac{\tan A - \tan B}{1 + \tan A \tan B}.$$

Addition of Algebraic Expressions
In adding algebraic expressions, *similar terms* can be combined by adding their coefficients; for example $(3x^2 - 2xy + 3) + (y^2 + 3xy - 5)$ can be reduced to $3x^2 + xy + y^2 - 2$ by this means.   See **Common denominator** for addition of algebraic fractions.

Addition of Angles   The sum $A + B$ of two directed angles (rotations) A and B is an **angle** constructed as the rotation A followed by the rotation B (positive angles being counterclockwise and negative angles, clockwise). The measure of $A + B$ is the sum of the measures of A and B. For example, the sum of a 60° angle and

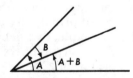

a 30° angle is a 90° angle; the sum of a 60° angle and a $-30°$ angle is a 30° angle.

Addition of Complex Numbers   See **Complex number**.

Addition of Sets   See **Union of sets**.

Addition of Vectors   (Syn.: Composition of vectors)   When vectors $\mathbf{V}_1$, $\mathbf{V}_2$ are represented as directed line segments, their sum, or resultant,

3

$\mathbf{V}_1 + \mathbf{V}_2$ is the directed diagonal of the parallelogram whose adjacent sides are $\mathbf{V}_1$ and $\mathbf{V}_2$ (this is the parallelogram law). When plane vectors $\mathbf{V}_1$ and $\mathbf{V}_2$ are represented by number pairs, as (x_1, y_1), (x_2, y_2), their sum is the vector $(x_1 + x_2, y_1 + y_2)$, obtained by adding like coordinates; this rule applies to vectors in a space of any number of dimensions.

Adjacent Two *angles* are adjacent if they share a common vertex and a common side, but do not overlap. Two *sides* of a triangle, or polygon, are adjacent in case they share a common vertex.

Aleph-Null, $\aleph_0$ In the theory of sets, the smallest infinite **cardinal number**; it is the cardinal number of the unending sequence of whole numbers $\{1, 2, 3, 4, \ldots\}$. ($\aleph$ is the first letter of the Hebrew alphabet.)

Algebra Ordinary algebra is the study of operations and relations among numbers through the use of **variables,** or literal symbols, such as "a," "b," "x," "y," etc., instead of just constants, such as "2," "$\frac{5}{6}$," etc. The use of variables gives algebra vastly greater scope than arithmetic, which is limited principally to constants. For example, in algebra, the distributive law of numbers is expressed by the formula "$a \cdot (x + y) = ax + ay$." In arithmetic, only specific instances could be cited, such as $3(5 + 8) = 3 \cdot 5 + 3 \cdot 8, 2(1 + 6) = 2 \cdot 1 + 2 \cdot 6$; or the law might be stated as a verbal rule: "The product of a given number into a sum of two numbers is the product of the given number into the first plus its product into the second." Not only are symbolic formulas more compact than verbal rules, but also they permit manipulations for solving equations and deriving new relationships which would be extremely difficult or impossible without them.

The role of the Arabs in spreading algebra throughout Western Europe (beginning about 800 A.D.) is important in the history of the subject. However, present-day symbolism was not perfected in Europe until the sixteenth and seventeenth centuries. Algebra was eventually founded on a logical basis in the nineteenth century; here, the rules and formulas of ordinary algebra can be derived from a few initial axioms, much as the theorems of plane geometry are deduced from axioms and postulates. Many of the features of algebra follow from the axioms of the **field**.

As an elementary subject, algebra treats techniques for handling algebraic expressions, the solution of equations, and related topics. Interpreted more broadly, it is one of the major divisions of **mathematics**; it is the part which deals with "finite" processes, rather than "infinite" processes, such as are typical of the calculus. The description "higher algebra" is often applied to the advanced aspects of the subject, as distinguished from the more familiar, ordinary algebra. Examples of topics in higher algebra are *algebraic numbers, groups, fields, rings, number fields,* and the *algebra of matrices.* In a very general sense, an "algebra" is a mathematical system which expresses itself in variables and symbols for its entities, operations, and relations, and develops formal rules for the manipulation of its expressions.

Ref. [18, 81, 120].

Algebra, Boolean See **Boolean algebra.**

Algebra of Matrices The symbolic study of matrices, and operations and relations among them; it is a generalization of ordinary algebra. In this algebra a **matrix**, such as a second order matrix

$$\begin{pmatrix} a & b \\ c & d \end{pmatrix}$$

is represented by a single letter, A, B, C, etc.; addition and multiplication are denoted by $A + B$ and $A \cdot B$ (or AB) as in ordinary algebra, and expressions such as $A^2(X^2 - BX + AD)$ have meaning in terms of matrix operations. This algebra shares many of the fundamental properties of ordinary algebra; some of these are the associative laws for addition and multiplication $(A + B) + C = A + (B + C)$ and $A \cdot (B \cdot C) = (A \cdot B) \cdot C$, and the distributive law, $A \cdot (B + C) = A \cdot B + A \cdot C$. One of the striking differences is the failure of the commutative law for multiplication, that is, $A \cdot B \neq B \cdot A$ for matrices A and B in general (the commutative law of addition does hold). Such a restriction has a drastic effect on algebraic technique; for example, while xax can be replaced by $ax \cdot x$, or ax^2, in ordinary algebra, the expression XAX cannot be so modified for matrices. Another striking difference is the failure of the principle of ordinary algebra which asserts that a product can equal 0 only if at least one factor is 0; the product of two nonzero matrices can equal the zero matrix (the matrix whose entries are all zeros). Matrices make up a type of "number" system known as a **ring**.

The theory of matrices was developed in the middle of the nineteenth century by Cayley, and is a central feature of higher algebra. One of its principal uses is in geometry, where a matrix can denote a *transformation* of a space. Matrices are important in the study of vectors, and in many parts of pure and applied mathematics.

Ref. [26, 32].

Algebra of Propositions (Syn.: Propositional calculus; Sentential calculus) The part of the logic which treats propositional forms built out of the sentence connectives "and," "or," "if . . . , then . . . ," and "not"; particularly, the logical validity of such forms. For example, the proposition "The earth is round or the earth is not round" is recognized as being true (logically valid), not because of any property of the earth but because of the form of the sentence; this form is symbolized "P or (not P)," and any proposition with this sentence structure is true. The connectives define the *conjunction*, "P and Q," the *disjunction*, "P or Q," the *conditional*, "If P, then Q," and the *denial* "not P." Out of these, more complicated forms can be put together; examples are "(P and Q) or (not Q)," "If (P or R), then Q." The law of excluded middle asserts the (logical) validity of "P or (not P)" (illustrated in the example above); the law of contradiction asserts the validity of "not [P and (not P)]" (that is, that a proposition and its denial are not both true). Propositions are *logically equivalent* in case they say the same thing in different propositional forms. An example is given by the law of double negation, which asserts that "not (not P)" is (logically) equivalent to "P." The law of contraposition asserts that the form "If P, then Q" and the form "If (not Q), then (not P)" are equivalent. For exam-

5

ple, the sentence "If the lot is small, then the house is small" is equivalent to "If the house is not small, then the lot is not small."

In the algebra of propositions, symbols are introduced for sentence connectives: "$P \wedge Q$" is often used for "P and Q," "$P \vee Q$" for "P or Q," "$P \rightarrow Q$" for "if P, then Q," and "$\sim P$" for "not P." In this notation, the sentence "It is not the case that all is lost and the gold is not safe" takes the form "$\sim(P \wedge (\sim Q))$." With variables "P," "Q," etc., standing for propositions, and symbols "$\wedge$," "$\vee$," etc., for connectives, the study of propositional forms assumes a highly algebraic aspect; the algebra of propositions, which evolved in the second half of the nineteenth century, is a type of mathematical system called a **Boolean algebra**.

Ref. [75, 89, 115].

Algebra of Sets (Syn.: Algebra of classes; Calculus of classes) A part of logic (or mathematics) that treats classes, or **sets**, of things, and operations and relations among these sets; here, symbols (variables) such as "A," "B," etc., are used to stand for sets, and expressions are formed out of these and certain signs for operations and relations (much as expressions are formed with variables denoting numbers in ordinary algebra). The *universe*, or universal set, is understood as the set of all individual things, and the *null*, or empty set, as the set with no individuals; these are sometimes denoted by 1 and 0, respectively. For example, in a particular use, all integers might be taken as the universe, and a set would mean any collection of integers; the null set might arise as the set of integers whose squares are negative. In plane geometry, all the points in the plane might be regarded as the universe, and a set would be any collection of points; the null set can arise as the set of points of intersection of a circle and a line that does not meet it. Various *relations* among sets arise. That A and B are *equal*, written "$A = B$," means that A and B are the same sets (have exactly the same members); for example, the set of equilateral triangles equals the set of equiangular triangles. That set A is *included in* set B, or A is a subset of B, written "$A \subset B$," means that every member of A is a member of B; for example, the set of powers of 3 is a subset of the set of odd numbers. That two sets *overlap* means that they have at least one member in common; that they are *disjoint*

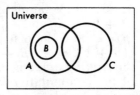

means that they have no members in common. These relations can be represented geometrically, as in the figure; here the universe is represented by the interior of the rectangle and the sets A, B, C by the interiors of the circles. In the figure, B is included in A, A and C overlap, and B and C are disjoint; such geometric representations are called *Venn diagrams*. Various general statements hold for these relations; among these are the following. The null set is a subset of every set, while every set is a subset of the universe. The relation of inclusion between sets is a transitive relation; that is if $A \subset B$ and $B \subset C$, then $A \subset C$. Equality and inclusion are connected by the fact that $A = B$ just in case $A \subset B$ and $B \subset A$.

Operations on sets include union and intersection (see **Property**). The *union,* or *sum,* of *A* and *B* is the smallest set containing both; it is denoted by "$A \cup B$." Its members are the members of *A* taken together with the members of *B*; for example, the union of {1, 3, 5} and {2, 3, 5, 7} is {1, 2, 3, 5, 7,}. The *intersection,* or *product,* of *A* and *B* is the largest set common to both; it is denoted by "$A \cap B$". Its members are those common to both sets (the intersection of the given sets in the last example is {3, 5}). Finally, the *complement* of *A,* denoted by *A'*, is the set consisting of all elements of the universe which are not in *A*; for example, the com-

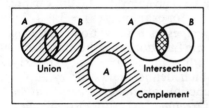

plement of the set of even whole numbers in the universe of all whole numbers is the set of odd whole numbers. Many general statements hold involving operations on sets. The union of any set *A* with the null set is *A*; the union of *A* with the universe is the universe. The intersection of *A* with the null set is the null set, and with the universe is *A* itself. The complement of the universe (null set) is the null set (universe). Union and intersection are commutative and associative; in this respect they are analogous to addition and multiplication in ordinary algebra. However, other properties are strikingly different; for example, the equations $A \cup A = A$ and $A \cap A = A$ hold for all sets *A*; their analogs in arithmetic, $x + x = x$, and $x \cdot x = x$, do not hold for all numbers *x*. *De Morgan's laws* are the following equalities, mixing the three operations (*A*

$\cap$ *B*)' = *A'* $\cup$ *B'* (the complement of an intersection is the union of the complements), and (*A* $\cup$ *B*)' = *A'* $\cap$ *B'*. Operations on sets can be connected with relations between sets. Two sets are disjoint in case their intersection is the null set. If one set is a subset of the other, then the complement of the second is a subset of the complement of the first; that is, if $A \subset B$, then $B' \subset A'$.

The algebra of sets was originated by Boole in the middle of the nineteenth century; it is a type of mathematical system known as a **Boolean algebra**.

Ref. [75, 89, 95].

Algebra of Vectors   The symbolic study of certain operations and relations among vectors.   See **Vector, Vector space**.

Algebraic   Referring to concepts or methods of algebra. Sometimes used in connection with signed numbers, in contrast to unsigned numbers, as in "algebraic addition," "algebraic angle," or "algebraic multiplication."

Algebraic Addition   In arithmetic, the addition of signed numbers, that is, of positive and negative numbers. Such addition can be reduced to the addition (or subtraction) of positive numbers by the following law of signs:

> **(1)** $(-a) + (-b) = -(a + b)$;
> **(2)** $a + (-b) = a - b$;
> **(3)** $a + (-b) = -(b - a)$.

Rule **(1)** implies that the sum of two negative numbers is the sum of the numerical values with the minus sign prefixed; for example,

$$(-3) + (-8) = -(3 + 8), \text{ or } -11.$$

Rules **(2)** and **(3)** imply that the sum of a positive and a negative number is obtained by subtracting the smaller

7

numerical value from the larger numerical value, and prefixing the sign of the number with the larger numerical value; e.g., $5 + (-2) = 5 - 2$, or 3, and $2 + (-5) = -(5 - 2)$, or -3. A law of signs is also available for **subtraction**.

Algebraic Equation An equation with each side being an algebraic expression. For example, $3 - \sqrt{x} = 5x^2 + y$, is an algebraic equation; the equation $3 - \sin x = 5x^2 + y$, is not algebraic because the term $\sin x$ is not (it is a transcendental equation).

Algebraic Expression Any expression in variables and constants which designates numbers and involves only the application of algebraic operations; these are the expressions encountered in ordinary algebra. Special types of algebraic expressions are given particular names. A *monomial* involves only multiplication between variables and constants, such as $3xy$ and $-5ax^2$; monomials, which differ only in their numerical factors, such as $3ax$ and $7ax$, are *similar terms,* or *like terms* (a monomial is sometimes called a "term"). A *binomial* is a sum of two monomials (terms), as in $2x + ay^2$; a *trinomial* is a sum of three monomials. A *multinomial* or *polynomial* (or a *rational integral expression*) is a sum of any number of monomials; for example, $ax^2 - \frac{1}{2}xy + 3y - 5y^2z$ is a rational integral expression whose terms are ax^2, $-\frac{1}{2}xy$, $3y$, and $-5y^2z$. A *rational expression* is a quotient of multinomials, or an algebraic expression which can be transformed to such a quotient. This type of expression may involve any algebraic operation on the variables but root extraction; for example, $2 + [x/(x + 1)]$ is a rational expression [it can be transformed to $(3x + 2)/(x + 1)$].

An *irrational expression* is one which is not rational; it involves root extraction of an expression containing a variable, as in $\sqrt{2x + 1} - 5y$.

The variables of an algebraic expression are sometimes singled out, as in the terminology "a rational expression in x," or "an algebraic expression in x and y." For example, $x\sqrt{y} - 2x^2$ is a polynomial in x but not in y; it is an algebraic expression in either variable or both. See **Transcendental**.

Algebraic Function An *explicit algebraic function* (or, simply, *algebraic function*) is a function whose value is given by an algebraic expression; for example, $f(x) = 3x^2 + 2\sqrt{x}$ specifies such a function. These algebraic functions may be classified according to the algebraic expressions which define them; for example, a function is *rational integral, rational,* or *irrational* according to whether the expression is of the same type.

In advanced mathematics, an algebraic function is taken to mean a correspondence from values of x to values of y as determined by a polynomial equation $P(x, y) = 0$; an example is

$$2xy^3 + x^2y - 3xy + 5x^3 + 7 = 0.$$

This is sometimes called an *implicit function*, to distinguish it from the first type. The theory of algebraic functions is an extensive one in advanced mathematics.

Algebraic Identity An **identity** which is an algebraic equation.

Algebraic Multiplication In arithmetic, the multiplication of signed numbers, that is, of positive and negative numbers. Such multiplication can be reduced to multiplication of positive numbers by use of the following *law of signs:*

(1) $(-a) \cdot (-b) = a \cdot b$;
(2) $(-a) \cdot b = -(a \cdot b)$.

These provide the rule that like signs give "plus," and unlike signs give "minus"; e.g., $5 \cdot (-3) = -(5 \cdot 3)$, or -15, and $(-4) \cdot (-\frac{3}{5}) = 4 \cdot (\frac{3}{5})$, or $\frac{12}{5}$. A similar law of signs is also available for **division**.

Algebraic Number   A real number (or complex number) which is a solution of some polynomial equation whose coefficients are rational numbers; it is an *algebraic integer* if the coefficients are ordinary integers and the leading coefficient is one. The theory of algebraic numbers is an important part of higher algebra.   See **Integer**, **Number field**.   Ref. [28].

Algebraic Operations   In ordinary algebra, the operations of addition, subtraction, multiplication, division, root extraction, and raising to an integral or fractional power. The nonalgebraic, or *transcendental*, operation is illustrated by the logarithm; the definition of the logarithm rests upon the limit process of the calculus.

Algorithm   Usually, an explicit method of computation which proceeds in a step-by-step manner, repeating an underlying process. One example is the method of square root calculation taught in school; another is the familiar procedure of long division. Sometimes "algorithm" is used for any rule of calculation or explicit method of solution.   See **Euclidean algorithm**.

Alternate Angles of Transversal   See **Transversal**.

Alternating Series   An infinite series whose successive terms are alternately positive and negative. If the terms are decreasing in numerical value and have the limit 0, then the series is necessarily convergent; an example is $1 - \frac{1}{2} + \frac{1}{3} - \frac{1}{4} + \cdots$, with n^{th} term $(-1)^{n-1}/n$.

Alternation   In *logic,* the same as **disjunction**; in *proportions,* the deduction of $a/c = b/d$ from $a/b = c/d$.

Altitude   In geometry, generally, a line segment (or its length) which measures the height of a figure.   See particular figures such as **Cone**, **Triangle**, etc.

Ambiguous Case   In *plane trigonometry,* the case of the **solution of the triangle in the plane** where the given data lead to two solutions. It occurs when two sides and the angle opposite one of them are given, as sides a, b, and angle A, in the figure;

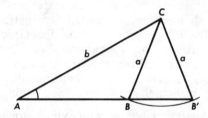

each of the triangles ABC, $AB'C$ satisfies the given conditions. In *spherical trigonometry,* the ambigious case in the **solution of the oblique spherical triangle** occurs when two sides and an angle opposite one of them are given, or when two angles and the side opposite one of them are given (this latter case is peculiar to the spherical triangle).

Amplitude of Complex Number (Syn.: Argument; Phase)   The angle of rotation about the origin of the positive x-axis into the point with rectangular coordinates (a, b), representing the complex number $a + bi$.

Amplitude of Periodic Function   See **Periodic function**.

9

Amplitude of Polar Coordinates   The angle θ in the pair (r, θ) of **polar coordinates in the plane**.

Analog Computer   See **Computer**.

Analysis   One of the major branches of mathematics, which sprang out of the development of the calculus in the seventeenth century; it makes use of the notions of limit and continuity and various extensions of these concepts. Examples of parts of analysis are the *calculus of variations, functions of a real variable, functions of a complex variable, power series,* and *trigonometric series.*

Analytic   Generally speaking, referring to algebraic or arithmetic techniques, in contrast to geometric methods, which deal directly with geometric concepts; the latter methods are sometimes called "synthetic." Euclid's geometry, and ancient Greek mathematics in general, was synthetic in nature; modern mathematics, born in the seventeenth century, is principally analytic.   See **Proof**.

Analytic Geometry   (Syn.: Coordinate geometry)   The algebraic study of geometry by use of coordinate systems. A coordinate system introduces a connection between the fundamental element of geometry, the point, and the fundamental element of algebra, the number; this permits the application of algebraic methods to geometry. For example, in plane geometry, a circle is the set of points at a fixed distance (the radius) from a fixed point (the center); in analytic geometry, a circle is represented by an equation $(x - h)^2 + (y - k)^2 = r^2$, where (h, k) is the center and r is the radius. *Plane analytic geometry* includes a systematic study of the conics; *solid analytic geometry* includes such a study of the quadric surfaces.

Algebraic methods in geometry have proved so effective that they have practically eliminated purely geometric, or synthetic, methods. Major credit for the invention of analytic geometry in the first half of the seventeenth century is given to Descartes; its introduction and the invention of the calculus later in that century marked the beginning of modern mathematics.

Ref. [2, 89, 148].

Analytic Proof   See **Proof**.

Anchor Ring   See **Torus** (Syn.).

Angle   In plane geometry, the *geometric angle* (or, simply, *angle*) is the basic figure made up of two half-lines, or rays, with a common end point; the half-lines are the *sides* of the angle and the common point is the *vertex* of the angle. The symbol " $\angle$ " is used for "angle"; for example, $\angle AOB$ designates the angle with vertex O

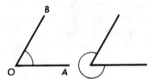

and sides OA and OB. An angle divides the plane into two separate portions; the complete specification of an angle calls for designating one of these as the *interior* of the angle by, say, a small arc about the vertex. Thus, two sides and a vertex determine two possible angles, one of which may be a reflex angle; when the interior is not indicated, the smaller angle is usually meant. Two angles are *congruent* in case one can be brought into coincidence with the other by a rigid motion; this expresses the idea that the angles are the same except for location. Congruent angles are often called "equal angles" in elementary geometry (this is not strictly in accord with the logical use of "equal," which means "the same in every respect"). The term "angle" is also used for the figure consisting of two line segments with a common end point; such a figure determines an angle in the preceding sense.

A common unit of *measure* for plane angles is the *degree of angle*, $\frac{1}{360}$ part of a complete circle; another measure, used in trigonometry, is the *radian*. Angles with the same measure are congruent. Angles can be classified according to their measures. A *right* angle is one of 90°, a *straight*, or *flat*, angle is one of 180°; in a right angle the sides are perpendicular, in

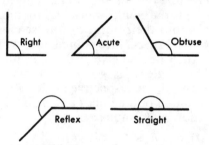

Right   Acute   Obtuse

Reflex   Straight

a straight angle they form one complete line. A *perigon* is an angle of 360° and a *zero* angle is one of 0°; in both the perigon and the zero angle the sides coincide, but in the first case the interior of the angle is the whole plane (except for the side), and in the second case the interior is entirely collapsed. An *acute* angle is one between 0° and 90°, an *obtuse* angle is one between 90° and 180°, and a *reflex* angle is one between 180° and 360°. An *oblique* angle is one which is not a multiple of 90° (the oblique angle is sometimes reserved for just the acute and obtuse angle; also, the obtuse angle is sometimes used for any angle greater than 90°). Relations between two angles can

also be expressed in terms of their measures. Two angles are *complementary* if the sum of their degree measure is 90°; either is called the "complement" of the other. Two angles are *supplementary* if the sum is 180°; either is called the "supplement" of the other. Two angles are *explementary,* or *conjugate,* if the sum is 360°; either is called the "explement" or "conjugate" of the other.

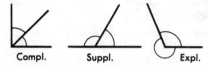

Compl.   Suppl.   Expl.

The *directed* (or *algebraic*, or *general*) *angle* is used in trigonometry. In this case, an angle represents a rotation of an *initial side* into a *terminal side* about their common initial point, the vertex; the rotation can be indicated by a directed arc, as shown.

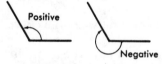

Positive   Negative

If the rotation is counterclockwise, the angle is *positive;* if clockwise, the angle is *negative* (the rotation may include any number of complete revolutions). The measure of a directed angle is a signed number giving both the direction and amount of the rotation; for example, $-90°$ is a clockwise rotation through one-quarter of a revolution, 375° is a counterclockwise rotation of one revolution followed by a 15° rotation. *Co-terminal* angles are angles with the same initial and terminal sides, for example, 120° and $-240°$; such angles differ by a multiple of 360°. When rectangular coordinates are used in the plane, the angle is in *standard position* if the positive x-axis is its initial side; the *quadrant of the angle* is then the quadrant in which the terminal side falls (for example, 130° is in the second quadrant, and −130° is in the third). When the terminal side coincides with an axis, the angle is a *quadrantal* angle, that is, a multiple of 90°.

For angles in space, see **Dihedral angle, Polyhedral angle, Solid angle, Spherical angle**.

Angle between Curves The angle between the tangent lines to the curves at a point of intersection of the curves. In the figure, angle *APB*

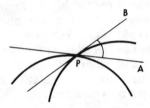

is the angle between the curves at *P*. Two curves are *perpendicular,* or *orthogonal,* in case the angle between them is a right angle.

Angle between Line and Plane The angle between the line and its projection in the plane. More specifically, let line *l* intersect plane *p* in the point *O*; from a point *A* on *l*, drop a

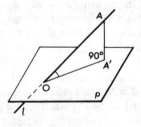

perpendicular to the plane, meeting it in *A'*; then the angle *AOA'* is the angle between *l* and *p*. If *l* does not

intersect *p*, or lies on *p*, the angle is the zero angle.

Angle between Lines In the *plane*, the smaller of the angles formed by two intersecting lines, as shown in the first figure; if the lines are parallel,

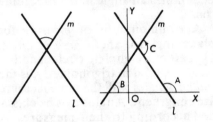

the angle is the zero angle. In plane analytic geometry, the angle from one line *l* to another *m* (second figure) is the counterclockwise rotation *C* about their point of intersection which brings *l* into coincidence with *m* (its value is between 0° and 180°). The angle *C* is given in terms of *A* and *B*, the respective angles of inclination of the lines *l* and *m*, by the following formulas:

(1) $C = B − A$, if B is greater than A;
(2) $C = 180° + B − A$, if B is less than A.

In terms of the slopes a and b of l and m, C is given by the formula

$$\tan C = (b − a)/(1 + ab).$$

For two lines, l_1, l_2, in *space*, the angle θ between them is the angle between two intersecting lines respectively parallel to them; it is given by the formula

$$\cos \theta = \cos \alpha_1 \cos \alpha_2 + \cos \beta_1 \cos \beta_2 + \cos \gamma_1 \cos \gamma_2,$$

in terms of the direction angles α_1, β_1, γ_1 and α_2, β_2, γ_2 of the lines.

Angle of Depression or Elevation The angle between the horizontal *OA* and the line of sight *OP* from *O* to *P*. It is an angle of depression if the observed point *P* is below *OA*;

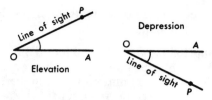

Elevation — Depression

it is an angle of elevation if P is above OA.

Angle of Inclination See **Inclination of line**.

Angles of Transversal See **Transversal**.

Annulus The plane region bounded by two concentric circles. Its area is $\pi(R^2 - r^2)$, the difference between

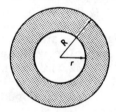

the area of the larger circle and that of the smaller circle.

Antecedent In *logic,* the proposition P in the **conditional** "If P, then Q"; Q is the consequent. In *algebra,* the numerator in a ratio, a/b, the denominator being the consequent; the algebraic usage is rare.

Antiderivative See **Indefinite integral** (syn.).

Antilogarithm (Syn.: Inverse logarithm) The inverse function of the logarithm; the antilogarithm of a number x is the number whose logarithm is x (designated by antilog x). For example, antilog $2 = 100$, since $\log 100 = 2$. See **Computation with logarithms, Logarithm**.

Antitrigonometric Functions See **Inverse trigonometric functions** (syn.).

Apex The highest point of a figure

relative to a base line or plane; for example, the apex of a cone is its vertex (highest relative to the base of the cone).

Apothem (Syn.: Short radius) The perpendicular line segment (or its length) from the center of a **regular polygon** to a side.

Approximate Number (Syn.: Approximation) A number which serves as an estimate of a desired number. Approximate numbers occur in measurement, where precision is limited, and in estimates of unending decimals by a finite number of decimal places. The notion of *significant digit* is used in describing the relationship between a true value and an approximate number N for it expressed in decimal form. The *most significant digit* of N is its first non-zero digit (reading left to right); its decimal place is the most significant decimal place of N. For example, in 3.068, the most significant digit is 3 and the most significant place is the unit's place; in .00270, the most significant digit is 2 and the most significant place is the thousandth's place. To specify a particular digit of N as its *least significant digit* (with corresponding least significant decimal place) is to state the following: the distance of the true value b from N is no more than one-half the unit of that place (dropping the digits of N following that place). For example, the statement "the third digit 6, of 3.068 is its least significant digit" means it is no better than 3.06 as an approximation, and that the true value lies between 3.055 and 3.065. Altogether, the significant digits of N are its most and least significant digits and all digits between; in the last example, 3.068, these are three digits, 3, 0, and 6.

Approximation

In numerical computation, the convention is generally accepted that when N contains one or more digits after the decimal point, then the last digit is to be understood as the least significant digit, when nothing is stated to the contrary. For example, 3.068, with no qualification, would contain four significant digits, with 8 as least significant; .00270 would contain three significant digits, with the last 0 as least significant; in the first case, the true value is between 3.0675 and 3.0685, and in the second, between .002695 and .002705. This convention is followed in tables of functions, for instance. When N contains no decimal point (a whole number), and terminates in one or more zeros, then the least significant digit needs to be specified. For example, in 5,800 it needs to be stated whether there are two, three, or four significant digits; in the first case, the true value would be between 5,750 and 5,850, and in the third, between 5,799.5 and 5,800.5. Notice that this ambiguity does not arise for terminal zeros when N is not a whole number, according to the above convention; for example, 20.00 is understood to have four significant digits.

Most numerical computations are performed with approximate numbers; when a series of operations are carried out retaining a fixed number of places after each operation, significant digits, and accuracy, are generally lost. Dealing with this matter is part of the art of computation. The problem is considered in the subject of "numerical analysis"; this subject has had a great stimulus through the rise of the electronic digital computer, which performs thousands of operations in less than a second and where accumulated loss of accuracy might make a final result useless.

14

See **Error, Precision, Rounding off.** Ref. [80, 89].

Approximation   As applied to numbers, an **approximate number** or a method for obtaining such a number. The numbers in a sequence of approximate numbers a_1, a_2, a_3, $\ldots$, which approach a desired value as a

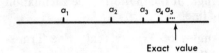

Exact value

limit, are *successive approximations*. A procedure for generating successive approximations is a *method of successive approximations*. For example, the common procedure for extracting the square root is such a method; applied to $\sqrt{3}$, it generates 1, 1.7, 1.73, 1.732, and so on. Various methods of successive approximations have been developed for the important problem of the solution of equations.

Arabic Numerals   The digits 0, 1, 2, 3, 4, 5, 6, 7, 8, 9 used in the **decimal number system**.

Arbitrary Constant (Syn.: Parameter) A symbol holding a place for an unspecified constant. For example, in the polynomial $3x^2 = x + A$, "A" is an arbitrary constant, when it is understood to be replaceable by any particular number; also, the coefficients "a," "b," "c" in the general quadratic equation $ax^2 + bx + c = 0$ are arbitrary constants.   See **Variable**.

Arc   The portion of a **curve** between two of its points P and Q. The arc PQ is a *simple arc* in case it does not intersect itself; a *circular arc* is a (simple) arc of a circle. Technically, an arc in the plane or in three-space, can be defined as follows: it is the image of the unit interval $0 \leq x \leq 1$ under a one-to-one continuous mapping.

Arc Length   The length of an arc. See **Element of arc length**.

Arc-Cosecant; Arc-Cosine; Arc-Cotangent; Arc-Secant; Arc-Sine; Arc-Tangent (Syn.: Inverse cosecant; Inverse cosine; Inverse cotangent; Inverse secant; Inverse sine; Inverse tangent)   The **inverse trigonometric functions** of the trigonometric functions *cosecant, cosine, cotangent, secant, sine,* and *tangent,* respectively.

Area (plane)   A numerical measure expressing two-dimensional extent in a plane. A geometric square of side 1 has area 1, or *unit* area; the area of any planar region can be thought of as the number of such unit squares it contains (this number is not necessarily a whole number). By the area of a closed curve or a polygon is meant the area of the interior region. (Sometimes, "area" is used to mean the interior region itself.)

The area of a *rectangle* is the product of the lengths of two adjacent sides; this may be used as a basis for a rigorous definition of areas of other figures. From this, it can be inferred that the area of a *triangle* is one-half the base times the altitude; then the area of a *polygon* is the sum of the areas of the triangles into which it can be divided. The area of a *simple closed curve,* such as an el-

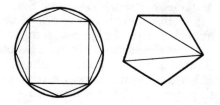

lipse or circle, can be gotten at by the area of an inscribed polygon; the area of the curve is taken as the *limit* of the areas of an infinite sequence of inscribed polygons which approach the curve as their limiting figure. This method leads, for example, to the well-known formula πr^2 for the area of a circle. The areas of *similar figures* are in the same ratio as the second powers of corresponding lengths; for example, doubling the radius of a circle quadruples its area; halving the side of a square quarters its area. General formulas for area are derived in the calculus.   See **Integral of function**. [Archimedes (third century B.C.) was able to compute various areas in the spirit of modern calculus by the early "method of exhaustions."]

See **Ellipse, Parallelogram**, etc., for areas of particular figures; also, see **Isoperimetric**.   Ref. [8].

Area of Surface   A numerical measure expressing two-dimensional extent of a plane or curved surface in space. The area of an elementary surface (that is, one made up of planar faces, such as a cube), or of a surface which can be rolled out on a

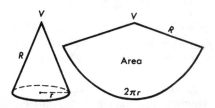

plane (such as a cone), has immediate meaning in terms of plane area. In other cases, such as the sphere, the area can be gotten at by the area of an elementary surface which circumscribes the given surface (that is, an elementary surface whose faces are tangent to the given surface); the

15

area of the surface is taken as the *limit* of the areas of an infinite sequence of circumscribed elementary surfaces that approach the given surface as their limiting figure. The methods of the integral calculus translate this descriptive procedure into an explicit formula for computing areas. See **Double integral**, **Surface of revolution**.

See **Cone**, **Sphere**, etc., for areas of particular curved surfaces; also, see **Theorem of Pappus**.

Argand Diagram (Syn.: Complex plane)   The representation of complex numbers by rectangular coordinates in the plane; the complex number $a + bi$ is identified with the point having coordinates (a, b). The

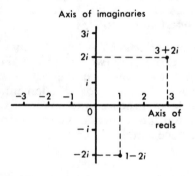

Axis of imaginaries

real numbers a appear along the x-axis, which is the *axis of reals,* or the *real axis.* The pure imaginary numbers bi appear along the y-axis, which is the *axis of imaginaries,* or the *imaginary axis.* This representation allows operations and relations involving complex numbers to be given a geometric meaning. The realism introduced thereby was important in dispelling the strangeness and even mysticism attached to these numbers as late as the nineteenth century.

Argument (logic)   An explicit demonstration or **proof** of a proposition.

Argument of Complex Number   See **Amplitude of complex number** (syn.).

Argument of Function   In expressions such as $f(x), f(a), f(5)$, etc., for functional values, $x, a, 5$, etc., are arguments of the function f; for example, in log $3x$, the argument of the log function is $3x$.

Arithmetic   As ordinarily understood, the art of reckoning; that is, calculation with integers, using the fundamental operations of arithmetic—addition, subtraction, multiplication, and division. In ancient Greek mathematics, the term "logistic" was used instead, with "arithmetic" being reserved for what is called the "theory of numbers" today.   See **Algebra**.   Ref. [64, 81, 120].

Arithmetic Mean (Syn.: Average; Mean)   Of n numbers, their sum divided by n; in particular, the arithmetic **mean** of two numbers a and b is $(a + b)/2$. The arithmetic mean is a numerical expression of the "central tendency" of a collection of numbers; it has the feature that the sum of the deviations of the numbers to the right exactly balances the sum of the deviations of the numbers to the left. For example, the mean of two numbers is the number halfway between them.   See **Expected value**, **Standard deviation**.

Arithmetic Modulo *m*   See **Congruent integers**.

Arithmetic Progression and Series   An *arithmetic progression* is a sequence of equally spaced numbers. The simplest arithmetic progression is the sequence of whole numbers, 1, 2, 3, 4, 5, ... In general, an arithmetic progression has the form $a, a + d,$

$a + 2d, \ldots, a + (n - 1)d, \ldots;$ the

$$a \quad a+d \quad a+2d \quad a+3d, \text{ etc.}$$

first term is *a*, the *common difference* is *d*, the nth *term* is $a + (n - 1)d$; if the sequence terminates, it has a *last term l*. An arithmetic progression is determined when *a* and *d* are given; for example, if *a* is 3 and *d* is $\frac{7}{2}$ the arithmetic progression is 3, $\frac{13}{2}$, $\frac{20}{2}$, $\frac{27}{2}, \ldots;$ if the progression terminates at the thirteenth term, then this last term is $3 + (13 - 1) \cdot \frac{7}{2}$, or 45.

An *arithmetic series* is the sum of the terms of an arithmetic progression. For example,

$$1 + 2 + 3 + \cdots + n$$

is an arithmetic series; it equals $n(n + 1)/2$. The general formula for the sum of *n* terms of an arithmetic progression is $n \cdot (a + l)/2$; this can be remembered as the number of terms times the average of the first and last term. In the last example, with $a = 3, d = \frac{7}{2}$, and $n = 13$, the sum is $13 \cdot (3 + 45)/2$, or 312.

The following important theorem of the theory of numbers concerns arithmetic progressions: if the first term *a* and the common difference *d* are integers with no positive factor in common (other than 1), then infinitely many of the terms in the unending progression will be *prime numbers*. This difficult result was proved by Dirichlet near the middle of the nineteenth century.

Arithmetic Unit Of a **digital computer**, a principal internal component that carries out arithmetical and logical operations as directed by internally stored instructions. An example of a logical operation on coded information is comparing two strings of digits for identity in particular places; another is testing the sum of the digits of a number for evenness or oddness. See **Code**.

Arm Of an *angle,* a side of the angle; of a *right triangle,* a side other than the hypotenuse.

Artificial Intelligence See Machine Intelligence (Syn.)

Associative Law Of *addition,* the formula $(a + b) + c = a + (b + c)$; of *multiplication,* $(a \cdot b) \cdot c = a \cdot (b \cdot c)$. The inverse operations, subtraction and division, are not associative; for example, the associative law for subtraction would require $(a - b) - c = a - (b - c)$, which is not generally true. The associative law for any *binary operation,* denoted by " $*$ ", is expressed by $(a * b) * c = a * (b * c)$. See **Field**.

Asymmetric Relation A **relation** having the following property: whenever thing *a* is in the given relation to thing *b*, then *b* is *not* in the given relation to *a*. For example, the relation "*a* is less than *b*," among numbers, is asymmetric; so is the relation "*a* is the father of *b*," among people. See **Symmetric relation**.

Asymptote Of a plane curve, a line related to it in the following manner: the distance from a point *P* on the curve to the line approaches zero as *P* moves along one direction of the

curve so that its distance from a fixed point increases without bound. (Usually, the curve is required to remain on one side of the line, not "snake" about it.) The hyperbola, for example, is a conic with two asymptotes.

Automation (computer) The performance of certain tasks by a computer that are ordinarily associated with human judgment and human decision-making; tasks in a manufacturing process provide an example. See **Machine intelligence** (computer).

Auxiliary Circle Of an **hyperbola (ellipse)**, the circle with radius equal to half the transverse (major) axis and its center at the center of the conic.

Average See **Mean**.

Axiom (Syn.: Postulate) Of a mathematical system or **deductive theory**, a proposition which is accepted without proof. The axioms make up the initial propositions from which all other propositions of the theory are derived, by proof. In modern usage, "axiom" and "postulate" mean the same thing, although a distinction is made in Euclid's geometry; axioms are propositions of a general logical nature (about equals and unequals), while postulates are propositions concerning geometric objects and constructions. See **Inconsistent axioms**, **Independent axiom**.

Axiom of Choice (Syn.: Zermelo's axiom) The following principle of the theory of sets: given a collection, finite or infinite, of sets A, B, C, . . . , it is possible to construct a set X by choosing one member from A to belong to X, one member from B to belong to X, and so on, for all the sets. See **Ordered set**. Ref. [99].

Axiom of Continuity The principle that the real numbers and the points of the line can be put into exact correspondence.

Axiom of Infinity The principle that the natural numbers 1, 2, 3, . . . , form an unending, or infinite, sequence.

Axiom of Superposition See **Superposition**.

Axiomatics In foundations of mathematics, the following view of mathematical "truth": a mathematical statement being "true" means that it is a logical consequence of a set of initial assumptions, or axioms. This approach is inherent in the **deductive theory** of ancient Greek geometry; it was given deeper meaning and greatly refined in the twentieth century by Hilbert and others in an attempt to avoid certain **paradoxes** that had come forth in the **foundations of mathematics**. The axiomatic method expresses the philosophy of most modern mathematicians, even though certain logical questions still remain unresolved. Ref. [95, 134, 149].

Axioms of Equality See **Equality**.

Axioms of Euclid Those assumptions of Euclid's *Elements* which deal with logical properties of equality and inequality. Euclid called them "common notions." His postulates, by contrast, deal with geometric properties. An example of a "common notion" is the statement "The whole is equal to the sum of its parts." Today, "axiom" and "postulate" are synonymous.

Axis In geometry, generally, a line or line segment related to the symmetry of a geometric figure (as in the "major axis" of an ellipse). See **Cylinder**, **Ellipse**, etc., for axes of special figures.

Axis of Circle on Sphere The diameter of the sphere which is perpendicular to the plane of the **circle on the sphere**.

Axis of Coordinates See **Coordinate axis** (syn.).

Axis of Imaginaries or Reals See **Argand diagram**.

Axis of Revolution See **Surface of revolution**.

Axis of Symmetry See **Symmetry in plane**, **Symmetry in space**.

Azimuth In plane **polar coordinates**, the same as *polar angle*; in space **spherical coordinates**, the same as *longitude*.

B

Base In *geometry,* a particular side or face of a geometric figure, such as a triangle, cone, etc.; in *algebra,* the number to which an exponent applies, such as b in b^3 or 10 in 10^2.

Base Angle In a triangle, either of the two angles having the base as a side.

Base of Logarithms For the *common logarithm*, the number 10; for the *natural logarithm* the number $e(= 2 \cdot 71828 \cdots)$. In general, a logarithm can be defined for any base b which is a positive number different from 1; the **logarithm** of a positive number N is then the exponent when N is written as a power of b.

Base of Number System (Syn.: Radix) For the *decimal* number system, the whole number 10, for the *binary* number system the whole number 2. In general, a **number system** can be defined for any base b which is a whole number different from 1.

Basis Vectors In the plane (space), two (three) vectors such that any **vector** is a linear combination of them; they serve as a "framework" for all vectors. In the plane (space), any two (three) vectors that do not

lie on a line (plane) can be used as a basis; if they are perpendicular, or orthogonal, to each other, then they form an *orthogonal basis*. A commonly used orthogonal basis are the three unit vectors along the positive axes of a rectangular coordinate system; they form an *orthonormal basis* (that is, an orthogonal basis of unit vectors). Similar notions apply to vectors in spaces of higher dimension.

Bayes' Theorem The following principle in the foundations of probability. Let $p(a_1), p(a_2), \ldots, p(a_n)$, be the probabilities of the n mutually exclusive and exhaustive alternatives $a_1, a_2, \ldots, a_n$ of a given **random event** A. Consider an outcome b of a related random event B; let $p(b|a_i)$ be the probability of b, given the occurrence of a_i. Then Bayes' theorem expresses $p(a_i|b)$, the probability of a_i given b, by the formula

$$[p(b|a_i)p(a_i)] \div [p(b|a_1)p(a_1) \\ + p(b|a_2)p(a_2) \\ + \cdots + p(b|a_n)p(a_n)].$$

In practice, b represents certain information related to the random event A, and the formula is used as a basis of drawing inferences about A from this information.

Biconditional In logic, the propositional form "P if and only if Q," or any statement of this form; it is sometimes written "$P \leftrightarrow Q$" (see **Algebra of propositions**). An example is the statement "Triangle ABC is equilateral if and only if triangle ABC is equiangular." A biconditional statement is understood to be true just in case the individual statements P, Q are both true or both false; for example, the following statement is true, "The moon is made of green cheese if and only if $2 + 2 = 5$." The *truth-*

table in the figure shows which combinations of truth values for P, Q make the biconditional true (T) and which false (F).

P	Q	P if and only if Q
T	T	T
F	T	F
T	F	F
F	F	T

A biconditional is so-called because it is logically equivalent to the following conjunction of **conditionals**: "If P then Q and if Q then P." Hence, the truth of a biconditional statement can be argued by arguing the truth of the separate conditional statements; for example, the preceding statement about triangle ABC can be argued by proving the separate statements, "If triangle ABC is equilateral, then it is equiangular," "If triangle ABC is equiangular, then it is equilateral."

The *denial* of the biconditional has several forms; a useful one is the form "(not P, and Q) or (not Q, and P)." For example, a denial of the biconditional about triangle ABC is "(Triangle ABC is not equilateral and it is equiangular) or (triangle ABC is not equiangular and it is equilateral)."

Alternative phrasings used in mathematics for the biconditional statement include: (**1**) "P is necessary and sufficient for Q"; (**2**) "P is equivlent to Q"; (**3**) "P just in case Q."

Binary Number System (Syn.: Dyadic number system) A system of notation for (real) numbers, like the decimal system, that uses the place value method but with *base 2* rather than *base 10*. Only two digits are required, 0 and 1, which are sometimes called "bits" (abbreviation of "binary digits"). In this system, the decimal whole numbers 1, 2, 3, 4, 5, 6, 7, 8, etc., appear as 1, 10, 11, 100, 101, 110, 111, 1000, etc. This notation is based

on powers of 2; for example, 11011 stands for

$$1 \cdot 2^4 + 1 \cdot 2^3 + 0 \cdot 2^2 + 1 \cdot 2^1 + 1 \cdot 2^0;$$

this can be computed in decimal notation, as $16 + 8 + 0 + 2 + 1$, or 27. More generally, a five-digit binary number, says, *edcba,* where the letters stand for 0 or 1, denotes

$$e \cdot 2^4 + d \cdot 2^3 + c \cdot 2^2 + b \cdot 2 + a;$$

similar meaning is attached to any number of digits. By analogy with decimal notation, a is said to be in the units place, b in the 2's place, c is the 2^2's place, and so on. See **Number system**.

The change from binary notation to decimal notation can always be made, as in the example, by writing out a binary number as a sum of powers of 2 and then carrying out the operations in decimal notation. The reverse process, decimal notation to binary notation, can be accomplished by successive division by 2 and using the remainders as binary digits—this can be illustrated by writing 87 in binary notation; divide 87 by 2 to obtain quotient 43 and remainder 1 (the latter is used in the binary units place); divide the quotient 43 by 2 to obtain a new quotient 21 and a new remainder 1 (the latter is used in the 2's place); continuing this process gives the following succession of pairs of quotient, remainder, (10, 1), (5, 0), (2, 1), (1, 0), (0, 1); the process terminates when the quotient is 0; putting together the remainders in reverse order, gives 87 as 1010111.

Arithmetic in the binary system, for all its apparent strangeness, is basically the same as that in the decimal system both being place value systems. *Addition* and *multiplication* of binary numbers involves the use of addition and multiplication tables for low numbers, and the process of "carrying" in applying the table to higher numbers.

Addition Table	Multiplication Table
$0 + 0 = 0$	$0 \cdot 0 = 0$
$0 + 1 = 1$	$0 \cdot 1 = 0$
$1 + 1 = 10$	$1 \cdot 1 = 1$
$10 + 1 = 11$	

Addition is illustrated as follows (notice that $1 + 1 + 1 = 10 + 1 = 11$).

```
(carries)      (1) (1) (1)
                1   1   0   1
                    1   1   1
              ─────────────────
            1   0   1   0   0
```

Multiplication is illustrated as follows.

```
                    1   1   0   1
                        1   0   1
                  ─────────────────
                    1   1   0   1
                0   0   0   0
            1   1   0   1
(carries)  (1) (1) (1) (0) (0)
          ─────────────────────
        1   0   0   0   0   0   1
```

To represent fractions and irrational numbers, as with the decimal system, the binary system uses binary fractions involving negative powers of its base and a *binary point* to separate the positive and negative powers. For example, 110.101 represents

$$1 \cdot 2^2 + 1 \cdot 2 + 0 \cdot 1 + 1 \cdot 2^{-1}$$
$$+ 0 \cdot 2^{-2} + 1 \cdot 2^{-3}.$$

Computing this in ordinary arithmetic gives

$$1 \cdot 4 + 1 \cdot 2 + 0 \cdot 1 + 1 \cdot \tfrac{1}{2} + 0 \cdot \tfrac{1}{4} + 1 \cdot \tfrac{1}{8}$$

or

$$4 + 2 + \tfrac{1}{2} + \tfrac{1}{8}, \text{ or } \tfrac{53}{8}.$$

As with decimal numbers, it is necessary to allow unending binary fractions in order to represent all real numbers. The rational numbers (fractions), lead to repeating binary fractions, the irrational numbers lead to nonrepeating binary fractions. The irrational numbers $\sqrt{2}$ and π have the following representations to 21 binary places:

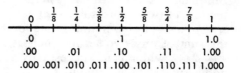

$$\sqrt{2} = 1.011010100000100111100$$
$$\pi = 11.001001000011111101101$$

Binary notation corresponds to a *binary scale* of markings on a line; this scale is based on successive halves, instead of successive tenths as with decimals. The figure shows

0	$\frac{1}{8}$	$\frac{1}{4}$	$\frac{3}{8}$	$\frac{1}{2}$	$\frac{5}{8}$	$\frac{3}{4}$	$\frac{7}{8}$	1
.0				.1				1.0
.00		.01		.10		.11		1.00
.000	.001	.010	.011	.100	.101	.110	.111	1.000

this: the interval 0 to 1 is bisected at .1; the two half-intervals are bisected at .01 and .11, respectively; the four quarter-intervals are bisected at .001, 011, .101, and .111, respectively; and so on. An inconvenience of binary notation for ordinary computation is the number of digits required to represent comparatively low numbers; for example, 1010111 represents 87. Binary arithmetic is advantageous and commonly used in connection with the electronic digital computer because the binary digits 0 and 1 can be distinguished by two contrasting electrical states such as "off" and "on."

Ref. [28, 92].

Binary Operation In general, a process that is applied to pairs of things to produce single things. Familiar examples are the addition and the multiplication of numbers; other examples are the addition of vectors, the multiplication of matrices, and the union of sets. Various general properties of binary operations are significant in mathematical systems. One is closure—a set of things is *closed* under a given binary operation if the operation applied to an arbitrary pair of members of the set yields a member of that set; for example, the whole numbers are closed under addition, but not under subtraction. The attempt to achieve closure under the various arithmetical and algebraic operations is a motivation for extensions of the concept of **number** from whole numbers to real numbers and complex numbers.   See **Field**, **Group**, **Operation**.

Binomial   A polynomial which is the sum of two terms, such as $aw^2 + 5bw$, or $3x - 2y$ (sometimes used for the sum of any two terms, such as $x + 2\sqrt{y}$, which is not necessarily a polynomial).   See **Trinomial**.

Binomial Coefficients   The numerical coefficients in the expansion of $(x + y)^n$, where n is a whole number; these coefficients are whole numbers. When n is 2 or 3,

$$(x + y)^2 = x^2 + 2xy + y^2$$
$$(x + y)^3 = x^3 + 3x^2y + 3xy^2 + y^3.$$

In the first case, the binomial coefficients are 1, 2, 1, and in the second case 1, 3, 3, 1. The **binomial theorem** gives a general formula for the coefficients, for any n.

The binomial coefficients have many interesting properties. For example, they make up a special triangular array known as *Pascal's triangle*, shown in the figure. Each row gives the binomial coefficients for one value of n—the second row when $n = 1$, the third when $n = 2$, and so on.

$$\begin{array}{c}
1 \\
1 \quad 1 \\
1 \quad 2 \quad 1 \\
1 \quad 3 \quad 3 \quad 1 \\
1 \quad 4 \quad 6 \quad 4 \quad 1 \\
1 \quad 5 \quad 10 \quad 10 \quad 5 \quad 1 \\
1 \quad 6 \quad 15 \quad 20 \quad 15 \quad 6 \quad 1
\end{array}$$

The triangle is easily constructed as follows: (**1**) border the triangle with 1's; (**2**) place the sum of adjacent numbers in a row in the next row and between the two numbers; Pascal's triangle exhibits the symmetry of the binomial coefficients about the middle value. The sum of the numbers in row $(n + 1)$, the binomial coefficients for n, is 2^n; for example, when $n = 4$, the sum is $1 + 4 + 6 + 4 + 1$, or 16, which does equal 2^4. The binomial coefficients are important in the subject of probability, where they occur in the so-called binomial distribution for success in repeated trials.   See **Combination of things**.

Binomial Distribution   See **Probability in repeated trials**.

Binomial Series   The expansion of $(a + x)^p$ as an infinite **power series** in x when p is not a whole number or zero; it converges to $(a + x)^p$ for x between $-a$ and a. The series was discovered by Newton in the seventeenth century. When p is a positive integer, this reduces to the finite series of the **binomial theorem**.

Binomial Theorem (Syn.: Binomial expansion; Binomial formula)   The following expansion of $(x + y)^n$ as a sum of $n + 1$ terms, n being a whole number:

$$(x + y)^n = x^n + nx^{n-1}y$$
$$+ \frac{n(n - 1)}{2} x^{n-2}y^2$$
$$+ \cdots + y^n.$$

The next term is obtained from a given one as follows: (**1**) for the next coefficient, multiply the given coefficient by the exponent of x and divide by one more than the exponent of y; (**2**) for the next exponents, reduce the exponent of x by 1 and increase the exponent of y by 1. The *general term*, or $(r + 1)^{st}$ term, is expressed in factorial notation as

$$\frac{n!}{(n - r)!r!} x^{n-r}y^r,$$

$r = 0, 1, 2, \ldots, n$. The coefficient of $x^{n-r}y^r$ is called the **binomial coeffi-**

cient; it is denoted by $\binom{n}{r}$ or $C(n, r)$.

When n is not a whole number, the binomial expansion becomes the **binomial series**, an infinite series.

Ref. [28, 120].

Biquadratic   See **Quartic** (syn.).

Birectangular   In geometry, having two right angles; for example, a birectangular spherical triangle is one with two right angles, and a birectangular trihedral angle is one with two right dihedral angles.

Bisector   The bisector of an *angle* (*dihedral angle*) is the half-line (half-plane) which divides the angle into two angles of equal measure; it is made up of points whose (perpendicular) distances to the sides (faces) of the angle are equal. The bisector of a *line segment* is the midpoint of the line segment.   See **Geometric construction, Perpendicular bisector**.

Bit (Syn.: Binary digit)   In the binary number system, either of the digits 0 or 1 ("bit" is an abbreviation of "binary digit"). Strings of bits represent numbers in the binary system; for example, 11010 represents the decimal number 26. Strings of bits are used in a **digital computer** to stand for numbers, and also to code other kinds of information, such as instructions to the computer.

Bit of Information   See **Information theory**.

Boolean Algebra   In logic, a symbolic theory introduced by Boole in the middle of the nineteenth century; it marked the beginning of modern logic. This algebra can be interpreted as an **algebra of propositions** or as an **algebra of sets** and shows the "isomorphism" of these separate systems. Some of the rules of Boolean algebra resemble those of ordinary algebra; others are different. One striking difference is that in a Boolean algebra the "product" of any element with itself is always that element. In the case of sets, this means that the intersection of a set with itself is the set; in the case of propositions, it means that a proposition of the form "P and P" is logically equivalent to "P" itself. (Formally, a Boolean algebra is a *ring* with an identity element of multiplication and with $x \cdot x = x$ for every element x.)   Ref. [2, 44, 93, 134].

Bound   An *upper* (*lower*) *bound* of a set of numbers is a number which is greater (less) than or equal to every member of the set. For example, the infinite set $\{1, 1/2, 1/4, 1/8, \ldots, 1/2^n, \ldots\}$ has 2 as one of its many upper bounds, and $-\frac{1}{4}$ as one of its lower bounds. A set is *bounded* if it has both a lower bound and an upper bound. The preceding set is bounded, but the infinite set $\{2, 4, 6, 8, \ldots, 2n, \ldots\}$ is an unbounded set; the latter has a lower bound, but no upper bound. The infinite set $\{0, 3, -3, 6, -6, 9, -9, \ldots, 3n, -3n; \ldots\}$ has neither a lower bound nor an upper bound.

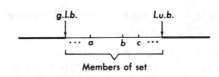

Members of set

The *least upper bound* (abbreviated l.u.b.) of a set is the smallest of all its upper bounds, the *greatest lower bound* (abbreviated g.l.b.) is the greatest of all its lower bounds

Bound of Function

(provided these exist). In the first example, 1 is the least upper bound, and 0 is the greatest lower bound; in the second, 2 is the greatest lower bound.   See **Sequence**.

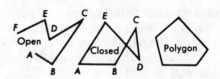

Bound of Function   A bound of its set of functional values. An *upper* (*lower*) *bound* is an upper (lower) bound of this set of values; a function is *bounded* if it has both an upper and lower bound. The notations l.u.b., g.l.b. stand, respectively, for the *least upper bound* and *greatest lower bound* of a function (when they exist). For example, the trigonometric function sin x is bounded with least upper bound 1 and greatest lower bound -1. The exponential

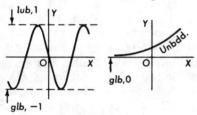

function 2^x is unbounded; it is bounded from below by its greatest lower bound 0, but unbounded from above.

Brace and Bracket   See **Parentheses**.

Brachistochrone Problem   See **Cycloid**.

Briggs' Logarithm   See **Common logarithm** (syn.).

Broken line   A continuous path consisting of a finite number of connected line segments, AB, BC, CD, ..., PQ, QR (it is assumed that not all the segments lie on one line). The broken line is *closed* if its initial point and final point coincide; otherwise it is *open*. A closed, broken line in the plane which does not intersect itself is a **polygon**. A broken line is *inscribed in a curve* in case each of its

points A, B, C, ... is on the curve. An inscribed broken line which fits "close" to a curve serves as an approximation to the curve. It is often useful to represent a curve as a limit of a sequence of inscribed broken lines; this idea is applied in defining the length of a curve, for example.

Buffon's Needle Problem   The following problem of chance. Suppose that the plane is marked with a series of equally spaced parallel lines b units apart: what is the probability that a needle of length a tossed randomly on the plane will land so as to touch one of these lines? Surpris-

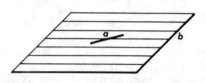

ingly, the number pi, π, figures in the answer; the required probability is $2a/\pi b$. When $a = b$, this is approximately 0.64; hence, the chance is about 64 to 100 that the needle will touch a line. The problem was stated in the middle of the eighteenth century by Comte de Buffon.   Ref. [73].

Bundle of Planes (Syn.: Sheaf of planes)   The family of all planes through a given point in space, called the *center* of the bundle.

C

Calculator   See **Computer**.

Calculus (Syn.: Infinitesimal calculus)   The field of mathematics created in the second half of the seventeenth century by Newton and Leibniz, which rests upon the fundamental concept of **limit**. Its invention was one of the great achievements in science, and ranks with Greek geometry in the profound effect it has had on scientific thinking. As with all great advances, partial ideas related to the calculus had appeared before; for example, Archimedes and other Greek mathematicians of antiquity had used related ideas in their method of exhaustions for the calculation of areas and volumes. The invention of analytic geometry and the calculus gave rise to the modern development of mathematics.

Differential calculus deals with the rate of change of a function. This is defined as a limit, and is expressed as the **derivative of a function** and the corresponding operation of differentiation of functions. Geometrically, the derivative gives the slope of the tangent line to a curve. Its applications include velocity, acceleration, the curvature of curves and surfaces, and maxima and minima of functions.

Integral calculus is connected with the idea of area; this is expressed by the definite **integral of a function** and the corresponding operation of integration of functions. The definite integral (from a to b) of a function $f(x)$ can be interpreted as the area bounded by the graph of $y = f(x)$ and the x-axis, between $x = a$ and $x = b$. Among the many applications

of integration are length, area, and volume of geometric figures.

The so-called **fundamental theorem of the calculus** relates the basic operations of differentiation and integration; it states that these processes are "inverse" to each other. This leads to the principal means of carrying out the operation of integration, and explicitly evaluating areas, volumes, etc. Introductory calculus usually includes the study of the elementary transcendental functions such as trigonometric functions, the logarithm function, and the exponential function. Also, the calculus is intimately related to the notion of the irrational real number, and the continuity of the line, as well as the concept of the continuous function. Following the invention of the calculus, there was a great burst of mathematical activity; in developing the new wealth of mathematics, questions of rigor were put aside. It was not until the second half of the nineteenth century that the subject was put on a thoroughly sound foundation.

Ref. [28, 39, 58, 79, 140].

Calculus of Variations The study of the maximum or minimum values of functions whose values depend upon a curve or another function, rather than a real number. The ordinary calculus treats functions sin x, log x and, in general, $f(x)$, where (the argument) x is a real number; the calculus of variations, an extension, studies functions where the argument may be an entire curve. For instance, the "brachistochrone" problem belongs to the calculus of variations (see **Cycloid**)—here, two points A and B in a vertical plane are fixed and an arbitrary curve C from A to B is considered; with C is associated the time $F(C)$ for a

25

particle to descend from A to B along the curve C under the influence of gravity [the functional value $F(C)$ depends upon the curve C]. The problem is to find the particular curve for which $F(C)$ has the smallest value. The calculus of variations also treats functions of surfaces and higher dimensional geometric figures. See **Isoperimetric**.

The calculus of variations requires more sophisticated methods than the ordinary calculus. Its development, starting about 1700, was an important outgrowth of the burst of new mathematics following the invention of the calculus; it occupies a major place in modern mathematics and mathematical physics.

Cancellation   For *equations*, the removal of a term or factor common to both sides of an equation. Examples are (1) changing $5x^2 + 6y = 2x + 6y - 3$ to $5x^2 = 2x - 3$, by cancelling the term $6y$; (2) changing $3x^2y = 6x$ to $xy = 2$, by cancelling the factor $3x$. General cancellation **laws** are the following:

(1) if $a + x = a + y$, then $x = y$;
(2) if $a \cdot x = a \cdot y$ and $a \neq 0$, then $x = y$.

For *fractions*, cancellation is the removal of a factor common to the numerator and denominator. For example, $\frac{15}{24} = \frac{5}{8}$ *and*

$$(x - y)(x + y/2y(x + y) = (x - y)/2y.$$

This is based on the general cancellation law

$$(a \cdot x)/(a \cdot y) = x/y.$$

A fraction with no factors that can be cancelled is said to be in lowest terms.

Cardinal Number   A *finite cardinal number* is a whole number when considered as the expression of how many members are in a collection of objects. For example, a particular set of distinct persons named Tom, Dick, and Harry has the cardinal (number) 3. Any two finite sets which can be matched one-to-one with each other have the *same* finite cardinal. (Another view of whole number is as an **ordinal number**, in which its place in the succession of whole numbers matters.)

An *infinite cardinal number* is a concept of the theory of sets, expressing how many members are in an infinite set; this is a subtler idea. As with finite sets, two sets have the same cardinal number, or *power,* in case they can be put into one-to-one correspondence with each other. The simplest infinite set is the set of whole numbers $\{1, 2, 3, \ldots, n, \ldots\}$. Its cardinal number is the least infinite cardinal, and is denoted by the Hebrew letter $\aleph_0$ (aleph-null). Any set has this cardinal (number) if it can be matched one-to-one with the set of whole numbers; such a set is also said to be *countable* (or *enumerable*, or *denumerable*). The set of positive powers of 10, namely, $\{10, 10^2, 10^3, \ldots\}$, is countable (match 10^n with n). Since these powers of 10 form a subset of the set of natural numbers, this shows that an infinite set can have the same cardinal as a subset of itself; this is strikingly different from finite sets. Another surprising phenomenon is that the set of all fractions, or rational numbers, is countable, in spite of the fact that the whole numbers seem to make up only a small part of all rational numbers.   See **Enumeration of the rational numbers**.

A cardinal number larger than aleph-null (in an appropriately defined sense) is that of the set of all real (decimal) numbers (or the set of all points on the line); this cardinal is denoted by c. Sets with cardinal number c are said to have the *power of the continuum*. The *continuum hypothesis* is that there is no cardinal between aleph-null and c, i.e., between the cardinal of the whole numbers and that of the real numbers; it was shown in 1963 to be an *independent axiom* of set theory.

It is possible to construct an unending, increasing chain of cardinal numbers beyond the cardinal number c. It is also possible to extend the ordinary arithmetic of finite cardinals to a transfinite arithmetic of **transfinite numbers**; this arithmetic has many unusual features in comparison with ordinary arithmetic. The theory of infinite sets and cardinals was created in the latter part of the nineteenth century by G. Cantor. It gave rise to certain logical paradoxes which caused a major investigation of the **foundations of mathematics**.
Ref. [29, 30, 121, 149].

Cartesian Coordinates in Plane A standard method of locating points in the plane by pairs of numbers denoting distances along two fixed intersecting lines, called the *axes*. The two axes are marked with uniform number scales, with one axis being the first, or x-axis, and the other being the second, or y-axis; the *origin* is their point of intersection. In a *rectangular coordinate system*

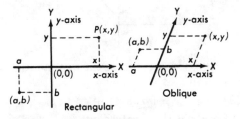

Rectangular   Oblique

the axes are perpendicular to each other. Any point P is located by its pair of *coordinates* (x, y); the *abscissa*, x, specifies the intersection of the x-axis with the line through P parallel to the y-axis; the *ordinate*, y, specifies the intersection of the y-axis with the line through P parallel to the x-axis. The origin has coordinates $(0, 0)$, a point on the x-axis has coordinates $(x, 0)$, a point on the y-axis has coordinates $(0, y)$, and a point on neither axis has both coordinates different from 0. The axes divide the plane into four *quadrants;* in the *first quadrant*, x and y are both positive; in the *second quadrant*, x is negative, y is positive; in the *third quadrant*, x and y are both negative; in the *fourth quadrant*, x is positive, y is negative.

An *oblique* Cartesian coordinate system is one in which the axes are nonperpendicular; oblique coordinates (x, y) are defined as above.

A Cartesian coordinate system in the plane matches points in the plane with pairs of numbers; this connection leads to analytic geometry and the use of algebra in the study of plane geometry. The name "Cartesian" comes from Descartes, the mathematician-philosopher, who introduced these coordinates in the first half of the seventeenth century.

See **Polar coordinates in plane, Transformation of coordinates**.

Cartesian Coordinates in Space A standard method of locating points in space by triples of numbers denoting distances along three fixed lines, or *axes*. The axes are marked with uniform number scales, and meet in a common point, the *origin*; they are arranged as the first, or x-axis, the second, or y-axis, and the third, or z-axis. In a *rectangular coordinate system* the axes are perpendicular in pairs; each pair of axes determines a *coordinate plane*—the *xy*-plane, the *xz*-plane, and the *yz*-plane; the three coordinate planes are mutually perpendicular. Any

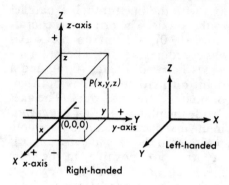

point *P* is located by its triple of *coordinates* (x, y, z); the *x*-coordinate is the intersection of the *x*-axis with the plane through *P* parallel to the *yz*-coordinate plane; the *y*-coordinate and *z*-coordinate are determined similarly (see figure). The origin has coordinates $(0, 0, 0)$; points in the *yz*-coordinate plane have coordinates $(0, y, z)$, points in the *xz*-coordinate plane have coordinates $(x, 0, y)$, points in the *xy*-coordinate plane have coordinates $(x, y, 0)$; points not in a coordinate plane have all coordinates different from 0. The three coordinate planes divide space into eight *octants,* and the octant in which a point lies is determined by the signs of its coordinates. The positive axes (half-lines) make up a configuration called a **trihedral**. There are two "orientations" for a trihedral in space, right-handed and left-handed; they are illustrated in the figure. See **Cylindrical coordinates**, **Spherical coordinates**, **Transformation of coordinates**.

Casting Out Nines In arithmetic, a method used to check multiplication or addition. It is based on the *excess*

of nines* in the digits of a whole number; this is the remainder when the sum of the digits is divided by 9. (The excess of nines in 9,357 is 6, since 9 + 3 + 5 + 7 = 24, and the remainder when 24 is divided by 9 is 6.) To check that $23 \cdot 47 = 1,081$, replace $23 \cdot 47$ by the excesses of 23 and 47 to obtain $5 \cdot 2$, or 10; now replace 10 by its excess 1, and verify that this is indeed the excess of nines in 1,081. Similarly, to test whether $456 + 987$ equals 1,543, replace the terms in the sum by their excesses to obtain 6 + 6, or 12, and reduce this to the excess 3; now notice that the excess of 1,543 is 4, which is different from 3; redoing the addition shows that the answer should be 1,443. The same method can be applied to an arithmetical expression involving any combination of additions and multiplications. The method is related to the notion of **congruent integers** modulo 9. It was probably known in Hindu mathematics of the first millenium.

Catenary A plane curve which is the vertical shape assumed by a uniform, flexible cable under gravity when it is held at two fixed points. The equation of the catenary can be

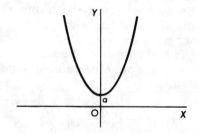

expressed in terms of the exponential function as

$$y = (a/2)(e^{x/a} + e^{-x/a});$$

here, *a* is the *y*-intercept.

Cauchy Condition For an infinite

sequence of numbers $s_1, s_2, s_3, \ldots$, the following condition that it have a **limit**: the difference $s_{N+k} - s_N$ approaches 0 as N and k (independently) approach infinity. It has the advantage of a condition for convergence which makes no reference to the limit value itself.

Cavalieri's Theorem In solid geometry, the following condition for two solids to have the same **volume**: their sections by any plane parallel to a

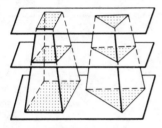

fixed plane must have equal areas. Cavalieri was an Italian mathematician of the first half of the seventeenth century whose work preceded the invention of the calculus. He developed a theory of "indivisibles" which was an unclear and unsatisfactory approach to the problems of the calculus.

Center In geometry, generally, the center of symmetry of a geometric figure, as in "center of an ellipse." See **Circle**, **Ellipsoid**, etc. Also, see **Symmetry in plane**, **Symmetry in space**.

Centi- One hundredth, used as a prefix; for example, a centimeter is one-hundredth of a meter.

Central Angle Of a circle, an angle

with vertex at its center. The circular arc (or the chord) intercepted by the angle is said to subtend the central angle. A central angle has the degree measure of the intercepted arc. See **Sector of circle**, **Segment of circle**.

Central Conic Either of the conics ellipse or hyperbola; these have centers of symmetry, in contrast to the parabola, which does not.

Central Limit Theorem The following fundamental theorem of probability. Let $X_1, X_2, X_3, \ldots$, be a sequence of mutually independent random variables; then, under very general conditions, the distribution of the sum $X_1 + X_2 + \cdots + X_n$ approaches a normal distribution as n increases without bound. This theorem shows the basic nature of the normal distribution; it is remarkable in not depending on the form of the distributions of the X_i.

Central Polyhedral Angle Of a sphere, a **polyhedral angle** with vertex at its center. Such an angle intersects the sphere in a spherical polygon.

Central Quadric Either of the quadric surfaces ellipsoid or hyperboloid; these have centers of symmetry, in contrast to the paraboloid, which does not.

Centroid of Plane Figure In physical terms, the single point of support (center of mass) of a horizontal homogeneous planar region at which it just balances under the pull of gravity; also termed the centroid of the boundary of the region. The centroid of a *circle* is its center; the centroid of a *triangle* is the common point of intersection of its three medians. A formula is derived in the integral calculus for the centroid of a general plane figure (see **Double integral**). The centroid occurs, for example, in the **theorem of Pappus** for the area and volume of solids of revolution.

Chain Rule In the calculus, the following rule for the derivative of a composite function $f[u(x)]$:

$$df/dx = (df/du) \cdot (du/dx).$$

To obtain $d[\sin(3x^2)/dx]$, for example, write it as $d(\sin u)/dx$, where $u(x) = 3x^2$; then the derivative is

$$[d(\sin u)/du] \cdot [d(3x^2)/dx] = (\cos u) \cdot (6x)$$
$$= 6x \cos (3x^2).$$

Chance A chance event and a chance variable are the same as a **random event** and a **random variable**.

Change of Coordinates See **Transformation of coordinates**.

Characteristic of Logarithm The integral part of the common logarithm; the positive decimal part is the *mantissa*. See **Computation by logarithms**.

Check To check a *calculation* is to apply some test of correctness: examples are (**1**) checking a sum by reversing the order of addition, (**2**) checking a product by **casting out nines**. To check a *solution of an equation* means, generally, to insert the supposed solution in place of the unknown in the original equation, calculate each side separately, and verify the equality. For example, to check 2 as a solution of the equation $x^2 - x = 6 - 2x$, replace x by 2 on both sides; the left side gives $2^2 - 2$, or 2, while the right side gives $6 - 2 \cdot 2$, or 2, also; the solution checks. On the other hand, testing 3 as a solution gives $3^2 - 3$, or 6 on the left, and $6 - 2 \cdot 3$, or 0 on the right; hence 3 is not a solution.

Chord In geometry, a line segment joining two points on a curve or surface. A *secant line* is an (unlimited)

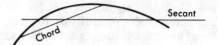

line which contains a chord. See **Focal chord, Supplemental chords**.

Chord of Contact Of a circle, the chord joining the points of tangency

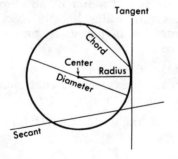

of the two tangent lines from a point P outside the circle.

Circle A plane curve consisting of all points at a given distance from a given point, the *center;* it is one of the principal figures of plane geometry. The *radius* is the given distance (or any line segment from the center to the circle); a *chord* is a line segment joining two points of the circle; a

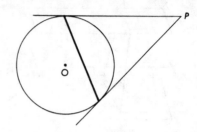

diameter is a chord (or its length) passing through the center. The diameter is twice the radius.

A line in the plane of a circle intersects the circle in no, one, or two points. In the third case, it is a *secant line*, in the second case, a *tangent line*. The radius to the point of contact, or point of tangency, of a tangent line is perpendicular to the tangent line. Conversely, if a line has a point *P* in common with a circle and is perpendicular to the radius to *P*, then it is the tangent line at *P*.

The *circumference C* of a circle is its (total) length. The ratio of the circumference to the diameter is the same for all circles; the common value is denoted by π and has the approximate value 3.1416. Hence, $C = \pi d$, or $C = 2\pi r$, where *d* is the diameter and *r* is the radius. The *area A* of a circle (which means the area of its interior) is given by $A = \pi r^2$. A unit circle (that is, a circle of radius 1) has circumference 2π and area π. The circle has the following **isoperimetric** property; among all closed plane curves of given length, it includes the largest possible area.

Three points *P, Q, R* (not on a line) determine a circle; the center is the intersection of the perpendicular bisectors of *PQ* and *QR*. Also, a circle is determined by requiring that it be tangent to a given line *l* at a point *P* and contain a given point *R* not on *l*; the center is the intersection of the perpendicular bisector of *PR* and the perpendicular to *l* at *P*.

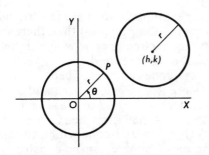

In analytic geometry, the circle with center at (*h, k*) and radius *r* is represented by an *equation* $(x - h)^2 + (y - k)^2 = r^2$; when the center is at the origin (0, 0), this becomes $x^2 + y^2 = r^2$. The *parametric equations* of a circle with center at the origin are the two equations $x = r \cos \theta$, $y = r \sin \theta$; the parameter θ is the rotation of the positive *x*-axis into a point *P* of the circle. See **Circumscribed circle, Inscribed circle, Squaring the circle.** Ref. [111].

Circle on Sphere   Any plane which meets a sphere in more than one point, intersects the sphere in a circle; conversely, every circle on the sphere is determined by such an intersection. If the plane contains the center of the sphere, the intersection is a

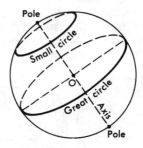

great circle; otherwise, it is a *small circle*. The *axis* of the circle is the diameter of the sphere which is perpendicular to the plane of the circle; the end points of the axis are the *poles* of the circle.

Circular Arc   An arc of a circle; the symbol $\widehat{PQ}$ is sometimes used to denote the arc between points *P, Q*.

Circular Cone   A **cone** whose base is a circle.

Circular Cylinder   A **cylinder** whose bases are circles.

31

Circular Functions See **Trigonometric functions** (syn.).

Circular Helix See **Helix**.

Circular Ring See **Annulus** (syn.).

Circulating Decimal See **Repeating decimal** (syn.).

Circumcenter of Triangle The center of the **circumscribed circle** of the triangle.

Circumference of Circle The (total) length of a circle; it equals π times the diameter. "Circumference" is sometimes used to mean the circle itself (as against its interior).

Circumference of Sphere The circumference of any great circle on the sphere.

Circumscribed Circle The circle circumscribed *about a triangle* is the (unique) circle which passes through the vertices of the triangle; the triangle is said to be inscribed in the circle. The center O is the *circumcen-*

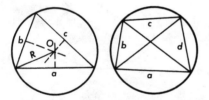

ter of the triangle; it is the common point of intersection of the perpendicular bisectors of the sides. The radius R of the circumscribed circle is given in terms of the lengths a, b, c of the sides of the triangle by the formula

$$R = \frac{abc}{4\sqrt{s(s-a)(s-b)(s-c)}};$$

s is half the perimeter, $\frac{1}{2}(a + b + c)$.

More generally, a circle circumscribed *about a polygon* is one which passes through the vertices of the polygon; the polygon is then in-

scribed in a circle. Not every polygon can be inscribed in a circle. For example, a (convex) quadrilateral can be, just in case its opposite angles happen to be supplementary. *Ptolemy's theorem* states the following condition on the sides of the quadrilateral in order that it can be inscribed in a circle: the lengths a, b, c, d must be such that $ac + bd$ equals the product of the diagonals. A *regular polygon* of n sides can always be circumscribed by a circle; the center of the circle is the center of the regular polygon; the radius R of the circumscribed circle is given by $R = (b/2)\csc(180°/n)$, where b is the length of a side.

Circumscribed Cone A cone circumscribed *about a pyramid* is a cone whose vertex coincides with that of the pyramid and whose base circumscribes the base of the pyramid; the pyramid is then inscribed in the cone. The lateral edges of the pyramid are elements of the cone. If the base of a

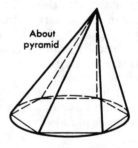

About pyramid

pyramid can be inscribed in a circle (for example, if the base is a triangle or a regular polygon) then there is a (unique) circular cone which circumscribes the pyramid.

A cone circumscribed *about a sphere* is one whose base and every element is tangent to the sphere; the sphere is then inscribed in the cone. A right circular cone which circumscribes a sphere can be constructed

by revolving an isosceles triangle and

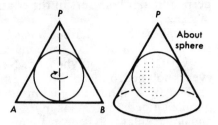

an inscribed circle about the altitude through 360° in space (see triangle *PAB* in figure).

Circumscribed Cylinder A cylinder circumscribed *about a prism* is a cylinder which contains the lateral edges of the prism as elements; the bases of the cylinder necessarily circumscribe those of the prism. The prism is then inscribed in the cylinder. If a circle can be circumscribed about a base of the prism (for example, if the base is a triangle or regular poly-

gon) then there is a (unique) circular cylinder which circumscribes the prism.

A cylinder circumscribed *about a sphere* is one whose bases and every

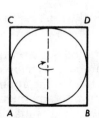

element are tangent to the sphere; the

sphere is then inscribed in the cylinder. A right circular cylinder which circumscribes a sphere can be constructed by revolving a square and an inscribed circle about a diameter through 360° in space (see *ABCD* in the figure).

Circumscribed Polygon A polygon circumscribed *about a circle* is a polygon whose sides are tangent to the circle; the circle is then an in-

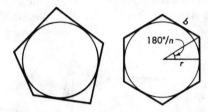

scribed circle of the polygon. The length *b* of the sides of a *regular polygon of n sides* is related to the radius *r* of the inscribed circle by the formula $b = 2r \tan (180°/n)$.

Circumscribed Polyhedron A polyhedron circumscribed about a closed surface, such as a sphere, is a polyhedron whose faces are tangent to the surface; the surface is then inscribed in the polyhedron.   See **Area of Surface, Inscribed sphere**.

Circumscribed Prism A prism circumscribed *about a cylinder* is a

About cylinder

prism whose bases are circumscribed

about the bases of the cylinder and whose lateral faces are tangent to the cylinder; the cylinder is then inscribed in the prism. Each lateral face of the prism is tangent along an element of the cylinder (see AA', BB' in the figure).

Circumscribed Pyramid A pyramid circumscribed *about a cone* is a pyramid whose vertex coincides with that of the cone and whose base circumscribes the base of the cone; the cone is then inscribed in the pyramid.

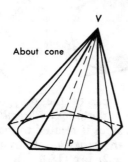

About cone

Each lateral face of the pyramid is tangent along an element of the cone (see VP in the figure).

Circumscribed Sphere The sphere circumscribed *about a tetrahedron* is

About tetrahedron

the unique sphere which contains the four vertices of the tetrahedron; the tetrahedron is then inscribed in the sphere. The center of the sphere is the common point of intersection of the four perpendiculars to the triangular faces at their circumcenters; it is also the common point of intersec-

tion of the four planes which are the perpendicular bisectors of the edges in space.

A sphere circumscribed *about a polyhedron* is one that contains all the vertices of the polyhedron. Not every polyhedron can be circumscribed by a sphere; a rectangular parallelepiped, a regular pyramid, and any regular polyhedron are polyhedrons that can be.

Class See **Set** (syn.).

Clearing of Fractions In the solution of equations, modification of an equation so as to remove the denominator of its fractional terms. For example, $x/2 - 3 = 5/3$ is changed to $3x - 18 = 10$ by multiplying both sides by the least common denominator 6. Also $x/(x + 2) + 1/(2x - 3) - 3/5 = 0$ becomes $5(2x - 3)x + 5(x + 2) - 3(x + 2)(2x - 3) = 0$ on multiplying both sides by the least common denominator $5(x + 2)(2x - 3)$.

Clockwise In the sense of the hand of a clock. An **angle**, considered as a rotation, is ordinarily counted as

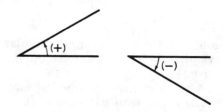

positive if counterclockwise, negative if clockwise.

Closed (under operation) A set of things, such as numbers, is closed under an **operation** in case the application of the operation to any members in the set always results in members of that set. For example, the positive fractions are closed under the operation of division, but the positive integers are not.

Closed Curve   A **curve** with no endpoints. A *simple closed curve* in the plane has the additional property that it does not cross itself; it bounds

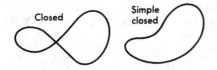

Closed   Simple closed

a finite portion of the plane, called its *interior* (see **Interior of closed curve**). By the *area* of such a plane curve is meant the area of its interior. A technical definition of a (continuous) closed curve in the plane (or in space) is the following: it is the image of a circle under a continuous mapping (it is *simple* in case the mapping is one to one).

Closed Plane Figure   In elementary geometry, the boundary of a simple two dimensional region; examples are polygons, circles, sectors of circles, etc.; sometimes, the region is included.

Closed Surface   Informally, a surface which in the complete boundary of a finite, three-dimensional portion of space, called its *interior*; the surface has no bounding curves. Examples are the sphere, cone, torus, etc. By the *volume* of the surface is meant the volume of the interior. The *solids* of ordinary solid geometry include such closed surfaces as polyhedrons, spheres, cones, cylinders, spherical pyramids, etc.

Code   The *machine code* of a computer is the system of symbols used in direct communication with the computer. The machine is built to interpret and act on instructions given to it in this form; these make up its *instruction code*. A coded instruction typically specifies an operation and one or more addresses (internal storage locations). In a *single address code*, the address may tell where an operand is to be obtained, or where the result of an operation is to be stored, or where the next instruction is to be found. In a *two-address code*, the addresses may tell the locations of two numbers to be operated on (by addition, for example); a *three-address code* can do this, as well as specify where the result is to be placed; a *four-address code* can further specify where the next instruction is to be found. The instruction code consists of comparatively few instructions; these can be put together in elaborate combinations, however, to direct the computer through a required computation. See **Computer program**.

Coding   See **Computer program**.

Coefficient   In algebra, the numerical factor of a term; for example, the coefficient in $2x$ is 2, in $-3x^2y$ is -3, in x^2 is 1. It is common to include literal factors in a coefficient; for example, in $3ax^2$ the coefficient of x^2 is $3a$. Also, one part of a product may be regarded as the coefficient of the other part; for example, in $3bx^2y$, the coefficient of x^2 is $3by$, the coefficient of y is $3bx^2$, the coefficient of x^2y is $3b$, and the coefficient of bx^2y is 3. See **Polynomial**.

Coefficients, Binomial   See **Binomial coefficients**.

Coefficients of Equation   The coefficients of the terms of an equation (the constant term also being regarded as a coefficient). For example, the coefficients of the equation $2x^2 - 3x + 5 = 0$ in the variable x, are

35

2, −3, and 5, respectively; the coefficients of $x^2 + bx - c = 0$ in the variable x are 1, b, and $-c$, respectively. In the first example, the leading coefficient is 2, in the second it is 1. In general, the *leading coefficient* of a polynomial equation is the coefficient of the term of highest degree. See **Quadratic equation and formula, Roots of polynomial equation**.

Co-functions (trigonometry) See **Complementary trigonometric functions** (syn.).

Coincident Identical, as used in geometry. For example, in an isosceles triangle the median and altitude from the apex to the base are coincident.

Co-latitude In the **spherical coordinates** of a point P, the angle from the polar axis to the line segment joining the origin to P.

Collecting terms In algebra, simplifying expressions by combining similar terms. For example, the expression $5x - 2yz + x + yz$ is reduced to $6x - yz$ by collecting terms. The procedure depends upon the distributive law of algebra; namely, $ab + ac = a(b + c)$.

Collinear Having a line in common. *Collinear points* are points lying on a single line; for example, all points in the plane equidistant from two fixed points P and Q are collinear (they lie on the perpendicular bisector of PQ). In space, *collinear* (or *co-axial*)

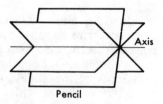

Axis

Pencil

planes are planes which pass through a common line. All planes passing through a given line (the axis) are said to make up a *pencil of planes*.

Cologarithm The cologarithm of a number x, denoted by colog x, is the number $-\log x$ (that is, log $1/x$) expressed with a positive decimal part. For example, to find colog 23 write $= -\log 23 = -1.3617 = 8.6383 - 10$; the latter is the desired form. The cologarithm is used in **computation by logarithms** involving denominators to avoid negative decimals. For example, in computing $(67 \cdot 108)/23$, its logarithm is expressed as log 67 + log 180 + colog 23; these three terms are written with positive decimal parts and the sum is then expressed in the same way.

Combination of Things In algebra, any subset of objects taken out of a given finite set of objects. For example, $\{a, b\}$, $\{a, c\}$, $\{b, c\}$ are all possible combinations of two things out of the set $\{a, b, c\}$. A combination of *n things taken r at a time* is any collection of r distinct members chosen out of a set of n things. The general formula for the total number of such combinations (in factorial notation) is

$$\frac{n!}{(n - r)!\, r!},$$

this is abbreviated $\binom{n}{r}$, or $C(n, r)$. In the example, $n = 3$ and $r = 2$, and the formula gives $3!/(1\,!\,2\,!)$; this equals $(3 \cdot 2 \cdot 1)/(1)(1 \cdot 2)$, or 3. $C(n, r)$ occurs also as the value of the general binomial coefficient in the expansion of $(x + y)^n$.

A more general concept is a combination of *n things r at a time with repetitions allowed*; this is a set of r occurrences of symbols picked out of a set of n distinct symbols where repetitions of symbols are allowed (for example *aab* is a combination of three things selected from $\{a, b, c, d\}$). The total number of such combinations is

$$\frac{(n + r - 1)!}{(n - 1)!\, r!}.$$

Ref. [102, 108].

Combined Variation A relationship in which one variable is equated to an algebraic expression in two or more other variables. An example is $z = 3x^2/y$, in which z varies with x and y. See **Variation**.

Command In a computer, the set of internal signals which cause the computer to execute the operation specified by an **instruction**; sometimes used to mean "instruction," but this is not preferred.

Commensurable Two *line segments* are commensurable if there is a single line segment of which each is a whole number multiple. For example, segments of length $\frac{1}{2}$ and $\frac{4}{5}$ are commensurable; they are, respectively, 15 and 8 times the length $\frac{1}{10}$. An equivalent definition, using numbers instead of segments, is this: two *numbers* are commensurable if their ratio is equal to a rational number (fraction). For example, the commensurability of $\sqrt{3} - 1$ and $3/(\sqrt{3} + 1)$ may be tested by forming the quotient $(\sqrt{3} - 1) \div [3/(\sqrt{3} + 1)]$; since this equals

$$(\sqrt{3} - 1)(\sqrt{3} + 1)/3,$$

or $\frac{2}{3}$, the numbers are commensurable [both are multiples of $1/(\sqrt{3} + 1)$, $\sqrt{3} - 1$ being twice this, and the other being three times this].

The Greek mathematicians of antiquity identified numbers with line segments; they expressed that a segment (number) was a *rational number* by the assertion that it was commensurable with the unit segment. That there were segments not commensurable with the unit segment asserted the existence of irrational numbers. An example of such a segment is the diagonal of a square with a unit segment as a side; this is the number $\sqrt{2}$.

Common Denominator Of two or more fractions, an integer or polynomial that is exactly divisible by each denominator; hence, a common multiple of the denominators. For example, the fractions of $\frac{2}{3} - \frac{1}{10} + \frac{7}{15}$ have a common denominator 30; they also have 60, 90, etc., as common denominators. The two fractions of

$$[x/2(x + 1)(x - 2)] + [3/(x + 1)(x - 1)]$$

have the common denominator

$$2(x + 1)(x - 1)(x - 2);$$

another is

$$2(x + 1)(x - 2)(x + 1)(x - 1),$$

or

$$2(x + 1)^2(x - 2)(x - 1).$$

Fractions with identical denominators are *similar fractions*; such fractions may be added (or subtracted) by merely adding (or subtracting) the numerators, and retaining the original denominator. The common denominator is used to rewrite fractions as similar fractions in order to add or subtract them in this manner. The change to a common denominator is made by multiplying the numerator and the denominator by an appropriate factor; for example, using 30 as a common denominator, the first sum above becomes

$$\frac{2 \cdot 10}{3 \cdot 10} - \frac{1 \cdot 3}{10 \cdot 3} + \frac{7 \cdot 2}{15 \cdot 2},$$

or $\frac{20}{30} - \frac{3}{30} + \frac{14}{30}$; this yields

$$\frac{20 - 3 + 14}{30},$$

37

or $\frac{31}{30}$ as the result. In the second example, the common denominator $2(x + 1)(x - 1)(x - 2)$ leads to

$$\frac{x(x - 1) + 3 \cdot 2(x - 2)}{2(x + 1)(x - 1)(x - 2)}$$
$$= \frac{x^2 + 5x - 12}{2(x + 1)(x - 1)(x - 2)}$$

The *least common denominator* of several fractions, abbreviated l.c.d., is the least common multiple of their denominators.

Common Difference   Of an **arithmetic progression**, the difference between successive terms.

Common Divisor (Syn.: Common factor)   Of two or more integers (polynomials), an integer (polynomial) which is a **divisor** of each. For example, the integers 12 and 18 have the common divisors 2, 3, 4, 6; the polynomials $2(x - 1)^2(x + 2)$, $4(x - 1)^3(x + 2)^2$ have the common divisors $2(x - 1)$, $2(x + 2)$, $2(x - 1)$ $(x + 2)$, $2(x - 1)^2(x + 2)$. The *greatest common divisor*, abbreviated g.c.d., is defined **(1)** for integers, as the largest common divisor, and **(2)** for polynomials, as a common divisor of highest degree. In the examples, 6 and $2(x - 1)^2(x + 2)$ are the greatest common divisors. The greatest common divisor is the same as the *highest common factor,* abbreviated h.c.f. Two integers (polynomials) are *relatively prime* in case their g.c.d. is 1 (is a constant).

The g.c.d. of several expressions can be found by factoring them into prime factors; the g.c.d. is the product of the common factors, each raised to the least power (possibly 0) with which it appears. For example, 60 and 36 factor into $2^2 \cdot 3 \cdot 5$ and $2^2 \cdot 3^2$; the g.c.d. is therefore $2^2 \cdot 3$, or 12. The **Euclidean algorithm** is a procedure for finding the g.c.d. which does not require factoring into primes.

Common Fraction (Syn.: Vulgar fraction)   A **fraction** which is a ratio of whole numbers, such as $\frac{2}{3}$, or $\frac{5}{8}$.

Common Logarithm (Syn.: Briggs logarithm)   The **logarithm** to the base 10.

Common Multiple   Of two or more integers (polynomials), an integer (polynomial) which is a **multiple** of each. For example, 42 is a common multiple of 2, 6, and 14; other common multiples are 84 and 126. The polynomials $(x - 1)^2(x + 2)$, $(x - 1)$ $(x + 2)^2$ have $(x - 1)^2(x + 2)^2$ as a common multiple; other common multiples are $(x - 1)^3(x + 2)^2$ and $(x - 1)^2(x + 2)^3$. The *lowest, or least, common multiple*, abbreviated l.c.m., is defined **(1)** for integers, as the smallest positive common multiple, and **(2)** for polynomials, as a common multiple of least degree. In the examples, the l.c.m.'s are 42 and $(x - 1)^2(x + 2)^2$. A common multiple of several expressions is always available in their product; this is not necessarily the l.c.m., however. The l.c.m. can be determined from their prime factors; it is the product of these factors, each raised to the highest power with which it appears. For example, 12 and 98 factor into $2^2 \cdot 3$ and $2 \cdot 7^2$; the l.c.m. is therefore $2^2 \cdot 3 \cdot 7^2$, or 588.

A common multiple of the denominators of two or more fractions is called a **common denominator** of the fractions.

Common Tangent   Of two circles in

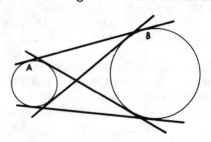

a plane, a line which is tangent to both circles. Two circles which are exterior to each other have four common tangents—two of them are *internal* and two of them are *external*. The "common tangent" sometimes means the line segment between the points of tangency (as AB in the figure).

Commutative Group (Syn.: Abelian group) A **group** in which the binary operation is commutative.

Commutative Law The commutative law of *addition* is expressed by the equation $a + b = b + a$; that is, a sum is unaffected by the order of the terms. Similarly, the commutative law of *multiplication* is given by $a \cdot b = b \cdot a$. The commutative law for any *binary operation*, denoted by "$*$", is the property that $a * b = b * a$. The feature holds in many mathematical systems, such as the **group** and the **field**, but fails in other systems, such as the **algebra of matrices** (for multiplication). The acceptance of an algebraic system in which "multiplication" is not commutative was considered by Hamilton in the middle of the nineteenth century and was a major break with the traditions of mathematics.

Comparison Test The following test for the convergence of an infinite series $a_1 + a_2 + a_3 + \cdots$ to a finite sum: each term in absolute value is less than or equal to the corresponding term of a series which is known to converge; that is, $|a_n| \leq b_n$, where $b_1 + b_2 + b_3 + \cdots$ is a convergent series of positive (or zero) terms. See **Ratio test**.

Compiler In a computer, a set of stored instructions which takes a computational routine in one code and automatically converts it to another code which is, typically, more acceptable for execution by the machine. See **Computer program**.

Complement of Set The collection of all things (in a designated "universe") that are not members of a given set A; it is denoted by A' or CA. (See **Algebra of sets**.) For example, the complement of the set of even whole numbers in the universe of all whole numbers, is the set of odd whole numbers.

Complementary Angles Two **angles** whose sum is $90°$.

Complementary Trigonometric Functions (Syn.: Co-functions) The following pairs of **trigonometric functions**: *sine* and *cosine, tangent* and *cotangent, secant* and *cosecant*. The reason for the term "complementary" is that the functions in a pair have equal values for complementary angles; that is, if $A + B = 90°$, then $\sin A = \cos B$, $\tan A = \cot B$, $\sec A = \csc B$; e.g., $\sin 30° = \cos 60°$, $\tan 115 = \cot (-25°)$.

Completing the Square In algebra, a technique for modifying a quadratic polynomial to obtain a perfect (trinomial) square. It is based on the observation that an expression $x^2 + bx$ lacks being a perfect square only by omission of the constant term $b^2/4$ [since $(x + b/2)^2 = x^2 + bx + b^2/4$]; the missing term is the square of half the coefficient of the variable. For example, to complete the square in $x^2 - 4x - 7$, add and subtract 4 [the square of $(\frac{1}{2})(-4)$]; this leads to $(x^2 - 4x + 4) -4 -7$, and finally to the desired result $(x - 2)^2 -11$. Completing the square provides a general method for the solution of the **quadratic equation**; also, see **Trinomial**.

Complex Fraction A fraction whose numerator or denominator (or both)

39

contains a fraction; examples are

$$\frac{2}{3/5}, \quad \text{and} \quad \frac{1 - (x/y)}{1 + (y/x)}.$$

A complex fraction can always be reduced to a simple fraction. For example,

$$\frac{2}{3/5} = \frac{2/1}{3/5} = \frac{2}{1} \cdot \frac{5}{3} = \frac{10}{3}.$$

This method is based on the following general rule for the division of fractions.

$$\frac{a/b}{c/d} = \frac{a}{b} \cdot \frac{d}{c} = \frac{ad}{bc}.$$

Another method of reduction is to multiply the fractions in numerator and denominator by a common denominator; in the second example above, this calls for multiplying by xy, yielding $(xy - x^2)/(xy + y^2)$.

Complex Number   A number representable in the form $a + bi$, where a and b are real numbers and i is the *imaginary unit* satisfying the equation $i^2 = -1$. This is an extension of the concept of **number** which serves to remedy the inadequacy of ordinary real numbers for the complete solution of quadratic equations. (Historically, a satisfactory conception of complex numbers did not emerge until the end of the eighteenth century, although they were used for 100 years before that.) Examples of complex numbers are $2 + 3i$, $1 - i$, 5, and $4i$. As the notation $a + bi$ shows, the complex numbers have as their building blocks the real numbers and the imaginary unit i (sometimes denoted by $\sqrt{-1}$). The real numbers are included among the complex numbers; they occur when $b = 0$. When $b \neq 0$, the complex number is *imaginary*, such as $2 + 3i$; when a is 0, the complex number is *pure imaginary*, such as $4i$. In $a + bi$, a is the *real part* and b is the *imaginary part*.

Two complex numbers are equal just in case their real and imaginary parts are separately equal; for example, $(2 + 1) + (\frac{1}{2})i$ equals $3 + (\frac{5}{10})i$.

The complex number can be interpreted as a point in the coordinate plane; $a + bi$ is identified with the point P having coordinates (a, b). For example, the imaginary unit i is represented by $(0, 1)$ at the unit point of the y-axis. (This **Argand diagram**, or complex plane, helps remove the notion that a complex number is less "real" than a real number, a notion that endured into the nineteenth century.) The length r of the line seg-

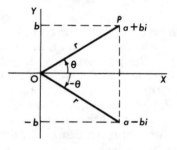

ment OP from the origin O to P is the *absolute value*, or *modulus*, of the complex number $a + bi$; it equals $\sqrt{a^2 + b^2}$. The angle θ from the positive x-axis to OP is the *amplitude*, or *argument*, or *phase*, of $a + bi$. The *polar*, or *trigonometric*, *form* of the complex number $a + bi$ is $r(\cos\theta + i\sin\theta)$; see **Euler's formula**. Two complex numbers which are symmetrically located across the x-axis are called *conjugate complex numbers*; they have the forms $a + bi$, $a - bi$, having amplitudes of opposite sign. Their product, $(a + bi) \times (a - bi)$, is a real number, $a^2 + b^2$.

The ordinary techniques of arithmetic and algebra are used in arithmetical operations with complex numbers, the number i being treated as a literal symbol; the novel feature is that i^2 may be replaced by -1. An example of addition is the following:

$$(3 + 2i) + (4 - i) = (4 + 3) + (2 - 1)i$$
$$= 7 + i;$$

for addition in general,

$$(a + bi) + (c + di) = (a + c) + (b + d)i.$$

An example of multiplication is

$$(3 + 2i)(4 - i) = 12 + 5i - 2i^2$$
$$= 12 + 5i + 2.$$

or $14 + 5i$; in general,

$$(a + bi)(c + di) = (ac - bd)$$
$$+ (ad + bc)i.$$

Division of complex numbers is accomplished by multiplying numerator and denominator by the conjugate of the latter and thereby "rationalizing" the denominator, that is, removing i from the denominator. For example, to compute $(3 + 2i)/(4 - i)$, multiply top and bottom by $4 + i$; then

$$\frac{(3 + 2i)(4 + i)}{(4 - i)(4 + i)} = \frac{12 + 11i + 2i^2}{16 - i^2}$$
$$= \frac{10 + 11i}{17},$$

or $\frac{10}{17} + \frac{11}{17}i$. For division in general,

$$\frac{a + bi}{c + di} = \frac{(a + bi)(c - di)}{c^2 + d^2}.$$

Powers of i higher than the second can always be reduced to ± 1 or $\pm i$; for example, $i^3 = i^2 \cdot i = (-1)i = -i$, and $i^4 = i^2 \cdot i^2 = (-1)(-1) = 1$. When $r(\cos \theta + i \sin \theta)$, the polar form, is used, multiplication and division are expressed by the formulas

$$r(\cos \theta + \sin \theta) \cdot r'(\cos \theta' + i \sin \theta')$$
$$= rr'[\cos(\theta + \theta') + i \sin (\theta + \theta')],$$

and

$$[r(\cos \theta + i \sin \theta)]/[r'(\cos \theta' + i \sin \theta')]$$
$$= (r/r')[(\cos \theta - \theta') + i \sin (\theta - \theta')];$$

that is, in multiplication, multiply the absolute values and add the amplitudes, while in division, divide the absolute values and subtract the amplitudes. Raising to a power is accomplished in the polar form by the elegant formula

$$[r(\cos \theta + i \sin \theta)]^n = r^n(\cos n\theta + i \sin n\theta);$$

this is De Moivre's theorem. It holds for fractional exponents as well as integral exponents; because of this, it provides a method for the extraction of **roots of complex numbers**.

A complex number can be regarded as an individual number apart from its expression as a combination of real numbers. In this case, frequent variables for complex numbers are z and w, and algebraic expressions are cast directly in these symbols, as in $2z^2 - 4z + 5$ or $wz - w + 3z$. Viewed as a number system in itself, the complex numbers obey many of the fundamental laws of ordinary algebra, such as the commutative and associative laws of addition and multiplication, the distributive law, and so on. This similarity is pointed up by the fact that the complex numbers and the real numbers are both examples of a common mathematical system, the so-called **field**. An important respect in which the two systems differ is that the real numbers form a simple **ordered set**, while the complex numbers do not. The motivation mentioned earlier for inventing complex numbers was to solve any quadratic equation; for example, the equation $x^2 - 2x + 3 = 0$ has the solutions $1 + i\sqrt{2}$ and $1 - i\sqrt{2}$. But a remarkable fact emerges from satisfying this requirement—*any polynomial equation, no matter what its degree, has solutions in complex numbers* (the coefficients may be any complex, or real, numbers); for example, the equation

$$100x^5 - \sqrt{2}\,x^4 + \tfrac{1}{2}x^3 - 999x^2 + \pi = 0$$

has complex solutions. This result is the **fundamental theorem of algebra**.

The elementary transcendental functions such as the logarithm function, the trigonometric functions, etc., are initially defined for real numbers. These functions can be extended to functions defined for complex numbers; such functions of a complex variable are essential to many parts of advanced mathematics. See **Logarithm of complex number**, **Power series**.

Ref. [28, 73, 120, 148].

Complex Plane See **Argand diagram** (syn.).

Complex Root. Of an equation, a root which is a complex number. See **Imaginary root**.

Complex Variable A **variable** which takes on only complex numbers as values; a commonly used letter is "z."

Component of Vector The projection of a vector on a given line. If OP is a vector and l is a line through O, then OP' is the component of OP along l, where PP' is perpendicular to l; the length of OP' is the length of OP times the cosine of the angle between OP and l. When the vector

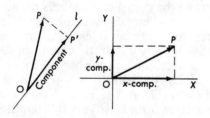

depicts force, for example, then the component represents the effective force in the direction of l.

The projection of a vector on the x-axis is its x-component (similarly

for any axis). When a plane vector is represented as a pair of numbers (a, b) a component is understood to be either of the coordinates a or b; these are the (directed) lengths of the projections on the axes.

Composite Number In arithmetic, an integer which is the product of two integers, both different from 1 and -1; for example, the integer 6 is composite (since $6 = 3 \cdot 2$), but the integer 7 is not. A **prime number** is one that is not composite. See **Unique factorization theorem**.

Composition of Functions Formation of a **function** as one function (mapping) g followed by another f; the resulting *composite function* has the functional value $f[g(x)]$. For example, log sin x [that is, log(sin x)] results from the composition of sin

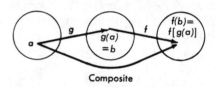

Composite

and log. More specifically, $f[g(x)]$ is described as follows: starting with the argument a, obtain the functional value $g(a)$; then, using $g(a)$ as an argument b, obtain the functional value $f(b)$; the result is $f[g(a)]$. For example, let $f(x) = 2x^2 + 1$, $g(x) = x - 2$. To obtain $f[g(x)]$ when $x = 4$, first compute $g(4) = 4 - 2$, or 2, then compute $f(2) = 2 \cdot 2^2 + 1 = 8 + 1$, or 9; hence $f[g(4)] = 9$. In practice, the expression for $f[g(x)]$ is obtained by substituting the expression for $g(x)$ in place of x, in the expression for $f(x)$; in the last example,

$$f[g(x)] = 2[g(x)]^2 + 1 = 2(x - 2)^2 + 1$$
$$= 2x^2 - 8x + 9.$$

Composition can be viewed as a binary operation among functions;

out of two functions it produces a single function. Viewed thus, it shares some of the basic features of ordinary algebraic operations. For example, just as there is a number, the *identity element* 1, which reproduces any number on multiplication, so there is a function, the *identity function*, which reproduces any function on composition; this is the function I for which $I(x) = x$; symbolically, $f[I(x)] = f(x)$ and $I[f(x)] = f(x)$. On the other hand, unlike multiplication, composition of functions is not commutative; that is, $f[g(x)]$ and $g[f(x)]$ do not always describe the same functions; for example, with $f(x)$ and $g(x)$ as in the preceding example,

$$f[g(x)] = 2x^2 - 8x + 9;$$

but

$$g[f(x)] = f(x) - 2 = (2x^2 + 1) - 2$$
$$= 2x^2 - 1.$$

See **Inverse of function**.

For the derivative of a composite function, see **Chain rule**.

Composition of Ordinates   See **Graphing**.

Composition of Relations   A "chain" process of combining two **relations** in a given order to produce a *composite relation*: namely, given two relations in a certain order, then x bears the composite relation to z in case x bears the first relation to y and y bears the second relation to z, for some y. For example, the relation "is a brother of" and the relation "is a parent of" yield the composite relation "is a brother of a parent of" (that is, "is an uncle of"). Various family relationships are built by composition—the composition of the relation "is the father of" with itself yields "is the father of a father of"

(that is, "is the paternal grandfather of"). Reversing the order of relations generally changes a composite relation; for example, the relation "is a parent of a brother of" is different from the first example.

Let "$R * S$" denote a composite of relations R and S; then, symbolically, "$x(R * S)z$" denotes "for some y, $x R y$ and $y S z$." As an example, let "$m G n$" stand for "m is greater than n," and "$m S n$" stand for "m is the square of n" (for whole numbers m and n). Then "$m(G * S)n$" stands for "m is greater than the square of n"; on the other hand, "$m(S * G)n$" stands for "m is the square of a whole number greater than n." Composition is a binary operation on relations; as the example shows, it is not commutative. This operation belongs to the "algebra," or "calculus," of relations, which is a subject of symbolic logic.

Composition of Vectors   See **Addition of vectors**.

Computation   The carrying out of a series of arithmetical (or other) operations.   See **Algorithm**, **Computer program**.

Computation by Logarithms   Numerical computation by use of logarithms (usually common logarithms). The simplification of numerical computation was the motivation for the invention of the **logarithm** at the beginning of the seventeenth century. Its usefulness rests on the following basic properties:

(1) $\log a \cdot b = \log a + \log b$;
(2) $\log (a/b) = \log a - \log b$;
(3) $\log a^n = n \log a$; and
(4) $\log \sqrt[n]{a} = (1/n) \log a$.

These show that multiplication of numbers translates into addition of logarithms, division into subtraction,

43

raising to a power into multiplication, and root extraction into division. The small price paid for this simplification is the use of a table of logarithms for passing between numbers and their logarithms.

The *common logarithm* log A (base 10) is used in computations; log A (A positive) is written as an integer (its *characteristic*), plus a positive decimal fraction (its *mantissa*). When A is a decimal number, the characteristic is specified by the location of the decimal point; the mantissa is specified by its string of digits (regardless of the decimal point), and can be found in a table of logarithms. For example, when $A = 17.6$, then log $A = 1.2455$, with characteristic 1 and mantissa .2455 (see Appendix D); also, log .0176 $= -2 + .2455$, or $8.2455 - 10$, and log $1.76 = 0.2455$. The logarithm found in this way is generally an approximate number, since the true value is usually an unending decimal.

The reverse process of finding the *antilogarithm*, or "antilog x" is called for in computation; this is the number whose logarithm equals x. To find the antilogarithm, x is written as an integer (characteristic) and a positive decimal (mantissa); the mantissa is located in a table of logarithms to determine the string of digits of x, and then the decimal point is located by means of the characteristic. Suppose log $A = 1.6794$, for example; that is, antilog $1.6794 = A$; a table look-up with the mantissa .6794 gives 478; the decimal point is then located in accordance with the characteristic 1, to give $A = 47.8$, or antilog $1.6794 = 47.8$.

The following examples illustrate computation by logarithms, using the four-place table of logarithms in Appendix D. Compute $(17.6)(0.486)$;

(1) log $[(17.6)(0.486)] =$ log 17.6 $+$ log 0.486 $= 1.2455$ $+ 9.6866 - 10 = 0.9321$;

(2) antilog $0.9321 = 8.552$; thus, $(17.6)(0.486) = 8.55$, rounded off.

Compute $1.76/0.486$;

(1) log $\dfrac{1.76}{0.486} =$ log 1.76 $-$ log 0.486
$= 0.2455 - (9.6866 - 10)$
$= (10.2455 - 10) - (9.6866 - 10)$
$= 10.2455 - 9.6866 = 0.5589$;

(2) antilog $0.5589 = 3.622$, or rounded off, 3.62.

Compute $\sqrt{0.486}$;

(1) log $\sqrt{0.486} =$ log $(0.486)^{1/2}$
$= \frac{1}{2}$ log $0.486 = \frac{1}{2}(9.6866 - 10)$
$= 4.8433 - 5$;

(2) antilog $(4.8433 - 5) = 0.6972$, or, rounded off, 0.697; thus, $\sqrt{0.486} = 0.697$.

The **cologarithm** is commonly used in computations involving division. **Linear interpolation** is applied when exact values are not found among the entries of the table of logarithms. Logarithms are common in trigonometric computations. In order to avoid using separate tables of logarithms and trigonometric functions, tables of composite functions, such as log sin, have been constructed to simplify these computations (see Appendix D). These are used, for example, in the solution of a triangle in the plane.

Computer (Syn.: Computing machine)   A mechanical, electrical, or other machine that is capable of carrying out a series of operations on numbers and other information in symbolic form. An *automatic computer* is one that can perform long sequences of operations without human intervention. A distinction is made between a *digital computer* and an *analog computer*—in the former, numbers are represented as strings of digits (for example, in decimal or binary form); in the latter, numbers are represented by physical quantities, such as rotations, voltages, or distances, and arithmetical operations are carried out directly on these quantities.

The modern electronic digital computer is a *stored-program computer*; that is, the sequence of instructions that direct the computer through the solution of a problem are internally stored in advance, and the computation proceeds automatically thereafter. A distinction is often drawn between a *computer* and a *calculator* on this basis—a computer has a stored program and can internally modify its instructions in the course of a computation; a calculator does not have this capability (in a desk calculator, for example, the instructions are impressed manually by the human operator).

Ref. [36, 37, 60, 61, 97, 125].

Computer Program   In an automatic computer, a *program* is a plan for the machine to follow in the solution of a problem; *programming* is the construction of such a plan. A program is often described in the graphical form of a *flow diagram*, or *chart*; this is an array of boxes, arrows, symbols, etc. which indicates the logical pattern of the computation. The figure shows the over-all structure of a typical program; it repeats

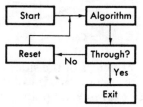

a general solution procedure, or algorithm, over and over, until an answer is obtained to an acceptable degree of accuracy (see **Approximation**).

For the computer to carry through a program, the program must be detailed further and organized into a *routine*; this is a sequence of coded instructions which the machine can interpret and execute directly; it is stored in the computer, together with necessary data, in advance of computation (or various stages of computation). A routine is generally a highly detailed list written in a specialized "language" matched with the computer at hand; *coding* is the construction of a routine. Thus, a program is a design for a routine, while a routine is a means of actually carrying out a program. This distinction, although preferred, is not universally followed; thus, "program" and "routine" are used interchangeably, and "programming" may include "coding," as well as planning for coding.

Automatic coding (or *automatic programming*) are methods of coding in which the computer itself is used in the preparation of a routine. In this connection, a routine may be written in a pseudocode (or *programming language*), which is more efficient for human use, and not in the instruction code of the computer (or *machine language*), which is more efficient for computer use. This calls for the use of *executive routines* which transform pseudocodes into machine language; an executive routine, then, is one that processes and controls other routines. An *interpreter* is an executive routine with the following feature: it automatically translates a stored routine in pseudocode step by step causing the necessary machine operations to be carried out that lead to a desired problem so-

45

lution; the output is the solution of the problem. A *compiler*, on the other hand, is an executive routine which automatically translates a routine in pseudocode into an equivalent routine in machine code (or, more generally, in another programming language); thus, a compiler takes as input a program expressed in one coded form and yields as output an equivalent program expressed in another coded form.

See **Computer programming language**, **Digital computer**.   Ref. [92].

Computer Programming Language The *machine language* of an automatic computer is the system of symbols for representing information which the computer can directly interpret and act upon; it is the language the machine was built to understand. Through computer programs and routines a modern electronic **digital computer** can solve an unlimited variety of problems; however, its machine language is not the "natural" language for humans to use in formulating solutions to these problems (as ordinary mathematical symbolism might be, for example). To bring the computer closer to the problem, *programming languages* are designed. Such a "higher order" language is expressed in a "pseudocode" which is a compromise between machine language and the scientific language of problems; *FORTRAN* and *ALGOL* are existing examples. Of considerable interest are languages intended to program **machine intelligence**. A *list-processing language* is one adapted to this type of problem; here, entire lists of information, rather than single items, are manipulated as individual entities. When a higher order language is used on a computer, an *executive routine* is called for to translate it into machine

code. Some present research is concerned with the design of computers whose own machine language will be close to such an advanced programming language.   See **Computer program**.

Computer Sciences The field of knowledge that treats the design and use of computers, including methods of programming and development of areas of application.

Ref. [19, 35, 36, 37, 61, 87].

Computing Machine   See **Computer** (syn.).

Concave   A plane curve with end points P and Q is *concave toward a point O* in case the region bounded by the line segments OP, OQ, and the curve is a convex set.   See listings under **convex**.

Concentric   Sharing a common center, as in "concentric circles."

Conclusion   In logic, the individual statement Q in a **conditional** statement "If P, then Q"; the statement P is the *hypothesis*. "Conclusion" also has a less formal meaning as a statement derived by proof from a set of assumptions, or hypotheses.

Concurrent   In geometry, having a point in common, as in concurrent lines or concurrent planes. In plane geometry, for example, the perpen-

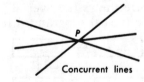

Concurrent lines

dicular bisectors of the sides of a triangle are concurrent. In solid geometry, for example, all planes that are tangent to a given cone are concurrent at the apex of the cone. All planes in space concurrent through a fixed point form a *bundle* of planes. See **Collinear**, **Pencil**.

Condition In general, a requirement or **property**; as in the condition that a whole number be a prime, or that a triangle be isosceles. Condition P is *sufficient* for condition Q in case P implies Q; condition P is *necessary* for Q in case Q implies P, that is, in case Q cannot hold unless P does. For example, the condition that an integer m is (exactly) divisible by 4 is a sufficient condition for m to be an even integer; equality of corresponding angles is a necessary condition for two triangles to be congruent (equality of corresponding angles, however, is not sufficient for congruence). Condition P is *necessary and sufficient* for condition Q in case P implies Q and Q implies P; for example, equality of two sides of a triangle is a necessary and sufficient condition for equality of two angles. In general, a necessary condition need not be sufficient, nor a sufficient condition be necessary; for example, to become rich it may be necessary to desire money, but it is not sufficient. See **Biconditional**, **Conditional**.

Conditional (Syn.: Implication) In logic, the propositional form "If P then Q," or any statement having this form; it is sometimes symbolized "$P \to Q$." P is the *antecedent* (or *hypothesis*), and Q is the *consequent* (or *conclusion*). An example is: "If a, b, c are the sides of a right triangle, then $a^2 + b^2 = c^2$"; here, P stands for "a, b, c are the sides of a right triangle" and Q stands for "$a^2 + b^2 = c^2$." Mathematical theorems are frequently expressed as conditionals; alternative phrasings are "P implies Q," "P is sufficient for Q," and "P only if Q." See **Algebra of propositions**, **Biconditional**.

A conditional is taken to be false in case the antecedent is true (T) and the consequent is false (F); otherwise it is taken to be true (see the truth-table in the figure). This agreement leads to regarding as true such bizarre statements as "If $0 = 1$, then $2 + 2 = 4$"; however, the agreement is useful for theoretical considera-

P	Q	If P then Q
T	T	T
F	T	T
T	F	F
F	F	T

tions and harmless in practice. The *denial* of the conditional is the conjunction "P and not Q"; for example, the conditional "If our experiment succeeds, then we are famous" is denied by the statement "Our experiment succeeds and we are not famous."

Associated with the conditional "If P then Q" are several related conditionals, the *contrapositive*, *converse*, and *inverse*; these are, respectively, "If not Q, then not P," "If Q then P," "If not P, then not Q." A conditional and its contrapositive are logically equivalent; "If I go, then you go" has the same logical meaning "If you do not go, then I do not go." This is not so of a conditional and its converse; particular statements of these forms may be true together, or one may be true and the other false; the latter case is illustrated by the conditionals "If m is a prime number greater than 2, then m is an odd number" (true), "If m is an odd number, then m is a prime number greater than 2" (false). The converse and inverse conditionals are logically equivalent—in fact, they are contrapositive conditionals.

47

Conditional Convergence An infinite series, which is convergent, is *conditionally convergent* in case its series of absolute values is not convergent (an example is the convergent series $1 - \frac{1}{2} + \frac{1}{3} - \frac{1}{4} + \cdots$; its series of absolute values is the divergent harmonic series $1 + \frac{1}{2} + \frac{1}{3} + \frac{1}{4} + \cdots$). See **Absolute convergence**.

Conditional Equation An equation, containing variables, which is false for at least one replacement of the variables by constants, and true for at least one replacement. An example is $x^2 - 1 = x + 1$; it becomes a true statement when x is replaced by 2, but a false one when x is replaced by 1. An *unconditional equation*, or *identity*, is one which is true for all values of the variables (examples are $x^2 - y^2 = (x + y)(x - y)$, and $\sin^2 A + \cos^2 A = 1$); an *inconsistent equation* is one true for no values of the variables.

Conditional Inequality See **Unconditional inequality**.

Conditional Probability If A is an alternative outcome of one random event and H that of another, then the probability of A, assuming that H holds, is the *conditional probability* of A under the hypothesis H; sometimes written "$\Pr(A \mid H)$." For example, the probability that 2 occurs in a roll of two dice, under the hypothesis that a particular die shows 1, is 1/6 (without any hypothesis about one die, the probability is 1/36).

Cone In solid geometry, a closed surface defined by a closed plane curve C (the *directrix*) and a point V (the *vertex*, or *apex*) not in the plane of C; the cone consists of the lateral surface of all line segments from V to

C and the *base*, which is C and its interior (see **Pyramid**). Any line segment from V to C is an *element* of the cone; the *altitude* is the perpendicular line segment (or its length) from the vertex to the plane of the base. A cone is named after the di-

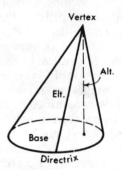

rectrix; for example, a *circular cone* has a circle as directrix, and an *elliptic cone*, an ellipse. A *convex cone* is one whose directrix is a convex curve. If the base has a center, the line segment from the vertex to the center is the *axis* of the cone. When the axis is perpendicular to the base, the cone is a *right cone*; otherwise it is an *oblique cone*; examples are the right circular cone and the oblique circular cone. A right circular cone can be generated by rotating a right

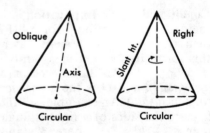

triangle about a leg through a complete revolution; accordingly, it is also called a *cone of revolution*.

The volume V of a cone is $\frac{1}{3}$ the area of the base times the altitude h; for a right circular cone, this becomes

$V = (\frac{1}{3})\pi r^2 h$, where r is the radius of the base. The lateral area of a right circular cone equals πrs, where s is the slant height (the distance from the vertex to any point on the circular directrix).

A *frustrum of a cone* is the solid between the base and a plane parallel to the base (and intersecting all the elements); its bases are given by the plane section and the original base, and the *altitude h* is a perpendicular line segment (or its length) between the planes of the bases. The volume of a frustrum of a cone equals $(\frac{1}{3})h(A_1 + A_2 + \sqrt{A_1 A_2})$, where A_1, A_2 are the areas of the bases. For a frustrum of a right circular cone, the *slant height s* is the

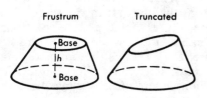

Frustrum   Truncated

portion of the original slant height between the bases; in this case, the volume V is $(\frac{1}{3})\pi h(r_1^2 + r_2^2 + r_1 r_2)$, where r_1, r_2 are the radii of the bases, and the lateral area is $\pi s(r_1 + r_2)$. The solid between the base of a cone and a plane section not parallel to the base (and intersecting all the elements) is a *truncated cone.*

A tangent plane to a cone touches the lateral surface along an entire element, the element of contact, or tangency. The planes tangent at the various elements make up a family of concurrent planes through the vertex, which is produced by rolling a plane around the lateral surface of the cone. The cone is an example of a *developable surface,* that is, a surface which can be laid out evenly on a plane; it is also a *ruled surface.*

The term "cone" is sometimes used for **conical surface**.

Confocal In geometry, having the same foci, as in confocal conics. For example, the ellipse $x^2/25 + y^2/9 = 1$ and the hyperbola $x^2/9 - y^2/7 = 1$ are confocal with common foci $(\pm 4, 0)$. A confocal ellipse and hyperbola always intersect at right angles (see figure). The equation

$$\frac{x^2}{a^2 - k} + \frac{y^2}{b^2 - k} = 1$$

represents a **family** of confocal conics. $a^2 > b^2$ are fixed, and $k\ (<a^2)$ is a parameter; when k is less than b^2 the conic is an ellipse, when k is greater than b^2, it is an hyperbola. All these

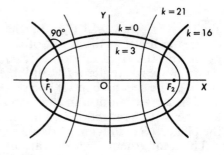

conics share the foci $(\pm\sqrt{a^2 - b^2}, 0)$; the figure shows several members of the family when $a^2 = 25$ and $b^2 = 9$.

Congruent Figures in Plane In plane geometry, two figures such that one can be brought into coincidence with the other by a rigid motion in space; this expresses the ordinary notion of geometric "sameness," or the "same except for location." The symbol "$\cong$" is used for the congruence relation; for example, "$\triangle ABC$ is congruent to $\triangle DEF$" is written "$\triangle ABC \cong \triangle DEF$" (this notation goes back to the seventeenth century). Examples of congruent figures are **(1)** line segments of equal length; **(2)** circles

49

of equal radii; **(3)** angles of the same measure; **(4)** circular arcs of the same length and radius. Actually, two types of congruence arise for figures in the plane. One occurs when the rigid motion is restricted to the plane; in this case, a figure is slid and turned into coincidence with another without being lifted out of the plane (tri-

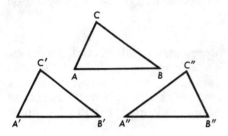

angles ABC and $A'B'C'$); in the other, the figure is lifted out of the plane and the rigid motion carried out in space (triangles ABC and $A''B''C''$). The second can also be realized as a rigid motion in the plane together with a reflection in a line in the plane. See **Polygon**, **Triangle**.

That congruent figures can be superposed, or brought into coincidence, was formulated as an axiom of superposition by Euclid. Sometimes the terms "equivalent figures" or "equal figures" are used for congruent figures; this use of equality is not consistent with its logical meaning as "the same in every respect."

See **Congruent figures in space**, **Geometry**.

Congruent Figures in Space In solid geometry, two figures such that one can be brought into coincidence with the other by a rigid motion; this expresses the ordinary motion of geometric "sameness"; it is symbolized by "$\cong$". Two figures in which one is congruent to the reflection of the other in a plane are said to be *oppo-*

sitely congruent, or *symmetric*; in the

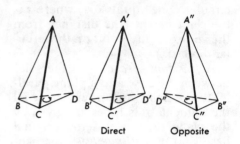

Direct   Opposite

other case, the figures are *directly congruent*, or simply *congruent*. Directly congruent figures have the same "orientation" in space, oppositely congruent figures have opposite "orientation." In the figures, this is expressed by the arrangement of the vertices of the base as viewed from the apex A; in the second figure, $B'C'D'$ has the same rotational sense as BCD, while in the third figure, $B''C''D''$ has the opposite rotational sense. Two left shoes, for example, are directly congruent, but a left shoe and a right shoe are oppositely congruent. For congruence of particular figures see **Polyhedral angle**, **Polyhedron**, **Spherical polygon**, **Spherical triangle**, **Trihedral angle**.

Congruent Integers In the theory of numbers, two integers a and b whose difference $a - b$ is (exactly) divisible by a given positive integer m, called the *modulus*; the integers are said to be "congruent modulo m." The congruence relation is symbolized "$a \equiv b \pmod{m}$" (read "a is congruent to b modulo m"). For example, 25 and 11 are congruent modulo 7; 14 and 3 are not congruent modulo 7; that is $25 \equiv 11 \pmod{7}$, $14 \not\equiv 3 \pmod{7}$. Put otherwise, congruent integers are those that have the same remainder on division by m. An example of a theorem of the theory of numbers expressed in congruence notation, is Fermat's theorem: it asserts that $a^{p-1} \equiv 1 \pmod{p}$ whenever p is a prime and a is not divisible by p [for example, if $a = 2$ and $p = 5$, then $16 \equiv 1 \pmod 5$].

A modified form of arithmetic, known as *arithmetic modulo m*, can be constructed based on congruence. In this arithmetic, the "sum" $a + b$, and the "product" $a \cdot b$, are defined as the remainder upon division by m of the ordinary sum and product; these operations are designated as *addition modulo m* and *multiplication modulo m*. For example, when $m = 7$, in this arithmetic, $4 + 5 = 2$ and $4 \cdot 5 = 6$. This is a "finite" arithmetic or "finite" number system (one having a finite number of elements). For example, when the modulus is 5, it consists of the five elements 0, 1, 2, 3, 4 under the operations of addition and multiplication modulo 5. The "addition" and "multiplication" tables are shown below.

+	0 1 2 3 4
0	0 1 2 3 4
1	1 2 3 4 0
2	2 3 4 0 1
3	3 4 0 1 2
4	4 0 1 2 3

Addition Modulo 5

·	0 1 2 3 4
0	0 0 0 0 0
1	0 1 2 3 4
2	0 2 4 1 3
3	0 3 1 4 2
4	0 4 3 2 1

Multiplication Modulo 5

Such a finite system can be represented geometrically by means of rotations of a circle. Consider the case $m = 5$; let any element a be identified with the arrangement of the five equally spaced points shown on the circle, produced by rotating the circle counterclockwise through an angle of $a \cdot (360°/5)$ that is, $a \cdot 72°$. Interpret $a + b$ as the arrangement of these points produced by the rotation a followed by the rotation b; interpret $a \cdot b$ as rotation b applied a

times; these sums and products are

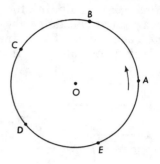

given as shown in the tables. The arithmetical and geometrical descriptions are *isomorphic* mathematical systems.

In a system of finite arithmetic, variables x, y, z, etc., stand for its elements, and an algebraic expression such as $x^2 + 2xy + y$ has meaning according to the operations in this "universe" of numbers. The system shares many properties of ordinary algebra—the commutative and associative laws of addition and multiplication hold, the distributive law holds, there are identity elements, 0 and 1, for addition and multiplication, etc. Technically, arithmetic modulo m is a commutative **ring**. The resemblance to ordinary algebra is closest when the modulus m is a prime number; in this case, the finite system is a **field**. The need for requiring that the modulus be a prime can be illustrated by the nonprime modulus 6; in this case, $3 \cdot 4$ equals 0 (modulo 6), even though neither 3 nor 4 equals 0 (modulo 6); this means that a product can be zero without either factor being 0, which is contrary to ordinary algebra. The introduction of the concept and notation of congruent integers by Gauss at the beginning of the nineteenth century was significant in the development of the theory of numbers.

51

Conic (Syn.: Conic section) A plane curve defined as follows: Fix a line, the *directrix,* and a point, the *focus;* select a positive constant *e,* the *eccentricity.* Then the set of all points *P* in the plane whose distance from the

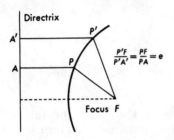

focus is in the ratio *e* to its distance from the directrix make up a conic. The three types of conics are distinguished by the value of the eccentricity; **(1)** when *e* is less than 1, the conic is an **ellipse**; **(2)** when *e* = 1, it is a **parabola**; **(3)** when *e* is greater than 1, it is an **hyperbola**. These curves are rather different in appearance. The ellipse is a simple closed

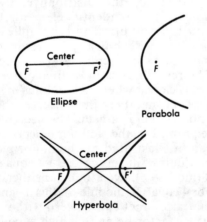

curve with two foci, *F* and *F'*; the parabola is a single widening branch with one focus; the hyperbola has two distinct branches and two foci, and lies between two asymptotes. An ellipse or hyperbola has a center of

symmetry, and is called a *central conic.* Conics whose eccentricities are equal are *similar conics;* such conics are expanded or contracted versions of each other. See **Eccentricity of conic.**

In algebraic form, a conic occurs as the graph of an equation of the type

$$ax^2 + bxy + cy^2 + dx + ey + f = 0$$

(general equation of the second degree in *x* and *y*); conversely, the graph of an equation of this type is a conic (with certain degenerate cases). Because of this, conics are called *quadric,* or *quadratic, curves.* The equation of a cone is simplified when it is appropriately located with respect to the axes of a rectangular coordinate system; for example, the ellipse has the equation $(x^2/a^2) + (y^2/b^2) = 1$ when the origin is at the center of the ellipse and the *x*-axis is along the major axis. In polar coordinates (r, θ), the equation of the conic has the form

$$r = de/(1 - e \cos \theta);$$

here, the pole is at the focus, the di-

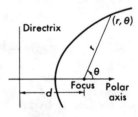

rectrix is perpendicular to the polar axis, and *d* is the distance between the focus and directrix. See **General equation, Tangent line to conic.**

The conics were studied exhaustively by Appollonius (third century B.C.); he named the types of conics and developed his theory by the Greek geometric methods. Today

they are studied as a part of analytic geometry. They occur in many applications, a notable example being the motion of planets and other astronomical bodies.
Ref. [148].

Conic Section (Syn.: Conic)   The conic as a plane section of a circular conical surface; it was in this form that they were defined originally by the Greek geometer Apollonius. The type of conic—ellipse, hyperbola, or

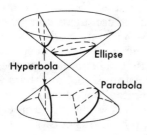

parabola—which is cut out by an intersecting plane (not passing through the vertex of the conical surface) depends upon the inclination of the plane: **(1)** the ellipse appears when the plane cuts all the elements of one nappe; **(2)** the parabola, when the plane cuts one nappe and is parallel to an element; **(3)** the hyperbola, when the plane cuts both nappes. Ref. [148].

Conical Helix   See **Helix**.

Conical Surface   In solid geometry, an indefinitely extended surface swept out by a line (the *generator,* or *generatrix*) which is fixed at a point (the *vertex,* or *apex*) and moves so as to pass through a given closed curve (the *directrix*). An *element* is any line passing through the vertex and the directrix. If the directrix has a center, then the line passing through the vertex and the center is the *axis* of the conical surface. A conical surface

has two *nappes* which meet at the vertex. A **cone** is a solid determined by

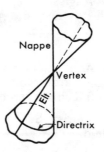

one nappe and a plane intersecting all its elements; "cone" is sometimes used for conical surface.   See **Pyramidal surface**.

When the directrix is a circle and the axis is perpendicular to the plane of the circle, the surface is a *circular conical surface* (special type of *quadric surface*). The plane sections of a circular conical surface are **conic sections**. Consider a circular conical surface with its vertex at the origin of a rectangular coordinate system in space and its axis along the z-axis; then its equation has the form $(x^2/a^2) + (y^2/a^2) = (z^2/c^2)$, that is, $x^2 + y^2 = k^2z^2$.

The conical surface is both a "developable" and a "ruled" surface.

Conicoid (Syn.: Quadric surface).

Conjecture   A mathematical statement which has neither been proved, nor denied by counterexample. Some long-standing conjectures of mathematics are the continuum hypothesis in the foundations of mathematics, Fermat's last theorem and the Goldbach conjecture in the theory of numbers, and the four-color problem in topology. The four-color problem was settled affirmatively in 1976; the continuum hypothesis was shown to be independent of the axioms of set theory in 1963.   **53**

Fermat's last theorem and the Goldbach conjecture remain open.

Conjugate Angles (Syn.: Explementary angles) In plane geometry, two angles whose sum is 360°; rarely used.

Conjugate Arcs In plane geometry, two circular arcs which together make up a full circle; rarely used.

Conjugate Axis See **Hyperbola**; **Hyperboloid**.

Conjugate Complex Numbers (Syn.: Conjugate imaginaries) Two complex numbers of the form $a + bi$, and $a - bi$, that is, $a + b\sqrt{-1}$ and $a - b\sqrt{-1}$. In the Argand diagram, conjugate complex numbers appear at symmetrical locations across the real axis. They are examples of **conjugate radicals**, having the property that their product is a real number $a^2 + b^2$; this fact is used, for example, in carrying out the division of complex numbers. Conjugate imaginaries occur as roots of polynomial equations. For example, the quadratic $x^2 - 2x + 2 = 0$ has the roots $1 - i$ and $1 + i$. This is a general phenomenon for any polynomial (with real coefficients)—if $a + bi$ is one root, then $a - bi$ is another.

Conjugate Diameter See **Diameter**.

Conjugate Hyperbola Of a given **hyperbola**, the hyperbola whose transverse and conjugate axes are, respectively, the conjugate and transverse axes of the given hyperbola.

Conjugate Hyperboloid See **Hyperboloid**.

Conjugate Radicals (Syn.: Conjugate surds) In ordinary algebra, often, expressions involving square roots of the form $a + b\sqrt{c}$ and $a - b\sqrt{c}$, with a, b, and c rational numbers. An example is $3 + 2\sqrt{2}$ and $3 - 2\sqrt{2}$. A significant feature of such a pair is that their product is free of radicals; for example $(3 + 2\sqrt{2})(3 - 2\sqrt{2}) = 3^2 - (2\sqrt{2})^2 = 9 - 8 = 1$. Hence, conjugate radicals are used for rationalization of denominators; for example,

$$\frac{3}{1 - \sqrt{2}} = \frac{3(1 + \sqrt{2})}{(1 - \sqrt{2})(1 + \sqrt{2})} = \frac{3(1 + \sqrt{2})}{1 - 2},$$

or $-3(1 + \sqrt{2})$.

The analogy between conjugate radicals and conjugate complex numbers $u + v\sqrt{-1}$, $u - v\sqrt{-1}$ is evident. The analogy is deepened by noting that the complex numbers are an extension of real numbers which is "generated" by adjoining the roots of $x^2 = -1$, while the numbers $a + b\sqrt{2}$ can be thought of as an extension of the rational numbers generated by adjoining the roots of $x^2 = 2$. In each case, the conjugates come about by using both roots; $\pm i$ (that is, $\pm\sqrt{-1}$) in one case, and $\pm\sqrt{2}$ in the other. The set of numbers $a + b\sqrt{2}$ form a mathematical system called a **number field**.

Conjunction In logic, the propositional form "P and Q," or any statement having this form; it is symbolized by "$P \wedge Q$" (see **Algebra of propositions**). An example is "3 is even and 3 is a prime." A conjunction is true just in case P, Q are separately true (T), otherwise it is false (F) (see truth-table in the figure); the

P	Q	P and Q
T	T	T
F	T	F
T	F	F
F	F	F

example given is a false conjunction.

The *denial* of the conjunction has the form "not *P* or not *Q*"; for example, the denial of the given statement about 3, is the statement "3 is not even or 3 is not prime."

Connected Set A set of points with the following property: any two of its points can be joined by a simple arc which lies entirely in the set. Of the four sets of points *A*, *B*, *C*, *D* in the figure, *A*, *B*, *C* are connected but *D* is not (in *C*, the interiors of the two small closed curves are excluded). A connected set in this sense is sometimes called an "arc-wise" connected

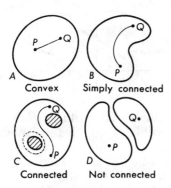

set. A connected set is **convex** in case the line segment between any two of its points is completely in the set. A set of points in the plane is *simply connected* in case **(1)** it is connected and **(2)** any simple closed curve in the set has its entire interior in the set (see the dotted curve in *C*, which is not simply connected). Connected sets are studied in *topology*.

Consecutive (Syn.: Successive) Immediately following each other in a linear or sequential ordering. Consecutive integers have the form *n*, *n* + 1; consecutive odd (even) integers have the form $2n - 1$, $2n + 1$ ($2n$, $2n + 2$), *n* itself being an integer. This notion does not apply to rational

numbers in their natural order on the line, since there is no "next" rational number after a given one. See **Density of rational numbers**.

Consequent In *logic,* the proposition *Q* in the **conditional** "If *P* then *Q*"; *P* is the antecedent. In *algebra,* the denominator in a ratio *a/b*, the numerator being the antecedent; seldom used, in this sense.

Consistent Axioms In logic, axioms which cannot lead to a contradiction. See **Inconsistent axioms**.

Consistent Equations Two or more simultaneous equations which have at least one common solution; otherwise, they are *inconsistent*. For example, $x^2 + y^2 = 13$ and $x - y = -1$ are consistent, having the common solution (2, 3), as well as $(-3, -2)$ [geometrically, the two graphs are a circle and an intersecting line]; also, $x - 2y = 1$ and $3x - 6y = 3$ are inconsistent (their graphs are parallel lines). (In the preceding, "solutions"

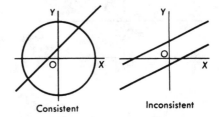

are understood to mean real numbers, not complex numbers.)

For *linear equations,* consistency has the geometric interpretation suggested by the following cases. In the plane, two linear equations in two variables are consistent in case their graphs (lines) intersect or are coincident (in the latter case the equations are *dependent linear equations*); the equations are inconsistent in case the lines are parallel. In space, three

55

linear equations in three variables represent three planes: the equations are consistent in case the planes intersect in one point, or have a common line, or are all coincident (in the latter two cases the equations are dependent); the equations are inconsistent in case one plane is parallel to the line of intersection of the others, or all three planes are parallel.

Constant A particular number or thing; more properly, the *name* of a particular thing, such as "3," "π," "Mark Twain." This is in contrast to a **variable**, or **arbitrary constant**; the latter stands in place of any one of a set of constants, and is usually represented by literal symbols such as "x," "a," "P," etc. In the case of numbers, a constant is sometimes called an *absolute number*.

Constant Function A function whose value is the same number for all

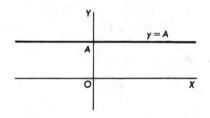

values of the argument, or independent variable; that is, for every value of x, $f(x) = A$, where A is a constant. The graph is the horizontal line $y = A$.

Constant of Integration The additive arbitrary constant occurring in the **indefinite integral** of a function.

Constant of Proportionality (Syn.: Constant of variation; Factor of proportionality) The constant k in a direct **proportionality** $y = kx$.

Constant Term (Syn.: Absolute term) Of a **polynomial** P, or polynomial equation $P = 0$, the term not containing a variable; for example, the equation $5x^2 - x + 4 = 0$ has 4 as its constant term.

Continuous Function For a **function of a real variable**, an informal notion of continuous function is suggested by the graphs of $f(x)$ and $g(x)$ shown in the figure. The function f is continuous at the value c, while g is discontinuous (not continuous) at c;

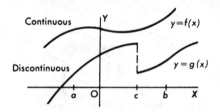

the functional values $f(x)$ pass "smoothly" through the functional value $f(c)$, while the values $g(x)$ jump when $x = c$. (Physically, the graph of f on the interval from a to b can be traced without lifting pencil from paper, while that of g cannot.)

These notions can be expressed precisely in terms of the **limit** concept. Let $f(x)$ be defined on the interval $a \leq x \leq b$. The function is *continuous at a value c* of the interval in case the limit of $f(x)$ as x approaches c exists and equals $f(c)$; it is *continuous on the entire interval* in case it is continuous at every value of the interval. Thus, a function defined on an interval is *discontinuous on an interval* in case it fails to be continuous at one or more values of the interval (see **Trigonometric series**). Such functions as polynomial functions, trigonometric functions, exponential and logarithmic functions are continuous on every interval on which they are defined. (A function that has a derivative at a point is necessarily continuous at that point.) The concept of continuity can be extended to functions of several variables, and to more abstract correspondences such as *transformations* between spaces.

Continuity lies at the foundation of the calculus, but a satisfactory theory for functions of a real variable was not forthcoming until the first half of the nineteenth century. In this theory, considerably more subtle types of discontinuities occur than the "jump" type shown in the figure.

Ref. [148].

Continuum Hypothesis   The assertion that there is no **cardinal number** between the cardinal of all whole numbers and that of all real numbers. It was settled in 1963 by P. Cohen who proved it was an **independent axiom** of set theory.   Ref. [132, 149].

Continuum of Real Numbers   The **ordered set** of all real numbers. The terminology "continuum" emphasizes that the ordered real numbers cover every point of the continuous line.   See **Number, Linear coordinates**.

Contradiction   A statement which is the denial of a statement known or assumed to be true.   See **Fallacy, Paradox**.

Contradiction, Proof by   See **Proof**.

Contrapositive   Of a given **conditional** "If *P* then *Q*," the conditional "If not *Q*, then not *P*," obtained by interchanging and denying the antecedent *P* and consequent *Q* of the given one. A conditional and its contrapositive are logically equivalent.

Control Unit   Of an automatic **digital computer**, a principal internal component that controls the computer as it executes a series of stored instructions; it interprets each coded instruction, it initiates the necessary signals to carry out the required operation, and it directs the computer to the next instruction.   See **Code**.

Convergent   A convergent **sequence (series)** is one which has a finite limit (sum); otherwise it is *divergent*.

Converse   Of a **conditional** "If *P* then *Q*," the conditional "If *Q* then *P*" obtained by interchanging the antecedent *P* and consequent *Q* of the given one. More loosely, the converse of a *theorem* is a statement obtained by (possibly partial) interchange of hypothesis and conclusion.

Convex Cone or Cylinder   In solid geometry, a **cone** or a **cylinder** whose base is a convex region.

Convex Function   For function of a real variable, one whose graph has the following property: any chord joining two points of the graph lies above (or on) the graph; it is *concave*

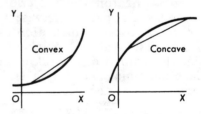

if any chord lies below (or on) its graph. For example, $y = x^2$ describes a convex function, and $y = \log x$, a concave function. A function will be convex (concave) just in case the plane region of all points above (below) the graph is a convex set. If $f(x)$ has a continuous second derivative d^2f/dx^2, then it will be convex (concave) in case d^2f/dx^2 is everywhere

57

nonnegative (nonpositive); this means that the slope never decreases (never increases). Ref. [50].

Convex Polygon In plane geometry, a polygon whose interior is a **convex set** in the plane; otherwise it is *concave*. A convex polygon can

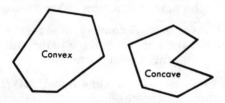

also be described as a polygon which lies entirely in one half-plane of any line containing one of its sides; also, its interior is the intersection of half-planes determined by these lines. The regular polygons are examples of convex polygons. A *spherical polygon* is convex in case it lies entirely on one side of any great circle containing one of its sides. In plane and solid geometry, the study of polygons is usually restricted to convex polygons.

Convex Polyhedron In solid geometry, a polyhedron whose interior is a **convex set** in space; otherwise it is *concave*. A convex polyhedron can also be described as a polyhedron which lies entirely on one side of any plane containing one of its faces; its interior is the intersection of half-spaces determined by these planes. The regular polyhedrons are examples of convex polyhedrons.

A *polyhedral angle* is convex in case the polyhedron determined by the faces and some plane section is a convex polyhedron; this condition will hold in case the plane section is a convex polygon.

Convex Set A set of points with the property that the line segment

joining any two of its points lies entirely in the set. An example is the interior of a circle. A *simple closed curve* or *polygon* is said to be convex in case its interior is convex; otherwise it is concave. Convex polygonal sets occur as the set of solutions of simultaneous linear inequalities. The region in the figure shows

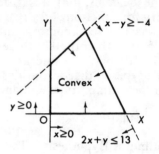

the convex set of solutions of the four linear inequalities $x - y \geq -4$, $2x + y \leq 13$, $x \geq 0$, $y \geq 0$—the arrow with each line shows the half-plane determined by a single inequality; the convex region is the region common to the four half-planes. See **Mathematical programming**. Ref. [50].

Coordinate For a **coordinate system**, any one of the numbers used to locate a point. For example, if (x, y) represents a point in a system of rectangular coordinates, then x and y are coordinates of the point; if (r, θ, φ) represents a point in a system of spherical coordinates in space, then r, θ, and φ are coordinates.

Coordinate Axis Of a system of **Cartesian coordinates**, any one of the axes. The first axis is the x-axis, the second axis is the y-axis, and (in space) the third axis is the z-axis. The *positive x*-axis (or other axis) is the half-line from the origin containing the positive values of x, the *negative x*-axis is the other half-line.

Coordinate Geometry (Syn.: Analytic geometry)   The algebraic study of geometry through the use of a coordinate system; rectangular Cartesian coordinates are generally understood in ordinary geometry.

Coordinate Plane   Of a system of **Cartesian coordinates in space**, any one of the three planes containing two axes; for example, the xz-plane is the coordinate plane containing the x-axis and z-axis.

Also, any plane marked with a system of rectangular Cartesian coordinates is called a coordinate plane.

Coordinate System   In the plane or space (or n-dimensional space), any method of representing points by numbers. Points on a line are represented by single numbers, such as **linear coordinates** or **logarithmic coordinates**. Points in the plane are represented by pairs of coordinates, such as **Cartesian coordinates in the plane**, or **polar coordinates**. Points in space require triples of coordinates, such as **Cartesian coordinates in space**, **spherical coordinates**, or **cylindrical coordinates**. Spaces of higher **dimension** are represented by four, five, or more coordinates; in fact, such spaces are often defined through this method of representation. The **transformation of coordinates** arises when two coordinate systems are set up in the same plane or in space; this relates the coordinates of one system to those of the other.

Coplanar   Lying in the same plane in space, as "coplanar points" or "coplanar lines." Three points not on a line are coplanar, as are two intersecting lines; either of these determine a unique plane. Four points in space are, in general, not coplanar; in this case they determine a tetrahedron. Two skew lines in space are not coplanar.

An example of a family of *coplanar lines* is all lines in space perpendicular to a given line l at a given point P; they make up the plane perpendicular to l at P (see figure). An

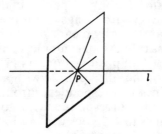

example of a family of *coplanar points* is all points in space equidistant from two given intersecting planes; they make up a plane which bisects the dihedral angle formed by the two given planes.

Corollary of Theorem   A proved proposition which is an immediate consequence or a special case of the **theorem** to which it is attached. As an example from plane geometry, consider the theorem "An inscribed angle is measured by one-half the intercepted arc"; it has the following corollary, "An angle inscribed in a semicircle is a right angle." Whether any particular proved proposition is to be taken as a theorem or a corollary is a matter of judgment or taste, not logical necessity.

Correlation   In statistics, informally, a measure of the interdependence of two random variables or two sets of data. The *correlation coefficient r* of two sets of data $\{a_1, a_2, \ldots, a_n\}$ and $\{b_1, b_2, \ldots, b_n\}$ is given by

$$r = \frac{\Sigma(a_i - \bar{a})(b_i - \bar{b})}{S_1 \cdot S_2};$$

here $\bar{a}, \bar{b}$ are the arithmetic means of the a_i and b_i, respectively, and

59

$$S_1^2 = \Sigma(a_i - \bar{a})^2, \quad S_2^2 = \Sigma(b_i - \bar{b})^2$$

(all sums are taken over $i = 1, 2, \ldots,$ n). This coefficient lies between -1 and 1; it measures how nearly the points (a_i, b_i) lie on a line.

Correspondence (Syn.: Mapping, Transformation)   A pairing of things in one set with things in another (or the same) set by means of an unambigous rule. As an example, consider the set N of positive integers $\{1, 2, 3, 4, \ldots\}$; the rule "pair $2n$ with n" determines a correspondence from N to N; in this correspondence, 1 goes to 2, 2 goes to 4, 3 goes to 6, and so on. For another example, consider the correspondence from all males to all females determined by the rule "y is a sister of x"; this associates with each male x having at least one sister, his (possibly several) sisters y.

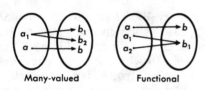

Many-valued   Functional

In a correspondence from a set A to a set B, two cases arise: **(1)** each member of A is associated with no, or one, member of B; **(2)** at least one member of A is associated with two or more members of B. The first defines a **function**, or functional correspondence; the second case defines a many-valued, or multiple-valued, function. The above example involving the set N is a function; the other example is not, since a male may have several sisters. (Technically, a correspondence is the same as a **relation** from one set to another.) A *one-to-one correspondence* between sets A and B is a correspondence such that **(1)** each member of A is associated with exactly one member of

B, and **(2)** each member of B is matched with exactly one member of A; in such a correspondence the members of A and of B are paired off

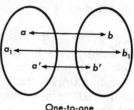

One-to-one

exactly. For example, when an auditorium is filled, a one-to-one correspondence exists between the seats and the people occupying them. This kind of correspondence is the basis of the **cardinal number** concept—two sets have the same cardinal number in case they can be put in one-to-one correspondence.

See **Inverse correspondence**; **Transformation**.

Corresponding Angles of Transversal.   See Transversal.

Corresponding Parts   In geometry, two *polygons* with the same number of sides are in correspondence when consecutive vertices of one are matched with the consecutive vertices of the other; corresponding parts of the two polygons are parts (points, angles, line segments) which are also matched under the given correspondence. Corresponding parts occur in the study of congruent figures, and of similar figures. With similar fig-

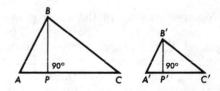

ures, for example, the correspondence is arranged so that corresponding angles are equal and the ratios of corresponding segments are equal. In the figure, showing similar triangles, $\angle A = \angle A'$, $\angle B = \angle B'$ $\angle C = \angle C'$, and the ratios $AB/A'B'$, $BC/B'C'$, $BP/B'P'$, etc., of corresponding segments are equal.

Cosecant Function   One of the **trigonometric functions**; abbreviated "csc." It is the reciprocal of the **sine function**, that is, $\csc A = 1/\sin A$; it

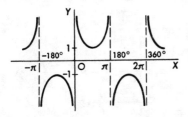

is a periodic function of period 360°, or 2π radians. The *cosecant curve* is the graph of $y = \csc x$, with x denoting radian measure.

Cosine Function   One of the **trigonometric functions**; abbreviated "cos." Let A be an angle of rotation of the positive x-axis terminating in the point (x, y); then $\cos A$ is defined as the ratio x/r, r being the distance of (x, y) from the origin. The cosine is

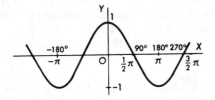

a periodic function of period 360°, or 2π radians. The *cosine curve* is the graph of $y = \cos x$, with x denoting radian measure.

Cosines, Law of   See **Law of cosines.**

Cotangent Function   One of the **trigonometric functions**; abbreviated

"cot," or "ctn." It is the reciprocal of the **tangent function**, that is, $\cot A = 1/\tan A$; it is a periodic function of

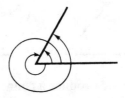

period 180°, or π radians. The *cotangent curve* is the graph of $y = \cot x$, with x denoting radian measure.

Coterminal Angles   Angles of rotation with the same initial and terminal sides; for example, 60° is co-

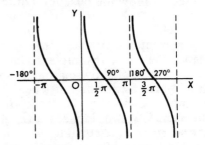

terminal with 420° and $-300°$. Such angles differ by a multiple of 360°, that is, by one or more full revolutions.

Countable Set (Syn.: Denumerable set; Enumerable set)   A set that can be put into one-to-one correspondence with all positive integers $\{1, 2, 3, \ldots\}$. Examples are (1) the set $\{1, 3, 5, \ldots\}$ of odd positive integers; (2) the set $\{2, 3, 5, 7, 11, 13, 17, 19, 23, 29, \ldots\}$ of prime integers; and (3) the set of rational numbers. The last example expresses the **enumeration of rational numbers**. All countable sets have the same **cardinal number**; this is the smallest infinite cardinal number.

Counterclockwise   See **Clockwise.**

Counterexample Ordinarily, an example which demonstrates the falsehood of a general statement. For instance, to show the falsehood of the statement "All men are taller than five feet," it is sufficient to point to one man under five feet. In mathematics, the counterexample is a common method of showing that a suggested proposition is not true. For example, consider the following statement: "If two sides and an angle of one triangle are equal to two sides and an angle of another triangle, then the triangles are congruent"; the counterexample shown in the figure disproves this statement (this is the ambiguous case in the solution of triangles).

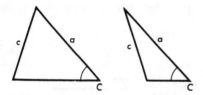

Failure to produce a counterexample does not constitute a **proof** of a statement. With both proof and counterexample lacking, a statement has the status of a conjecture. Conjectures exist in mathematics, and they offer tempting challenges to the research mathematician.

Coversine Function (Syn.: Coversed sine function) A **trigonometric function** defined as $1 - \sin A$ and written "covers A"; rarely used.

Cramer's Rule A method for solving linear simultaneous equations in several unknowns using determinants. For example, the solution of

$$3x - 5y = 2$$
$$x + 2y = 0,$$

according to Cramer's rule, is given by

$$x = \frac{\begin{vmatrix} 2 & -5 \\ 0 & 2 \end{vmatrix}}{\begin{vmatrix} 3 & -5 \\ 1 & 2 \end{vmatrix}} = \frac{2 \cdot 2 - 0 \cdot (-5)}{3 \cdot 2 - 1 \cdot (-5)} = \frac{4}{11}$$

$$y = \frac{\begin{vmatrix} 3 & 2 \\ 1 & 0 \end{vmatrix}}{\begin{vmatrix} 3 & -5 \\ 1 & 2 \end{vmatrix}} = \frac{3 \cdot 0 - 1 \cdot 2}{11} = -\frac{2}{11}$$

More generally, the solution of

$$ax + by = e$$
$$cx + dy = f$$

is given by

$$x = \frac{\begin{vmatrix} e & b \\ f & d \end{vmatrix}}{\begin{vmatrix} a & b \\ c & d \end{vmatrix}} = \frac{ed - fb}{ad - cb}$$

$$y = \frac{\begin{vmatrix} a & e \\ c & f \end{vmatrix}}{\begin{vmatrix} a & b \\ c & d \end{vmatrix}} = \frac{af - ce}{ad - cb}.$$

The denominator in the solution for either x or y is the determinant of the coefficients of the unknowns in the given equations; the numerator in the solution for a particular unknown is this determinant with the column of coefficients of that unknown replaced by the constant terms e, f. A similar procedure holds for three equations in three unknowns, or n linear equations in n unknowns; in these cases the rule involves determinants of the third and higher order. The method is named after the Swiss mathematician Cramer of the 18th century; it has theoretical advantages, but it is not an effective practical method of solution (compare **elimination of variables**).

Critical Point In the calculus, a critical point of the graph of $y = f(x)$ [or the function $f(x)$], is often taken to mean a point where the tangent line is either horizontal or vertical;

the critical points include the maximum and minimum points, and the horizontal and vertical inflection points. The critical points occur where the derivative of the function is zero or approaches infinity. A point where the derivative is zero is sometimes called a *stationary point.*

Cube In *solid geometry,* a rectangular parallelpiped whose edges are all equal. It has six square faces,

twelve equal edges, and eight vertices. The volume of a cube with edge a is a^3; its total area is $6a^2$.

In *arithmetic* or *algebra,* a cube is a third power, such as 5^3 or $(2x + 3)^3$. The term "perfect cube" is applied to an integer or polynomial which equals the cube of some integer or polynomial.   See **Perfect power.**

Cube Root The cube root of a number b is a number whose third power equals b; it is denoted by $\sqrt[3]{b}$. Thus, $x = \sqrt[3]{b}$ in case $x^3 = b$. Examples are $\sqrt[3]{8} = 2$, $\sqrt[3]{0} = 0$. The cube root of a positive integer is an irrational number unless b is a perfect cube. Similar notation applies to algebraic expressions; for example, $\sqrt[3]{a^3y^6} = ay^2$ and $\sqrt[3]{(1 + x)^3} = 1 + x$.   See **Radical, Root of number.**

Cube, Duplication of See **Duplication of cube.**

Cubic In algebra, of the third degree. For example, a *cubic polynomial* is a polynomial of the third degree, such as $2x^3 - x^2 + 3x + 5$; it has the general form $ax^3 + bx^2 +$ $cx + d$. A *cubic function* is a function whose value is given by a cubic polynomial; for example, the equation $y = x^3 - 2x^2 - 5x + 6$ defines a cubic function. Two typical graphs of cubic functions are shown in the figure.

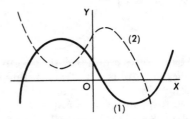

A *cubic equation* is one equivalent to a cubic polynomial equated to zero. A cubic equation has either three real roots or one real root and two conjugate imaginary roots. For example, $x^3 - 2x^2 - 5x + 6 = 0$ has the roots -2, 1, and 3; on the other hand, $x^3 - 3x^2 + 4x - 2 = 0$ has the roots 1, $1 + i$, and $1 - i$. The real roots are the points of intersection of the graph of the cubic polynomial with the x-axis. In the figure, curve (1) shows a case of three real roots, and curve (2) shows a case of one real root. There is an explicit formula for the solution of the general cubic equation similar to, but more involved than, that for the quadratic equation; it was discovered in the middle of the sixteenth century. Much earlier (about 1100), Omar Khayyam, the author of the *Rubaiyat,* had developed a geometric procedure for finding positive roots of cubic equations.

See **Roots of polynomial equation.** Ref. [148].

Curvature The curvature of a *circle* (or circular arc) is taken as the reciprocal $1/R$ of the radius R; the curvature measures the angular rotation of the tangent line per unit length of arc (small circles have high curvature, and large circles have small curvature).

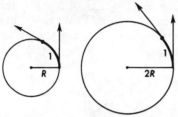

For a more general plane curve, the curvature is a number defined at each point P on the curve and may vary from point to point. At a point where the curve "bends" away from the tangent line, the curvature is, informally, that of the tangent circle at P which "hugs" the curve most closely. More precisely, in the calculus, the curvature at P is the rate of change of the angle of inclination of the tangent line with respect to distance along the curve. For a curve $y = f(x)$, the curvature K is given by

$$K = \frac{d^2f/dx^2}{[1 + (df/dx)^2]^{3/2}};$$

for a curve given by parametric equations $x = g(t), y = h(t)$.

$$K = \frac{(dg/dt)(d^2h/dt^2) - (dh/dt)(d^2g/dt^2)}{[(dg/dt)^2 + (dt/dt)^2]^{3/2}}$$

The *radius of curvature* R at the point P is the absolute value of the reciprocal $1/K$. The circle with radius R

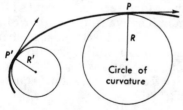

Circle of curvature

which is tangent to the curve at P (and bends in the same direction) is the *circle of curvature* at P; its center is the *center of curvature* at P. The locus of the centers of curvature

is called the *evolute* of a curve (see **Involute of curve**).

The notion of curvature can be extended to curves and surfaces in space. One important concept is that of (total) *curvature* of a surface at any point of the surface. This curvature of a sphere of radius R is $1/R^2$ at every one of its points; the curvature of a more general surface at a point P (where the surface bends away from the tangent plane) is that of the tangent sphere that "hugs" it most closely at P (in an appropriate sense). The curvature at every point of a plane or any *developable surface* equals zero; at each point of an ellipsoid, it is positive; at a *saddle point,* it is negative.

Curve Informally, a one-dimensional configuration, or a figure obtained by stretching, contracting, bending, etc., a line segment or line ("curve" includes the straight line and line segment). An *arc* is a portion of a curve between two of its points. A curve may be described by geometric conditions; in that case, it is referred to as a locus of points (for example, a circle is the *locus of points* at a fixed distance from a given point).

A *plane curve* is one that lies in a plane; it is frequently represented as the graph of an equation $y = f(x)$, or $F(x, y) = 0$, in rectangular coordinates x, y. For example, $x^2 + y^2 = 4$ is an equation of the circle with center at the origin and radius 2; also $y = 2x + 6$ is an equation of the line through $(0, 6)$ and $(-3, 0)$. These are examples of *algebraic curves,* that is, curves whose equations are algebraic equations. *Transcendental curves* are described by equations involving transcendental functions; an example is the sine curve, $y = \sin x$. A general way of representing plane curve is by **parametric equations** $x = g(t), y = h(t)$.

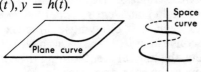
Plane curve / Space curve

A curve in three-dimensional space, such as a curve on a sphere (spherical curve) or a helix, is a *space curve*; if it does not lie in a plane it is a *skew*, or *twisted*, *curve*. A space curve may be represented by two simultaneous equations in three coordinate variables x, y, z; each equation represents a surface, and the pair represents their curve of intersection. A space curve may also be described by three parametric equations expressing x, y, and z separately as functions of a common parameter.

Technically, a plane (continuous) curve is the configuration described by a pair of equations $x = g(t), y = h(t)$ where g and h are continuous functions on an interval $a \leq t \leq b$; its endpoints are $[x(a), y(a)]$ and $[x(b), y(b)]$; when these coincide, the curve is a **closed curve**. An analogous definition applies to three-space or n-dimensional space (using 3, or n, functions). Continuous curves of the most general type can exhibit bizarre properties; for example, Peano, toward the end of the nineteenth century, constructed a curve in the plane which entirely fills a square and its interior.

Cybernetics   A theory introduced by the American mathematician N. Wiener in 1948 which studies the common features of such diverse systems as organisms, neural networks, computers, and automata; it attempts to build a common theoretical framework for biology and engineering. It is concerned with problems of control and communication in these systems, and how these bear upon the over-all performance of a system within a larger environment ("cybernetics" comes from the Greek word for "steersman"). A principal concept is that of *feedback,* whereby a system senses the effect of its action in the environment, compares this information with a desired objective, and modifies its next action accordingly. Areas of application of cybernetics include design of automata and of control mechanisms such as guidance systems of missiles and other regulating devices.   Ref. [5, 49, 62, 141].

Cyclic Permutation   See **Permutation.**

Cycloid   The plane curve traced out by a fixed point P on a circle as the circle rolls along a line, the *base* of the cycloid. The curve consists of a

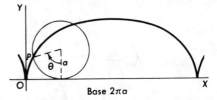
Base $2\pi a$

series of identical archs; the width of one arch along the base line is the circumference of the circle, $2\pi a$. (See **Trochoid.**) One of its interesting features is that it provides the solution to the famous "brachistrochrome" problem posed (and solved) in the seventeenth century: Given two points A and B in space, with A above B, find the path of quickest

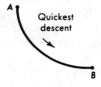
Quickest descent

descent from A to B. The answer is

not the shortest distance curve (the line segment from A to B), as one might guess, but the portion of a cycloid that joins A to B. See **Calculus of variations**.

The cycloid is represented by the parametric equations,

$$x = a(\theta - \sin \theta), \quad y = a(1 - \cos \theta);$$

the parameter θ is the angle shown in the figure (measured in radians); as it increases from 0 to 2π the cycloid completes one full arch.

Cylinder In solid geometry, a closed surface defined by a closed plane curve C (the *directrix*) and a line segment l (not in the plane of C), as follows. When l is moved parallel to itself with one end point tracing out the curve C, it generates a *lateral* surface, as well as a copy C' of C at the other endpoint; a cylinder consists of this lateral surface and two congruent

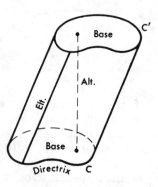

bases, made up of C, C', and their interiors. (See **Prism**.) The line l in any position is an *element* of the cylinder; an *altitude* is a perpendicular line segment (or its length) between the planes of the bases. A *right section* of a cylinder is a plane section which is perpendicular to the elements of the cylinder. A cylinder is named after the directrix; for example, an *elliptic cylinder* has an ellipse as directrix, and a *circular cylinder*, a

circle. (The open *parabolic* and *hyperbolic cylinders* are generally considered *cylindrical surfaces*.) A *convex cylinder* is one whose directrix is a convex curve. If the bases have centers, the line segment joining the centers is the *axis*; the axis is parallel to the elements. When the axis is perpendicular to the bases the cylinder is a *right cylinder*, otherwise it is an *oblique cylinder*; examples are the right circular cylinder and the oblique circular cylinder. The former can be produced by rotating a rec-

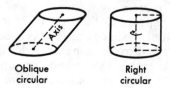

Oblique circular   Right circular

tangle about a side through 360°; accordingly, it is called a *cylinder of revolution.*

The volume V of a cylinder is the altitude times the area of the base (a cone sharing one base with a cylinder and having its vertex in the other base, scoops out one-third the volume of the cylinder); the lateral area A is the length of an element times the perimeter of a right section. For a right circular cylinder of altitude h and radius r, $V = \pi r^2 h$ and $A = 2\pi rh$.

A tangent plane to a cylinder touches the lateral surface along an entire element, the element of contact, or tangency. The family of all tangent planes is obtained by rolling a plane around the lateral surface. The cylinder is an example of a *developable surface*, that is, a surface which can be laid out evenly on a plane; it is also a *ruled surface*.

The term "cylinder" is sometimes used for **cylindrical surface**.

Cylindrical Coordinates In space, a coordinate system which consists of a plane with polar coordinates and a z-axis through the pole, or origin, perpendicular to the plane. A point P is located in space by its (directed) distance z from the plane and the polar coordinates (r, θ) of its projection on the plane; (r, θ, z) are the *cylindrical coordinates* of P. When P is above the plane, z is positive, when P is in the plane, $z = 0$, and when P is below the plane, z is negative. (Usually cylindrical coordinates are

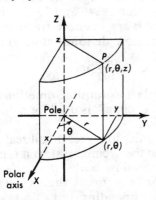

aligned with rectangular coordinates in the manner shown.)

When r is held constant at r_0, while θ and z vary, the point P generates a right circular cylindrical surface of radius r_0; this accounts for the name "cylindrical." When θ is held constant at θ_0 and r, z vary, P generates a half-plane at a dihedral angle θ_0 with the xz-plane. When z is held constant at z_0 and r, θ vary, P generates a plane at a distance z_0 from the xy-plane.

The cylindrical coordinates (r, θ, z) of a point P are transformed to its rectangular coordinates (x, y, z) by the following *equations of transformation:* $x = r \cos \theta$, $y = r \sin \theta$, $z = z$.

Cylindrical Helix　See **Helix**.

Cylindrical Surface　In solid geometry, an indefinitely extended surface swept out by a line (the *generator,* or *generatrix*) which moves parallel to itself so as to always pass through a given curve (the *directrix*). An *element* is the generator in any position. The cylindrical surface is *open* or *closed* depending upon whether the directrix is open or closed. A **cylinder** is a solid determined by two parallel planes intersecting all the elements of a closed cylindrical surface; "cylinder" is sometimes used for a cylindri-

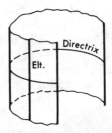

cal surface.　See **Prismatic surface**.

A *right section* of a cylindrical surface is a plane section perpendicular to the elements of the cylinder. A cylindrical surface whose right section is a circle is called *circular*; if the right section is an ellipse, parabola, or hyperbola then it is called elliptic, parabolic, or hyperbolic, respectively (these are quadric surfaces). Consider a cylindrical surface located so that its right section lies in the xy-plane of a system of rectangular coordinates in space; let $F(x, y) = 0$ be the equation of the right section. Then the cylindrical surface is represented by the same equation [thought of as satisfied by points (x, y, z) in space]; for example, $x^2 + y^2 = r^2$ is the equation of a circular cylindrical surface whose section has radius r.

The cylindrical surface is both a *developable* and a *ruled surface*.

D

Decagon　A polygon with ten sides;

D

it is a regular decagon if all its sides are equal and all its angles are equal.

Decimal Number System The ordinary system of notation for (real) numbers using place values and the base ten. The *digits* of the decimal system are 0, 1, 2, 3, 4, 5, 6, 7, 8, 9, and a number is denoted by a string of such digits; a number in this form is called a *decimal number*, or simply a *decimal*. See **Number system**.

In the representation of a whole number, the place of a digit tells which power of 10 it multiplies; the rightmost digit is in the *unit's place,* the next is in the *ten's place,* the next in the *hundred's place,* and so on. For example, 5,207 stands for

$$5 \cdot 10^3 + 2 \cdot 10^2 + 0 \cdot 10 + 7 \cdot 1.$$

Fractions are represented by use of the *decimal point*. Digits to the left of the decimal point multiply positive (or zero) powers of 10, while digits to the right multiply positive powers of $\frac{1}{10}$ (or negative powers of 10); the first digit to the right of the point is in the *tenth's place* or first decimal place, the next in the *hundredth's place* or second decimal place, and so on. A *decimal fraction* is a decimal that contains no digits (or only zero digits) to the left of the decimal point; an example is .5207, which stands for $5/10 + 2/10^2 + 0/10^3 + 7/10^4$. A decimal fraction equals a proper fraction whose denominator is a power of ten; for example, .5207 equals

$$\frac{5,207}{10,000}.$$

A *mixed decimal* has (nonzero) digits both to the left and to the right of the decimal point; an example is 52.07, which stands for

$$5 \cdot 10 + 2 \cdot 1 + 0 \cdot 10^{-1} + 7 \cdot 10^{-2},$$

or

$$5 \cdot 10 + 2 \cdot 1 + 0/10 + 7/10^2.$$

A mixed decimal equals an improper fraction whose denominator is a power of 10, as with

$$\frac{5,207}{100},$$

in the preceding example. *Similar decimals* have the same number of digits to the right of the decimal point, such as .46 and 35.16; similar decimals are, in effect, fractions with a common denominator, such as

$$\frac{46}{100} \text{ and } \frac{3,516}{100}$$

in the last example. Sometimes, the term "decimal" is used for a decimal fraction.

In order to represent all real numbers in the decimal system it is necessary to allow both *infinite decimals* and *finite decimals*, that is, decimals with an unending and a finite string of digits, respectively, to the right of the decimal point; examples are 42.083 and 5.23223222322223 $\cdots$. Finite and infinite decimal are also called terminating and nonterminating decimals, respectively. The decimal equivalent of a real number is its expression in decimal notation; for example, the decimal equivalent of $\frac{13}{20}$ is .65, the decimal equivalent of $\frac{9}{7}$ is 1.282828 $\cdots$ (obtained by long division of 7 into 9). A terminating decimal represents a rational number (fraction) whose denominator is a power of 10. The last example shows that a nonterminating decimal may also represent a rational number. The answer to the question of when a nonterminating decimal equals a rational number is: whenever it is a *repeating* decimal. This is one that eventually repeats a finite pattern of digits. The decimal expansion of ⅔ above is an example; another is .04193725725725 ··· (which repeats 725). A repeating decimal amounts to a **geometric series**, and the formula for the sum of the series changes the decimal into a fraction. Repeating decimals are also called circulating, periodic, or recurring decimals. The irrational numbers are infinite decimals which are not periodic; for example, the first few digits of the irrational numbers $\sqrt{3}$ and π are 1.72305 ··· and 3.14159 ···. Infinite decimals are estimated by finite decimal **approximate numbers** in calculations; for example, 3.1416 is used for π, and tables of functional values contain approximate decimals.

Arithmetic with finite decimals is carried out by familiar techniques. Addition is performed by adding digits in the same decimal place and carrying the overflow to the next place on the left; for example,

$$
\begin{array}{r}
\text{(carries)} \quad (1)\,(1)\,(1)\,(0) \\
2\ 6\ .\ 8\ \ 4\ \ 0 \\
7\ .\ 3\ \ 6\ \ 2 \\
\hline
3\ 4\ .\ 2\ \ 0\ \ 2
\end{array}
$$

Multiplication involves the addition of "partial products," obtained by multiplying each digit of the multiplier into the multiplicand and shifting them successively one place to the left. This method of long multiplication is illustrated as follows:

$$
\begin{array}{r}
2.57 \\
6.3 \\
\hline
771 \\
1542 \\
\hline
16.191
\end{array}
$$

[The number of decimal places in the product (to the right of the decimal point) is the sum of those in the factors.] Division is carried out by long division. One of the advantages of decimal notation over earlier number systems, such as Roman numerals, is the ease of performing arithmetical operations.

Decimal notation corresponds to a *decimal scale* of markings on a line, obtained by successive sub-division into tenths. This is illustrated for 1.377 in the figure. The process will

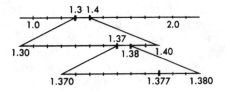

locate a finite decimal in a finite number of steps. In the case of an infinite decimal (not ending in an infinite string of zeros) the process will yield points closer and closer to the true point but never exactly equal to it; the true location is defined as a **limit** of these successive approximations. It is only through limits, or an equivalent concept, that the nature of irrational numbers is clarified.

The invention of the decimal place value system is credited to the Hindus some time before 800 A.D.; the Arabs spread it throughout Europe, where it was well established by the sixteenth century.

Decreasing   See **Increasing**.

Deduction   The process of reasoning logically from clearly stated hypotheses to a conclusion. The term "deduction" is sometimes also used for the conclusion of the deduction, as well.   See **Deductive Theory**.

Deductive Theory (Syn.: Axiomatic theory)   A formal organization of a mathematical or logical theory having the following character. It begins with a set of unproved *axioms*, or *primitive statements*, concerning a set of *undefined*, or *primitive terms*, and derives mathematical statements, or *theorems*, from the axioms by **proof**. What is logically assumed about the primitive terms is only what is expressed in the axioms. New terms are introduced by **definition**, which gives them meaning relative to the primitive terms (or previously defined terms). A great contribution of ancient Greek mathematics was the invention of deductive theory; it is best known through Euclid's Elements (about 300 B.C.), a theory of geometry which served as a prototype of rigorous reasoning for many centuries. (See **Euclidean Geometry**.)

In a *model*, or interpretation, of a deductive theory, the primitive terms are taken as entities having definition or existence outside of the theory, and as having the properties expressed by the axioms (translated as statements in the model); the model is said to *satisfy* the axioms. An advantage of a deductive theory is that it can deal "simultaneously" with its various models; proving a theorem in the theory establishes it in all models, in one stroke. A theory of **non-Euclidean geometry**, for example, is one with various models; in such a theory, the parallel postulate of Euclid is omitted, and in the various models the notions of "line" and "distance," for example, are not the ordinary ones. The spirit of twentieth century pure mathematics is that of rigorous deductive theory (see **Mathematical system**). A major aspect of modern logic is the study of the nature of deductive theories themselves; this is sometimes called "metamathematics" (for example, questions of inconsistent axioms, independent axioms, rules of inference, etc., belong to this field). See **Foundations of mathematics**.

Ref. [28, 149].

70

Defective Equation   In algebra, an equation derived from a given equation but lacking one or more roots of the given equation. For example, the equation $x^2 - 1 = 2x + 2$ reduces to $x - 1 = 2$ upon dividing both sides by $x + 1$; the latter equation is defective, for it has only the root 3, while the given equation has the roots 3 and -1. In general, an equation obtained by dividing both sides of another equation by an expression containing the variable should be checked for defectiveness. See **Solution of equation**.

Defective Number (Syn.: Deficient number)   In arithmetic, a whole number which is greater than the sum of its divisors (excluding itself, but including 1). See **Perfect number**.

Definite Integral   See **Integral of function**.

Definition   In a mathematical theory, a description of a new term by accepted, or undefined, terms and previously defined terms (together with logical terms). Definitions take various forms, as illustrated in the following examples. *Definition of parallelogram:* "A parallelogram is a quadrilateral whose opposite sides are equal"; here, it is supposed that "quadrilateral" and "opposite sides" have already been defined ("equal" is a logical term). *Definition of subtraction:* "$a - b$ is the number x such that $a = b + x$"; here, "addition" is assumed and $a - b$ given meaning in terms of it. *Definition of prime number:* "The whole number x is prime in case it has no divisors other than one and itself"; here "divisor," for example, is assumed defined and "x is prime" given meaning in terms of it.

In a formal deductive theory, the primitive, or undefined, terms are the initial stock of terms, and definitions are built on these. In logic, "rules of definition" are developed as principles for stating definitions.

Ref. [44].

Degenerate Conic A point, line, pair of parallel lines, or pair of intersecting lines, considered as a limiting case of a **conic section**. These are obtained when a plane meets a circular conical surface in a special way; for example, an ellipse approaches a single point as the intersecting plane approaches the vertex of the surface, remaining parallel to itself.

Degree (algebra) The degree of a *term* in one variable is the exponent of the variable; for example, the degree of $3x^2$ is two. The degree of a term in several variables is the sum of the exponents of the variables; for example, the degree of $2xy^2$ is three. The degree of a *sum of terms* is the highest degree among its terms, after combining similar terms. In particular, the degree of a *polynomial* in one variable is the highest power of the variable; the degree of an *equation* is the highest degree among its terms. For example, the degree of the equation $3x^2 - 2 = x^3 + 1$ is three.

Degree of Angle A unit of a numerical measure of angles. A unit angle (one degree) is a central angle which subtends an arc of $\frac{1}{360}$ of a circle; the degree measure of any

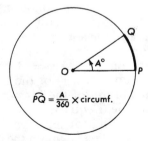

$$\widehat{PQ} = \frac{A}{360} \times \text{circumf.}$$

angle is the length of arc it subtends

divided by the length subtended by a unit angle. "Equal angles" mean angles of the same measure; angles are equal just in case they are congruent.

Degree measure is expressed in *degrees, minutes,* and *seconds;* a minute of angle is $\frac{1}{60}$ of a degree, and a second of angle is $\frac{1}{60}$ of a minute (minutes and seconds are sexigesimal units, being based upon subdivision into 60 parts). The notation "18°22'15"," for example, stands for 18 degrees, 22 minutes, and 15 seconds of angle. (The idea of sexigesimal measurement goes back 4,000 years to ancient Babylonia.) **Radian** measure of angles is generally preferred for theoretical work.

Degree, Spherical See **Spherical degree**.

Demoivre's Theorem The following formula for the power of a complex number expressed in polar form:

$[r(\cos \theta + i \sin \theta)]^n$
$$= r^n(\cos n\theta + i \sin n\theta).$$

That is, the nth power is obtained by raising the modulus r to the nth power and multiplying the ampli-

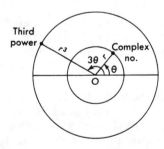

tude θ by n. This formula is valid for fractional exponents as well as integral exponents, and is therefore useful for obtaining a **root of a complex number**. The mathematician De Moivre stated the formula (for n a

71

positive integer) in the first half of the eighteenth century.

De Morgan's Laws The basic formulas $(A \cup B)' = A' \cap B'$, and $(A \cap B)' = A' \cup B'$ of the **algebra of sets**; they were stated by De Morgan in the middle of the nineteenth century, when modern symbolic logic was in its initial stages.

Denial (Syn.: Negation) In logic, the denial of a statement "P" is the statement "not P"; it is symbolized "$\sim P$". Any statement logically equivalent to $\sim P$ is also called a denial of P. For example, the denial of "It is raining" is "It is not raining"; the denial of "All numbers are even" is "There is a number which is not even"; the denial of the conditional statement "If he can be Captain, then I can be President" is "He can be Captain and I cannot be President." The statement "not P" is true or false respectively, in case P is false or true; that is, the prefix "not" reverses truth-values. See **Algebra of propositions**. Also, see **Biconditional**, **Conditional**, **Conjunction**, **Disjunction**, **Quantifier** for denials of various statement forms.

Denominate Number In measurement, a number of units of measure; examples are 5 yards, $\frac{1}{2}$ cubic centimeter, 7 gallons, 30° (30 degrees). When denominate numbers are compared, or subjected to arithmetical combination, they are to be reduced to the same denomination, that is, to a common unit. For example, to decide whether 1 foot 2 inches is larger than 35 centimeters, the two denominate numbers may be expressed in inches; thus, 1 foot 2 inches = 14 inches, 35 centimeters = 13.78 inches. Such a change is also made, for example, to calculate the area of a rectangle in terms of the lengths of its sides; if the lengths are expressed in inches, their product would be the area in square inches, if expressed in centimeters, it would be in square centimeters.

Denominator Of a fraction A/B, the expression represented by B; for example, the denominator of $\frac{5}{13}$ is 13, the denominator of $3y/(2x - 3)$ is $2x - 3$. A *common denominator* of two or more fractions is a multiple of the several denominators.

Density of Rational Numbers The following property of the **rational numbers** (as ordered on the line): between any two distinct rational numbers, no matter how close, there lies yet another rational number. For example, between $\frac{1}{3}$ and $\frac{1}{2}$ is the fraction $\frac{5}{12}$; between $\frac{5}{87}$ and $\frac{5}{88}$ is the fraction

$$\frac{875}{15,312}.$$

In general, $(a + b)/2$ lies between a and b; hence, there is no "next" rational number after a given one.

Denumerable Set See **Countable set** (syn.).

Dependent Linear Equation A given linear equation is dependent on a set of one or more linear equations in case the following holds: every (simultaneous) solution of the set of equations is also a solution of the given one; otherwise, the given equation is an **independent linear equation**. For example, $x - 4y = 6$ is dependent on $x - 2y = 3$ because every solution (x, y) of the latter is also a solution of the former. That a set of linear equations is dependent means that at least one of the equations is dependent on the others. (A reason for singling out the dependent equation is that its presence or absence does not affect the solutions of a set of linear **simultaneous equations**.)

Geometrically, one linear equation is dependent on another in case their graphs coincide. If distinct linear

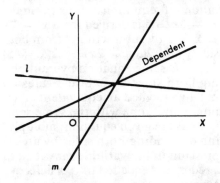

graphs of three linear equations in two variables intersect in a common point, they are dependent (each equation is dependent on the other two). Similarly, if distinct planar graphs of three linear equations in three variables share a common line of intersection, they are dependent. A similar geometric analysis can be made in other cases. See **Linear combination**.

Dependent Random Event   In **probability**, a basic concept expressing the idea that the outcome of one random event is related to that of another; that is, random event E is dependent on random event F in case the probabilities of the alternatives for E are affected by which alternative is assumed for F; otherwise E is an *independent* random event (as regards F). For example, suppose E is the simultaneous toss of a penny and a nickel, with the alternatives taken as **(1)** two heads, **(2)** two tails, and **(3)** a head and a tail (regardless of coin). Let F be the random event which is the toss of the penny only.

Then E is dependent on F; for example, the probability of the combination *head-head* for E will be different if a head is assumed for F than if a tail is assumed.

Dependent Variable   A *function* carries a value of one variable into a value of another; the latter is the dependent variable and the former the independent variable. For example, in the function from values of x to values of y expressed by the equation $y = 2x + 1$, y is the dependent variable and x the independent variable; the idea is that the value of x may be picked at will, but with this choice made, the value of y is determined. The equation $y = f(x)$ is a general notation which exhibits the dependent value y and the independent variable x.

Derivative of Function (Syn.: Differential coefficient of function)   The fundamental concept of the differential **calculus** which expresses in precise terms the idea of instantaneous rate of change of a function. More precisely, let $f(x)$ be a function of a real variable defined in an interval about $x = a$; then its derivative at $x = a$ is the *limit* of the quotient

$$\frac{f(a + \Delta x) - f(a)}{\Delta x}$$

as Δx approaches 0 (provided this limit exists). The derivative of $f(x)$ at x is denoted variously by

$$\frac{df(x)}{dx}, \ f'(x), \ Df(x), \ D_x f(x).$$

For example, $D_x(x^3) = 3x^2$ and

$$\frac{d(\sin x)}{dx} = \cos x.$$

When the function is expressed in the form $y = f(x)$, the following notations are also used:

$$dy/dx, \ y', \ Dy, \ D_x y.$$

73

In terms of the graph of $y = f(x)$, the derivative defines the slope of the **tangent line to the curve** at (x, y); if x is interpreted as time t, then the derivative $df(t)/dt$ defines the **velocity** of a moving particle at time t. The notation "df/dx" was introduced by Leizniz, "$f'(x)$" by Lagrange, and "Df" by Cauchy.

Differentiation is the operation which transforms $f(x)$ into its derivative $df(x)/dx$; it obeys the following rules for combinations of functions:

$$D_z[a \cdot f(x)] = a \cdot D_z f(x)$$
$$D_z[f(x) \pm g(x)] = D_z f(x) \pm D_z g(x)$$
$$D_z[f(x) \cdot g(x)]$$
$$= f(x) \cdot D_z g(x) + g(x) \cdot D_z f(x)$$
$$D_z \left[\frac{f(x)}{g(x)} \right]$$
$$= \frac{g(x) \cdot D_z f(x) - f(x) \cdot D_z g(x)}{[g(x)]^2}.$$

(See **Implicit differentiation, Inverse of function**.) For a composite function $f[g(x)]$, the following *chain rule* applies:

$$D_z\{f[g(x)]\} = [D_u f(u)] \cdot [D_z g(x)],$$

where u is to be replaced by $g(x)$ in the argument of $D_u f(u)$ [this formula can be put in the suggestive form $dz/dx = (dz/dy) \cdot (dy/dx)$, where $z = f(y)$ and $y = g(x)$]. An example is

$$D_z(\log \sin x) = D_u(\log u) \cdot D_z \sin x$$
$$= \frac{\cos x}{u} = \frac{\cos x}{\sin x} = \cot x.$$

The *second derivative* of $f(x)$ is the derivative of $df(x)/dx$; it is denoted variously by $d^2f(x)/dx^2$, $D_z^2 f(x)$, $f''(x)$; geometrically, it is related to the shape of a curve (see **Convex function** and **Curvature**); in the case of motion, it is related to **acceleration**. Higher order derivatives are defined similarly, that is, $D_z^n f(x)$ is the derivative of $D_z^{n-1} f(x)$; **Leibniz' theorem** gives a rule for calculating the nth derivative of a product.

See **Function of real variable, Fundamental theorem of calculus, Partial derivative**.

Derived Equation In algebra, an equation obtained from a given equation by the application of rules for modifying equations, as in the solution of equations. For example, $x^2 - 3x = 5$ is derived from $x^2 - 2x = x + 5$ by subtracting x from both sides, and $2(x^2 - 2x) = 2(x + 5)$ from the same equation by multiplying both sides by 2. Some rules do not always yield an equivalent equation, that is, one with the same solutions as the given equation; multiplying or dividing both sides by an expression in the variable may lead to a **redundant equation** or to a **defective equation**.

Desargues' Theorem The following basic proposition of **projective geometry**: If the lines through corresponding vertices of two triangles

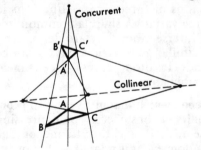

are concurrent, the points of intersection of corresponding sides are collinear; and conversely. It was discovered by Desargues in the first half of the seventeenth century, but its importance in projective geometry was not recognized until two centuries later.

Descartes' Rule of Signs The rule that the number of positive solutions of a polynomial equation $P(x) = 0$ is at most the number of variations of sign in $P(x)$. For example, the coefficient of $x^4 - 3x^3 - x^2 + 5x - 2 = 0$ in order are $+1, -3, -1, +5, -2$; there are three variations in sign ($+1$ to -3 is one variation, -3 to -1 is no variation, and so on); hence, the equation has at most three positive roots. For negative roots, the equation $P(-x) = 0$, obtained by replacing x by $-x$, is used; the number of its variations of sign gives the maximum number of negative roots of $P(x) = 0$. For the preceding example, this gives $x^4 + 3x^3 - x^2 - 5x - 2 = 0$; the coefficients now have one variation in sign; so that the original equation has at most one negative root. Descartes' rule applied to the equation $x^2 + 1 = 0$ shows that there are neither positive roots nor negative roots (the roots are the complex numbers i and $-i$). Descartes' rule can be sharpened as follows: the number of positive roots differs from the number of changes of sign by an even integer, a root of multiplicity m being counted m times.

Determinant Of a matrix, represented by a square array of numbers, a certain algebraic expression in its elements. A determinant of the **second order** is defined for a two-by-two matrix as the algebraic expression on the right side of the following equation,

$$\begin{vmatrix} a_1 & b_1 \\ a_2 & b_2 \end{vmatrix} = a_1 b_2 - a_2 b_1.$$

The left side is the notation for the determinant (the right side is sometimes called the expansion of the determinant). The elements a_1, a_2, b_1, b_2 of the matrix are also the elements of the determinant. If the elements of one row (column) are multiples of those of the other row (column), the determinant equals 0. In the matrix at the top of the next column, the second column is -2 times the first.

$$\begin{vmatrix} 2 & -4 \\ -3 & 6 \end{vmatrix} = 12 - 12 = 0;$$

A determinant of the *third order* is defined by the following equation:

$$\begin{vmatrix} a_1 & b_1 & c_1 \\ a_2 & b_2 & c_2 \\ a_3 & b_3 & c_3 \end{vmatrix} = \begin{aligned} & a_1 b_2 c_3 + a_2 b_3 c_1 + a_3 b_1 c_2 \\ & - a_3 b_2 c_1 - a_2 b_1 c_3 \\ & - a_1 b_3 c_2. \end{aligned}$$

Determinants of any order can be defined by an appropriate extension; a determinant of the nth order has $n!$ (that is, $1 \times 2 \times 3 \times \cdots n$) terms. The notation for determinants goes back to the middle of the nineteenth century.

Determinants arise in various parts of mathematics. They occur, for example, in the solution of simultaneous linear equations by **Cramer's rule**. For another example, they can be used in analytic geometry to express the equation of the line passing through two points (x_1, y_1) and (x_2, y_2); the equation is

$$\begin{vmatrix} x & y & 1 \\ x_1 & y_1 & 1 \\ x_2 & y_2 & 1 \end{vmatrix} = 0.$$

If the points are $(1, 0)$ and $(0, 1)$, the equation is

$$\begin{vmatrix} x & y & 1 \\ 1 & 0 & 1 \\ 0 & 1 & 0 \end{vmatrix} = 0;$$

expanding this determinant of the third order leads to

$$x + y - 1 = 0.$$

Determinants are important in the study of vectors. The rows of a determinant can be thought of as vectors; the fact that a determinant equals zero, for example, means that one of the row vectors is a linear combination of the others.

Ref. [32, 100, 127].

Determinant of Coefficients For a

system of simultaneous linear equations, the determinant of the matrix of coefficients of the variables (where the number of equations and variables is the same). For example, in

$$2x - 3y = 1$$
$$x + 5y = -6,$$

the determinant of coefficients is

$$\begin{vmatrix} 2 & -3 \\ 1 & 5 \end{vmatrix},$$

which equals 13. See **Cramer's rule**.

Determine Specify uniquely within a given class. For example, that two distinct points "determine" a line means that there is one and only one line containing these points. That two sides and the included angle "determine" a triangle means that there is one and only one triangle (to within congruence) with these sides and angle. As in the last example, uniqueness can be understood in a sense of equivalence other than logical identity.

Developable Surface Informally, a surface that can be rolled out evenly (that is, "developed") on a plane, such as a cylinder or cone; no two-dimensional portion of a sphere, for example, is developable.

Diagonal Of a *polygon* in the plane, any line segment joining non-adjacent vertices. A triangle has no diagonals, a quadrilateral has two diagonals, a pentagon has five diagonals, . . . , a polygon of n sides has

$n(n - 3)/2$ diagonals.

For a *polyhedron* in space, a diagonal is a line segment joining two vertices not in the same face; a paral-

lelepiped, for example, has four diagonals.

Diagram A pictorial representation. For example, the Argand diagram is used to represent complex numbers and the Venn diagram is used to exhibit relations between sets.

Diameter Of a *circle*, a line segment (or its length) joining two points of the circle and containing the center; of a *conic*, a chord which bisects each member of a family of parallel chords. The diameters of a central conic come in *conjugate pairs* through

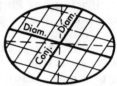

its center; each bisects the chords parallel to the other (see figure). A diameter of a *central quadric* surface is a chord through the centers of a family of parallel plane sections of the surface.

Diametral Plane Of a quadric surface, a plane that bisects every member of a family of parallel chords; two diametral planes are *conjugate* in case each is parallel to the family of parallel chords defining the other. A diametral plane of a central quadric passes through its center.

Difference of Like Powers An algebraic expression of the form $x^n - y^n$; for example, $x^2 - y^2$ and $x^3 - y^3$ are, respectively, the difference of squares and the difference of cubes. Such differences can be factored as follows:

$$x^2 - y^2 = (x - y)(x + y)$$
$$x^3 - y^3 = (x - y)(x^2 + xy + y^2)$$
$$\vdots$$
$$\vdots$$
$$x^n - y^n = (x - y)(x^{n-1} + x^{n-1}y + \cdots + xy^{n-1} + y^n).$$

Similar formulas holds for odd powers in the case of a **sum of like powers**.

Difference Quotient Of a function of a real variable $f(x)$, the ratio of increments

$$\frac{f(x + \Delta) - f(x)}{(x + \Delta) - x}, \quad \text{or} \quad \frac{f(x + \Delta) - f(x)}{\Delta}.$$

Differential Analyzer A computer designed for the solution of differential equations; it is typically an analog computer, or a combination analog-digital computer. See **Computer**.

Differential Calculus That part of the **calculus** dealing with the operation of differentiation of functions, and various applications. See **Derivative of function**.

Differential Coefficient of Function See **Derivative of function** (syn.).

Differential Equation In the calculus, an equation to be solved for an unknown function which involves the first or higher derivatives of the function. For example,

$$\frac{d^2f(x)}{dx^2} - f(x) = 0$$

is a differential equation in $f(x)$; solutions are $f(x) = \sin x$, or $f(x) = \cos x$, or any linear combination, $f(x) = A \sin x + B \cos x$.

Differential of Function The differential of a *function of a real variable* $f(x)$ at $x = a$, is the linear function $A \cdot dx$ in a variable dx, where A is the derivative of $f(x)$ at $x = a$. It is denoted by "*df*," or by "*dy*" when $y = f(x)$; that is,

$$df = (D_x f)dx, \quad \text{or} \quad dy = f'(a) \cdot dx.$$

If dx is taken as the horizontal coordinate measured from $[a, f(a)]$, then the graph of the differential is the tangent line to $y = f(x)$ at this point; the value of the differential is

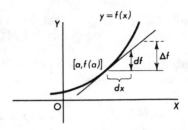

a linear approximation to the increment $\Delta f = f(a + dx) - f(a)$, for a given increment dx in the argument of f. For example, if x and y measure the radius and area of a circle, then $y = \pi x^2$; hence, $dy = 2\pi x dx$; when x increases from 3 to 3.1 ($a = 3$, $dx = 0.1$), y increases by approximately $dy = 2\pi \cdot 3 \cdot (0.1)$, or $(0.6)\pi$ (from its value 9π at 3). **Taylor's theorem** gives a more general method of approximation.

For a function $f(x, y)$ of *two variables*, the differential at a point (a, b) is the linear function $A dx + B dy$ in the independent variables dx, dy, where A, B are the partial derivatives of f at (a, b). It is denoted by df, or dz when $z = f(x, y)$; that is,

$$df = \frac{\partial f}{\partial x} \cdot dx + \frac{\partial f}{\partial y} \cdot dy.$$

Its graph is the tangent plane to the surface $z = f(x, y)$, relative to the origin $[a, b, f(a, b)]$, and with first and second coordinates dx and dy; it serves as a linear approximation to the functional increment $\Delta f = f(a + dx, b + dy) - f(a, b)$. An analogous definition applies to a function of any finite number of real variables.

Differentiation The operation which transforms a function $f(x)$ into its derivative $D_x f(x)$; its repeated application is *successive* differentiation, as in $D_x f(x)$, $D_x^2 f(x)$, $D_x^3 f(x)$, etc.

77

See **Derivative of function, Implicit differention**.

Digit Of the **decimal number system**, any one of the symbols 0, 1, 2, 3, 4, 5, 6, 7, 8, 9. These Hindu-Arab symbols were introduced into Europe about A.D. 1000.

Digit, Significant See **Approximate number**.

Digital Computer A **computer** that handles numbers and other information in symbolic form as strings of digits, and operates directly on these strings in carrying out operations. The modern digital computer is an automatic, high-speed machine capable of executing an arithmetical or logical operation in the order of millionths of a second. It is capable of processing large amounts of information rapidly and performing massive scientific calculations that were not feasible otherwise; this new dimension in calculating power can be applied in many branches of knowledge [see, for example, **Machine intelligence** (computer)]. It is bringing about a technological revolution in the modern world.

In a digital computer, a *word* is a string of digits representing one item of information, such as a single number; more generally, a word is a string that may occupy one internal storage location and is transported in the computer as a unit. One *bit* of a word is any one of its binary digits, 0 or 1, when the word is represented in binary form (string of 0's and 1's); thus, a *36-bit machine* contains 36 binary digits per word, and a *48-bit machine,* 48 per word (36 to 48 bits in binary notation corresponds to about 10 to 13 digits in decimal notation). A typical machine has a *fixed word length;* in a *variable word length* ma-

chine, the computer can control and vary the word length.

The computer has built into it a certain number of basic operations which it can be instructed to perform directly; a problem is solved as a series of these basic steps. A machine *instruction* specifies one of these steps; this might be a fundamental operation of arithmetic (such as addition), or a logical operation (such as substituting one number for another). The entire solution is specified by a computer *routine*; this is a sequence of coded instructions that is stored in the computer in advance and specifies the steps in the solution. The routine, or program, is devised by human intelligence and it is the unlimited variety of possible programs that gives the machine its remarkable versatility. For this reason, it is often called a *general-purpose computer*. See **Code**, **Computer program**.

An electronic digital computer typically contains three major kinds of internal units—the *storage unit,* the *arithmetic unit*, and the *control unit*. The storage unit holds information in individual *storage locations,*

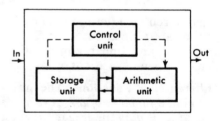

or *registers;* the information in one location might be one piece of numerical data or a single instruction of the routine. The arithmetic unit operates on the data it receives from storage; results are typically returned to storage for later use. The control unit interprets the coded instructions it receives from storage and initiates the electronic actions necessary to carry out the instruction; it directs the computer to the next instruction, and, in general, controls the flow of activity through the entire routine of instructions. In addition to its internal units, the computer is linked to *input* and *output* devices which permit information to be sent into or taken out of the computer; among these are tape units, electric typewriters, printers, card readers, etc. Some of the newer, more complex computers contain several internal arithmetic and logical units that can operate simultaneously.

Ref. [49, 67].

Dihedral Angle   In solid geometry, an elementary configuration consisting of two half-planes (the *faces*) with a common edge (the *edge* of the angle). The *plane angle* of a dihedral angle is the angle intercepted by a

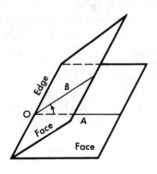

plane perpendicular to the edge (angle AOB in the figure). A dihedral angle is measured by its plane angle; a dihedral angle is acute, right, or obtuse, according to its plane angle. A dihedral angle of a polyhedron or of a polyhedral angle is one formed by two adjacent faces meeting along an edge.

Dimension   Of a **space**, the (fewest) number of coordinates required to represent its points. For example, a line has dimension one, a plane dimension two, and ordinary space dimension three. The points of an *n*-dimensional space have *n* coordinates $(x_1, x_2, \ldots, x_n)$. A configuration lying within a space is also assigned a dimension. A line seg-

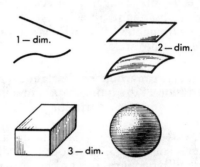

ment or curve, whether in a plane, three-, or higher-, dimensional space is one-dimensional (these can be viewed as portions of lines, distorted or otherwise). The interior of a simple closed curve in the plane (such as the interior of a circle), or a surface in space (as a distortion of such a planar region) is two-dimensional. The interior of a solid in three-space, such as the interior of a sphere, is three-dimensional. A general concept of the dimension of any configuration is not self-evident; it is treated in a field of topology, known as "dimension theory," which began about 1920.

Dimensions of Rectangular Figures   For a rectangle in the plane, its length and width; for a rectangular parallelepiped in space, its length, width, and height.

Diophantine Analysis   In the theory of numbers, the study of the solutions of (certain) equations in two or more variables, when the solutions are restricted to be integers. For example, Fermat's last theorem is a problem of diophantine analysis. The name is after the mathematician Diophantus of ancient Alexandria.

Direct Proof   See **Proof**.

Direct Trigonometric Function   Any one of the **trigonometric functions** sine, cosine, tangent, cosecant, secant, cotangent, in contrast to **inverse trigonometric functions** such as the arc sine, arc cosine, etc.

Direct Proportion or Variation   A **variation** of the type $y = kx$, in contrast to an *inverse* variation $y = k/x$.

Directed Angle (Syn.: Algebraic angle)   An **angle** of rotation; it is "directed" because it can be either counterclockwise (positive) or clockwise (negative).

Directed Line   A line with a selected direction along it; if P, Q are points on the line, then the distance from P to Q is positive or negative depending upon whether the direction from P to Q is the same or opposite to the selected one. A directed line segment represents a **vector**.

Directed Number   A signed number, used to distinguish measurement in one direction (positive) from that in the opposite direction (negative), as in a thermometer or number scale. This is in contrast to measurement of pure (positive) magnitude, such as ordinary area or volume.

Direction Angles, Cosines, Numbers In solid geometry, numbers which express the orientation of a directed line in space. Suppose such a line passes through the origin of a rectangular coordinate system; then its *direction angles* are the three angles of rotation α, β, γ of the positive x-, y-,

and z-axes into the assigned direc-

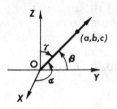

tion along the line (these angles lie between 0° and 180°). The *direction cosines* are cos α, cos β, cos γ; they satisfy the equation $\cos^2\alpha + \cos^2\beta + \cos^2\gamma = 1$. *Direction numbers a, b, c* are any three numbers proportional to the direction cosines; that is $a = k\cos\alpha$, $b = k\cos\beta$, $c = k\cos\gamma$ (with $k \neq 0$). The direction cosines of a line are the coordinates of the point a unit distance from the origin along its positive direction; direction numbers are coordinates of an arbitrary point on the line (except the origin). For a directed line not through the origin, the direction angles, cosines, and numbers are those of the parallel directed line through the origin.   See **Line**.

Orientation of a plane in space is expressed by the direction numbers of a normal, or perpendicular, line to the plane; if the plane has the equation $ax + by + cz + d = 0$, then a, b, c are direction numbers of a perpendicular.   See **Plane**.

Direction of Line or Curve   In the *plane,* the direction of a line is measured by its *inclination,* which is the positive (counterclockwise) angle of rotation of the positive x-axis into the line (this angle lies between 0° and 180°). In *space,* the direction of a line is represented by its three direction angles.

The direction of a curve at a given point P is taken as the direction of the **tangent line to the curve**. The

curvature is defined as the rate of

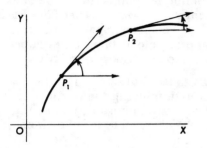

change of direction with respect to distance along the curve.

Directrix of Cone or Cylinder See **Cone**; **Cylinder**.

Directrix of Conic See **Conic**.

Discontinuous Function See **Continuous function**.

Discriminant In the theory of equations, a certain algebraic expression in the coefficients of a polynomial equation. The discriminant of the *quadratic equation* $ax^2 + bx + c = 0$ is the expression $b^2 - 4ac$ in the coefficients; for example, the discriminant of $x^2 - 2x + 3 = 0$ is $(-2)^2 - 4(1)(3)$ or -8; the discriminant of $2x^2 + x = 0$ is $1^2 - 4(2)(0)$, or 1. Three cases arise for the value of the discriminant: **(1)** the discriminant is positive—then there are two distinct real roots of the equation; **(2)** the discriminant is negative—then there are two distinct conjugate complex roots; **(3)** the discriminant is zero—then there is one real (double) root. For a polynomial equation $P(x) = 0$ of any degree, the discriminant, when defined, has the property that it is zero just in case the equation has a multiple root.

Disjoint Sets Sets with no members in common, such as the set of even integers and the set of odd integers; the intersection of disjoint sets is the null set.   See **Algebra of sets**.

Disjunction (Syn.: Alternation)   In logic, the propositional form "*P* or *Q*," or any statement of this form; it is symbolized "$P \lor Q$" (see **Algebra of propositions**). An example is "zero is positive or zero is negative" (which is a false statement). A disjunction is false (F) just in case both *P*, *Q* are false; otherwise it is true (T) [see truth-table in figure]. The *denial* of the disjunction can be expressed in the form "not *P* and not *Q*"; for example, the denial of the given statement about zero is "zero is not positive and zero is not negative" (a true statement).

This notion of disjunction is the *inclusive disjunction*, in contrast to the *exclusive disjunction*; the latter is taken to be false also when the components *P*, *Q* are both true. Both

P	Q	P or Q
T	T	T
F	T	T
T	F	T
F	F	F

disjunctions are used in ordinary discourse, but in mathematics, the inclusive disjunction is generally understood. For example, in asserting "*x* is divisible by 2 or *x* is divisible by 3," it is not intended to exclude that *x* is divisible by both 2 and 3, that is, by 6.

Distance In geometry, a fundamental concept which is a measure of the separation of geometric objects. The simplest geometric objects in the plane or in space are points; if distance between two points is taken as already defined, or as undefined and subject to appropriate axioms, then the distance between any two geometric configurations A and B is the following: it is the least distance between all possible pairs of points P, Q with P in A and Q in B. From this, the distance between various configurations can be determined. The distance between a point P and a line l (or a plane p) equals the distance

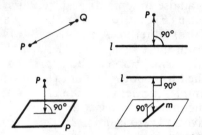

from P to the point of intersection of the perpendicular from P to l (or p). The distance between two parallel lines (or planes) equals the distance between the endpoints of a perpendicular line segment joining the lines (planes). The distance between skew lines l and m in space equals the distance between the endpoints of the perpendicular line segment joining the lines. In analytic geometry the distance between points is expressed by an algebraic formula; this enables other distances to be expressed similarly. In the calculus, the **length** of a curve is defined; by *distance along a curve* from point P to point Q is then meant the length of the arc from P to Q. See **Distance formula**; also for distance from a point to a line or plane, see **Normal form**.

In Euclidean geometry, the distance between two points is the length of the line segment between them; also, this path has the least length of all curves joining the two points. This last property provides a clue for the definition of *distance on a surface*; the distance between two points is defined as the least length

of all curves lying on the surface and joining the points; the curve of least length is a *geodesic*. (See **Non-Euclidean geometry**, **Space**.) An abstract approach to distance is developed in the modern theory of **metric spaces**.

Distance Formula The following equation giving the distance D between two points (x_1, y_1) and (x_2, y_2) in the plane, in terms of their coordinates:

$$D = \sqrt{(x_1 - x_2)^2 + (y_1 - y_2)^2}.$$

For example, the distance between $(0, 2)$ and $(3, -1)$ is

$$\sqrt{(0 - 3)^2 + (2 + 1)^2},$$

or

$$\sqrt{9 + 9} = \sqrt{18} = 3\sqrt{2}.$$

For points (x_1, y_1, z_1) and (x_2, y_2, z_2) in three-space, the formula is

$$D = [(x_1 - x_2)^2 + (y_1 - y_2)^2 + (z_1 - z_2)^2]^{1/2};$$

for points $(a_1, a_2, \ldots, a_n)$, $(b_1, b_2, \ldots, b_n)$ in Euclidean **space** of n dimensions, the formula is

$$D = [(a_1 - b_1)^2 + (a_2 - b_2)^2 + \cdots + (a_n - b_n)^2]^{1/2}.$$

Distance-Rate-Time Formula The rule that distance equals rate multiplied by time, $d = r \times t$.

Distance on Surface See **Geodesic**.

Distribution Function (Syn.: Cumulative distribution function) Of a **random variable**, usually, the probability $F(x)$ that it will take on a value not greater than x; if the variable takes on only a finite set of values, then $F(x)$ is the sum of the probabilities of the values not greater than x.

Distribution of Primes See **Prime number theorem**.

Distribution of Random Variable Informally, a mathematical representation of the numerical probabilities associated with the values of the variable. One representation is by the **distribution function**, another is by the *frequency function*. See **Probability**.

Distributive Law In algebra, the formula $a \cdot (x + y) = a \cdot x + a \cdot y$; it states that multiplication can be "distributed" over addition. In the following example it is used several times:

$$(x + 3)(2x + 4) = (x + 3)2x + (x + 3)4$$
$$= 2x^2 + 6x + 4x + 12$$
$$= 2x^2 + 10x + 12.$$

See **Field**; **Vector space**.

Divergent Not convergent. See **Sequence**; **Series**.

Dividend The number a in the expression "$a \div b$" denoting division; the number b is the *divisor*.

Divisible The integer m is divisible by the integer n in case n is a **factor of the integer** m; also, the polynomial $p(x)$ is divisible by the polynomial $q(x)$ in case $q(x)$ is a **factor of the polynomial** $p(x)$. In the case of integers, there are special tests for divisibility by particular integers. The following are tests for divisibility by 2, 3, 4, 5, 9, 10, or 11: **(1)** *divisibility by 2*—the last digit of the number is divisible by 2; **(2)** *divisibility by 3*—the sum of the digits is divisible by 3; **(3)** *divisibility by 4*—the number represented by the last two digits is divisible by 4; **(4)** *divisibility by 5*—the last digit is 0 or 5; **(5)** *divisibility by 9*—the sum of the digits is divisible by 9; **(6)** *divisibility by 10*—the last digit is 0; **(7)** *divisibility by 11*—the sum of the digits in even places minus the sum in odd places is divisible by 11 (for example, 4,807 is indivisible by 11 because $(4 + 0) - (8 + 7)$, or -11, is divisible by 11). These rules depend upon the fact that the digits in the decimal number system represent multiples of powers of ten.

Division Division of numbers is one of the fundamental operations of arithmetic; it can be defined as the inverse operation of multiplication as follows: let a and b be numbers (with $b \neq 0$); then the *quotient* $a \div b$ (or a/b) is the number x satisfying the equation $b \cdot x = a$. For example $(-6) \div 2$ is -3, because $2 \cdot (-3) = -6$; also $0 \div b = 0$ for any $b \neq 0$, since $b \cdot 0 = 0$. The number a is the *dividend*, and b is the *divisor* in $a \div b$. The notation "$a \div b$" was introduced in the seventeenth century.

In the **division of whole numbers**, a and b, the number $a \div b$ is another whole number just in case "b goes into a" an exact number of times, that is, in case b is a *divisor* of a. Hence the whole numbers are not "closed" under division. This is a reason for extending the concept of *number* to the rational number (fraction); the rational numbers are closed under (nonzero) division, as are the real numbers. Techniques are developed in arithmetic for carrying out division with various forms of numbers. For example, the division of signed numbers can be reduced to the division of positive numbers by use of the following *law of signs:*

$$\textbf{(1)} \quad \frac{-a}{b} = \frac{a}{-b} = -\frac{a}{b},$$

and

$$\textbf{(2)} \quad \frac{-a}{-b} = \frac{a}{b};$$

that is, like signs give "plus," unlike signs give "minus." See **Fraction**, **Rationalization of denominator**.

83

The general definition of $a \div b$ shows why *division by zero* is to be excluded. For suppose b were 0; then $a \div 0$ would be the number x satisfying $0 \cdot x = a$. However, $0 \cdot x$ equals 0 for every number x; hence, for any a, $0 \cdot x = a$ would have no solution when $a \neq 0$, and would have any number as a solution when $a = 0$. Thus, $a \div 0$ would not exist when $a \neq 0$, and would have infinitely many values when $a = 0$. The exclusion of 0 as a divisor ensures that $a \div b$ is uniquely defined and that the usual rules of algebra apply to all fractions.

Division Algorithm See **Division of polynomials, Division of whole numbers**.

Division by Zero See **Division**.

Division of Complex Numbers See **Complex numbers**.

Division of Line Segment In geometry, the separation of a line segment into two line segments in a given proportion. One type of division is *internal division:* consider a directed line segment from P to Q; a point R on this segment divides it internally in the ratio PR/RQ where the distances PR and RQ are directed distances. This ratio may be any

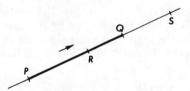

positive number; if R is at the midpoint M, the ratio is $1/1$, or 1; if R is between P and M (between M and Q), the ratio is less than (greater than) 1; if R is at P, the ratio is zero. The point R is an *internal point of division* of the line segment, and PR/RQ is the *ratio of division*. Ex-

ternal division occurs when R is on the line through PQ but external to PQ. In this case, the ratio of division is again PR/RQ, but it is negative (since PR and RQ are opposite in direction); for example, when R is placed so that Q is midway between P and R, the ratio of division is $2/(-1)$, or -2.

Let P, Q have rectangular coordinates (x_1, y_1) and (x_2, y_2), respectively; then the point (x, y) which divides PQ in the ratio r_1/r_2 is

$$x = \frac{r_2 x_1 + r_1 x_2}{r_1 + r_2}, \quad y = \frac{r_2 y_1 + r_1 y_2}{r_1 + r_2}.$$

For example, if $r_1/r_2 = 1/1$; this formula gives the midpoint $(x_1 + x_2)/2$, $(y_1 + y_2)/2$. Two points, one interior and one exterior, that divide PQ into numerically equal ratios provide a **harmonic division** of PQ.

Division of Polynomials The division of polynomials $A(x)$ and $B(x)$ is expressed by the following "division algorithm" of algebra: there exist polynomials $q(x)$ and $r(x)$ such that $A(x) = q(x) \cdot B(x) + r(x)$, with $r(x)$ having a lower degree than $B(x)$; the polynomial $A(x)$ is the *dividend,* $B(x)$ is the *divisor,* $q(x)$ is the *quotient,* and $r(x)$ is the *remainder*. There is a long division procedure of algebra, similar to that of arithmetic, for finding $q(x)$ and $r(x)$. When it is applied to

$$(2x^4 + 3x^2 + 8x - 1) \div (x^2 - x + 3)$$

it gives $q(x) = 2x^2 + 2x - 1$ and $r(x) = x + 2$; thus,

$$2x^4 + 3x^2 + 8x - 1$$
$$= (2x^2 + 2x - 1)(x^2 - x + 3)$$
$$+ (x + 2),$$

which can be verified by multiplication. (When the divisor has the linear form $x - a$, a simplified version of long division, known as "synthetic division," is available from the theory of equations.) The division of polynomials is used to change an improper fraction to a mixed expression, that is, a polynomial plus a proper fraction; for example,

$$\frac{2x^4 + 3x^2 + 8x - 1}{x^2 - x + 3} = 2x^2 + 2x - 1$$

$$+ \frac{x + 2}{x^2 - x + 3}.$$

See **Remainder theorem**.

Division of Whole Numbers Let m and n be whole numbers; then the "division algorithm" of arithmetic asserts that there are whole numbers q and r such that $m = q \cdot n + r$. The number m is the *dividend*, n is the *divisor*, q is the *quotient*, and r is the *remainder* (r is less than n). That is, divi-

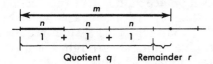

dend = quotient · divisor + remainder. The familiar long division procedure of arithmetic is a method of finding q and r. For example, when it is applied to $568 \div 13$, it gives $q = 43$ and $r = 9$; hence $568 = 43 \cdot 13 + 9$. Division of whole numbers is used to reduce an improper fraction to a mixed number, that is, an integer plus a proper fraction; for example, $\frac{568}{13} = 43 + \frac{9}{13}$.

Divisor In arithmetic or algebra, a **factor of an integer**, or a **factor of a polynomial**; for example, 2 is a divisor of 6, and $x - 1$ is a divisor of $x^2 + 2x - 3$. "Divisor" is also used for the term b in the expression for division $a \div b$. See **Common divisor**.

Dodecagon A polygon with twelve sides; it is a regular dodecagon if all its sides are equal and all its angles are equal.

Dodecahedron A polyhedron with twelve faces. A regular dodecahedron is a **regular polyhedron** with twelve faces; its faces are regular pentagons.

Domain of Function The set of values of x for which the functional value $f(x)$ exists. Log x, for example, is defined only when x is positive; hence the domain of the logarithm function is the set of positive real numbers. Also, the domain of

$$f(x) = \frac{1}{x - 1}$$

is all real numbers different from 1; the domain of $2x^2 - 5$ or $\sin x$ is all real numbers. The set of all functional values $f(x)$ is the *range* of the function.

Double Angle Formulas In trigonometry, formulas expressing a trigonometric function of twice an angle in terms of functions of the angle itself; among these are the following:

$$\sin 2A = 2 \sin A \cos A,$$
$$\cos 2A = \cos^2 A - \sin^2 A$$
$$\tan 2A = \frac{2 \tan A}{1 - \tan^2 A}.$$

They are consequences of the **addition formulas** of trigonometry.

Double Integral The double integral of a function $f(x, y)$ over a region R in the plane xy is a generalization

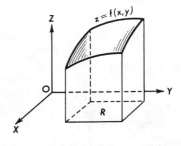

of the definite integral of a function

of one variable; it is denoted by

$$\iint_R f(x, y)\, dxdy.$$

The double integral has a direct interpretation as a measure of *volume;* when $f(x, y)$ is positive, it equals the volume included between the surface $z = f(x, y)$ and the region R. The double integral expresses other measures than volume, also; for example, if R has area A, then

$$\frac{1}{A}\iint_R xdxdy, \quad \frac{1}{A}\iint_R ydxdy$$

give the coordinates x, y of the *centroid* of the region R. Also, the *area* of the surface $z = f(x, y)$ above R is given by

$$\iint_R \left[1 + \left(\frac{\partial f}{\partial x}\right)^2 + \left(\frac{\partial f}{\partial y}\right)^2\right]^{1/2} dxdy,$$

where the partial derivatives of f occur under the radical. A double integral is generally evaluated as an **iterated integral**.

Technically, the double integral of $f(x, y)$ over the region R can be defined as follows. Divide the coordinate plane into a grid-work of squares of length d; let $\Delta A_1, \Delta A_2, \ldots, \Delta A_N$ be the squares of the grid-work which overlap the interior of R; let (x_1, y_1) $(x_2, y_2), \ldots, (x_N, y_N)$ be points of R in these respective squares. Form the sum

$$f(x_1, y_1)\Delta A_1 + f(x_2, y_2)\Delta A_2 + \cdots$$
$$+ f(x_N, y_N)\Delta A_N.$$

The number of terms N, and the sum, depends upon the dimension d of the grid-work; the *limit* of this sum, as d approaches 0, is taken as the double integral (provided the limit exists). When $f(x, y)$ is continuous, for example, and R is an ordinary region, this limit does exist.

Double Root Of an equation, a root that occurs twice; more precisely, r is a double root of the polynomial

equation $p(x) = 0$ in case $(x - r)^2$ is a factor of $p(x)$ (and this is the highest power which is a factor). For example, if the quadratic equation $x^2 - 6x + 9 = 0$ is solved by factoring, it becomes $(x - 3)^2 = 0$, so that 3 is a double root (solving by the **quadratic formula** in this case would give one root, instead of two). Double roots occur in polynomial equations of any degree; for example, in the cubic $(x - 1)^2(x - 2) = 0$, 1 is a double root and 2 is a single root. See **Multiple root**.

Duality (Projective geometry) See **Projective geometry**.

Duodecimal Number System A system of notation for (real) numbers using place values, like the decimal system, but with the base twelve rather than ten. This system requires twelve digits, 0 through 9 and two additional symbols for ten and eleven. In duodecimal notation the string of four digits 2,764 stands for the number $2 \cdot 12^3 + 7 \cdot 12^2 + 6 \cdot 12 + 4$, or 4,540 in the decimal number system. In principle, arithmetical operations can be carried out in this system as readily as in the decimal system. One advantage of the duodecimal system is that fractions can more often be written as finite strings; for example, in the decimal system

$$\frac{1}{6} = .166666\ldots, \quad \frac{1}{9} = .111\ldots,$$

while in the duodecimal system

$$\frac{1}{6} = .2 \left(\text{that is, } \frac{2}{12}\right)$$
$$\frac{1}{9} = .14 \left(\text{that is, } \frac{1}{12} + \frac{4}{12^2}\right).$$

However, $\frac{1}{5}$ and $\frac{1}{10}$ (finite decimals) are infinite strings in the duodecimal system.

Duplication of Cube In geometry,

the ancient Greek problem of the *geometric construction* (straight edge and compass) of a cube whose volume is twice that of a given cube; in

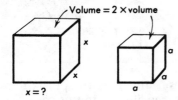

Volume = 2 × volume

x = ?

modern algebraic language, this is the problem of solving $x^3 = 2a^3$, where x and a are the sides of the required and given cubes, respectively. It was not until the nineteenth century that a proof was obtained of the impossibility of constructing a solution. If the imposed restriction to straight edge and compass is lifted, then it is possible to devise various constructions. Some of these were discovered by the early Greek geometers; in particular they invented solutions that made use of conics.

Dyadic Number System　See **Binary number system** (syn.).

Dynamic Programming　See **Mathematical programming**.

E

e　A fundamental number of mathematics which has the approximate value 2.71828 . . . (to five places). One definition gives it as the limit of the (increasing) sequence $(1 + 1/n)^n$, as the integer n grows without bound; the first few terms of this sequence are

$$1, \left(\frac{3}{2}\right)^2, \left(\frac{4}{3}\right)^3, \left(\frac{5}{4}\right)^4, \left(\frac{6}{5}\right)^5, \ldots$$

Another expression for e is the sum of the factorial infinite series

$$1 + \frac{1}{1} + \frac{1}{1 \cdot 2} + \frac{1}{1 \cdot 2 \cdot 3} + \frac{1}{1 \cdot 2 \cdot 3 \cdot 4} + \cdots.$$

The number e is the base of the natural logarithm, and ranks with **pi**, π, in its importance in mathematics. It was introduced by Euler in the middle of the eighteenth century; it was not until the latter half of the nineteenth century that it was shown by Hermite to be *transcendental*.　Ref. [28, 73, 140].

Eccentric Angle and Circles　See **Ellipse, Hyperbola.**

Eccentricity of Conic　The constant ratio $\dfrac{\text{distance to focus}}{\text{distance to directrix}}$,

for any point P on the **conic.** An *ellipse* has eccentricity between 0 and 1; of two ellipses, the one with the larger eccentricity is relatively flatter; when the eccentricity is 0, the ellipse is a circle. Every *parabola* has the eccentricity 1. A *hyperbola* has

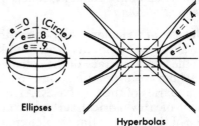

Ellipses

Hyperbolas

eccentricity larger than 1; when the eccentricity is near 1, the hyperbola is relatively narrow; when the eccentricity increases, the hyperbola becomes relatively wider. Two conics with equal eccentricities are *similar;* and in similar conics, lengths in one are proportional to corresponding lengths in the other (such as axes of similar ellipses).

Edge　Of a geometric figure in space, a line or line segment which is the intersection of two plane faces; examples are the edge of a dihedral angle, and the lateral edge of a prism.

Element of Arc Length (Syn.: Linear

element). In the calculus, the differential of arc length s along a curve, s being regarded as a function of the variable defining the curve. If the curve is given by $y = f(x)$, then the differential ds is given by

$$ds = \sqrt{1 + (df/dx)^2}\ dx;$$

if the curve is given by parametric equations $x = g(t)$, $y = h(t)$, then $ds = \sqrt{(dg/dt)^2 + (dh/dt)^2}\ dt$. In general, $ds^2 = dx^2 + dy^2$. The *arc length* between two points is obtained by integrating ds between these points.

Element of Cone   Any line segment on the **cone** joining the vertex to a point on the boundary of the base. An element of a **conical surface** is a line through the vertex which lies entirely on the surface. A plane tangent to a cone (or conical surface) touches it along an entire element, called the *element of contact*.

Element of Cylinder   Any one of the parallel line segments which make up the lateral surface of the **cylinder**; they join corresponding points of the boundaries of the two bases. An element of a **cylindrical surface** is any one of the parallel lines which make up the surface. A plane tangent to a cylinder (or cylindrical surface) touches it along an entire element, called the *element of contact*.

Element of Integration   Of a definite integral in the calculus, the expression under the integral sign; for example, in $\int_a^b f(x)dx$, the element of integration is $f(x)dx$, and in

$$\int_a^b \sqrt{1 + [f'(x)]^2}\ dx$$

it is $\sqrt{1 + [f'(x)]^2}\ dx$. The idea of the terminology comes from the definition of a definite integral as a limit of a sum of terms; the "element of integration" symbolizes a general term of this sum. In the first example, the

integral equals the area A under the curve $y = f(x)$, and $f(x)dx$ symbolizes the area of one of the rectangles

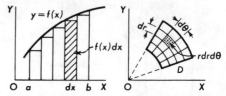

whose sum gives an approximation to A (see figure); in this case, $f(x)dx$ is an *element of area*. In the second example, the integral equals the length L of this curve from $x = a$ to $x = b$; the element of integration is the *element of arc length;* it symbolizes the length of one segment of a broken line whose total length is an approximation to L. The notion of element of integration applies to a double (or higher) integral as well; again, it is the expression under the double integral sign, and it symbolizes one of many pieces whose sum approximates the value of the integral. For example, in $\iint_D r\ dr\ d\theta$, the element of integration is $r dr d\theta$; in this case, the integral equals the area of the region D in terms of polar coordinates, and $r dr d\theta$ is the *element of plane area* in these coordinates (see figure).

Element of Set   See **Member of set** (syn.).

Elements of Geometry   The presentation of geometry by Euclid in the form of a deductive system which appears in his *Elements* (written about 300 B.C.). The term "elements" is often also used to mean the basic concepts and propositions of any subject.

Elevation   See **Angle of elevation**.

Elimination of Variable   In solving simultaneous equations, any method of removing one unknown and reducing the number of equations by one. As an example, consider the linear equations,

$$2x - y = 2$$
$$x + 3y = 1.$$

The unknown y can be eliminated by *substitution* as follows; solve the first equation for y, to obtain $y = 2x - 2$; substitute for y in the second equation, to obtain $x + 3(2x - 2) = 1$, or $7x = 7$; this has y eliminated. The solution is completed by solving the last equation to obtain $x = 1$, substituting this value in an original equation, and solving for y to obtain $y = 0$. Another method is elimination by *addition* or *subtraction;* in this case, both equations are modified so as to produce the same coefficient in each for a given variable, and then the equations are added, or subtracted to remove the variable. Consider the above example; the numerical coefficient 3 can be obtained for y in the first equation by multiplying both sides by 3; when the resulting equation is added to the second equation, the result is $7x = 7$, with y eliminated.

The general procedure for solution by elimination of three equations in three unknowns, x, y, z, would be the following. Eliminate one of the variables, say z, in each of two pairs of equations to obtain two equations in x and y. Now eliminate one of these variables, say y, between these two equations to obtain one equation in x. Solve for x; substitute in an equation in the two variables x and y to obtain y; and finally substitute in an original equation to obtain z. Successive elimination of variables is an effective computational procedure for the solution of simultaneous linear equations (compare **Cramer's rule**).

Ellipse A **conic** with eccentricity e between 0 and 1; it is the locus of

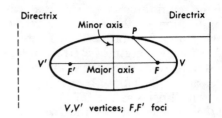

V,V' vertices; F,F' foci

points P whose distance from a fixed point (the *focus*) is in the fixed ratio e to its distance to a fixed line (the directrix). It occurs in nature as the path of a planet, for example. See **Eccentricity of conic**.

The ellipse is symmetrical about the line through the focus perpendicular to the directrix; this line intersects the ellipse in its *vertices,* and the line segment (or its length) between the vertices is the *major axis.* The midpoint of the major axis is the *center,* and a segment (or its length) from the center to a vertex is a *semimajor axis.* A *chord* is a line segment joining two points of the ellipse. The chord through the center perpendicular to the major axis is the *minor axis*; the center bisects this axis, and either half is a *semiminor axis.* The major axis is larger than the minor axis. (An ellipse is determined by the major axis and the focus, or by the major and minor axes). The ellipse is also symmetrical about the minor axis; it has a second directrix and focus which define the same ellipse, and the two foci and directrices are equally spaced from the center. A *focal chord* is a chord through a focus; a focal chord perpendicular to the major axis is a *latus rectum.* A *focal radius* is a line segment (or its length) from a focus to a point on the ellipse. A circle is a special case of an ellipse in which the foci coincide at the center; in this case the eccentricity is 0. The area of an ellipse equals πab where a is the semimajor axis and b the semiminor axis. (This is a generalization of the area of a circle, when $a = b =$ radius. The formula $2\pi r$ for the length of a circle, interestingly, does not have a simple extension to the ellipse.)

An ellipse has the following *sum property:* the sum of the two focal radii to any point P on the ellipse is the same for every point P, that is, $PF + PF' =$ constant. This property defines an ellipse as the locus of a point whose distances from two fixed points have a constant sum. (Thus, an ellipse is determined by two foci and a point on the curve.) The ellipse also has the following *focal* or *reflection property:* the two focal radii FP and $F'P$ to a point P on the ellipse make equal angles with the tangent line at P (angle $APF = BPF'$ in the figure). Hence, light or sound coming from one focus will re-

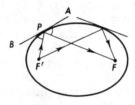

flect off the ellipse and return to the other focus; this accounts for the acoustical effect in a room with an elliptical ceiling ("whispering gallery").

In analytic geometry, the ellipse is in standard position when its center is at the origin and its major axis is on the x-axis. Its *equation* is then

$$\frac{x^2}{a^2} + \frac{y^2}{b^2} = 1,$$

where $2a$ is the major axis and $2b$ is the minor axis, and a is greater than

b. The distance c from the center to a

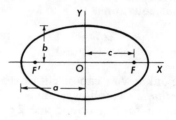

focus and the eccentricity e are given in terms of a and b by

$$c^2 = a^2 - b^2, \quad e = \frac{c}{a} = \frac{\sqrt{a^2 - b^2}}{a}.$$

The length of the latus rectum is $2b^2/a$; the distance from the center to a directrix is a^2/c; the sum of the focal radii to any point on the ellipse is the constant $2a$. Two ellipses are *similar* if their eccentricities e are equal; in this case, the values a, b, c of one are proportional to those of the other.

The circles of radius a and b with center at the origin are the *eccentric circles* of the ellipse; the larger is the *auxiliary circle*. A point P on the ellipse is related to these circles through the *eccentric angle* α by the

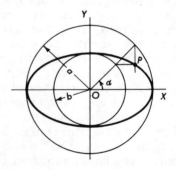

construction shown in the figure. This gives the parametric equations $x = a \cos \alpha$, $y = b \sin \alpha$ for the ellipse, with the parameter α ranging from $0°$ to $360°$.

Ellipsoid An *ellipsoid of revolution* (or *spheroid*) is the surface of revolution produced by rotating an ellipse in space about one of its axes, called its *axis of revolution.* When the ellipse is rotated about its longer axis the ellipsoid is *prolate,* when rotated about its shorter axis, it is *oblate.* The *poles* are the end points of the axis of revolution; the circle generated by the endpoints of the other axis of the ellipse is the *equator.* Any

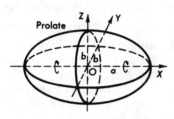

plane section parallel to the equator is a circle, any plane section perpendicular to the equator is an ellipse. Suppose the rotated ellipse is in standard position in the xz-plane (its center at the origin, major axis $2a$ on the x-axis, and minor axis $2b$ on the z-axis). Then the prolate ellipsoid of revolution has the *equation*

$$\frac{x^2}{a^2} + \frac{y^2}{b^2} + \frac{z^2}{b^2} = 1,$$

and the oblate ellipsoid of revolution,

$$\frac{x^2}{a^2} + \frac{y^2}{a^2} + \frac{z^2}{b^2} = 1.$$

The segments cut off on the coordinate axes by the ellipsoid are the *axes* of the ellipsoid.

The *general ellipsoid* is the *quadric surface* whose equation takes the more general form

$$\frac{x^2}{a^2} + \frac{y^2}{b^2} + \frac{z^2}{c^2} = 1$$

with proper alignment of the coordinate axes; the origin is the *center* of the ellipsoid, and the (arbitrary)

positive numbers $2a$, $2b$, $2c$ are the axes; the *major* axis, *mean* axis, and *minor* axis are the axes according to decreasing length. *Similar* ellipsoids are ones for which the axes of one are proportional to those of the other; for example, an ellipsoid with axes 5, 4, 3 is similar to one with axes 10, 8, 6. The volume of an ellipsoid equals $\frac{4}{3}\pi abc$; when $a = b = c$ the ellipsoid is a sphere and this becomes the familiar $\frac{4}{3}\pi r^3$.

Elliptic Cone or Cylinder A **cone** or **cylinder** with an ellipse as the boundary of a base.

Elliptic Paraboloid See **Paraboloid**.

Empirical Based on observation and experimental evidence. This is the basis of the inductive scientific method, and contrasts with the deductive or axiomatic method which is founded on logical argument from explicit assumptions. Mathematics is the field of science which makes particular use of **deductive theory**.

An *empirical function* or *curve* is one constructed as an approximate representation of numerical observations; it arises in the applications of mathematics to engineering and statistics, for example. On the other hand, functions, such as $x^2 - 2x + 3$, $\log x$, $\cos x$, etc., are defined by precise mathematical processes.

Empty Set (Syn.: Null set) The set with no members. See **Algebra of sets**.

Entropy of Information See **Information theory**.

Enumerable Set See **Countable set** (syn.).

Enumeration of Rational Numbers Any procedure for putting the set of rational numbers (fractions) into one-to-one correspondence with the natural numbers 1, 2, 3 · · · (showing that the rational numbers make up a *countable set*). Various enumerations exist; the figure demonstrates one (confined to the positive fractions). Arrange all positive fractions in an (unending) double array

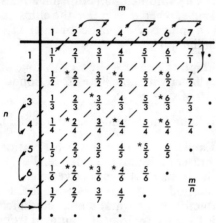

as shown; beginning at $\frac{1}{1}$, count off the fractions along the back-and-forth path shown, excluding any fraction which fails to be in lowest terms (marked with "∗" in the figure). This procedure counts every positive rational number exactly once; this is so because any particular rational number appears somewhere, and it appears exactly once as a fraction in lowest terms. Ref. [28, 149].

Envelope In the plane, an envelope of a *family of curves* is a curve that is

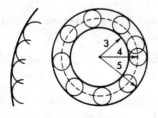

tangent to every member of the

family. For example, the family of circles of radius 1 whose centers lie on a circle of radius 4 has two envelopes—one is a circle of radius 5 and the other is a circle of radius 3, each with the same center as the given circle.

In space, an envelope of a *family of planes* or *surfaces* is a surface that is tangent to every member of the family. For example, the right circular cylindrical surface of radius r is the envelope of the family of encircling planes at a distance r from the axis.

Epicycloid and Hypocycloid The *epicycloid* is the plane curve traced by a fixed point on a circle as it rolls along the outside of a fixed circle. If the rolling circle has a radius equal to that of the fixed circle, the epicycloid has one arch; if it is half that of the fixed circle, the curve has two

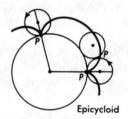

Epicycloid

arches; if the radius is $1/n$ of that of the fixed circle, the curve has n arches.

A *hypocycloid* is defined similarly

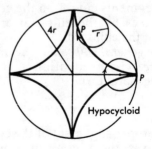

Hypocycloid

except that the circle rolls along the

inside of the fixed circle. It is not immediately obvious that when the radius of the inner circle is half that of the outer circle, the hypocycloid is simply a diameter of the large circle. When the inner radius is one-third the outer, the curve has three arches; when the inner radius is $1/n$ of the outer, the curve has n arches.

These curves were used by Ptolemy in 200 A.D. in a complicated attempt to describe the irregular motions of the planets in terms of circular paths; it was based on the assumption that the earth was at the center of the universe.

The **cycloid** is obtained by rolling a circle on a straight line.

Equal Fractions **Fractions** which denote the same number; the fractions a/b and c/d are equal in case $ad = bc$. This provides one test for equality of fractions; for example, to check equality of $\frac{55}{154}$ and $\frac{85}{238}$, verify that $55 \cdot 238 = 85 \cdot 154$, or $13{,}090 = 13{,}090$.

Equal Geometric Figures In elementary geometry, generally, figures with the same measure, such as angles of the same degree measure, plane figures of the same area, or solids of the same volume. This meaning of "equality" is different from its logical meaning, although it is well-established in elementary geometry.

Equal Sets Sets which are identical, that is, which contain exactly the same members. This notion has significance in mathematics, because sets are described in various ways and it may not be simple to determine that two different descriptions yield the same set. For example, to prove that the set of even whole numbers is identical with the set of whole numbers whose squares are even, may take only a little doing; to prove that the set of even numbers (excluding 2 and 4) is identical with the set of numbers which are the sum of two odd primes, is to resolve a famous unsettled problem, the *Goldbach conjecture*.

Equality The logical relation expressing identity or sameness, and symbolized by the sign "$=$". The statement "$A = B$" (read "A equals B"), where A and B are constants or expressions in constants, means that A and B name the same thing. For example, the statement "Mark Twain $=$ Samuel Clemens" asserts that Mark Twain and Samuel Clemens are the same man; similarly, the statement "$2 + 2 = 4$" means that "$2 + 2$" and "4" are different names (expressions) for the same number.

Basic rules of algebra for handling equalities, involving both constants and variables, include the following *laws,* or *axioms, of equality:* **(1)** equals added to equals give equals, that is, $x = y$ and $a = b$ implies $x + a = y + b$; **(2)** equals multiplied by equals give equals, that is, $x = y$ and $a = b$ implies $x \cdot a = y \cdot b$; **(3)** equals divided by nonzero equals give equals, that is, $x = y$ and $a = b$ and $a \neq 0$ implies $x/a = y/b$. From such basic rules, other techniques (such as transposing terms) can be justified.

Apart from these algebraic features, the equality relation satisfies the following logical conditions: **(1)** it is *reflexive,* that is, for every a, $a = a$; **(2)** it is *symmetric,* that is, $a = b$ implies $b = a$; **(3)** it is *transitive,* that is, $a = b$ and $b = c$ imply $a = c$. These properties are evident from the meaning of equality; in a logical theory of equality, they might occur as axioms or theorems. They show

93

that equality is an **equivalence relation**, such as congruence (in geometry) is. The symbol "$=$" for equality was introduced in the middle of the sixteenth century.

Ref. [136].

Equation A mathematical statement of the form "$A = B$"; A is the left member (or side), and B is the right member (or side).

When A and B are expressions containing variables, then the equation is an *identity* in case it is true for any (meaningful) replacement of the variables by constants; examples are

$$x^2 - y^2 = (x + y)(x - y),$$

with variables x and y, and $\sin^2\theta + \cos^2\theta = 1$, with variable θ. It is a *conditional equation* in case it is true for one or more replacements of the variables but false for others: an example is $x^2 - 3x + 2 = 0$ (true only for $x = 1$ and $x = 2$, false otherwise); another example is $x + y = 1$ (true when $x = 0$ and $y = 1$, or $x = \frac{1}{2}$ and $y = \frac{1}{2}$, etc.; false when $x = y = 1$, or $x = 2$ and $y = 1$, etc.) The symbol "$\equiv$" is sometimes used in place of "$=$" to distinguish an identity.

A *solution,* or *root,* of a conditional equation is a particular value of the variable for which the equation is true (or particular values of the several variables, if the equation has several); a solution is said to "satisfy" the equation. An *inconsistent* equation is one which is true for no values; for example $x^2 + 1 = 0$, with x a real number. Equations may have no, one, two, or any number of solutions. For example, $x^2 + 1 = 0$, has no (real) solutions, neither does $\sin\theta = 2$; $2x + 5 = 1$ has exactly one solution, $x = -2$; $(x - 1) \times (x - 2) = 0$ has exactly two solutions, $x = 1$ and $x = 2$; $\sin\theta = 1$ has infinitely

many solutions, namely, $\theta = 90°$, $450°$, $810°$, etc. In problems of determining solutions the variable is frequently called the *unknown*; see **Solution of equation**. Commonly, "solution" is taken to mean "real number solution"; what the solutions are depends, in general, on what type of number is allowed as a solution (see **Number**).

Two equations are *equivalent* in case they have the same set of solutions. There are rules for transforming an equation into an equivalent one (for example, adding the same thing to both sides). A technique of solving equations in algebra is to change it through a series of equivalent equations until a final equation is obtained for which the solutions are obvious. For example, $x^2 - x = x + 3$ may be solved as follows:

$$x^2 - 2x - 3 = 0,$$
$$(x - 3)(x + 1) = 0,$$
$$x - 3 = 0 \text{ or } x + 1 = 0,$$

$x = 3$ or $x = -1$; the solutions are 3 and -1. Certain useful techniques for solving equations (for example, multiplying or dividing both sides by an expression in the variable) need not produce equivalent equations; they may lead to *redundant* or a *defective* equations.

Equations are sometimes named according to the operations and functions that occur in them. A fractional equation is one that contains fractions, such as

$$\frac{3}{x} + 1 = \frac{3x}{2};$$

an irrational, or radical equation involves a radical (containing an expression in a variable), such as $\sqrt{x + 1} = x - 2$; an algebraic equation involves algebraic operations. A trigonometric equation is one, such as $\sin 2x = 2 \cos x$, which contains trigonometric functions involving the variable; an inverse trigonometric equation is illustrated by arc tan $x = 2 - x^2$; a logarithmic equation by log $x = 3x - 5$; and an exponential equation by $3^{2x} = 7$ (in which the variable appears in an exponent).

The *polynomial* equation is important in algebra; this is one of the form $P(x) = 0$, where $P(x)$ is a polynomial (or an equation equivalent to this). The *degree* of the polynomial equation is the degree of the polynomial $P(x)$. The equation is classified according to degree; it is linear, quadratic, cubic, etc., if the degree is one, two, three, etc. The general equation of the nth degree (in one variable) is

$$a_0 x^n + a_1 x^{n-1} + \cdots + a_{n-1}x + a_n = 0.$$

See **Roots of polynomial equation**.

The geometric interpretation of the set of solutions of an equation depends upon the number of variables it contains. The solutions of an *equation in one variable,* such as $x^2 + 2x - 1 = 0$, consist of individual numbers, or points on a line. The solutions of an *equation in two variables* consist of pairs of numbers, making up the *locus* or *graph* of the equation. For example, the solutions of $y = 2x$ comprise a straight line; the solutions of $(x - 1)^2 + y^2 = 4$ comprise a circle, center at $(1, 0)$, radius 2. The solutions of an *equation in three variables* consist of triples of numbers making up the surface which is the graph of the equation. For example, the solutions of $x^2/9 + y^2/4 + z^2/4 = 1$ comprise an ellipsoid of revolution. See **Simultaneous equations**.

Equation, General See **General equation**.

Equation of Curve or Locus For a *plane curve* (or locus), an equation whose graph is the given curve; more specifically, an equation in rectangular coordinates x, y which is satisfied by those points and only those points (x, y) which belong to the given curve. Other types of equations of plane curves are **parametric equations** and the **polar equation**. See particular curves such as **Circle, Ellipse, Line**, etc.

A *space curve* may be given by two equations in three variables (intersection of surfaces) or by parametric equations. See **Curve**.

Equation of Surface An equation whose graph is the given surface; more specifically, an equation in rectangular coordinates x, y, z which is satisfied by those points and only those points (x, y, z) belonging to the surface. See particular surfaces such as **Plane, Ellipsoid**, etc.

Equations, Theory of See **Theory of equations**.

Equator of Ellipsoid of Revolution The circle which is the plane section of an ellipsoid of revolution through the center and perpendicular to the axis of revolution.

Equiangular Having equal angles. An equiangular *polygon* of n sides has each angle equal to $[(n - 2)/n]180°$; in particular, an equiangular *triangle*

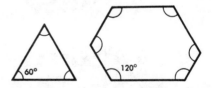

has each angle equal to $60°$. An equiangular triangle is necessarily *equilateral,* but an equiangular polygon of more than three sides need not be equilateral (see figure).

Equiangular Hyperbola See **Rectangular hyperbola** (syn.).

Equiangular Spiral   See **Spiral**.

Equidistant   A *point P* is equidistant from two given points *A* and *B* in case the distances *PA* and *PB* are equal. A *line* (*plane*) is equidistant from two points *A* and *B* in case each point of the line (plane) is equidistant from the points *A* and *B*;

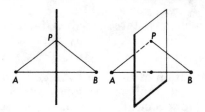

this line (plane) is the perpendicular bisector of *AB* in the plane (space).

Equilateral   In geometry, having equal sides. An equilateral triangle is necessarily equiangular, but an equilateral polygon of more than three sides (for example, a rhombus) need not be equiangular.   See **Polygon; Triangle**.

Equilateral Hyperbola   See **Rectangular hyperbola** (syn.).

Equilateral Triangle   A triangle with all sides equal; it is equiangular, with each angle equal to 60°. The following formulas hold for an equilateral

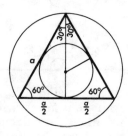

triangle with side *a*: altitude = $(\sqrt{3}/2)a$, area = $(\sqrt{3}/4)a^2$, radius of inscribed circle = $(\sqrt{3}/6)a$, radius

of circumscribed circle = $(\sqrt{3}/3)a$.

Equivalence Relation   A relation between members of a set with the following properties: **(1)** *reflexive*— every member is in the given relation to itself; **(2)** *symmetric*—if *a* is in the given relation to *b*, then *b* is in the given relation to *a*; **(3)** *transitive*—if *a* is in the given relation to *b*, and *b* to *c*, then *a* is in the given relation to *c*. Examples of equivalence relations are **(1)** equality; **(2)** congruence (in geometry); **(3)** "is of the same age" (between people). Examples of relations which are not equivalence relations are **(1)** "is greater than" (between numbers); **(2)** "is divisible by" (between whole numbers); the first relation is neither reflexive nor symmetric, and the second is not symmetric.

The equivalence relation provides a precise way of expressing that things are "the same in a certain respect." For example, triangles being the same with respect to "size" and "shape" means that they bear the relation of congruence to each other. Any equivalence relation among the members of a set *partitions* the entire set into mutually exclusive subsets called *equivalence classes;* two members are in the same equivalence class in case they bear the given relation to each other, and in different classes otherwise. For example, the relation "is of the same age" partitions people into equal age groups. For another example, consider the relation among all integers defined as follows: *m* is in the given relation to *n* in case *m − n* is divisible by 2. This is an equivalence relation; it partitions all integers into two subsets, the even numbers and the odd numbers. The displayed figure suggests the general partition process (the symbol "↔" is used to mean

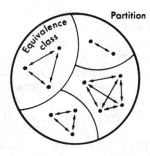

Partition

that the connected items are in the given relation).

Equivalent Equations Equations which have the same set of solutions; for example, $3x - 2 = x + 1$ and $2x - 3 = 0$ are equivalent. In algebra, the process of solving an equation often amounts to transforming it through a succession of equivalent equations to a final equation, which can then be solved directly.

Equivalent Sets Sets that can be put into one-to-one correspondence with each other; hence, sets with the same **cardinal number**.

Equivalent Statements Informally, two statements are *logically equivalent* if they say the same thing because of their form, not their content; more precisely, if their sentence forms are equivalent (in the sense of logic). For example, the statement "If n is even, then $3n$ is even" is logically equivalent to "If $3n$ is not even, then n is not even"; this is so because their logical forms are "If P, then Q," and "If not Q, then not P," and these are (logically) equivalent. In the **algebra of propositions** and in the study of the **quantifier**, methods are developed for identifying logically equivalent statements.

In mathematics, the term "equivalent statements" is used more loosely to mean statements or conditions which imply each other (because of their content). For example, "Tri-angle ABC is equilateral" is equivalent to "Triangle ABC is equiangular"; this is a fact of geometry, not of logic.

Eratosthenes See **Sieve of Eratosthenes**.

Ergodic Process See **Stochastic process**.

Error In numerical computation, the difference Δ between an **approximate number** N and the true number b which it approximates; that is $\Delta = N - b$; the *absolute error* is the numerical value of Δ, or $|\Delta|$. The *relative error* is $\Delta \div b$ (or, sometimes, $|\Delta| \div b$); the *per cent error* is the relative error expressed in per cent. For example, if a desk whose true length is 3.10 (in feet), is measured as 3.12, then the error is 0.02, the relative error is $0.02 \div 3.10$ or 0.0065, and the per cent error is 0.65 per cent. Since the true value is not generally known, the relative error is estimated by $\Delta \div N$ instead (this gives 0.0064 in the example). Also, what is known, generally, is a maximum value E of Δ, not Δ itself; then $E \div N$ is used to estimate the maximum relative error. For example, if a measurement gives the reading 4.83, this means that the true

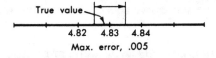

True value

4.82 4.83 4.84

Max. error, .005

number is between 4.825 and 4.835; hence the maximum absolute error is .005 and the maximum relative error is about

$$\frac{.005}{4.83},$$

or .1 per cent.   See **Rounding off**.

Escribed Circle of Triangle (Syn.: Excircle)   A circle which is tangent to one side of a triangle and to the other two sides extended; its center is the *excenter* of the triangle. The line segment from the excenter to the vertex of the angle formed by the extended sides bisects this angle (*AO* in the figure). Also, the line segment

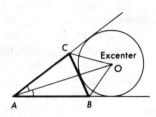

from the excenter to either of the other vertices bisects the exterior angle at that vertex (*OB* and *OC* in the figure).

Euclidean Algorithm   In arithmetic, the following procedure for finding the greatest common divisor (g.c.d.) of two positive integers m and n: divide the smaller, say m, into n, obtaining a remainder r_1; divide r_1 into m, obtaining a remainder r_2; divide r_2 into r_1, obtaining a remainder r_3; continue the process until a zero remainder is obtained; then the remainder preceding this is the g.c.d. For example, let $m = 84$, $n = 405$; the successive remainders are 69, 15, 9, 6, 3, 0; hence, 3 is the g.c.d. of 84 and 405. The analogous process with polynomials will determine their g.c.d., as well.

Euclidean Geometry   Commonly, the **deductive theory** of ordinary geometry based upon the assumptions of Euclid (or modifications of them); Euclid's work appears in his famous *Elements* (about B.C. 300). The theory served as the preeminent expression of the postulational method for many centuries, and eventually in modified versions became standard teaching material in schools. From the modern point of view, Euclid's original formulation has various shortcomings. A formulation meeting modern standards was published about 1900 by Hilbert; a postulate he found necessary to add to Euclid's assumptions, for example, was this: If a line cuts one side of a triangle, then it must cut another side (provided it does not pass through a vertex).

In modern mathematics, a Euclidean geometry (or space) can mean a **space** of any number of dimensions in which the distance between points is a direct extension of ordinary distance. A **non-Euclidean geometry** is one in which the parallel postulate of Euclid does not hold, and distance is not the ordinary one.

Ref. [42, 52, 53, 101].

Euclidean Space   See **Space**.

Euclid's "Elements"   The famous work on Greek mathematics by Euclid (about 300 B.C.). It contains thirteen books and has a total of 465 propositions. A deductive theory of geometry is developed in the work; also included (and this is not as well known) are other parts of Greek mathematics dealing with the theory of numbers and Greek algebra.

Euler's Formula   The following relation between the number e and the imaginary unit i of the complex numbers:

$$e^{i\theta} = \cos \theta + i \sin \theta.$$

When $\theta = \pi$, this becomes $e^{i\pi} = -1$, an elegant formula relating three of the fundamental numbers of mathematics, π, i, and e. From the polar form $r(\cos \theta + i \sin \theta)$ of a complex number, it follows that any complex number can be expressed in the form $re^{i\theta}$.

Euler's Theorem on Polyhedrons

The following fundamental relation among the number of vertices V, edges E, and faces F of a polyhedron: $E = F + V - 2$ (see figure). Euler's theorem can be used to prove the fact

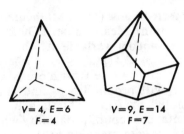

V = 4, E = 6
F = 4

V = 9, E = 14
F = 7

that there are only five regular polyhedrons. This theorem (middle of eighteenth century) was one of the early results of what was later recognized as the field of **topology**. Ref. [28].

Even Function For a function of a real variable $f(x)$, one whose graph is symmetric with respect to the y-axis. Examples are the functions $x^2 + 2$ and $\cos x$. The function is *odd* in

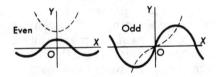

case its graph is symmetric with respect to the origin. Examples are the functions $x^3 + 2x$ and $\sin x$. The graph of a continuous odd function must pass through the origin.

Definitions that make no direct reference to graphs are the following. The function is even in case the equation $f(-x) = f(x)$ holds for every x; that is, replacing x by $-x$ does not change the functional value $f(x)$. The function is odd in case

$f(-x) = -f(x)$, holds; that is, replacing x by $-x$ yields the negative of $f(x)$. For example, let $f(x) = x^2 + 2$; since

$$f(-x) = (-x)^2 + 2 = x^2 + 2 = f(x),$$

the function is even. Let $f(x) = x^3 + x$; since

$$f(-x) = (-x)^3 + (-x) = -x^3 - x$$
$$= -(x^3 + x) = -f(x),$$

the function is odd. In general, when $f(x)$ appears as a polynomial function containing only even (odd) powers of x, the function is even (odd).

Even Number An integer which is divisible by 2. An expression for any even number is $2n$, where n in an integer. The sum, product, or difference of even numbers is an even number. An *odd number* is an integer which is not even; it can be written as $2n + 1$ (or as $2n - 1$), where n is an integer. The product of odd numbers is odd, but the sum and difference is even.

Even Permutation See **Permutation**.

Evolute of Curve See **Involute of curve**.

Evolution In algebra, the operation of root extraction; the square root and the cube root are examples. *Involution* or raising to power, is the inverse operation. For example, in the relationship $b = a^2$, b is obtained from a by involution, but a is obtained from b by evolution. See **Root of number**.

Excenter of Triangle The center of the **escribed circle of the triangle**.

Excess of Nines Of a positive integer, its remainder on division by 9; it equals the excess of nines in the sum of its digits. For example, 8,466

99

has remainder 6 on division by 9; this is also the remainder of 24, the sum of its digits. The excess of nines is used in checking computations by **casting out nines**.

Executive Routine   In a computer, a stored routine, or set of instructions, whose function is to process and control other routines automatically.   See **Computer program**.

Existence Theorem   A type of theorem which asserts the existence of a number, geometric entity, or other mathematical object having a certain property or satisfying a required condition. For example, the fundamental theorem of algebra states that, given any polynomial equation, there exists a root of the equation (possibly a complex number). Another existence proposition is that every positive (real) number has a (real) square root. A geometric example is the parallel postulate of Euclidean geometry.

Existence in mathematics is not posed as a philosophical question. The work of mathematics often requires an existence proof to show that certain properties can be realized when certain conditions are assumed. Objections have been raised to certain nonconstructive procedures for proving mathematical existence by the school of **intuitionism**.

Existential Quantifier   In logic, the **quantifier** "there exists an x such that"; abbreviated "$(\exists x)$."

Expansion of Determinant   See **Determinant**.

Expansion in Series   Of a function of a real variable $f(x)$, an expression for $f(x)$ as the sum of an infinite series (which may hold for only certain values of x). For example, an ex-

pansion of $1/(1 - x)$ is given by

$$\frac{1}{(1 - x)} = 1 + x + x^2 + x^3$$
$$+ \cdots + x^n + \cdots;$$

the equality holds for x between -1 and 1. Expansions in **power series**, as in this example, are of the greatest importance.   See **Taylor series**.

Expected Value (Syn.: Mathematical expection; Mean value)   Of a *discrete* **random variable** X, the sum $p_1 x_1 + p_2 x_2 + p_3 x_3 + \cdots$, where X assumes the value x_1 with probability p_1, x_2 with probability p_2, and so on; denoted by $E(x)$. This is a fundamental concept of **probability** which gives precise meaning to the notion of "average value in the long run." As an example, consider a game of chance with three possible outcomes; the first outcome wins 2 dollars, the second wins 1, and the third wins -4 (that is, loses 4 dollars). Suppose the respective probabilities of these outcomes are $\frac{1}{3}$, $\frac{1}{2}$, and $\frac{1}{6}$; then the expected value of winnings is

$$\tfrac{1}{3} \cdot 2 + \tfrac{1}{2} \cdot 1 + \tfrac{1}{6} \cdot (-4),$$

or $\frac{1}{2}$ dollar. The interpretation is that playing many games will lead to an "average winning" of 50 cents per game. The game of matching pennies has expected value 0; either alternative, matching or not matching, has probability $\frac{1}{2}$, and the winnings are 1 or -1 (this is an example of a "fair game," that is, one with zero expected value).

For a *continuous random variable* X with a probability density function $f(x)$, $E(x)$ is the integral of $xf(x)$ over the set of values x on which $f(x)$ is defined.

Explementary Angles (Syn.: Conjugate angles)   Two angles whose sum is 360°; seldom used.

Explicit Function An explicit function of x is a function whose values are given by an explicit expression (algebraic or otherwise) in x. For example, the equation $y = 2x - 3$ gives values of y as an explicit function of x (solving for x in terms of y would express the value of x as an explicit function of y). In an **implicit function** a correspondence is expressed through a "mixed" equation such as $y^2 + 2y - x^2 - 3 = 0$.

Exponent (Syn.: Index) In an expression of the form b^a, a is called the exponent; b is the base, and b^a is a *power* of b (sometimes "power" is used for "exponent").

When the exponent is a *whole number* the power is an abbreviation for repeated multiplication; for example, 5^2 stands for $5 \cdot 5$, 5^3 for $5 \cdot 5 \cdot 5$, etc. In general, b^n stands for $b \cdot b \cdots b$ with n factors b, when n is a positive integer. The operation of forming b^n from b and n is involution, or raising to a power.

Powers can be defined for *integral exponents;* in this case b^p is given meaning when p is any integer (positive, negative, or zero). By definition, $b^0 = 1$ and $b^{-n} = 1/b^n$, where n is a positive integer and $b \neq 0$; for example, $5^0 = 1$, $3^{-2} = 1/3^2 = 1/9$. These definitions lead to the following *laws of exponents:*

(1) $b^p \cdot b^q = b^{p+q}$;
(2) $b^p/b^q = b^{p-q}$;
(3) $(b^p)^q = b^{pq}$;
(4) $(bc)^p = b^p c^p$;
(5) $(b/c)^p = b^p/c^p$.

The first three laws state that (with a common base) products, quotients, and powers of powers translate into sums, differences, and products of the exponents; the last two laws state that exponents "distribute" over the terms of a product or quotient (dif-

ferent bases). Examples of the laws are, respectively,

$$x \cdot x^2 = x^3; \quad \frac{2^3}{2^2} = 2^1;$$

and

$$(a^n)^3 = a^{3n}; \quad (2x)^3 = 2^3 x^3 = 8x^3;$$
$$\left(\frac{a^2}{2b}\right)^3 = \frac{(a^2)^3}{(2b)^3} = \frac{a^6}{8b^3}$$

When powers are defined for *fractional exponents,* b^a is given meaning for b a positive real number and a any fraction, or rational number. The definition is this: let p and n be integers with n positive; then $b^{1/n}$ is the nth root of b, or $\sqrt[n]{b}$, and $b^{p/n}$ is the pth power of $b^{1/n}$, that is, $b^{p/n} = (\sqrt[n]{b})^p$ (the last is the same as $\sqrt[n]{b^p}$). Examples are:

(1) $4^{3/2} = (\sqrt{4})^3 = 2^3 = 8$
  or $4^{3/2} = \sqrt{4^3} = \sqrt{64} = 8$;
(2) $5^{-2/3} = (\sqrt[3]{5})^{-2} = 1/(\sqrt[3]{5})^2$.

The above laws of exponents apply as well to fractional exponents (p, q taken as fractions); for example,

$$2^{1/2} \cdot 2^{1/3} = 2^{5/6},$$
$$(a^{4/3}b^2)^{3/2} = (a^{4/3})^{3/2} \cdot (b^2)^{3/2} = a^2 b^3.$$

With *irrational exponents,* the power b^r is given meaning when b is a positive real number and r is any real number. This extension requires the limit process of the calculus. First, an irrational number r is recognized as the limit of a sequence of rational numbers $a_1, a_2, a_3, \ldots$; second, the successive powers $b^{a_1}, b^{a_2}, b^{a_3}, \ldots$, are well defined, since the exponents are rational; finally, b^r is defined as the **limit** of this sequence of rational powers. For example, consider $5^{\sqrt{2}}$; since $2 = 1.414\ldots$, $5^{\sqrt{2}}$ may be defined as the limit of $5^1, 5^{1.4}, 5^{1.41}, \ldots$, that is, $5^1, 5^{\frac{7}{5}}, 5^{\frac{141}{100}}, \ldots$. The laws of exponents continue to hold for such exponents. The extension to real exponents is the theoretical basis of the logarithm (the logarithm of a number A is the solution x of $b^x = A$, and this solution may be irrational). The extension to complex numbers is possible, whereby b^z is defined for a complex number exponent z (see **Exponential series**).

The actual computation of real powers is best carried out through **computation by logarithms**. Also, **De Moivre's Theorem** gives a means of computing powers with a complex number as base. A clear exposition of zero, negative, and fractional exponents was first put forth by the English mathematician Wallis in the seventeenth century.

Ref. [81, 120].

Exponential Function Usually, a function whose value is given by a^x, where a is a positive constant (sometimes "exponential function" is reserved for e^x, where a is taken as the particular number e). The graph of an exponential function is an *exponential curve*. When a is greater than 1, this curve rises more and more sharply to the right (it eventually

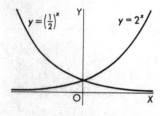

rises more rapidly than any given graph $y = x^n$, with n a positive integer). The exponential function is the inverse function of the **logarithm function**.

The function e^x is a basic transcendental function of the calculus; it has many important properties. For example, the slope of the tangent line to the curve $y = e^x$ is e^x itself (that is, the derivative of e^x is e^x itself). This function satisfies the *functional equation* $f(A + B) = f(A) \cdot f(B)$, that is, $e^{A+B} = e^A \cdot e^B$; the functions a^x are the only continuous functions satisfying this equation.

Ref. [2, 28]. See **Exponential series**.

Exponential Series The following power series expansion of the exponential function e^x,

$$1 + \frac{x}{1!} + \frac{x^2}{2!} + \frac{x^3}{3!} + \cdots + \frac{x^n}{n!} + \cdots.$$

It converges to e^x for every real number x. Interpreting x as a complex number z in this series, provides a definition of e^z for a complex exponent; from this, b^z may be defined as e^{kz} where $k = \log_e b$.

Expression Generally, any combination of operations, variables and constants denoting numbers (or more general things); examples are $2 + \sqrt{3}$, $3x^2 - 4x + 2$, $\sqrt{x + 1}$, or $\log(x + \tan x)$. Limitation of the operations may be designated; for example, an **algebraic expression** uses only algebraic operations.

Exsecant Function A trigonometric function defined as $\sec A - 1$ and abbreviated "exsec A"; rarely used.

Exterior See **Interior**.

External Division or Ratio See **Division of line segment**.

External Tangent, Common See **Common tangent**.

Externally Tangent Circles See **Tangent circles**.

Extraction of Root Computation of a **root of a number**.

Extraneous Root An irrelevant root; it can occur as a root of a **redundant equation** in the course of solving an equation.

Extreme and Mean Ratio See **Golden section**.

Extreme Terms of Proportion The first and fourth terms, a and d, in a proportion $a/b = c/d$; the second and third terms, b and c, are the *mean* terms.

Extreme Value of Function A maximum or minimum value of a function. See **Function of a real variable**.

F

Face See particular figures in space such as **Dihedral angle**, **Polyhedron**, **Prism**, etc.

Face Angle Of a **polyhedral angle** in space, a plane angle formed by adjacent edges; its vertex coincides with that of the polyhedral angle.

Factor of Integer (Syn.: Divisor of integer) The integer n is a factor of the integer N in case $N = q \cdot n$, for some integer q; when this holds, N is said to be divisible by n. For example, 4 is a factor of 12 because $12 = 3 \cdot 4$, and 13 is a factor of 195 because $195 = 15 \cdot 13$. One way to test whether n is a factor of N is to divide n into N and check whether the remainder is 0. For example, dividing 17 into 1,412 yields a quotient of 83 and a remainder of 1; hence 17 is not a factor of 1,412. There are special tests for determining whether an integer is exactly **divisible** by low integers such as 3, 4, 5, etc.

A positive integer is *factorable* if it has a positive factor other than 1 and itself; otherwise it is a positive prime number. A *prime* factor is a factor which is a prime number; for example, the prime factors of 12 are 2 and 3. Every integer can be expressed as a product of prime factors, according to the **unique factorization theorem** of arithmetic. See **Common divisor**.

Factor of Polynomial (Syn.: Divisor of polynomial) The polynomial $p(x)$ is a factor of the polynomial $P(x)$ in case $P(x) = q(x) \cdot p(x)$, for some polynomial $q(x)$. For example, $x - 2$ is a factor of $x^2 + x - 6$ because the latter equals $(x + 3) \times (x - 2)$; a second factor $x + 3$. One way to test whether $p(x)$ is a factor of $P(x)$ is to divide $p(x)$ into $P(x)$ and check whether the remainder is 0. This method is not effective for discovering factors however, and in elementary algebra, techniques for finding factors are studied. Examples of factoring formulas are

$$x^2 - a^2 = (x + a)(x - a),$$
$$x^2 + 2ax + a^2 = (x + a)^2,$$
$$x^2 + (a + b)x + ab = (x + a)(x + b).$$

(Also, see **Difference of like powers, Perfect power, Sum of like powers**.)

A polynomial is *factorable* if it has a factor of lower degree than itself (not a constant); otherwise it is a prime, or **irreducible polynomial** (see **Common divisor**). In ordinary algebra, polynomials are taken to have coefficients which are integers or rational numbers; to factor a polynomial means to factor it into polynomials of this kind. In this sense, $x^2 + 4x + 2$ is an irreducible polynomial. Every polynomial $P(x)$ with rational coefficients and leading coefficient 1 can be written as a product of irreducible such polynomials; this factorization is unique apart from the order of the factors. In higher algebra, polynomials are treated whose coefficients belong to a *field*; in this more general case, the unique factorization property still holds.

Factor of Proportionality (Syn.: Constant of proportionality; Constant of variation)   In the direct **proportionality** $y = kx$, the constant k.

Factor Theorem   The following theorem of algebra, relating a root of a polynomial $p(x) = 0$ to a factor of the polynomial: the value a is a root of $p(x) = 0$ just in case $(x - a)$ is a factor of $p(x)$. For example, $x^2 - x - 2 = 0$ has 2 as a root, and the polynomial factors into $(x - 2)(x + 1)$. The factor theorem is a consequence of the **remainder theorem** of algebra.

Factorable   See **Factor of integer**, **Factor of polynomial**.

Factorial   Of a positive integer n, the product

$$1 \times 2 \times 3 \times \cdots \times (n - 1) \times n,$$

of the n consecutive positive integers from 1 to n; it is denoted by "$n!$" (read "n factorial"). For example, $5! = 1 \cdot 2 \cdot 3 \cdot 4 \cdot 5$, or 120. The low factorials have the following values: $1! = 1$, $2! = 2$, $3! = 6$, $4! = 24$, $5! = 120$. Factorials can be computed one from the other by the "recursive" equation

$$(n + 1)! = (n + 1)(n!);$$

for example, $5! = 5(4!) = 5 \cdot 24$, or 120. For completeness, 0! is assigned the value 1.

Factorials occur in formulas; examples are the binomial theorem, and the following *factorial series* for the number e,

$$e = 1 + \frac{1}{1!} + \frac{1}{2!} + \frac{1}{3!} + \cdots + \frac{1}{n!} + \cdots.$$

The factorial notation "$n!$" for the factorial was introduced at the beginning of the nineteenth century; it is also written $\lfloor n$.

Fallacy   A **paradox**, in which a con-tradictory or false proposition is "proved" by what appears to be a sound argument, is called a fallacy. A fallacy is uncovered by exposing an unjustified point in the argument; in some fallacies the errors are quite subtle. There are arguments which "prove" that **(1)** $0 = 1$; **(2)** every triangle is isosceles; **(3)** every angle is a right angle; **(4)** every point *inside* a circle is necessarily *on* the circle. The following is a (not too subtle) false argument for the proposition $2 = 1$: Let $a = b$; multiply both sides by a to obtain $a^2 = ab$; subtract b^2 from both sides to obtain $a^2 - b^2 = ab - b^2$; this factors into

$$(a + b)(a - b) = b(a - b),$$

or $2b(a - b) = b(a - b)$ since $a = b$; dividing both sides by the common factor $b(a - b)$ gives $2 = 1$.   See **Infinite series** for another example.

More difficult fallacies sometimes arise in "solutions" of the trisection of the angle offered by amateur mathematicians who do not understand that a solution has been proved impossible.

Ref. [21, 103, 105].

False Position   In the numerical solution of equations, a method of successive approximation for computing a root; it improves an estimate at each stage by linear approximation.

Family   In geometry, generally, a collection of related geometric configurations. Examples are **(1)** all

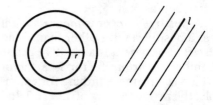

circles with fixed center but arbitrary

radii; and **(2)** all lines parallel to a fixed line *l*. In **(1)**, an individual circle is distinguished by a value of the radius *r*; *r* is the *parameter* of the family. In **(2)**, an individual line can be distinguished by its distance from the given line, and this number can be used as a parameter for the family. See **Confocal** for a further example.

When curves are represented as graphs of equations, a family presents itself as a collection of equations; this is usually expressed as a single equation containing a parameter, or arbitrary constant. In example **(1)**, if (2, 3) is the fixed center, then each circle of the family has an equation $(x - 2)^2 + (y - 3)^2 = r^2$; different circles are obtained by assigning different values to the parameter *r*. A *one-parameter family* contains a single parameter, as in the examples; a *two-parameter family* contains two parameters, etc. For example, all circles with radius 1 but arbitrary center (*h*, *k*) is such a family; its equation is $(x - h)^2 + (y - k)^2 = 1$, *h* and *k* being the parameters. In space, all tangent planes to a fixed cone comprise one-parameter family; all tangent planes to a fixed sphere comprise a two-parameter family.

Fermat Number A whole number of the form 1 plus 2 to the power 2^n, that is, $1 + 2^{2^n}$, where $n = 0, 1, 2, 3, \ldots,$. The first few Fermat numbers are 3, 5, 17, 257, 65537; these are prime numbers, and Fermat conjectured (first half of the seventeenth century) that all these numbers were prime. He was wrong; Euler (eighteenth century) showed the next number $1 + 2^{2^5}$, or 4,294,967,297, factors into (641) (6,700,417). Fermat numbers are related to the geometric construction of regular polygons in the

following way: suppose that the number of sides of a regular polygon is a prime number *p*; then the polygon can be constructed by straight edge and compass just in case *p* is a Fermat number. Ref. [6].

Fermat's Last Theorem The famous conjecture of mathematics that the equation $x^n + y^n = z^n$, where *n* is 3 or greater, has no solution in which *x*, *y*, *z* are all positive integers. When $n = 2$, that is, $x^2 + y^2 = z^2$, the equation has infinitely many such solutions, the so-called Pythagorean numbers; one of these is $x = 3$, $y = 4$, $z = 5$. Ever since Fermat, in the seventeenth century, wrote on a page of a manuscript that he had an elegant proof he could not jot down in the margin for lack of space, mathematicians have been intrigued with the problem. The theorem has been proved for *n* less than 600 and other values of *n*, but the general statement has defied proof or disproof; perhaps the greatest contribution of this conjecture has been the important mathematics inspired by it. Ref. [6, 85, 132].

Fermat's Theorem See **Congruent integers**.

Fibonacci Numbers (Syn.: Fibonacci sequence) The unending sequence of integers

1, 1, 2, 3, 5, 8, 13, 21, 34,
55, 89, 144, 233, ...

formed according to the rule that each integer is the sum of the preceding two; that is $a_{n+2} = a_{n+1} + a_n$, with $a_1 = a_2 = 1$. The Fibonacci numbers have many unusual features. The following one is related to botany: The constant fraction of a turn between successive leaves on the stalk of a particular plant is supposed

105

to equal the ratio of alternate Fibonacci numbers; for the apple this is $\frac{2}{5}$, for the leek, $\frac{5}{13}$, etc. A curious feature of the sequence appears if the numbers are squared; doing this (with the omission of the first) gives 1, 4, 9, 25, 64, 169, 441, 1156, . . . ; now if successive terms of this sequence are added the result is a sequence of alternate Fibonacci numbers 5, 13, 34, 89, 233, ... These numbers are named after Leonardo Fibonacci, or Leonardo of Pisa, a famous mathematician of the thirteenth century; he had a great influence in converting Europe to Hindu-Arab decimal arithmetic. Ref. [6, 65].

Field   A collection of real (or complex) numbers comprise a number field in case the sum, product, difference, and quotient (with nonzero divisor) of any two of its numbers is again one of its numbers. Examples are the set of rational numbers, the set of real numbers, and the set of complex numbers.

In higher algebra, the notion of a field is generalized in the following way to describe any mathematical system which is "arithmetically closed." A field consists of a set of entities ("numbers") subject to two binary operations ("addition" and "multiplication"), which satisfy the following *axioms of the field:* **(1)** the set is a commutative **group** under the operation of addition (0 denoting the identity element of addition); **(2)** the set with 0 deleted is a commutative group under the operation of multiplication; **(3)** the two operations are related by the distributive law

$$a \cdot (b + c) = a \cdot b + a \cdot c.$$

From these it is possible to derive many of the concepts and relationships of ordinary arithmetic and algebra; for example, the operations of subtraction and division can be introduced as inverse operations to addition and multiplication. The theory of the field can be carried out as a logical sequence of theorems and definitions, much as plane geometry is ordinarily presented, to show that the rules of algebra have a logical basis.

Less familiar examples of fields are the *finite fields* that arise in the study of **congruent integers** and various **number fields** of modern higher algebra. The field was formalized as an axiomatic system at the beginning of the twentieth century. The **integral domain** and the **ring** are more general mathematical systems than the field, also of importance in higher algebra.

Ref. [2, 11, 89, 134].

Figure   In arithmetic, the symbol for a whole number, such as "3" or "47."   See **Geometric figure**.

Finite   A finite set is one whose distinct members can (theoretically) be completely counted off from 1 to a last whole number n. For example, the set of grains of sand on the earth is finite. A more subtle description is this: a set is finite in case it cannot be put into one-to-one correspondence with a part of itself. A set which is not finite is **infinite**.   See **Cardinal number**.

"Finite" is also used to mean bounded in spatial extent or magnitude; for example, a circle is a finite figure, whereas a line is infinite, being unbounded in extent.

Fixed Point, Floating Point   With fixed point computations in a digital computer, numbers are represented by strings of digits with a fixed location of the decimal, or binary, point; in *floating point computation* the location of the point may vary from number to number, as determined by the computer. A digital computer may be built to perform in one manner or the other; if it is designed as a fixed point machine, floating point computation can be achieved by a stored routine of instructions. The floating point makes use of **scientific notation** of numbers, and its advantage is in automatically retaining significant digits regardless of the size of a number; in the case of the fixed point, the programmer must estimate in advance the magnitudes of numbers that may arise during a computation and introduce "scale factors" to prevent the loss of significant digits.   See **Approximate number**.

Flat Angle (Syn.: Straight angle) An angle of 180°.

Flow Chart or Diagram   Of a **computer program**, a display of the logical pattern of a computation; it contains boxes and arrows and various symbols indicating such directions as "compute," "substitute," "compare," etc. A *flow chart* is sometimes understood to be a more detailed display than a *flow diagram,* which may represent a computation in larger units, or subroutines.

Focal Chord or Radius   A *focal chord* of a conic is a line segment joining two of its points and passing through a focus; a *focal radius* is a line segment from a focus to one of its points. In a circle (as a special ellipse) the focal chord and focal radius are the diameter and radius.

Focal Property of Conic (Syn.: Reflection property of conic)   See particular conics **Ellipse, Hyperbola Parabola**.

Focus   See **Conic**.

Foot of Line   The point of intersection of a line with a given line or plane; usually used with the perpendicular line.

Formal   In accordance with specified and unambiguous rules. For example, a formal argument or proof is one that is presented as a strict deduction. A "formal theory" sometimes means a **deductive theory**.

Formula   A symbolic statement of a mathematical relationship. For example, the area of a circle is given by the formula $A = \pi r^2$, where r is the radius. A formula expressed verbally is sometimes called a "rule"; for example the preceding formula translates into a (verbal) rule as follows: "the area of a circle is π times the square of the radius." Certain common formulas of mathematics have particular names, such as the "addition formulas" of trigonometry, the "law of sines," and so on.

Expressing relationships as formulas is indispensable to mathematics; among other things, it greatly facilitates the derivation of new relationships. For example, the above formula can be solved for r, yielding the formula $r = \sqrt{A/\pi}$ for the radius in terms of the area.   See **Algebra, Symbol**.

Foundations of Mathematics   The study of the underlying concepts of mathematical reasoning and the nature of mathematical truth. Great interest developed in this field at the turn of the twentieth century as a result of the logical **paradoxes** in the theory of infinite sets. The attempts to resolve these contradictions and establish a sound foundation for all of mathematics spawned three points of view. **(1)** *Logicism,* which views

107

mathematics as a complex structure of purely logical relationships and, hence, as a branch of symbolic logic (this found its fullest expression in the three-volume *Principia Mathematica* of Russell and Whitehead (1910–13)). **(2)** *Intuitionism*, which rejects cherished concepts of mathematics and attempts to build a restricted mathematics on what is presumably a more direct and acceptable basis of reasoning. **(3)** *Formalism,* which emphasizes **axiomatics** and regards mathematical truths as deductive consequences of assumed axioms. Most practicing mathematicians accept the latter view.

Attempts to settle problems of the foundations of mathematics led to a remarkable expansion of modern logic; the symbolic and algebraic techniques so typical of mathematics itself were applied to logical studies of mathematical methods. Today, symbolic **logic** is an important and active part of mathematical science. Ref. [42, 123, 149].

Four-Color Problem In topology, the problem of showing that no more than four colors are needed to color any map in the plane; it is assumed that each country is a single, connected region, and adjacent countries (countries with a common boundary curve) are colored differently (nonadjacent countries may be colored the same). That at least four colors are needed is illustrated by the displayed map of five countries which is colored by four colors but cannot be colored by three.

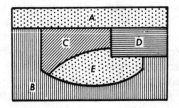

The problem was stated in the middle of the nineteenth century and despite the attention it attracted, it remained an outstanding problem that defied solution until 1976 when a proof was announced by Appel and Haken. (See *Scientific American*, October 1977, pp. 108–110). Their proof is characterized by heavy use of a high-speed computer.

The analogous problem for maps on the *torus* had been solved earlier; it is that seven colors, and no fewer, will do. Ref. [7, 41, 124, 135].

Four-Dimensional Space A **space** whose points are represented by quadruples of real numbers (x, y, z, w). Geometries in such a space can be classified into **Euclidean geometries** and **non-Euclidean geometries**. In the first case, the "distance" between two points is given by the formula

$$[(x - x_1) + (y - y_1)^2 + (z - z_1)^2 + (w - w_1)^2]^{1/2}.$$

In the second case, distance may be prescribed by any one of a variety of formulas different from this. A famous non-Euclidean geometry is the space-time continuum of relativity theory where a single point (x, y, z, t) represents a physical location (x, y, z) in ordinary space at a certain time t, distance between two points is expressed by

$$[c^2(t - t_1)^2 - (x - x_1)^2 - (y - y_1)^2 - (z - z_1)^2]^{1/2},$$

and c is the speed of light. The condition that the expression under the radical is non-negative, determines a "light cone" with vertex at (x_1, y_1, z_1, t_1); the interior of the cone consists of those space-time points (x, y, z, t) which are physically attainable from (or to) the vertex. One nappe of the

cone represents the "future" (t

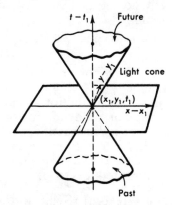

Future

Light cone

(x_1,y_1,t_1)

$x - x_1$

Past

greater than t_1), and the other nappe the "past" (t less than t_1); the limitation to the interior of the light cone means that no speed can exceed the speed of light. (The figure shows the light cone for two physical space coordinates x, y.)

Ref. [47, 73, 122, 135].

Fourier Series   See **Trigonometric series**.

Fourth Proportion   Of the **proportion** $a/b = c/d$, the term d.

Fraction   In arithmetic, an expression of the form $\dfrac{A}{B}$, where $B \neq 0$; its *numerator* is A and its *denominator* is B. A fraction is sometimes written "A/B"; it is also called a *ratio*. Examples of fractions are

$$\frac{2}{5}, \quad \frac{5-11}{1+\frac{2}{3}}, \quad \frac{\sqrt{3}}{7-2}.$$

The term "fraction" is commonly restricted to expressions that can be reduced to a ratio of integers; the first two examples are such (the second equals $-18/5$). This will be its meaning below.

The simplest fraction is the ratio m/n of whole numbers m and n, such as $\frac{2}{5}$ or $\frac{4}{3}$. Such a positive fraction can

be thought of as a number of equal parts of unity; for example, $\frac{2}{5}$ is two of the five equal parts of unity, m/n is m of the n equal parts of unity. When the denominator is 1, the fraction denotes a whole number, $m/1 = m$. Negative (and zero) fractions occur when the numerator and denominator are integers; a ratio p/q of integers denotes a **rational number**. When $p = 0$, the rational number is 0; for example

$$\frac{0}{2} = 0, \quad \frac{0}{-5} = 0, \quad \frac{0}{b} = 0.$$

When $q = 1$, the rational number is an integer; for example,

$$\frac{2}{1} = 2, \quad \frac{-5}{1} = -5.$$

Different fractions may denote the same number; for example, $\frac{1}{2} = \frac{2}{4}$. (One test for equal fractions is the following: $a/b = p/q$ in case $aq = bp$.) The *negative* of p/q is denoted by $-(p/q)$; the following *law of signs* holds:

$$\textbf{(1)} \quad \frac{-p}{q} = \frac{p}{-q} = -\frac{p}{q},$$

and

$$\textbf{(2)} \quad \frac{-p}{-q} = \frac{p}{q};$$

that is, unlike signs give negative fractions, like signs give positive fractions.

Special terminology has grown for fractions. A *common* (or *vulgar*) fraction is a ratio of whole numbers; if the numerator is less than the denominator (as in $\frac{2}{3}$) it is a *proper* fraction, otherwise an *improper* fraction (as in $\frac{3}{2}$). An improper fraction can always be written as a *mixed number*, that is, an integer plus a proper fraction (see **Division of whole numbers**). A *unit* fraction is one whose numerator is 1 (as in $\frac{1}{4}$). A *simple* fraction is a ratio of integers. A *decimal* fraction

Fraction

is a finite decimal with no digit (or only zero digits) to the left of the decimal point, as in .52103; such a fraction equals a proper fraction whose denominator is a power of 10. Fractions with identical denominators are *similar* fractions.

The following law holds for fractions having a common factor in numerator and denominator: $(r \cdot p)/(r \cdot q) = p/q$. This leads to cancellation of a common factor as a means of simplifying fractions; for example

$$\frac{42}{66} = \frac{2 \cdot 21}{2 \cdot 33} = \frac{21}{33} = \frac{3 \cdot 7}{3 \cdot 11} = \frac{7}{11}.$$

In the last example, $\frac{7}{11}$ is said to be in lowest terms; in general, a ratio of integers is in lowest terms if the numerator and denominator are integers with no factors in common (other than 1 or -1). Any fraction can be written as a decimal number (which may be an infinite repeating decimal), by dividing the denominator into the numerator.

The *positive fractions* form a closed system as far as addition, multiplication, and division are concerned; that is, the sum, product, and quotient of positive fractions is a positive fraction. Enlarging to all fractions (negative and zero, as well as positive), results in a system of numbers which is closed under subtraction as well, that is, under all four arithmetic operations (division by zero being excluded). Addition and subtraction of fractions are based on the formulas $p/r + q/r = (p + q)/r$ and $p/r - q/r = (p - q)/r$. Thus, to add or subtract any fractions, they are modified so as to have a common denominator; for example $\frac{3}{10} + \frac{2}{15} = \frac{9}{30} + \frac{4}{30} = \frac{13}{30}$. Multiplication of fractions is based on the formula $(p/q) \cdot (r/s) = (p \cdot r)/(q \cdot s)$, that is, numerators and denominators are multiplied

separately; for example, $\frac{2}{3} \cdot \frac{5}{6} = \frac{10}{18} = \frac{5}{9}$. Division of fractions is based on the formula

$$(p/q) \div (r/s) = (p/q) \cdot (s/r),$$

where none of q, r, s is 0; thus, the rule "invert the divisor and multiply"; for example, $\frac{2}{3} \div \frac{5}{6} = \frac{2}{3} \cdot \frac{6}{5} = \frac{12}{15}$. A ratio in which a fraction occurs in the numerator or denominator (or both) is a *complex* fraction, such as $(\frac{1}{3} + 1)/\frac{4}{3}$. Such a fraction can always be reduced to a simple fraction (the example reduces to $\frac{2}{3}$).

Fraction (algebra) (Syn.: Rational expression) An algebraic expression of the form A/B; it is usually understood that A and B are polynomials, or that the expression equals one in which A and B are polynomials (see *complex fraction* below). A is the *numerator* and B the *denominator*. The fraction is *proper* if A and B are polynomials and the degree of the numerator is less than that of the denominator [as in $(x - 1)/(x^2 - x + 5)$]; otherwise it is *improper* [as in $(x^2 - 2x + 5)/(x + 1)$]. An improper fraction can always be written as a *mixed expression,* that is, the sum of a polynomial and a proper fraction. Fractions can be simplified by cancelling common factors of the numerator and denominator; for example

$$\frac{x^2 - 1}{x^2 + 2x - 3} = \frac{(x - 1)(x + 1)}{(x - 1)(x + 3)} = \frac{x + 1}{x + 3}$$

A fraction, such as the last, whose numerator and denominator are polynomials with no factor in common (other than ± 1) is said to be in lowest terms.

Algebraic fractions can be added, subtracted, multiplied, and divided to form new fractions; the techniques for carrying out these operations are based upon the same rules that apply to numerical fractions. Addition and subtraction of fractions is accomplished by use of the common denominator, multiplication involves separate multiplication of numerators and of denominators, and division is reduced to multiplication by inverting the divisor. An expression, such as

$$\frac{[(x-1)/x] - [1/(x+1)]}{x-1},$$

which contains fractions in the numerator or denominator is a *complex fraction;* such an expression can be reduced to a *simple fraction,* that is, a quotient of polynomials.   See **Partial fraction**.

Fractional equation   In algebra, an equation containing fractions, such as $1/x + 8/3 = x$. A technique for solving such equations is clearing of fractions. In the example, both sides are multiplied by the common denominator $3x$ to clear of fractions, giving $3 + 8x = 3x^2$; this is written $3x^2 - 8x - 3 = 0$, which factors into $(3x + 1)(x - 3) = 0$, and gives $x = -\frac{1}{3}$ and $x = 3$ as solutions.

Fractional Exponent   In arithmetic, $b^{p/n}$ equals the nth root of b^p (b positive, p an integer, n a positive integer); for example $5^{2/3} = \sqrt[3]{25}$.   See **Exponent**.

Frequency Function   See **Random Variable**.

Frequency of Periodic Function   The reciprocal of the period; it specifies the number of repetitions of the graph of a **periodic function** per unit interval; for example, the frequency of $\sin kx$ or $\cos kx$ is $k/2\pi$.

Frequency (statistics)   In a collection of data, the number of occurrences in each of several categories.

As an example, suppose that 200 persons are classified into three age groups—under 20 years of age, between 20 and 40, and over 40; suppose that 56 persons fall in the first group, 66 in the second, and 78 in the third. Then 56 is the frequency of the first group, 66 of the second, and 78 of the third. The ratio of frequency to total number of observations is the *relative frequency;* hence, .28 ($= \frac{56}{200}$), .33, .39 are the respective relative frequencies in the example. The relative frequencies must add up to 1 if all occurrences are accounted for.

Frustrum   Of a given solid, a related one determined by two parallel planes meeting the given solid. A frustrum of a **cone** or **pyramid** is determined by the plane of the base and a plane parallel to the base.

Function (Syn.: Functional relation; Mapping; Single-valued function) The following concept of a **correspondence** or relationship between two sets: a *function from a set A to a set B* is given when an unambiguous rule is known which tells how to associate with each member of A one (or no) member of B. For example, if A is the set of integers $\cdots -2, -1, 0, 1, 2, \cdots$ and B is the same set, then the algebraic expression x^2 prescribes a function from A to B—it associates with an integer x in A the integer x^2 in B, thereby carrying 2 into 4, 0 into 0, -3 into 9, and so on. As another example, let A be the set of male citizens of the United States and B be the set of female citizens; then a function from A to B is specified by the rule that each member x of A is to be associated with the wife of x in B (if x has a wife). The abbreviation, *function in a set A,* is used when the sets A and B are the

111

same; the first example is a function in the set of integers.

The function is a basic concept, and it is useful to describe it in several ways. It may be described as a *mapping* from a set A into a set B;

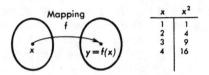

the function "maps" or "carries" an individual member x of A into its *image y* in B. A function may also be described as a collection of pairs (x, y), where x belongs to A, and y is the member of B associated with x; the pair (x, y) is said to belong to the function. A function in tabular form, such as a table of squares or a table of a trigonometric function, is a listing of pairs belonging to the function; this is illustrated in the displayed table. The plane *graph of a function* is an especially useful device; it is the configuration of all pairs (x, y) belonging to the function, plotted in rectangular coordinates. The figure shows the graph of the function in the set of real numbers as specified by x^2; the broken arrows represent the function as a mapping.

Special *functional notation* is adopted for the general study of functions. A function is denoted by a single letter, such as f, g, F, G, etc. When f is a function from A to B, and x belongs to A, then $f(x)$ (read "f of x") denotes its associate in B (introduced by Euler in the eighteenth century); $f(x)$ is the *value of the function f at x*, or the *functional value* at x, and x is the *argument* of $f(x)$. For example, if f maps x into x^2, then $f(2) = 4$, $f(0) = 0$, and $f(-3) = 9$ (in the first

case, 2 is the argument and 4 is the functional value); in this case the

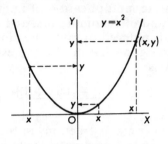

equation $f(x) = x^2$ expresses the general functional value in explicit algebraic form. The *argument x*, the *function f*, and the *functional value* $f(x)$ are distinguished as follows: the function f carries the argument value x into the functional value $f(x)$; x is a member of set A, $f(x)$ is a member of set B, while the function f, itself, may be thought of as the rule or process associating $f(x)$ with x. See **Composition of functions, Inverse of function.**

The most common means of specifying a function is an explicit formula for the functional value. For example, $f(x) = 2x^2 - 3$ specifies the function which carries x into $2x^2 - 3$; in particular, $f(2) = 5$, $f(0) = -3$; $f(\frac{1}{2}) = -\frac{5}{2}$. In general, when $f(x)$ is an explicit expression in x, $f(a)$ is evaluated by substituting a for x in the given expression; in the last example,

$$f(-2) = 2(-2)^2 - 3 = 2 \cdot 4 - 3 = 5.$$

The term "function" is often used for the functional value; thus, the phrase "the function $f(x)$" is common; this is convenient in practice. It is also common to let another variable, like y, stand for the functional value; this is expressed as $y = f(x)$. In this presentation, x is called the *independent* variable, y the *dependent variable,* and y is said to be a function of x (the idea is that the value of y "depends" on the value of x—a value of x may be chosen arbitrarily, but once chosen, the value of y is determined). For example, in the equation $A = \pi r^2$ for the area A of a circle in terms of the radius r, A is the dependent variable and r is the independent variable.

For a function f from set A to set B, there may be some members of A that have no associates in B; all those members of A which do have associates in B comprise the set called the *domain* of the function. Similarly, there may be some members of B that are not associates of any member of A; the set of all associates is the *range* of the function [that is, the set of all functional values $f(x)$]. In the example where $f(x) = x^2$, with x any integer, the domain is all integers and the range is all perfect squares $0, 1, 4, 9, 16, \ldots$.

The above description is sometimes said to define a "single-valued function," because whenever the image y of x exists, it is a single value. There are correspondences where several values of y go with one value of x; for example, in the correspondence from x to y given by $y^2 = x$, the value 4 for x goes with two values, 2 and -2, for y. Such a correspondence is often called a "many-valued function." The inverse trigonometric functions are examples of many-valued functions; this type of function frequently occurs as the **inverse of a function**.

Ref. [2, 89, 148].

Function of Complex Variable A function from complex numbers to complex numbers. The theory of such functions is very extensive, and is important in pure and applied mathematics. See **Power series**. Ref. [2, 148].

Function of Real Variable A function from real numbers to real numbers. For example, $f(x) = 2x + 1$, $f(x) = 1/x^2 + 3$, and $f(x) = \log x$ describe such functions, x being a real number. The *graph* of the function is that of the equation $y = f(x)$; it cuts any vertical line in no more than one point (that is, it does not fold back on itself, horizontally).

Functions of real variables are classified according to the expression for $f(x)$. Thus, a real function is a *polynomial* function, *rational* function, *irrational* function, or *transcendental* function according to whether the expression for $f(x)$ is of the same type. Respective examples are $f(x) = x^2 - 2x + 5$, $f(x) = x/(x^2 - 1)$, $f(x) = \sqrt{x + 1} - 2x$, $f(x) = 3 \sin 2x$. A correspondence $y = f(x)$, where $f(x)$ is an explicit expression in x, is said to give y as an *explicit function* of x; a "mixed" equation, such as $x^2 + y^2 = 4$, is said to give y as an **implicit function of** x. Strictly, an implicit function is not necessarily a "function"; that is, it may be "many-valued" instead of "single-valued", in that one value of x can go with several values of y (in this case the graph can fold back on itself).

A function is *bounded* in case $f(x)$, in absolute value, never exceeds a constant, called a *bound* of the function. The function is said to be *increasing* (*decreasing*) on any interval of x where the graph is rising (falling), that is, where $f(x)$ increases (decreases) as x increases; in either case, the function is *monotonic* on the interval. A "high" point of the graph is called a *relative maximum,* or simply, a *maximum point* of the function; at such a point, $f(a)$ is greater

113

than $f(x)$ for x is an interval about a, $x \neq a$; often called *proper* maxi-

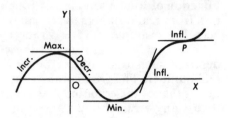

mum (a similar description applies to a *minimum point*). A *turning point*, or *relative extreme point*, is one which is either a relative maximum or relative minimum point. The value $f(a)$ is an *absolute maximum* (*minimum*) in case it is not less than (not greater than) $f(x)$ for all values of x for which $f(x)$ is defined. An *inflection point* is one where the graph reverses its sense of curvature. A *stationary point* is a turning point or a point of horizontal inflection. In the calculus, these features of a function are studied by means of its derivative $df(x)/dx$. For example, a condition for being increasing (decreasing) is that the derivative be non-negative (nonpositive); also, maximum and minimum points are found by solving $df(x)/dx = 0$, and inflection points, by determining where the second derivative vanishes. See **Continuous function**, **Derivative of function**.

The theory of functions of real variables is an extensive and important part of mathematics. For special functions see **Exponential function**, **Logarithm function**, **Trigonometric functions**, etc. Also, see **Periodic function**, **Power series**, **Trigonometric series**.

Ref. [1, 6, 71].

Function of Several Variables A function of two variables is one which associates with a pair of things (x, y), a single thing z. For example, the expression $x^2 + y^2$ defines a function from pairs of real numbers (x, y) to single numbers z, where $z = x^2 + y^2$; in particular, with the pair $(2, 3)$ is associated $2^2 + 3^2$, or 13.

The notation for functions of two variables is similar to that for one variable. Letters f, g, F, etc., are used for functions. If f is a function, then the *functional value*, denoted by $f(x, y)$ is the correspondent of the pair (x, y); x and y are the *arguments* of $f(x, y)$. In the example, this notation appears as $f(x, y) = x^2 + y^2$, $f(2, 3) = 13$, $f(0, 1) = 1$. When the correspondence is written as $z = f(x, y)$, then x and y are the *independent variables*, z the *dependent variable*, and z is said to be a function of x and y; an example is $z = (2x^2 + y)/(x + y^2)$. The *graph* of $f(x, y)$ is that of the equation $z = f(x, y)$ [that is, the set of points (x, y, z) that satisfy the equation]; in general, this represents a surface in space. For example, the graph of $f(x, y) = x^2 + y^2$ is the paraboloid of revolution given by $z = x^2 + y^2$.

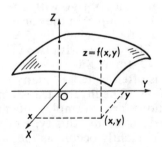

In a similar way, functions of three independent variables, or any finite number of independent variables can be defined.

Functional As a **function**, usually, a correspondence from one set of functions to another, or the same, set of functions (or to a set of numbers). It is a *linear functional L* in case it has the following feature: $L(af + bg) = aL(f) + bL(g)$ for all numbers a, b and all allowable functions f, g. The operations of differentiation and integration in the calculus are examples of linear functionals.

Functional Correspondence or Relation See **Function**.

Functional Equation An equation in which the unknown to be solved for is a function, rather than a number. For example, $f(u \cdot v) = f(u) + f(v)$ is a functional equation in an unknown function f. [$f(x) = \log x$ is a solution, since $\log u \cdot v = \log u + \log v$].

Functional Value The value $f(x)$ associated with a given value x by means of a **function** f; similar notation, such as $f(x, y), f(x, y, z)$, etc., is used for functions of several variables.

Fundamental Operations of Arithmetic The four operations of addition, subtraction, multiplication and (nonzero) division. Subtraction (division) is the **inverse operation** to addition (multiplication). The notations "$+$" and "$-$" for addition and subtraction, were adopted about 1500; the notations "$\cdot$" or "$\times$", for multiplication, and "$\div$" for division, were introduced in the seventeenth century.

Fundamental Identities of Trigonometry See **Trigonometric identity**.

Fundamental Theorem of Algebra The following proposition of the theory of equations concerning polynomials (with rational, real, or complex coefficients): every polynomial equation has at least one root, which

may be either a real number or an imaginary number. (It was proved first by Gauss about 1800.) This is an existence theorem; it does not specify how to actually determine **roots of polynomial equations**. A consequence of this theorem and the so-called *factor theorem* is that any polynomial can be factored into a product of linear polynomials (allowing complex coefficients); for example,

$$2x^3 - x^2 + 8x - 4 = (x + 2i)(x - 2i)(2x - 1),$$

where i is the complex unit ($i^2 = -1$). See **Irreducible polynomial**.

Ref. [28, 120].

Fundamental Theorem of Arithmetic See **Unique factorization theorem**.

Fundamental Theorem of Calculus A theorem of the calculus connecting the derivative with the definite integral. In one form (of several) it states the following. Let $f(x)$ be a continuous function on the interval $a \le x \le b$; let $F(x)$ be the definite integral of f on the interval from a to x, that is,

$$F(x) = \int_a^x f(u)du.$$

Then any function whose derivative equals $f(x)$ [antiderivative of $f(x)$] has the form $F(x) +$ constant, on the interval.

This theorem provides the principal means of evaluating a definite integral; an antiderivative $G(x)$ of $f(x)$ is determined and $\int_a^b f(x)dx$ is expressed as the number $G(b) - G(a)$. It was the discovery of this inverse relationship between integration and differentiation by Newton and Leibniz that created the calculus as a mathematical discipline.

115

G

Games, Theory of See **Theory of games**.

General Equation For *one variable,* the general equation of the nth degree is the polynomial equation

$$a_0 x^n + a_1 x^{n-1} + \cdots + a_{n-1}x + a_n = 0.$$

The study of the **roots of polynomial equations** belongs to the theory of equations.

For *two variables,* the general equation of the second degree is $ax^2 + bxy + cy^2 + dy + ex + f = 0$. The systematic study of its graphs is undertaken in plane analytic geometry. The graph is always a **conic** (including certain degenerate conics). The type depends upon the sign of $b^2 - 4ac$; it is an ellipse, parabola, or hyperbola depending upon whether this number is less than, equal to or greater than 0, respectively.

For *three variables,* the general equation of the second degree is the general polynomial equation of this degree in three variables. Its graphs are the *quadric surfaces*—the ellipsoids, paraboloids, hyperboloids (and certain degenerate cases). These graphs are systematically studied in solid analytic geometry.

General Term Of a sequence or series, a formula for all its terms; for example,

$$a + (n - 1)d, n = 1, 2, 3, \ldots,$$

is the general term of the arithmetic progression

$$a, a + d, a + 2d, \ldots.$$

See **Binomial theorem**.

Generator (Syn.: Generatrix) See **Conical surface, Cylindrical surface**.

Genus See **Topology**.

Geodesic If an arc on a surface, with endpoints P and Q, has the least length of all arcs on the surface joining P and Q, then it is a geodesic of the surface. The length of a geodesic defines the notion of curvilinear **dis-**

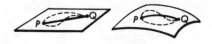

tance between points on a surface. In a plane, the geodesic joining P and Q is the line segment between them; on a sphere, it is the shorter arc of the great circle between the points. See **Non-Euclidean geometry**.

Geometric Construction In Euclidean geometry, a construction that uses only an unmarked straight edge and a compass; such a construction is restricted to the drawing of straight lines and circles. This type of construction is studied in elementary geometry; examples are bisecting a given angle (see Figure), drawing a perpendicular line from a given point

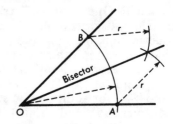

to a given line, circumscribing a circle about a given triangle, and so on.

The Greek geometers of antiquity concerned themselves a great deal with problems of geometric construction. Three, which they could not resolve, were the **duplication of the cube**, the **squaring of the circle**, and the **trisection of the angle**. It was many centuries later that each of these constructions was shown to be impossible, but the attempts to resolve them were fruitful in the development of mathematics.

The problem of the construction of regular polygons also attracted the ancient geometers. It was easy to construct regular polygons of three, four, five, or six sides, but the regular polygon of seven sides defied construction. It was not until late in the eighteenth century that Gauss proved the following general proposition: The only regular polygon with a prime number of sides that can be constructed is one for which the prime is of the form $1 + 2^{2^n}$ (a *Fermat number*). The first such prime after 5 is 17; hence the seven-sided regular polygon is not constructible, but the 17-sided one is.

It is interesting that any constructions using both ruler and compass is possible by compass alone; this was shown about 1800 by the Italian geometer Mascheroni.

Ref. [16, 28, 137].

Geometric Figure An entity of geometry such as a line, circle, triangle, cube, cylinder, and so on. A plane figure is one which lies in a plane, such as an ordinary triangle; this is in contrast to a figure which cannot be fitted onto the two-dimensional plane, such as a spherical triangle or a polyhedron.

Geometric Mean (Syn.: Geometric average) The geometric mean of n numbers is the nth root of their product. In particular, the geometric mean of a and b is $\sqrt{ab}$ (this is the mean proportional between a and b). For example, when $a = 2$ and $b = 3$, the geometric mean is $\sqrt{6}$ or 2.45 approximately. See **Mean**.

Geometric Progression and Series
A *geometric progression* of numbers is a sequence of numbers such that the ratio r of any term to the preceding term is the same from term to term; r is the *ratio of the progression*. The general form of the progression is a, ar, ar^2, ... , ar^{n-1}; a is the *first term*, and ar^{n-1} is the nth or *last term*. The sum equals $a(1 - r^n)/(1 - r)$. For example, 1, 3, 9, 27, 81 is a geometric progression with $r = 3$; its sum is $(1 - 3^5)/(1 - 3)$, or 121.

A geometric series is an unending series of the form $a + ar + ar^2 + \cdots$; an example is the series $1 + \frac{1}{2} + \frac{1}{4} + \frac{1}{8} + \cdots$, where $r = \frac{1}{2}$ and $a = 1$. Such an infinite series has a sum (is convergent) whenever r is less than 1 in numerical value; the sum equals $a/(1 - r)$. For the example, the sum of the preceding series is $1/(1 - \frac{1}{2})$, or 2.

The geometric series occurs as a repeating decimal in the decimal number system; the formula for the sum allows such a decimal to be expressed as an ordinary fraction. For example, the repeating decimal $2.757575 \cdots$ can be written as

$$2 + \tfrac{75}{100} + \tfrac{75}{10000} + \tfrac{75}{1000000} + \cdots,$$
or
$$2 + [\tfrac{75}{100} + \tfrac{75}{100} \cdot \tfrac{1}{100} + \tfrac{75}{100} \cdot (\tfrac{1}{100})^2 + \tfrac{75}{100} \cdot (\tfrac{1}{100})^3 + \cdots];$$

the bracketed series is geometric with $a = \tfrac{75}{100}$ and $r = \tfrac{1}{100}$, so its sum is $a/(1 - r)$, or $\tfrac{75}{100}/(1 - \tfrac{1}{100})$; this reduces to $(\tfrac{3}{4})/(\tfrac{99}{100})$, or $\tfrac{25}{33}$. Consequently $2.757575 \ldots$ equals $2\tfrac{25}{33}$. This method works for any repeating decimal.

Geometric Solid (Syn.: Closed surface; Solid) The bounding surface of a three-dimensional portion of space, called its interior. Examples are the sphere, cube, and pyramid. The term "solid" sometimes refers to the boundary together with its interior. (This is analogous to the ambiguity of "circle" as a curve or as a curve and its interior.)

By the *measure of a solid* is meant the numerical **volume** of its interior. "Equal solids" mean solids with the same volume measure, regardless of their shapes.

Geometry That major branch of **mathematics** which deals with the nature of space and the shape, size, and other properties of figures. Mathematics began as a theoretical science with the **Euclidean geometry** of the pre-Christian era. This is the study of those properties of figures in the plane and in ordinary three-dimensional space retained under rigid motion. A more general type of geometry is **projective geometry**, which had its beginnings much later, in the seventeenth century; in this geometry those properties of figures are studied that are retained under projection of the figure into any other figure (as in perspective drawings). A modern and much more general geometry is **topology**, which had its beginnings in the middle of the nineteenth century and has grown vigorously in this century; in topology those properties of a figure are studied that remain when the figure is subjected to any continuous transformation without the loss of idenity of any of its points.   See **Transformation** (geometry).

Another division of geometry, of historical significance, is that between Euclidean geometry and **non-Euclidean geometry**. The break with more than 2,000 years of Euclidean concepts at the beginning of the nineteenth century had a profound effect upon mathematics. It not only produced fundamental changes in notions of physical and mathematical **space**, it also affected deeply ideas concerning the logical nature of mathematics and the meaning of **axiomatics**.

The introduction of analytic geometry by Descartes in the seventeenth century merged two principal branches of mathematics, geometry and algebra; this was the birth of modern mathematical analysis. The algebraic method proved so effective in geometry, that it largely replaced the *synthetic* (nonalgebraic) method of the Greek geometers in the further development of geometry. Another historical event was the unification and generalization of Euclidean and non-Euclidean geometry by Riemann in the middle of the nineteenth century; his general theory profoundly influenced modern geometry.

Ref. [3, 28, 42, 52].

Goldbach Conjecture The conjecture that every even number (except 2) equals the sum of two primes. For example, $4 = 2 + 2, 6 = 3 + 3, 8 = 5 + 3, 10 = 5 + 5, 12 = 7 + 5$. This conjecture, stated in the middle of the eighteenth century and generally believed to be true, poses a remarkably difficult problem—the prime numbers are the building blocks of the natural numbers in terms of the operation of multiplication, and questions concerning additive properties of primes often involve unusual complications.

Golden Section The division of a line segment AB by an interior point P in the ratio $\tau:1$, where τ is the positive root of $x^2 - x - 1 = 0$. This

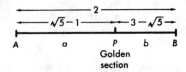

Golden section

root is $(\sqrt{5} + 1)/2$, giving $1/\tau$ and

$1/\tau^2$ [that is, $(\sqrt{5} - 1)/2$ and $(3 - \sqrt{5})/2$] as parts in the golden section of a unit segment. This division of a segment is pleasing to the eye and occurs often in designs. (The point P is also said to divide the segment AB into extreme and mean ratio.)

Ref. [82].

Graph   A geometric representation of a relationship between numbers, usually in a rectangular coordinate system. The **graph of an equation**, the **graph of a function**, the **graph of an inequality**, and so on, are important notions.

Graph of Equation   For an *equation in two (three) variables,* the set of points in the plane (space) whose coordinates satisfy the equation; usually, rectangular coordinates are understood. For example, the graph of the equation $y = x^2 - 1$ is the parabola shown in the figure; the particular points $(0, -1)$, $(1, 0)$, $(-2, 3)$ belong to the graph, which can be

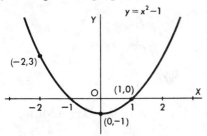

verified by substitution in the equation (in the figure, different unit lengths are used on the two axes). In general, the graph of an equation in x and y is some type of curve which depends upon the nature of the equation; for example, the graph of a linear equation $ax + by + c = 0$ is a straight line and the graph of the general equation of the second degree is a conic.   See **Polar equation**.

In general, the graph of an *equation in three variables* is a surface in space. For example, the graph of the equation $x^2 + y^2 + z^2 = 4$ is a sphere with center at the origin and radius 2; the particular points $(0, 2,$

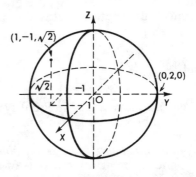

$0)$ and $(1, -1, \sqrt{2})$ belong to the graph, which can be verified by substitution in the equation. The graph of a linear equation $ax + by + cz + d = 0$ is a plane; the graph of a second degree equation, as in the example of the sphere, is a quadric surface.

See **Simultaneous equations**.

Graph of Function   For a **function of a real variable**, $f(x)$, the graph of the equation $y = f(x)$; for a function of two variables, $f(x, y)$, the graph of the equation $z = f(x, y)$. For example, when $f(x, y) = 3x + 2y + 5$, the graph is that of $z = 3x + 2y + 5$ (a plane).

Graph of Inequality   For an *inequality in two variables, x* and *y,* the set of points (x, y) in the plane which satisfy the inequality; such a set is

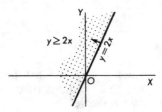

generally a two-dimensional region **119**

in the plane. For example, the graph of the inequality $y \geq 2x$ consists of all points lying on or above the line $y = 2x$; the particular points $(2, 5)$ and $(-1, -2)$ belong to the graph because substitution yields the true statements

$$5 \geq 2 \cdot 2$$

and

$$-2 \geq 2 \cdot (-1).$$

In general, any linear inequality in two variables has a half-plane as its graph.

For an *inequality in three variables*, $x, y,$ and z, the graph consists of all points (x, y, z) satisfying the inequality. In general, it will be a three-dimensional portion of space; in the case of a linear inequality in three variables the graph is a half-space, that is, all points lying on one side of a plane.

See **Solution of inequality, Simultaneous inequalities**.

Graph, Logarithmic   See **Logarithmic coordinates**.

Graphing   The construction of a visual representation of a graph. For example, an equation in two variables, say x and y, is graphed by computing several values (x, y) satisfying the equation, plotting them in a rectangular coordinate system, and then drawing a path through the points. For instance, to graph $y = 1/x$ the following table may be prepared:

x	-4	-2	-1	$-\frac{1}{2}$	$-\frac{1}{4}$	$\frac{1}{4}$	$\frac{1}{2}$	1	2	4
y	$-\frac{1}{4}$	$-\frac{1}{2}$	-1	-2	-4	4	2	1	$\frac{1}{2}$	$\frac{1}{4}$

When these points are plotted, the graph is seen to consist of two separate smooth curves.

A special technique of graphing is *composition of ordinates*, whereby a

graph is obtained by "vertical addi-

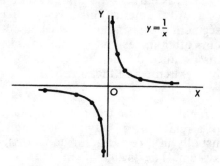

tion" of two other graphs. For example, to apply this method to the equation $y = -\frac{1}{2}x^2 + 2x + 3$, the graphs of $y = -\frac{1}{2}x^2$ and $y = 2x + 3$ are first drawn (with the same set of axes); then the ordinates of points of the two graphs lying above each other are added to obtain the desired graph. In general, to graph $y = f(x)$

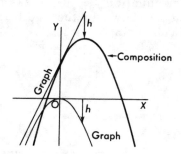

$+ g(x)$, apply ordinate addition to the graphs of $y = f(x)$ and $y = g(x)$.

Great Circle   Of a sphere, its intersection with a plane passing through the center of the sphere. Two points on a sphere and the center determine a unique plane, and therefore a unique great circle through the points; the shorter arc between the points is the *geodesic* on the sphere, that is, the shortest path on the sphere between the points (this is used in navigation). In geometry on a sphere, the great circle plays the basic role that the line does in geometry in the plane. See **Loxodromic spiral, Circle on sphere, Non-Euclidean geometry**.

Greater than See **Inequality relation**.

Greatest Common Divisor See **Common divisor**.

Greatest Lower Bound See **Bound**.

Greek Alphabet See Appendix C.

Group A mathematical system consisting of a set G and a *binary operation* $*$ which satisfy the following *axioms of the group*: (1) $x * y$ is a member of G, whenever x and y are; (2) $(x * y) * z = x * (y * z)$; (3) there is an identity element e of G, that is, $e * x = x * e = x$ for every member x of G; (4) each member x of G has an inverse element y in G, that is, a member y such that $y * x = x * y = e$. (Briefly, the set G under the operation $*$ is closed, associative, contains an identity element, and contains the inverse of each of its members.) The group is *commutative* (or *abelian*) if $x * y = y * x$ for every x and y in G.

An example of a group is the integers under addition (G is the set of integers, and $*$ is addition). Axiom (1) holds because the sum of two integers is another integer. The identity element of axiom (3) is 0, and the inverse element of x in axiom (4) is $-x$, the negative of x. Another example is the positive fractions m/n under multiplication; here, the identity element is 1, and the inverse element of m/n is the reciprocal n/m. A third example is the vectors in the plane under vector addition.

Less familiar than the examples given are the *finite groups,* in which the set G has only a finite number of members. These arise, for instance, in the study of **congruent integers** (and the study of permutations). An "arithmetic modulo 5," for example, can be defined for the finite set $\{0, 1, 2, 3, 4\}$ involving operations of "addition" and "multiplication"; then this set under "addition" is a commutative group; also, this same set with 0 deleted is a commutative group under "multiplication." The finite group also arises as a **group of symmetries**. Such groups as the latter and, more generally, groups of *transformations* are especially significant for geometry [see **Transformation** (geometry)].

The "abstract group" described by axioms is a generalization of the above examples, and others. It is one of the unifying ideas of modern mathematics, and is studied extensively in higher algebra and other fields. The term "group" was introduced by Galois in the first half of the nineteenth century; later in this period, Cayley laid down the basic assumptions of such a system.

Ref. [20, 34, 55, 68].

Group of Symmetries Of a geometric figure in space, the collection of rigid motions that transform the figure into itself. More specifically, a *symmetry* of a square, circle, cube, sphere, etc., is any rigid motion in space that carries the figure back into itself; for example, any rotation (in the plane) of the circle about its center is a symmetry of a circle; also, any plane rotation of the square about its center which is a multiple of 90° is a symmetry. Symmetries may be combined by following one motion with a second motion. For example, the rotation of the square through 180° followed by the rotation through 270° can be identified with the single rotation through 90° Thus, all the symmetries of a figure make up a set of entities which are subject to a rule of combination or binary operation. This is a mathematical system which satisfies the axioms of the **group**; it is known as as the group of symmetries of the figure. It provides a rigorous mathematical tool for the study of geometric symmetry.

For a more detailed illustration, consider the group of symmetries of the square further. From the displayed figure, at least eight rigid motions can be recognized which carry

the square into itself: **(1)** four of these are the (counterclockwise) rotations of 0°, 90°, 180°, and 270°, which will be denoted by R_0, R_1, R_2, and R_3, respectively; **(2)** four others are the "flips" or reflections in the lines (1), (2), (3), and (4), which will be denoted by F_1, F_2, F_3, and F_4, respectively. As mentioned, these symmetries are combined by successive application. For example, as shown

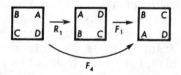

in the figure, R_1 followed by F_1 has the same effect as F_4; this combination is denoted symbolically by

$$R_1 * F_1$$

and is identified with F_4, that is,

$$R_1 * F_1 = F_4.$$

These eight motions can be shown to give all the symmetries of the square; hence the group of symme-tries of the square is the finite set $\{R_0, R_1, R_2, R_3, F_1, F_2, F_3, F_4\}$ under the binary operation $x * y$ (taken as x followed by y). The displayed table shows $x * y$ for all x, y. (In this table,

	R_0	R_1	R_2	R_3	F_1	F_2	F_3	F_4
R_0	R_0	R_1	R_2	R_3	F_1	F_2	F_3	F_4
R_1	R_1	R_2	R_3	R_0	F_4	F_1	F_2	F_3
R_2	R_2	R_3	R_0	R_1	F_3	F_4	F_1	F_2
R_3	R_3	R_0	R_1	R_2	F_2	F_3	F_4	F_1
F_1	F_1	F_2	F_3	F_4	R_0	R_1	R_2	R_3
F_2	F_2	F_3	F_4	F_1	R_3	R_0	R_1	R_2
F_3	F_3	F_4	F_1	F_2	R_2	R_3	R_0	R_1
F_4	F_4	F_1	F_2	F_3	R_1	R_2	R_3	R_0

$x * y$

$x * y$ is found at the intersection of the row x and the column y; for example, $F_1 * R_1 = F_2$ and $R_3 * F_2 = F_3$). The table is the story, in symbolic form, of the symmetries of the square. This finite system, as mentioned, satisfies the axioms of the group. For example, the identity element is R_0 (the "motion" that leaves the square fixed). Every symmetry x has an inverse symmetry x' such that $x * x' = R_0$; for example, the inverse of R_1 is R_3, the inverse of R_2 is itself, and the inverse of any reflection F is F itself.

Symmetries, as the example of the square indicates, can be expressed as **permutations** of the vertices, so that the study of symmetries of polygons and polyhedra is the study of certain groups of permutations. The square also illustrates the typical noncommutative feature of groups of symmetries; for example, $R_1 * F_1 \neq F_1 * R_1$, since $R_1 * F_1 = F_4$ and $F_1 * R_1 = F_2$. (This is to be contrasted with ordinary numbers or complex numbers under addition or multiplication.) The square also illustrates the notion of a *subgroup*, this is a sub-set of the group which is a complete group in itself—the combination of any two of its members always leads back to one of its members. This is illustrated in the table by the sub-group $\{R_0, R_1, R_2, R_3\}$.

Groups of symmetries are used in the study of considerably more com-plex figures than the square, notable among these are the regular polyhe-drons in space.

Grouping In algebra, arrangement of terms in an expression for a spe-cial purpose. For example, to factor the expression $ax + 6y + 3x + 2ay$, the terms are grouped as $(ax + 3x)$ $+ (2ay + 6y)$ to yield

$$x(a + 3) + 2y(a + 3) = (x + 2y)(a + 3).$$

Half-Angle Formulas As trigono-metric identities, formulas that ex-press a trigonometric function of half an angle in terms of functions of the angle itself. Among these are:

$$\sin \frac{x}{2} = \sqrt{\frac{1 - \cos x}{2}}$$

$$\cos \frac{x}{2} = \sqrt{\frac{1 + \cos x}{2}}$$

$$\tan \frac{x}{2} = \frac{\sin x}{1 + \cos x} = \frac{1 - \cos x}{\sin x}.$$

These formulas are derivable from the **double angle formulas**.

There is another set of half-angle formulas which is used for the solu-tion of a triangle in the plane; these express the tangent of half an angle of a triangle in terms of the sides of the triangle:

$$\tan \tfrac{1}{2}A = \frac{r}{s - a}$$

$$\tan \tfrac{1}{2}B = \frac{r}{s - b}$$

$$\tan \tfrac{1}{2}C = \frac{r}{s - c};$$

here a, b, c are, respectively, the sides opposite angles A, B, C; s is half the perimeter $\tfrac{1}{2}(a + b + c)$, and

$$r = \sqrt{\frac{(s - a)(s - b)(s - c)}{s}}$$

(r is the radius of the inscribed circle of the triangle). Similar half-angle formulas exist for the solution of an oblique spherical triangle:

$$\tan \tfrac{1}{2}A = \frac{r}{\sin(s - a)}$$

$$\tan \tfrac{1}{2}B = \frac{r}{\sin(s - b)}$$

$$\tan \tfrac{1}{2}C = \frac{r}{\sin(s - c)}$$

where r is now given by

$$r = \sqrt{\frac{\sin(s - a)\,\sin(s - b)\,\sin(s - c)}{\sin s}}.$$

The half-angle formulas for triangles are useful for obtaining the angles when three sides are given.

Half-Line, Half-Plane, Half-Space
A *half-line,* or *ray,* is the portion of a line on one side of a fixed point P of the line (including P): P is the *initial point* of the half-line (sometimes P is excluded). For example, an angle consists of two half-lines with a com-mon initial point; also, in a rectangu-lar coordinate system, the origin divides the x-axis into two half-lines, namely, the positive x-axis and the negative x-axis. A *half-plane* is the

portion of a plane on one side of a fixed line l of the plane (including or excluding l); l is the edge of the half-plane. For example, a dihedral angle in space consists of two half-planes

123

with a common edge; also, the y-axis in a plane coordinate system divides the plane into two-half planes, one containing the points (x, y) with x positive and the other with x negative. A *half-space* is the portion of space on one side of a fixed plane in space (including or excluding the plane); for example, the xy-coordinate plane divides space into two half-spaces, one with z positive, the other with z negative. See **Convex polyhedron, Convex polygon**.

Half-Side Formulas (spherical trigonometry)   Formulas for the solution of an oblique spherical triangle which express the tangent function of half a side in terms of the angles of the triangle.

$$\tan \tfrac{1}{2}a = R\cos(S - A)$$
$$\tan \tfrac{1}{2}b = R\cos(S - B)$$
$$\tan \tfrac{1}{2}c = R\cos(S - C)$$

where S is half the sum of the angles $\tfrac{1}{2}(A + B + C)$, and

$$R = \sqrt{\frac{-\cos S}{\cos(S - A)\cos(S - B)\cos(S - C)}}.$$

These formulas are useful for obtaining the sides of a spherical triangle when the angles are given.

Harmonic Analysis   In advanced calculus, the study of the representation of functions by **trigonometric series**.

Harmonic Division   The line segment PQ is said to be divided harmonically by a pair of points R and S, one interior (say R) and one exterior, in case R and S divide PQ in the same numerical ratio; that is, PR/RQ and PS/SQ are equal in numerical value.   See **Division of line segment**. The relative positions of R and S, for a fixed segment PQ, may be described as follows (see figure). When R is closer to P than to Q, S

is left of P; when R is closer to Q

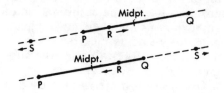

than to P, S is right of Q; as R approaches the midpoint, S recedes farther and farther out. When R is *at* the midpoint, there is no finite point S which achieves harmonic division; in **projective geometry**, however, S is taken as the "ideal point" of the line through PQ.

Harmonic Mean (Syn.: Harmonic average)   Of two numbers a and b, the number h such that $1/h = \tfrac{1}{2}[(1/a) + (1/b)]$; that is, the reciprocal of h is the arithmetic mean of the reciprocals of a and b. (For example, when $a = 1$, $b = \tfrac{1}{3}$, then the arithmetic mean of the reciprocals is $\tfrac{1}{2}(1 + 3)$, or 2, so that $h = \tfrac{1}{2}$.) The numbers a, h, c, form a **harmonic progression**.
The harmonic mean of several numbers is the reciprocal of the arithmetic mean of the reciprocals of the numbers.   See **Mean**.

Harmonic Progression and Series   A *harmonic progression* of numbers is a sequence of numbers whose reciprocals form an arithmetic progression. An example is the progression $1, 1/2, 1/3, \ldots, 1/n$. (Musical strings, made of homogeneous material and under the same tension, will harmonize if their lengths are in proportion to these values. This was supposed to have been known by Pythagoras (sixth century B.C.) and to have supported his mystical philosophy that the universe is based on relationships between numbers). In a harmonic progression, each term equals the harmonic mean of the two neighboring terms; for example, in the progression $\frac{1}{2}, \frac{1}{5}, \frac{1}{8}, \frac{1}{11}, \frac{1}{15}, \ldots$, the term $\frac{1}{8}$ is the harmonic mean of $\frac{1}{5}$ and $\frac{1}{11}$. This terminology is sometimes extended as follows: the *harmonic means* of any two terms of a harmonic progression are all the terms between the given ones; in the last example, the harmonic means between $\frac{1}{2}$ and $\frac{1}{15}$ are $\frac{1}{5}, \frac{1}{8}$, and $\frac{1}{11}$.

A *harmonic series* is an infinite series of terms in harmonic progression, such as $1 + 1/2 + 1/3 + 1/4 + \cdots + 1/n + \cdots$. A harmonic series is divergent, that is, does not have a finite sum (in the sense of infinite series).

Haversine Function   A **trigonometric function** defined as $\frac{1}{2}(1 - \cos A)$ and written "hav A"; rarely used.

Helix   A *cylindrical helix* is a curve in space which lies on a cylinder and crosses its elements at a constant angle α. A *circular helix* is one that lies on a right circular cylinder; it can be represented by parametric equations $x = a \cos \theta, y = a \sin \theta, z = b\theta$, where θ is the parameter (the z-axis is the axis of the cylinder, of radius a, and $\cos \alpha = b/\sqrt{a^2 + b^2}$). When the right cylinder is rolled out on a plane as a rectangle, a circular helix appears as a series of parallel line segments. A *conical helix* is a

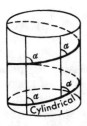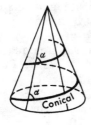

space curve on a cone that crosses the elements of the cone at a con-

stant angle. When a right circular cone is rolled out on a plane as a sector of a circle, the helix appears as an equiangular spiral, a plane curve that cuts the radii of the sector at a constant angle. The *spherical helix* is the same as the **loxodromic spiral**.

Hemisphere   The portion of a sphere cut off by a plane through its center (including the circle of intersection).

Heptagon   A polygon with seven sides; it is a regular heptagon if all its sides are equal and all its angles are equal. The regular heptagon is the regular polygon of fewest sides that cannot be realized by **geometric construction**.

Hero's Formula (Syn.: Heron's formula)   The following formula for the area of a triangle in terms of its sides a, b, c:
$$\text{Area} = \sqrt{s(s - a)(s - b)(s - c)},$$
where s is half the perimeter, $\frac{1}{2}(a + b + c)$. The formula was derived by the mathematician Heron of ancient Alexandria.

Hexagon   A polygon with six sides; it is a regular hexagon if all its sides are equal and all its angles are equal. The length of a side of a regular hexagon equals the radius of the circumscribed circle.

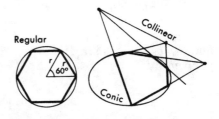

Pascal's theorem expresses an interesting property of a *hexagon inscribed in a conic;* namely, the three points of intersection of the three pairs of opposite sides, lie on a line. This is an early theorem in the history of projective geometry; it was discovered by Pascal in the first half of the seventeenth century, when he was sixteen years old.

Hexahedron A polyhedron with six faces. A regular hexahedron is a **regular polyhedron** with six faces; the only regular hexahedron is the cube.

Higher Algebra The advanced and abstract aspects of modern algebra. See **Algebra, Mathematics**.

Higher Plane Curve In analytic geometry, a curve defined by an algebraic equation of degree higher than two, or, often, by an equation involving elementary transcendental functions.

Highest Common Factor (Syn.: Greatest common divisor) See **Common divisor**.

Hilbert Space A generalization of ordinary space to an infinite-dimensional space. A *point* in Hilbert space may be represented by an infinite sequence of numbers $(a_1, a_2, a_3, \ldots)$ having the property that the infinite series $a_1^2 + a_2^2 + a_3^2 + \cdots$ is convergent. Any finite dimensional (Euclidean) space is a *subspace* of Hilbert space; for example, a point (x, y, z) in ordinary three-dimensional space can be identified with $(x, y, z, 0, 0, \ldots)$ in Hilbert space. The *distance* between two points $(a_1, a_2, a_3, \ldots)$ and $(b_1, b_2, b_3, \ldots)$ in Hilbert space is given by

$$[(a_1 - b_1)^2 + (a_2 - b_2)^2 + (a_3 - b_3)^2 + \cdots]^{1/2}$$

(the value in the bracket is the sum of an infinite series).

A point in Hilbert space can also be interpreted as a **vector** with infinitely many components (just as a

point in ordinary space can be thought of as the vector from the origin to that point.) The *inner product* of two vectors $(a_1, a_2, a_3, \ldots)$ and $(b_1, b_2, b_3, \ldots)$ is the sum of the infinite series

$$a_1 b_1 + a_2 b_2 + a_3 b_3 + \cdots ;$$

two vectors are *orthogonal,* or *perpendicular,* in case their inner product is zero. See **Vector space**.

The space described above is a *real* Hilbert space; when the components $a_1, a_2, a_3, \ldots$ are allowed to be complex numbers, it is a *complex* Hilbert space (in this case, the formulas for distance and inner product must be modified slightly). Hilbert space can be treated as an *abstract space*; viewed as such a deductive theory, it has a variety of interpretations. Hilbert spaces arise in various parts of mathematics and physics.

Ref. [116].

Homogeneous A *homogeneous polynomial P* is a polynomial in two or more variables whose terms all have the same degree; then the equation $P = 0$ is a *homogeneous equation.* For example $3x^2 y - 2xy^2 + y^3 = 0$ is a homogeneous equation of the third degree in x and y. More generally, a function $f(x, y)$ is *homogeneous of degree n* in case $f(kx, ky) = k^n f(x, y)$; for example $\tan(y/x)$ is homogeneous of degree 0. Analogous definitions apply to a function of any finite number of variables.

Homogeneous Linear Equation In *two variables x, y*, an equation of the form $ax + by = 0$; in *three variables x, y, z*, an equation of the form $ax + by + cz = 0$; and so on, for any number of variables. The graph of $ax + by = 0$ is a line through the origin; the graph of $ax + by + cz = 0$ is a plane in space through the origin.

Two simultaneous homogeneous

equations $ax + by = 0$ and $cx + dy = 0$, in two variables, always have the common solution $(0, 0)$; if the graphs are distinct lines, there is no other solution. Similarly, two homogeneous linear equations in three unknowns always has the solution $(0, 0, 0)$ and if the graphs are distinct planes any point on the line of intersection is a solution. A similar geometric analysis can be made of solutions of three or more equations in three unknowns. Concepts related to the *matrix of coefficients* of any number of homogeneous linear equations in three or more variables permit a general analysis of their solutions.

Horizontal In the plane (space), parallel to the *x*-axis (*xy*-plane); *vertical* means perpendicular to horizontal.

Horner's Method A method of successive approximations for computing the roots of a polynomial equation, studied in the theory of equations. It isolates a root, step-by-step, between successive units, tenths, hundredths, etc.

Hyperbola A **conic** with eccentricity *e* greater than 1; it is the locus of points *P* whose distance from a fixed point (the *focus*) is in the constant ratio *e* to its distance from a fixed line (the *directrix*). The hyperbola

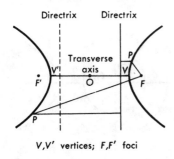

V,V' vertices; F,F' foci

occurs in nature as the path of a comet, for example.

The hyperbola is symmetrical about the line through the focus perpendicular to the directrix; this line intersects the two branches in the *vertices,* and the line segment (or its length) between the vertices is the *transverse axis.* (A hyperbola is uniquely determined by the transverse axis and the focus.) The midpoint of this axis is the *center,* and a segment (or its length) from the center to a vertex is a *semitransverse axis.* A *chord* is a line segment joining two points of the hyperbola. One branch of a hyperbola is a reflection of the other in a line through the center and perpendicular to the transverse axis; thus, the hyperbola has a second directrix and focus which define the same hyperbola, and the two foci and directrices are equally spaced from the center. A *focal chord* is a chord through a focus; a focal chord perpendicular to the transverse axis is a *latus rectum.* A *focal radius* is a line segment (or its length) from a focus to a point on the hyperbola.

A hyperbola has the following *difference property.* The difference of the two focal radii to any point *P* on the hyperbola is the same (in numerical value) for every point *P.* This property defines a hyperbola as the locus of points whose distances from two fixed points have a constant difference (thus, a hyperbola is determined by two foci and a point on the curve). The hyperbola also has the

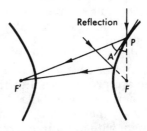

following *focal,* or *reflection property.* **127**

Hyperbola

The two focal radii FP and $F'P$ to a point P on the hyperbola make equal angles with the tangent line at P (angle APF = angle APF' in the figure). This means that rays of external light coming toward F will reflect off the hyperbola and converge at the single point F'.

In analytic geometry, the hyperbola is in standard position when its center is at the origin and its transverse axis is on the x-axis. The *equa-*

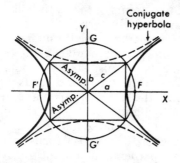

tion of the hyperbola is then

$$\frac{x^2}{a^2} - \frac{y^2}{b^2} = 1,$$

where $2a$ is the transverse axis; $2b$ is the *conjugate axis,* a line segment (or its length) perpendicular to the transverse axis and bisected by the center. The distance c from the center to a focus and the eccentricity e are given in terms of a and b by

$$c^2 = a^2 + b^2, \quad e = \frac{c}{a} = \frac{\sqrt{a^2 + b^2}}{a}.$$

The length of the latus rectum is $2b^2/c$; the numerical value of the difference of focal radii to any point on the hyperbola is $2a$. Two hyperbolas are *similar* if their eccentricities e are equal; in this case, the values a, b, c of one are proportional to those of the other. A hyperbola has two *asymptotes;* they are the lines through the origin with equations $x/a - y/b = 0$ and $x/a + y/b = 0$. Associated

with the hyperbola is its *conjugate hyperbola* whose axes are those of the given hyperbola interchanged. Its equation is

$$\frac{x^2}{a^2} - \frac{y^2}{b^2} = -1.$$

It shares the center and asymptotes of the given hyperbola, and its foci (G and G' in the figure) are also at distance c from the center; its eccentricity is c/b. A *rectangular (equilateral, equiangular)* hyperbola is one where $a = b$ (transverse and conjugate axes are equal). In standard position, its equation is $x^2 - y^2 = a^2$; its asymptotes are $x + y = a, x - y = a$. The simple equation $xy = k, k$ as a constant, is that of a rectangular hyperbola which has been rotated $45°$ about the origin from its standard position (making the x-axis and

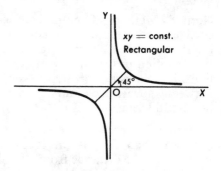

y-axis its asymptotes).

For a hyperbola in standard posi-

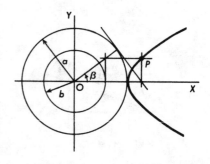

tion, the circles of radius a and b with

center at the origin are the *eccentric circles,* the circle with radius *a* being the *auxiliary circle.* A point *P* on the hyperbola is related to these circles through the *eccentric angle* β by the construction shown in the figure. This gives the parametric equations $x = a \sec \beta$, $y = b \tan \beta$ for the hyperbola, with the parameter β ranging from $0°$ to $360°$.

See **Eccentricity of conic, Lemniscate.**

Hyperbolic Cylinder A **cylindrical surface** whose right section is a branch of a hyperbola.

Hyperbolic Paraboloid See **Paraboloid.**

Hyperbolic Spiral See **Spiral.**

Hyperboloid A *hyperboloid of revolution* is the surface of revolution produced by rotating a hyperbola in space about one of its axes, called its *axis of revolution.* When the hyperbola is rotated about its conjugate axis, the result is a hyperboloid of revolution of *one sheet*; when the

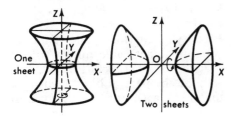

One sheet

Two sheets

hyperbola is rotated about its transverse axis the result is a hyperboloid of revolution of *two sheets.* Suppose the rotated hyperbola is in standard position in the *xz*-plane (its center at the origin, transverse axis 2*a* on the *x*-axis, and conjugate axis 2*b* on the *z*-axis). Then the *equation* of the hyperboloid of revolution of one sheet is

$$\frac{x^2}{a^2} + \frac{y^2}{a^2} - \frac{z^2}{b^2} = 1.$$

Plane sections parallel to the *xy*-plane are circles, while plane sections parallel to the *xz*-plane or *yz*-plane are hyperbolas. The equation for the hyperboloid of revolution of two sheets is

$$\frac{x^2}{a^2} - \frac{y^2}{b^2} - \frac{z^2}{b^2} = 1.$$

Plane sections parallel to the *yz*-plane are circles, while plane sections parallel to the other coordinate planes are hyperbolas.

The *general hyperboloid of one sheet* is the *quadric surface* represented by an equation

$$\frac{x^2}{a^2} + \frac{y^2}{b^2} - \frac{z^2}{c^2} = 1,$$

with proper alignment of the coordinate axes. The plane section in the *xy*-plane is the ellipse $x^2/a^2 + y^2/b^2 = 1$; any plane section parallel to the *xy*-plane is an ellipse, while plane sections parallel to the other coordinate planes are hyperbolas. Its transverse axes are 2*a* and 2*b*, and its conjugate axis is 2*c*. The *general hyperboloid of two sheets* can be represented by

$$\frac{x^2}{a^2} - \frac{y^2}{b^2} - \frac{z^2}{c^2} = 1.$$

Here, plane sections parallel to the *yz*-plane are ellipses, while plane sections parallel to the other coordinate planes are hyperbolas; its transverse axis is 2*a* and its conjugate axes are 2*b* and 2*c*. Two hyperboloids

$$\frac{x^2}{a^2} + \frac{y^2}{b^2} - \frac{z^2}{c^2} = 1$$

(one sheet) and,

$$-\frac{x^2}{a^2} - \frac{y^2}{b^2} + \frac{z^2}{c^2} = 1$$

(two sheets), are *conjugate hyperboloids;* the second has transverse axis

129

$2c$ along the z-axis. If the semiaxes a, b, c of a hyperboloid of one sheet (two sheets) are proportional to those of another hyperboloid of one sheet (two sheets), then the hyperboloids are *similar*.

The hyperboloid of one sheet is a ruled surface, that is, a family of lines

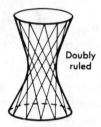

Doubly ruled

can be drawn on the surface covering all of its points. In fact, two distinct families of this sort can be drawn—the surface is *doubly ruled*.

Hypocycloid   See **Epicycloid**.

Hypotenuse   The side opposite the right angle in a **right triangle**; it is the longest side.

Hypothesis   In logic, the proposition P in a **conditional** "If P, then Q"; the proposition Q is the *conclusion*. In mathematics, the term "hypothesis" is used more loosely in place of "assumption."

I

Icosahedron   A polyhedron with twenty faces. A regular icosahedron is a **regular polyhedron** with twenty faces; its faces are equilateral triangles.

Ideal Point and Line   See **Projective geometry**.

Identical Figures   In elementary geometry, congruent figures, usually.

Identity   In *logic,* the relation of equality, or "sameness."

In *mathematics,* generally, an identity is an equation containing variables true for all (allowed) values of the variables. An *algebraic identity* is one involving only algebraic operations on the variables; an example is

$$x^2 - y^2 = (x + y)(x - y).$$

A *trigonometric identity* is one involving trigonometric functions of variables; e.g., $\sin A = \tan A \cos A$. An identity is sometimes written with the special sign of equality, "$\equiv$"; for example,

$$x^2 - y^2 \equiv (x + y)(x - y).$$

Identity Element   Of a set with a *binary operation,* a member e whose combination with any member x of the set is x itself; that is, $e * x = x * e = x$. For ordinary numbers, the identity element of *addition* is 0, since $0 + x = x + 0 = x$. The identity element of *multiplication* for numbers is 1, since $1 \cdot a = a \cdot 1 = a$. There are many other examples of identity elements; for instance, in the algebra of sets, the null set is the identity element for the union of sets. See **Group, Inverse element**.

Identity Function   The function which matches each thing x with itself; that is, $f(x) = x$. For example, let y be the person liked best by x; under the assumption that an individual likes himself better than anyone else, this correspondence from x

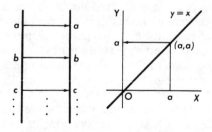

to y defines the identity function. In

the case of real numbers x, its graph is the line through the origin which makes an angle of $45°$ with the positive x-axis. See **Composition of functions, Inverse of function**.

Image In *geometry,* the reflection P' of a point P in a line (point, plane); similar terminology applies to more general transformations. For a *function,* the functional value $f(a)$ associated with a given value a.

Imaginary An *imaginary number* is a complex number $a + bi$ for which b is different from 0 (when $b = 0$, the complex number is a *real number*). When $a = 0$, it is a *pure imaginary* number, such as $3i$, or $-\frac{1}{2}i$. The *imaginary part* of $a + bi$ is the real number b; for example, the imaginary part of $-3 + 2i$ is 2 (the *real part* is -3). In the **Argand diagram**, where $x + iy$ is represented as the point (x, y), the *imaginary axis* is the y-axis.

Imaginary Root In algebra, a root of an equation which is an imaginary number. For example, the quadratic $x^2 - 2x + 10 = 0$ has the imaginary roots $1 + 3i$ and $1 - 3i$. This illustrates the general principle that imaginary roots of polynomial equations (with real number coefficients) always come in conjugate pairs, $a + bi$ and $a - bi$.

Implication In one meaning, a conclusion that follows from given assumptions (or the process that justifies the conclusion). For example, the assumption "There are a finite number of prime integers" has the implication "There is a largest prime integer." See **Inference**.

An implication also means any **conditional** statement "If P then Q." The conditional as defined and used in logic and mathematics is the so-

called *material implication*; here, the conditional is accepted as meaningful regardless of whether or not the separate statements P, Q have any apparent connection with each other. On the other hand, when the conditional is intended to express a relationship between P and Q, it is called *formal implication*; the attempt to make the latter notion precise leads to complications which appear to serve no useful purpose in mathematical logic.

Implicit Differentiation In the calculus, a method of obtaining the derivative of a function which is expressed implicitly by an equation. For example, suppose y is given as a function of x by the equation $x^2 - 3xy + y^2 - 5 = 0$; differentiating both sides, with y regarded as a function of x, leads to

$$2x - 3y - 3x(dy/dx) + 2y(dy/dx) = 0,$$
or,
$$dy/dx = (3y - 2x)/(2y - 3x).$$

A general formula for implicit differentiation can be given in terms of partial derivatives: let $f(x, y) = 0$ define y as a function of x; then,

$$\frac{\partial f}{\partial x} + \frac{\partial f}{\partial y} \cdot \frac{dy}{dx} = 0, \text{ or } \frac{dy}{dx} = -\frac{\partial f/\partial x}{\partial f/\partial y}.$$

When $f(x, y) = 0$ is regarded as giving x as a function of y, an analogous method yields dx/dy. In terms of differentials,

$$\left(\frac{\partial f}{\partial x}\right)dx + \left(\frac{\partial f}{\partial y}\right)dy = 0,$$

from which either derivative, dy/dx or dx/dy, can be obtained.

The equation $f(x, y) = 0$, in general, describes a curve in the plane; implicit differentiation provides a means of determining the slope dy/dx of the **tangent line to the curve** at any point. For example, in the example, the point (1, 4) lies on the curve; the slope of the tangent line at (1, 4) is given by $dy/dx = 2$.

Implicit Function A correspondence between values of x and y expressed by an equation of the form $R(x, y) = 0$. An example is the equation $y^2 + x + 2y - 3 = 0$; for instance, when $x = 0$, the corresponding values of y are determined by substituting 0 for x and solving the resulting equation $y^2 + 2y - 3 = 0$ (the solutions are -3 and 1). This type of correspondence may give y as a **many-valued function** of x, as in the example.

An *explicit function* occurs in the form $y = f(x)$; for example, $y = 3x^2 - 2$ gives y as an explicit function of x. In this form, the correspondence is a *single-valued function.*

Implicit functions yield explicit functions when the given equation is solved for one variable in terms of the other. In the first example, solving for x gives $x = 3 - 2y - y^2$;

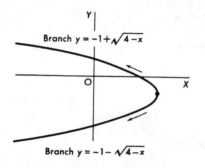

Branch $y = -1 + \sqrt{4-x}$

Branch $y = -1 - \sqrt{4-x}$

this expresses x as an explicit function of y. Solving for y gives two equations, $y = -1 + \sqrt{4 - x}$, $y = -1 - \sqrt{4 - x}$; this expresses y as two single-valued "branches," each being an explicit function of x.

Improper Fraction In arithmetic (algebra), a ratio of positive integers (polynomials) in which the value (de-

gree) of the denominator is not greater than that of the numerator; e.g., $\frac{5}{3}$ and $(3x^2 - 4x + 5)/(x - 2)$. See **Fraction, Fraction** (algebra).

Incenter of Triangle The center of the **inscribed circle** of a triangle; it is the common point of intersection of the angle bisectors.

Incircle See **Inscribed circle** (syn.).

Inclination of Line In a *plane,* the counterclockwise angle of rotation from the positive x-axis to the line; this *angle of inclination* lies between $0°$ and $180°$. The *slope* of the line is

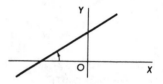

the tangent function of this angle. In *space,* the inclination of a line to a plane is the angle between the line and plane.

Inclination of Plane The inclination of one plane to another is the smaller of the two dihedral angles formed by the planes.

Incommensurable Of two lengths or numbers, not integral multiples of a common length or number; hence, not **commensurable**.

Incompatible Equations See **Inconsistent equations** (syn.).

Inconsistent Axioms Axioms which lead to a contradiction; that is, axioms from which it is possible to deduce both a statement and its denial. The problem of demonstrating that axioms of a given **deductive theory** are not inconsistent is generally difficult; one method is to exhibit a model of the theory which is known (or assumed) to contain no contradictions. The lack of a proof of consistency does not prevent mathematicians from working with a theory which is felt to be free of contradiction. In fact, the real number system underlies much of mathematics, yet its consistency is an unresolved problem of considerable importance in the foundation of mathematics. Ref. [42, 134, 149].

Inconsistent Equations **Simultaneous equations** in two or more variables that have no common solution. See **Consistent equations**.

Increasing An increasing (decreasing) *sequence* is one in which each term is greater than (less than) or equal to the preceding term; for example, the sequence 1/2, 2/3, 3/4, ..., $n/(n + 1)$, ..., is increasing. A *function* $f(x)$ is increasing (decreasing) in case $f(x)$ increases (decreases) as x increases (geometrically, its graph rises (falls) from left to right). For example, $x^2 + 2$ is increasing (decreasing) for positive (negative) values of x. If the derivative of $f(x)$ is nonnegative (nonpositive) on an interval, then the function is increasing (decreasing) on that interval.

Increment The increment of a *variable* x from $x = a$ to $x = b$ is the difference $b - a$. An increment in x is often denoted by Δx or dx; hence $a + dx$, with dx arbitrary, represents any value of x (usually thought of being near a). The increment of a *function* $f(x)$ from $x = a$ to $x = a + \Delta x$ is the difference $f(a + \Delta x) - f(a)$; it is often denoted by Δf (see figure). For example, the increment of $x^2 + 1$ from $x = 3$ to $x = 3.01$ is $[(3.01)^2 + 1] - [3^2 + 1]$, which equals $9.0601 - 9.000$, or 0.0601. The *ratio of increments* $\Delta f / \Delta x$ is the

"average" rate of change of $f(x)$ between a and $a + \Delta x$; it equals the

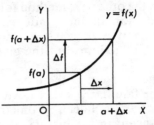

slope of the secant line through $[a, f(a)]$ and $[a + \Delta x, f(a + \Delta x)]$. Its limit is the **derivative of the function** at $x = a$ and the slope of the tangent line at $[a, f(a)]$. See **Differential of function**.

Indefinite Integral (Syn.: Antiderivative; Primitive) Of a given function $f(x)$, any function whose derivative equals $f(x)$; it is denoted by $\int f(x)dx$, with $f(x)$ called the *integrand* and x the *variable of integration* (the *integral sign* "$\int$" was introduced by Leibniz). If $F(x)$ is one indefinite integral of $f(x)$, then every indefinite integral has the form $F(x) + c$, where c is an arbitrary constant, called the *constant of integration*. For example, let $f(x) = 3x - x + 2$; then

$$F(x) = x^3 - \tfrac{1}{2}x^2 + 2x + c$$

gives all indefinite integrals of $f(x)$. The indefinite integral provides the principal means of evaluating the definite integral $\int_a^b f(x)dx$; this is based on the formula $\int_a^b f(x)dx = F(b) - F(a)$ (see **Fundamental theorem of calculus**). In the integral calculus, techniques are developed for finding indefinite integrals of various types of functions. A *table of integrals* is a list of known indefinite integrals; these are widely used in applications of the calculus. See **Integral of function, Integration by parts**.

Independent Axiom An axiom is

133

independent of several other axioms in case it is not possible to prove it from the others. A method for showing that an axiom is independent is to exhibit a (consistent) model in which all axioms but the given one hold.

The question of the independence of the familiar parallel postulate of ordinary Euclidean geometry was significant in the history of mathematics. For a long time it was conjectured that the parallel postulate could be proved from the other axioms and postulates of Euclid. This conjecture was finally disproved at the beginning of the nineteenth century with the discovery of non-Euclidean geometries; these were "geometries" that satisfied the other assumptions of Euclidean geometry but denied the parallel postulate itself. Ref. [42, 134, 149].

Independent Linear Equation A given linear equation is independent of a set of one or more linear equations in case there is at least one solution of the set of equations which is not a solution of the given equation; otherwise, the given equation is a **dependent linear equation**. (A *set* of linear equations is said to be independent if each equation is independent of the remaining ones.) For example, $x - 2y = 1$ is independent of $x + y = 3$; the second has the solution $(1, 2)$, which is not a solution of the first.

Independent linear equations can be given geometric meaning, as suggested by the following cases. Two linear equations are independent of each other if their graphs are not identical. Three linear equations in two variables are independent in case their graphs intersect by pairs in three distinct points (see figure).

Similarly, three linear equations in

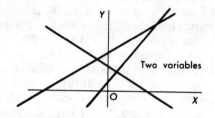

Two variables

three variables are independent when the graphs are planes with exactly one common point of intersection. See **Linear combination**.

Independent Random Event A basic concept of **probability** which expresses the idea that the outcome of one random event is not related to that of another. More precisely, one random event, E, is independent of another F, in case the probabilities of the various outcomes of E are not affected by which alternative is assumed for F; otherwise E is a **dependent random event** (as regards F). For example, the occurrence of heads or tails on one toss of a coin is independent of the outcome of a preceding toss. Also, it is generally conceded that a 7 or 11 turning up on a roll of two dice is independent of whether or not baby needs a new pair of shoes.

Independent Variable See **Dependent variable**.

Indeterminate Form An expression such as $\frac{0}{0}$, 0^0, ∞/∞, $0 \cdot \infty$, and so on, which has no direct meaning as a number; it can arise in attempting to evaluate an expression by direct substitution of certain values of the variable. An example occurs when $(x - 1)/(x^2 - 1)$ is evaluated at $x = 1$; the result is $\frac{0}{0}$. Although $(x - 1) \div (x^2 - 1)$ cannot be evaluated at $x = 1$ by direct substitution, the expression does have the limit $\frac{1}{2}$ as x approaches 1; to see this, simplify the expression to $1/(x + 1)$ and evaluate this when $x = 1$. Another example is $(\sin x)/x$, which gives the indeterminate form $\frac{0}{0}$ at $x = 0$; again, the expression does have a limit (1 in this case), although it is more difficult to show this. Limit values of indeterminant forms do not always exist; methods are developed in the calculus for determining when they do exist and how to find them. The derivative of a function can be viewed as the limit value of the indeterminate form $\Delta f/\Delta x$ arising as a ratio of **increments**. See **l'Hospital's rule**.

Index The index of a *power x^a*, is the **exponent** a. The index of a **radical** $\sqrt[n]{x}$ (the nth root of x) is the whole number n; in the case of square root $\sqrt{x}$, the index, 2, is generally omitted.

Indirect Proof (Syn.: *Reductio ad absurdum*) Usually, the method of **proof** which assumes the denial of what is to be proved and deduces a contradiction from this assumption.

Induction, Mathematical See **Mathematical induction**.

Inequality The statement of an inequality relation; hence, a statement of the form "$A < B$" or "$A > B$" (also "$A \leq B$" or "$A \geq B$"). Examples are the inequalities $2x + 1 < 3$, $x > \sin x$, $2x - 3y < 1$, $x^2 \geq 0$. Two categories of inequalities involving variables are usually distinguished: **(1)** an *unconditional inequality,* or absolute inequality, is one that is true for all values of the variable (or variables); **(2)** a *conditional inequality* is one that is false for some values of the variable. For example, the inequality $x^2 + 1 > 0$ is unconditional, while $2x < 3$ is conditional.

A *solution of an inequality* is a value of the variable (or variables) which satisfies the inequality, that is, converts it to a true statement. In general, a conditional inequality has an unlimited number of solutions. For example, $2x - 6 < 0$ has as a solution any number less than 3; $x - 2y > 0$ has as a solution any pair (x, y) with x greater than twice y. The *graph of an inequality* is a geometric representation of its solutions. Techniques for finding the solutions of inequalities depend upon the application of the laws of inequalities. See **Linear inequality, Quadratic inequality, Simultaneous inequalities**.

Ref. [5].

Inequality Relation (Syn.: Order relation) For numbers, either of the following relations: **(1)** a is less than b, denoted by "$a < b$"; **(2)** a is greater than b, denoted by "$a > b$." On a linear scale, the statement $a < b$ ($a > b$) means that a lies to the left of (right of) b; for example, $1 < 3$, $-2 < 0$, $-99 < 5$, $5 > 2$, $0 > -100$. The inequalities "$a < b$" and "$c > d$" are said to be opposite in sense. A number a is *positive* in case $a > 0$, *negative* in case $a < 0$. The assertions $x < y$ and $y > x$ are equivalent. Variations of these relations are the following: "$a \leq b$" stands for "$a < b$ or $a = b$," and "$a \geq b$" stands for "$a > b$ or $a = b$" (also written "$a \leq b$," and "$a \geq b$"); "$a < b < c$" stands for "$a < b$ and $b < c$," that is, "b is between a and c"

(for example, $1 < 3 < 5$, $-5 < 0 <$

2). The set of numbers x for which $x < a$ ($x > a$) make up the half-line excluding a, to the left (right) of a; those for which $a < x < b$ make up the interval between a and b, excluding the endpoints (see figure). (The symbols for inequalities were introduced in the seventeenth century.)

The following *laws of inequalities* provide basic rules for handling inequalities: **(1)** if $x < y$, then $x + a < y + a$ and $x - a < y - a$; **(2)** if $x < y$ and $a < b$, then $x + a < y + b$; **(3)** if $x < y$ and a is positive, then $ax < ay$ and $x/a < y/a$; **(4)** if $x < y$ and a is negative, then $ax > ay$ and $x/a > y/a$. (Like laws for ">" are obtained by interchanging "<" and ">.") Law **(1)** asserts that the same number may be added to or subtracted from both sides of an inequality; for example, $3 < 5$ leads to $1 < 3$ (subtracting 2), and $2x - 4 < 0$ implies $2x < 4$ (adding 4). Law **(2)** asserts that inequalities in the same sense can be added; for example, $3 > 2$ and $-3 > -4$ imply $0 > -2$, also, $2x - y < 2$ and $x + y < 3$ imply $3x < 5$. Law **(3)** asserts that both sides of an inequality can be multiplied or divided by a positive number; for example, $3x < 5$ implies $x < \frac{5}{3}$, and $x/2 > -1$ implies $x > -2$. On the other hand, law **(4)** asserts that when both sides are multiplied or divided by a negative number, the sense of the inequality is reversed; for example, $-x < \frac{1}{2}$ implies $2x > -1$, and $5 > 3$ implies $-5 < -3$.

See **Ordered set**.

Inference In logic, a single-step deduction from premises. For example, the premises "all rocks are hard" and "this is a rock," permit the inference "this is hard." This example is a traditional type of inference, the **syllog-**

ism. Allowable inferences are described by general *rules of inference* (*laws of inference, rules of proof*). From the point of the logician, a mathematical **proof** consists of a chain of individual inferences. In practice, the mathematician does not detail his proof to such an extent that he cites a rule of inference for each step in his proof; theoretically, this can be done for any correct proof.

An important rule of inference is the *rule of detachment,* or *modus ponens;* this asserts that the premises "If P then Q" and "P" allows the conclusion "Q." For example, from the two statements "if n is even, then $n + 1$ is odd" and "n is even," infer the statement "$n + 1$ is odd." This obvious rule is a basic process of reasoning. Legitimate *substitution* provides another rule of inference: for example, from the equation "$A^2 - B^2 = (A + B)(A - B)$" infer the equation "$(2X)^2 - 3^2 = (2X + 3) \times (2X - 3)$" by substitution of $2X$ for A and 3 for B.

Ref. [89, 134].

Infinite With respect to a set of things, unlimited in the number of its members; hence, not finite. A subtler characterization is this: a set is infinite in case it can be put into one-to-one correspondence with a part (not all) of itself.   See **Cardinal number**.

The term "infinite" is also used to mean "unbounded" in spatial extent or magnitude. For example, an angle is an infinite geometric figure, being unbounded in extent. Also the expression $1/x$ is said to be infinite at $x = 0$, meaning that its values are unbounded as x approaches 0; for instance, when $x = 1/1,000,000$, $1/x = 1,000,000$, when $x = 1/10^{100}$, $1/x = 10^{100}$, and so on.   See **Infinity**.

Infinite Sequence or Series   See **Sequence, Series**.

Infinitesimal Calculus   See **Calculus** (syn.).

Infinity   Loosely, the concept of a value beyond any finite value; it is denoted by the symbol "∞" (introduced in the seventeenth century). More specifically, a *sequence* of numbers $a_1, a_2, a_3, \ldots$ is said to *approach* ∞ with n in case any selected interval I on the line (no matter how large) contains only a finite number p of terms of the sequence (p may depend on I); this is written

$$\lim_{n \to \infty} a_n = \infty$$

(for example the limit of $\sqrt{n}$ is ∞, as n approaches ∞). The *function* $f(x)$ is said to approach infinity at $x = a$, written,

$$\lim_{x=a} f(x) = \infty,$$

in case the following holds: the limit

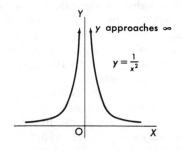

Infection Point   See **Point of inflection**.

Information Theory   A mathematical theory of information and its communication. The original work by the American mathematician C. E. Shannon in 1948 was related to communications engineering; it has application elsewhere as well. It relies heavily on concepts of probability, and is sometimes regarded as a branch of that field. Among the notions treated are (1) the measure of *amount of information,* (2) the *capacity* of a communication channel, (3) the *coding* of information, and (4) the *accuracy of transmission* (as affected, say, by "noise," or random disturbances, in a communication line). "Information" is regarded not in the ordinary sense of "meaning," but as messages, or strings of symbols (such as the letters in English sentences); the central problem is that of coding information so as to make efficient use of communication channels.

The *bit* is used as a unit in the numerical measure of information. To illustrate, suppose that just two messages are possible, and each is equally likely, that is, each has probability $\frac{1}{2}$; this situation is assigned an information measure of 1 bit, expressing that knowledge of one of the two alternatives has information value 1. If four equally likely alternatives exist, say A, B, C, D, a

Amount of Information

of the sequence of functional values $f(a_n)$ approaches ∞ for any sequence a_n which converges to a (for example, $1/x^2$ approaches ∞ as x approaches 0).   See **Projective geometry** for *point at infinity*.

Loose reasoning about infinity has its pitfalls; such errors were not uncommon in the early history of the calculus, even by excellent mathematicians (see **Series**).

Ref. [33, 56, 88, 121, 132, 153].

measure of 2 bits is assigned; knowledge of a particular alternative has twice the value now (the partial knowledge that, say, the message is one of A or B, would have information value of 1 bit). More generally, 2^N equally likely alternatives are assigned a value of N bits.

In practice, alternatives are not equally likely. Suppose a source of information produces messages, one after the other, from among alternative messages $A_1, A_2, \ldots, A_r$, each appearing with probability $p_1, p_2, \ldots, p_r$, respectively; then the source is assigned H bits of information, as given by

$$H = -[p_1 \log p_1 + p_2 \log p_2 + \cdots + p_r \log p_r];$$

here, the logarithm has the base 2. The number H may be thought of as the average number of bits in a message. It is also called the *entropy* of the information source, and can be viewed as a measure of the freedom available to the source in selecting messages (it has a maximum value when all the p's are equal, that is, when all alternatives are equally likely).

The notion of entropy can be extended to more complicated situations. A realistic one is an information source, as in telegraphy, that generates messages as sequences of symbols taken from a fixed "alphabet" of symbols; the selection of symbols is allowed to proceed in accordance with certain statistical limitations (for example, some letters of the English alphabet are more frequent than others). The entropy H can be defined in this situation, and may be thought of as the average number of bits of information generated by the source per symbol of its alphabet. The notion of *redundancy* of the information source can be defined in terms of entropy;

this measures the extent to which the structure of messages is determined by statistical laws rather than by the free choice of the sender. (The redundancy of the English language is about 50 per cent.)

An information source feeds messages into a communication channel. The channel is measured by a number C, called the *capacity*, which depends upon such factors as **(1)** the different lengths of time to transmit the different symbols of the basic "alphabet" of the channel, and **(2)** restrictions on the order in which these symbols may be sent. The capacity expresses the number of bits of information the channel is ideally capable of transmitting per second. When a given information source, of entropy H, is to send messages over a given channel, these messages are encoded (using certain equipment) before being fed into the channel; various encoding schemes can be used. Each scheme results in a particular value of the rate x, taken as the average number of symbols of the source transmitted per second. The problem is to devise a scheme which matches the statistical features of the source with the characteristics of the channel so as to make x as large as possible (for example, one aspect of matching might be to encode the most frequent symbol of the source by the channel symbol with least transmission time). The *fundamental theorem* of information theory states the following: the rate x can be made as close to the ratio C/H as desired by an appropriate scheme of encoding; but C/H can never be exceeded by *any* scheme. Thus, C/H is the theoretical limit for matching source with channel.

The theory extends the preceding concepts to channels with noise and to sources that transmit continuous information (rather than discrete messages).

Ref. [51, 72, 113, 152].

Inner Product of Vectors The product of the lengths l_1, l_2 of the **vectors** times the cosine of the angle θ between them; that is, $l_1 l_2 \cos \theta$. The in-

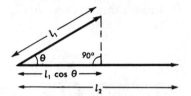

ner product is zero in case the vectors are perpendicular.

Inscribed Angle An angle is inscribed in a *curve* in case the angle is made up of two chords of the curve with the vertex as a common endpoint. An angle inscribed in a *circle* has measure equal to half of the intercepted arc; if the line segment

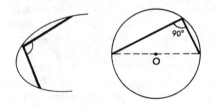

joining the ends of the chords is a diameter of the circle, then the angle is inscribed in a semicircle (in this case, the angle is a right angle).

Inscribed Circle (Syn.: Incircle) Of a *triangle,* the unique circle internal to a triangle and tangent to the three sides. Its center is the *incenter* of the triangle; this is coincident with the common point of intersection of the angle bisectors of the triangle. The radius r of the inscribed circle is given in terms of the lengths a, b, c of the sides of the triangle by

Inscribed Prism or Pyramid

$$r = \sqrt{\frac{(s-a)(s-b)(s-c)}{s}};$$

here, s is half the perimeter, $\frac{1}{2}(a + b + c)$.

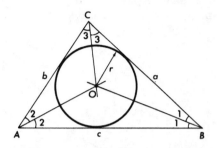

A circle is inscribed in a *polygon* in case the latter is a **circumscribed polygon** of the circle. A circle can be inscribed in any regular polygon; its radius is the apothem, or short radius, of the polygon.

Inscribed Cone or Cylinder A cone is inscribed in a pyramid in case the latter is a **circumscribed pyramid** of the cone; a cylinder is inscribed in a prism in case the latter is a **circumscribed prism** of the cylinder.

Inscribed Polygon A polygon is inscribed in a given curve (or other polygon) in case every vertex of the polygon lies on the curve. When a polygon is inscribed in a circle, the latter is a **circumscribed circle** of the polygon. See **Hexagon, Length, Pedal Triangle**.

Inscribed Polyhedron A polyhedron is inscribed in a surface if every vertex of the polyhedron lies on the surface. When a polyhedron, such as a tetrahedron or a regular polyhedron, is inscribed in a sphere, the latter is a **circumscribed sphere** of the polyhedron. See **Volume**.

Inscribed Prism or Pyramid A prism is inscribed in a cylinder in case the latter is a **circumscribed**

139

cylinder of the prism; a pyramid is inscribed in a cone in case the latter is a **circumscribed cone** of the pyramid.

Inscribed Sphere The inscribed sphere of a *tetrahedron* is the unique

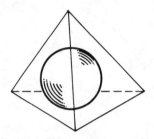

sphere interior to the tetrahedron and tangent to its four faces; the center is coincident with the common point of intersection of the four planes which bisect the dihedral angles of the tetrahedron. A sphere is inscribed in a *polyhedron* (*cone, cylinder*) in case the latter is a **circumscribed polyhedron** (**circumscribed cone, circumscribed cylinder**) of the sphere. A sphere can be inscribed in any regular polyhedron.

Instruction For an automatic computer, a direction to the computer to carry out a basic computational step, such as the addition of two numbers or transferring a number from one location to another. An instruction is expressed in a **code** which is directly meaningful to the computer; the instruction generally includes the operation to be performed and the storage location of the information to be acted on. A *routine* is a series of instructions intended to solve a given problem. The terms "command" and "order" are less preferred terms for "instruction" (see **Command**).

Integer In arithmetic, any one of the numbers

$$\cdots, -3, -2, -1, 0, 1, 2, 3, \cdots.$$

The *positive integers* 1, 2, 3, ..., are the same as the **natural numbers** (or whole numbers). The extension to include *zero*, 0, and the *negative integers* $-1, -2, -3, \ldots$, for one thing, allows the distinction to be made between measurement to the right (or above) a zero point and measurement to the left (or below) the zero point (an example is a thermometer). This extension also allows un-

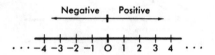

restricted subtraction among the integers. (See **Number**). Prominent among the integers are the **prime** numbers 2, 3, 5, 7, 11, ... The investigation of these numbers, and of the integers in general, belongs to the **theory of numbers**. The integers constitute a mathematical system known as an **integral domain**.

The *algebraic integer* is defined in higher algebra as a number which is a solution of some polynomial equation $x^n + ax^{n-1} + bx^{n-2} + \cdots = 0$, where the coefficients $a, b, \ldots$ are ordinary integers. For example, $3 - 2\sqrt{2}$ is an algebraic integer because it is a root of the equation $x^2 - 6x + 1 = 0$. Ordinary integers p are called "rational" integers, being algebraic integers which are also rational numbers (they occur as the solutions of linear equations $x - p = 0$).

Integral Calculus See **Calculus**.

Integral Domain In higher algebra, a mathematical system which generalizes the system of ordinary integers under addition and multiplication. More definitely, an integral domain is a system consisting of a set of entities together with two binary operations, called "addition" and "multiplication," which satisfies the following axioms: **(1)** it is a commutative **ring**; **(2)** it contains an *identity element e* of multiplication (that is, $e \cdot x = x$ for every x); **(3)** whenever a product $x \cdot y$ equals 0, then at least one of x and y is 0 (the element 0 being the identity element of addition). Besides the integers, an important example of an integral domain is provided by the set of all polynomials in a variable x.

Integral Equation   In advanced calculus, an equation to be solved for an unknown function which occurs under an integral sign. For example,

$$\int_0^1 e^{tz} f(x)dx = g(t)$$

is an integral equation for the unknown function $f(x)$, where $g(t)$ is a given function.

Integral Exponent, Solution, etc. An exponent, solution, etc., which is an integer, as against one which is not. For example, x^2 has an integral exponent, but $x^{\frac{1}{2}}$ has a fractional exponent; also the equation $2x + 6 = 0$ has the integral solution -3, while the equation $2x + 5 = 0$ has no integral solution. Integral solutions of equations are studied in Diophantine analysis.

Integral of Function   The *definite integral* is a basic concept of the integral calculus related to the measure of area and to various other geometric and physical measures. More specifically, the definite integral of a function $f(x)$ over the interval from $x = a$ to $x = b$ gives the area bounded by the graph of $y = f(x)$, the x-axis, and the two vertical lines through $x = a$ and $x = b$ [here, area above (below) the axis is counted as positive (negative)]. This integral is written

$$\int_a^b f(x)dx,$$

with $f(x)$ called the *integrand,* x the *variable of integration,* a the *lower limit* of integration, and b the *upper limit* of integration. For another interpretation of the definite integral, consider a particle moving along a line with variable velocity. Let $v(t)$ be the velocity at time t; then $\int_{t_1}^{t_2} v(t)dt$ equals the distance traveled by the particle during the time interval from t_1 to t_2. (Also, see **Length**.)

A formal definition of $\int_a^b f(x)dx$ for a continuous function $f(x)$ is the following. Let the interval from a to b be divided into n equal subintervals of length $\Delta [= (b - a)/n]$; let x_i be any point in the ith subinterval, and consider the sum S_n given by

$$S_n = f(x_1)\Delta + f(x_2)\Delta + \cdots + f(x_n)\Delta.$$

(This is an approximation to the area under the graph by a sum of rectangles; see **Element of integration**.) The number of terms on the right increases as n increases (and Δ decreases), and the value of S_n depends on n, in general. The definite integral is taken as the *limit* of S_n as n approaches infinity, that is, as Δ approaches 0. (This definition can be phrased so as to apply to functions which are not necessarily continuous on the interval from a to b.) The following general properties of the definite integral hold:

$$\int_a^b Af(x)dx = A\int_a^b f(x)dx \ \ (A = \text{constant}),$$
$$\int_a^b f(x)dx + \int_b^c f(x)dx = \int_a^c f(x)dx,$$
$$\int_a^b [f(x) \pm g(x)]dx = \int_a^b f(x)dx \pm \int_a^b g(x)dx.$$

(For a formula involving the integral of a product of functions, see **Integration by parts**.)

An *indefinite integral* of $f(x)$ is any

function $F(x)$ whose derivative is $f(x)$. The usual technique for evaluating definite integrals is based on the following formula;

$$\int_a^b f(x)dx = F(b) - F(a)$$

(see **Fundamental theorem of calculus**). This is sometimes written

$$\int_a^b f(x)dx = F(x)]_a^b$$

where the right side stands for $F(b) - F(a)$. For example, from $d(x^3)/dx = 3x^2$, it follows that

$$\int_0^2 3x^2dx = x^3]_0^2 = 2^3 - 0^3 = 8.$$

The type of definite integral described above is sometimes called *Riemann integral* to distinguish it from other types of integrals in advanced mathematics. The concept of definite integral can be extended to functions of two or more variables; see **Double integral**.

Integrand The function under the integral sign in a definite or indefinite integral; see **Indefinite integral**, **Integral of function**.

Integration The operation which transforms a function to the value of its definite or indefinite integral.

Integration by Parts A method of modifying an integral of a product of functions; for an *indefinite integral* it takes the form

$$\int f(x) \cdot g(x)dx$$
$$= f(x)\,G(x) - \int \frac{df(x)}{dx} \cdot G(x)dx,$$

where $G(x)$ is an indefinite integral of $g(x)$. This formula allows the integral of one product to be converted to the integral of another, by integrating one factor and differentiating the other. This is frequently a useful device; for example,

$$\int x \cos x \, dx = x \sin x - \int \sin x \, dx$$
$$= x \sin x + \cos x + C$$

(here, in the first step, cos x is integrated to sin x and x is differentiated to 1). For a *definite integral*, integration by parts takes the related form

$$\int_a^b f(x) \cdot g(x)dx = [f(b)G(b) - f(a)G(a)]$$
$$- \int_a^b \frac{df(x)}{dx} \cdot G(x)dx.$$

Integration by Substitution In integral calculus, the evaluation of an integral of a function by a change in the variable of integration. Suppose the definite integral $\int_a^b f(x)dx$ is to be evaluated; then the substitution $x = g(t)$ leads to

$$\int_a^b f(x)dx = \int_c^d f[g(t)] \cdot \frac{dg(t)}{dt} dt;$$

here, $a = g(c)$ and $b = g(d)$. That is, the substitution is carried out by replacing x by $g(t)$ and dx by the *differential* of $g(t)$, and making the necessary changes in the limits of integration. For example in $\int_0^1 \sqrt{1 - x^2}\, dx$, the substitution $x = \sin t$ gives $dx = \cos t\, dt$; this leads to

$$\int_0^1 \sqrt{1 - x^2}\, dx$$
$$= \int_0^{\pi/2} \sqrt{1 - \sin^2 t}\, \cos t\, dt$$
$$= \int_0^{\pi/2} \cos^2 t\, dt$$
$$= [\tfrac{1}{2}t + \tfrac{1}{4}\sin 2t]_0^{\pi/2} = \pi/4.$$

Intercept In geometry, the intersection, or common part, of one geometric figure with another.

In the plane, the *x-intercepts* and *y-intercepts* of the graph of an equation are its points of intersection with the x-axis and y-axis; the intercepts are found by setting one variable equal to 0 and solving for the remaining one. For example to obtain the x-intercepts of $y = x^2 - 3x - 4$, set y equal to 0 and solve for x; this gives $x = 4$ and $x = -1$, and so the x-intercepts are $(4, 0)$ and $(-1, 0)$. To obtain the y-intercepts, set x equal to 0 and solve for y; this gives $y = -4$, so the *y-intercept* is (0, −4). (Often, the individual coordinates 4 and −1 are called the *x*-intercepts, and −4 the *y*-intercept.) The solutions of an

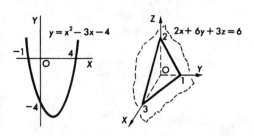

equation $f(x) = 0$ can be viewed as the *x*-intercepts of the graph of the equation $y = f(x)$; in the preceding example, the *x*-intercepts are the solutions of the quadratic equation $x^2 − 3x − 4 = 0$.

In *space,* there are three possible intercepts on the axes, the "*x*-intercept," "*y*-intercept," and "*z*-intercept." For the graph of an equation in three variables, the intercepts of an equation on a given axis are obtained by setting two variables equal to 0 and solving for the remaining one. For example, consider the linear equation $2x + 6y + 3z = 6$; setting *y* and *z* equal to 0, leads to the *x*-intercept (3, 0, 0) or, simply, 3. Similarly, the *y*-intercept is (0, 1, 0); or 1, and the *z*-intercept (0, 0, 2), or 2.

Intercept Form of Equation of Line or Plane   See **Line, Plane.**

Interior Angle of Polygon or Triangle (Syn.: Angle of polygon or triangle) The angle formed by two adjacent sides (whose interior lies inside the polygon, near the vertex); an interior angle is often denoted by the vertex of the polygon, such as $\angle A$ at vertex *A*. An interior angle of a (convex) plane polygon can never be a reflex angle. An *exterior angle* is formed by one side and the extension of an ad-

jacent side; there are two exterior angles at each vertex, which are opposite, hence equal, angles.

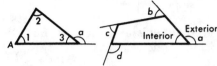

For a *triangle,* the sum of the (interior) angles is 180°; also, an exterior angle of a triangle equals the sum of the two opposite interior angles. In the figure $\angle 1 + \angle 2 + \angle 3 = 180°$, $\angle a = \angle 1 + \angle 2$. For an *n*-sided *polygon,* the sum of the interior angles is $(n − 2)$ times 180°. The sum of the exterior angles of any convex polygon is the same, 360°, no matter what the number of sides is (one exterior angle being counted at each vertex); for example, in the figure, $\angle a + \angle b + \angle c + \angle d = 360°$.

Interior or Exterior Angle of Transversal   See **Transversal.**

Interior of Closed Curve or Polygon A polygon or any simple closed curve in the plane divides the plane into two regions, an *interior* and an *exterior,* with the polygon or curve as their common boundary. As the figure suggests, any two points in the interior (or in the exterior) can be joined by an arc in the plane which

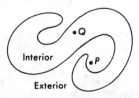

does not cut the boundary (that is, each region is a **connected set**), but to join a point *P* in the exterior to a point *Q* in the interior by an arc, it is necessary to cut the boundary. These

143

facts are established in the *Jordan curve theorem* of topology, which was not proved in all generality until the beginning of the twentieth century.

Ref. [28, 73].

Internal Division or Ratio See **Division of line segment**.

Internal Tangent, Common See **Common tangent**.

Internally Tangent Circles See **Tangent circles**.

Interpolation In a table of numerical values, any procedure for estimating intermediate values that are not listed. The common procedure is **linear interpolation**.

Interpreter In a computer, a set of instructions serving the following purpose: it enables the computer to carry out the solution of a problem automatically when the computational routine is in a code other than that of the given machine. See **Computer program**.

Intersection of Geometric Figures The configuration, or set of points, common to the figures. In the plane, for example, two nonparallel lines intersect in one point; a line and a circle intersect in no, one, or two points; two distinct circles intersect in no, one, or two points. In space, for example, two nonparallel planes intersect in a line of points; a plane and a sphere intersect in no, one, or a circle of points; two distinct spheres intersect in no, one, or a circle of points. Geometric intersection is expressed algebraically by simultaneous equations; the common solutions make up the intersection of the graphs of the equations. See **Intercepts**, **Plane section**.

Intersection of Sets (Syn.: Product of sets) Of two sets A and B, the largest set contained in both; it consists of the elements common to the sets; it is denoted "$A \cap B$" (see **Algebra of Sets**). For example, the intersection of the sets $\{0, 2, 4, 6\}$ and

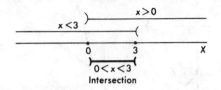

$\{1, 2, 3, 4, 5\}$ is $\{2, 4\}$; the intersection of the set of all real numbers less than 3 with the set of all real numbers greater than 0, is the set of real numbers between 0 and 3.

Interval Of numbers (points), the set of all numbers (points) lying between two fixed ones, called the *endpoints* of the interval. If the endpoints are included (excluded) the interval is *closed* (*open*). For example, the numbers between 0 and 2, exclusive

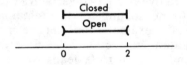

(inclusive) of 0 and 2, comprise the open (closed) interval with endpoints 0 and 2; it is described by the inequality $0 < x < 2$ ($0 \leq x \leq 2$). See **Inequality relation**.

Intuitionism (Syn.: Intuitionistic mathematics) A philosophy of mathematics which rejects non-constructive methods and insists upon "finite" processes of proof. It is one of several approaches to the **foundations of mathematics** which emerged at the beginning of the twentieth century in attempts to resolve the paradoxes of infinite sets. It was the most drastic proposal made, rejecting established logical principles in order to build mathematics on self-evident, finite principles. The intuitionist school is a small one in mathematics.

One of its basic ideas is to drop the law of excluded middle for infinite sets (this law asserts that a proposition or its denial is true). To see the reason for this view, consider a proposition of the following type: "Every x in set A has property such-and-such"; its denial is the proposition "There is an x in A which does not have property such-and-such." If A is infinite, then there may be no effective way of checking the elements one by one to determine whether or not each has the property in question, and hence no "constructive" way of deciding whether the proposition or its denial is true.

The insistence on finite, constructive methods using an "intuitive" notion of natural numbers $1, 2, 3, \ldots$ is central to intuitionism; many proofs of mathematics are unacceptable to this school because they depend upon certain transfinite procedures. This is especially true in the case of various **existence theorems** of mathematics. The nineteenth century mathematician Kronecker was a forerunner of this school; he objected strongly to Cantor's theory of infinite sets.

Ref. [42, 149].

Inverse Conditional   The **conditional** "If not P, then not Q," obtained by denying the antecedent and the consequent of a given conditional "If P then Q." It is logically equivalent to the converse "If Q, then P."

Inverse Correspondence (Syn.: Inverse of correspondence)   The **correspondence** which reverses the direction of a given correspondence; if the given correspondence carries x into y, then the inverse correspondence carries y into x. For example, consider the correspondence from a whole number n to twice the number, $2n$; the inverse correspondence goes from an even whole number m to half its value, $m/2$ (the first correspondence carries 4 into 8, the second carries 4 into 2). When a correspondence from numbers x to numbers y is expressed by an equation in x and y (for example, $xy - 3x + 2y = 4$), the inverse correspondence is described by the same equation; the difference is only in which variable is thought of as the first (independent) variable, and which the second (dependent) variable. This can be made explicit by solving for the second variable in terms of the first, if that is possible.   See **Implicit function, Inverse of function, Inverse relation.**

Inverse Element (Syn.: Inverse of element)   The *additive inverse* of a number x is its negative $-x$; the *multiplicative inverse* of a (nonzero) number x is its reciprocal $1/x$. The negative, $-x$, can be described as the number y such that $y + x = 0$; similarly, $1/x$ is the number y such that $y \cdot x = 1$.

A similar definition applies to any *binary operation* $*$ in a set with an identity element e; the inverse of an element x is an element y (when it exists) such that $y * x = e$ and $x * y = e$. In the case of addition of numbers, for example, $*$ is $+$, and e is 0. In a **group** every element has an inverse (this is one of its axioms).

Inverse Logarithm   See **Antilogarithm** (syn.).

Inverse of Function   The **inverse correspondence** of a function. A function from a set A to a set B carries a member of A into one (or no) member of B. The inverse correspondence carries members of B into members of A, but it need not be a functional correspondence; that is, it may associate a member of B with more than one member of A. For example, $y = x^2$ describes a functional correspondence from numbers x to numbers y; the inverse correspondence from y to x is given explicitly by $x = \pm\sqrt{y}$, which shows that x is a *many-valued* (specifically, two-valued) *function* of y (for instance, if $y = 4$ then $x = 2$ or -2).

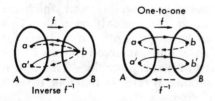

Many-valued functions of mathematics arise as inverses of (single-valued) functions; the inverse trigonometric functions are examples. The inverse will sometimes be a single-valued function; this occurs when the given function is a one-to-one correspondence. An example of this is given by $y = 10^x$, which is one-to-one from x to y; the inverse, given explicitly by $x = \log y$, is a single-valued function from y to x.

When a function is given by $y = f(x)$, with $f(x)$ an explicit expression in x, the inverse correspondence can also be described explicitly if the equation can be solved for x in terms of y. For example, solving $y = 2x^2 - 6$ for x gives $x = \pm\sqrt{\frac{1}{2}y + 3}$ (which is a two-valued function).

The graph of a function and the *graph of* its inverse are closely related —the graphs are the same except that the first and second axes are in-

terchanged; that is, for the inverse, the y-axis is viewed as the independent variable. This can be put in

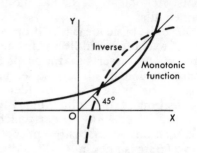

another way (which keeps the independent variable horizontal): the graph of the inverse is the original graph reflected in the 45° line through the origin. If the graph of a function is *monotonic,* that is, everywhere increasing or everywhere decreasing, the function is a one-to-one correspondence; in this case the graph of the inverse is also monotonic [and necessarily a (single-valued) function].

The *notation* f^{-1} is used for the inverse of a function f; for example, $\sin^{-1}$ is the inverse of the function $\sin$. In this notation, $f^{-1}(b)$ denotes any number a which f carries into b; that is, $a = f^{-1}(b)$ if and only if $b = f(a)$. It follows that $f[f^{-1}(b)]$ is b; or, in general, $f[f^{-1}(y)] = y$. Particular instances are the following: $\sin(\sin^{-1}y) = y$, $(\pm\sqrt{y})^2 = y$, $10^{\log y} = y$ (the inverse of x^2 is $\pm\sqrt{y}$ and the inverse of 10^x is $\log y$). See **Composition of functions**.

The *derivative* of a function $g(y)$ which is the inverse of a given function $f(x)$, equals the reciprocal of the derivative of $f(x)$—more explicitly, write $y = f(x)$ and $x = g(y)$; then $dg/dy = 1 \div (df/dx)$, for any (x, y) belonging to the given function. A suggestive form of this is $(dx/dy) = 1 \div (dy/dx)$. For example, if $y = e^x$,

$x = \log y$ (natural logarithm), then, by the rule, $dx/dy = 1 \div (dy/dx) = 1 \div e^z = 1/y$, which is, in fact, the derivative of $\log y$.

Inverse of Number See **Reciprocal of number** (syn.).

Inverse Operation (Syn.: Inverse of operation) The operation inverse to addition is *subtraction;* the operation inverse to multiplication is *division.* Subtraction can be defined in terms of addition as follows: the difference $a - b$ is the number x for which the equation $a = x + b$ holds. A similar definition can be given for division: the quotient $a \div b$ is the solution x of the equation $a = x \cdot b$.

The inverse operation can be defined in terms of the **inverse element**; for example $a - b = a + (-b)$ and $a \div b = a \cdot (1/b)$, $-b$ and $1/b$ being, respectively, the inverse of b with respect to addition and multiplication. This procedure can be followed for a *binary operation* $*$, in general; the inverse operation applied to a, b is defined as $a * b'$, where b' is the inverse of b. The inverse operation "undoes" a given operation; for example, in the case of addition, $(a + b) - b = a$.

Inverse Proportion or Variation A **variation** of the type $y = k/x$, in contrast to a direct variation $y = kx$.

Inverse Ratio (Syn.: Reciprocal ratio) Of two numbers a and b, the ratio of the reciprocal of a to the reciprocal of b, that is, $1/a \div 1/b$, or b/a. It equals the reciprocal of the (direct) ratio a/b.

Inverse Relation (Syn.: Inverse of relation) The **relation** which reverses the order of association of a given relation: more precisely, a is said to be in the inverse relation to b in case b is in the given relation to a. For example, the relation "y is a parent of x" pairs, say, off-spring x with parent y; the inverse relation is expressed by "x is an off-spring of y," which pairs parent y with off-spring x. Also, the relation "is less than" among numbers has as its inverse the relation "is greater than." The inverse relation of R is denoted by R^{-1}; hence, $a\ R^{-1}\ b$ if and only if $b\ R\ a$. The operation of forming the inverse relation is important in the logical theory of relations.

Inverse Trigonometric Functions (Syn.: Antitrigonometric functions) The functions inverse sine, inverse cosine, etc., which are the inverses of the trigonometric functions sin, cos, etc.; they are denoted by "arc sin," "arc cos," etc., or $\sin^{-1}$, $\cos^{-1}$, etc. For example, if x is a number between 0 and 1, then arc sin x (or $\sin^{-1}x$) is an angle measure y such that $\sin y = x$; similar definitions apply to the others. The "inverse" nature of these functions is expressed by the equations $\sin(\sin^{-1}x) = x$, $\cos(\cos^{-1}x) = x$, etc.

The functions $\sin^{-1}x$ and $\cos^{-1}x$ are defined for numbers x between -1 and 1, $\tan^{-1}x$ and $\cot^{-1}x$ for all

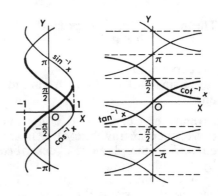

numbers x. The figure shows the

graphs of sin⁻¹, cos⁻¹, tan⁻¹, and cot⁻¹; the coordinate y is taken as the radian measure of an angle.

The inverse trigonometric functions are many-valued functions; for example, $\sin^{-1}(\frac{1}{2})$ is any of the angles $30°$, $-210°$, $150°$, $-330°$, $390°$, etc., which is coterminal with $30°$ or $150°$ ($\pi/6$ or $5\pi/6$ radians). By limiting each function to its **principal value**, it can be made a single-valued function. The heavy portions of the graphs show principal values; these are sometimes denoted by a capital letter, as in $\text{Sin}^{-1}x$.

(Graphs of the inverse functions are those of the original functions with axes interchanged.)

Involute of Circle A curve which is the path of the end of a taut string as it is unwound from a circle. In the figure, the length of the segment PP' equals the circular arc length AP', where P is any point on the evolute.

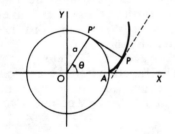

The involute has the property that the tangent line at P is parallel to the radius OP'. Parametric equations of the curve are $x = a(\cos\theta + \theta\sin\theta)$, $y = a(\sin\theta - \theta\cos\theta)$, with θ in radians.

Involute of Curve If C is a plane curve, then an involute of C is any curve E in the plane of C described by the end of a taut string as it is unwound from the given curve C. The *evolute* of a curve is the curve made up of the *centers of curvature* of the

given curve; a line perpendicular to the given curve is tangent to the evolute at the center of curvature (thus, the evolute of a curve is the envelope of the family of perpendicular lines to the curve). Evolute and involute are reciprocal, in the following sense: if E is the evolute of C, then C is an involute of E; and if C is an involute of E, then E is the evolute of C.

Involution In algebra, the operation of raising to an integral power, x^n; the inverse operation is *evolution,* or root extraction.

Irrational Equation or Expression An irrational expression (equation) is an algebraic expression (equation) which contains radicals, or fractional powers, involving variables; for example, $\sqrt{x + 1} - x = 3$ is an irrational equation in x. *Rationalization* is a technique for converting irrational expressions to rational expressions. The terminology "irrational expression" comes from the fact that a root of a positive integer or rational number is generally an irrational number.

Irrational Exponent See **Exponent**.

Irrational Number A real number which is not a rational number; examples are the numbers $\sqrt{2}$ and π. Irrational numbers occur early in the study of mathematics, for example, in connection with square roots and the length of a circle. Early Greek mathematicians studied these numbers in terms of commensurable and incommensurable lengths, and were puzzled by them; Eudoxus developed a theory of irrationals in the fourth century B.C. in an attempt to resolve the difficulties. An adequate modern theory did not emerge until the nineteenth century. A modern view is to regard an irrational number as a limit of an unending sequence of rational numbers; for example, $\sqrt{3}$ is the limit of the sequence 1, 1.7, 1.732, 1.7320, etc. In the **decimal number system**, irrational numbers are represented by the nonrepeating infinite decimals.

Ref. [88].

Irreducible Polynomial (Syn.: Prime polynomial) A polynomial which cannot be factored into polynomials of lower degree (in algebra, they play the part that prime numbers do in arithmetic). See **Factor of polynomial**.

Whether or not a given polynomial is irreducible depends upon the type of number that is allowed to serve as a coefficient. In elementary algebra, coefficients are restricted to rational numbers. Under these circumstances, factoring $2x^3 - x^2 + 8x - 4$ into $(x^2 + 4)(2x - 1)$ gives irreducible factors. Polynomials of any degree exist which are irreducible over the rational numbers; for example, the polynomial $x^4 + 1$ is an irreducible polynomial of degree 4. When real numbers are allowed as coefficients, then a polynomial which is irreducible must be of the first or second degree; for example, although $x^4 + 1$ is irreducible over the rational numbers, over the real numbers it factors into (irreducible) quadratics,

$$(x^2 - \sqrt{2}x + 1)(x^2 + \sqrt{2}x + 1).$$

If complex numbers are allowed as coefficients, then the **fundamental theorem of algebra** implies that the only irreducible polynomials are first degree polynomials. For example, the polynomial $(x^2 + 4)(2x - 1)$ above can be factored further into $(x + 2i)(x - 2i)(2x - 1)$, where i is the complex unit ($i^2 = -1$). In

higher algebra, the general problem of the irreducibility of polynomials over any number system which is a **field** is studied.

Irreducible Radical A radical which cannot be reduced to a rational expression. For example, $\sqrt{10}$ and $\sqrt{x + 1}$ are irreducible, while $\sqrt{4}$ is reducible to 2.

Isometry See **Rigid motion**.

Isomorphic Informally, two **mathematical systems** are isomorphic in case they represent the same underlying system by different concepts or notation (this is given more specific meaning with each mathematical theory). For example, the binary number system is isomorphic to the decimal number system; they are different methods of representing the same system, namely, the system of real numbers. Also, the ordinary geometric plane is isomorphic to the system of pairs of real numbers (x, y); the isomorphism is based upon Cartesian coordinates in the plane. Finally, the algebra of propositions is isomorphic to the algebra of sets (both regarded as Boolean algebras).

Isoperimetric Two closed curves in the plane are isoperimetric if they have the same length, or perimeter; the term is also applied to closed surfaces having the same area. Isoperimetric problems are those dealing with isoperimetric figures. A famous isoperimetric problem is this: among

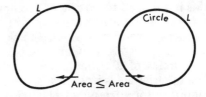

all closed curves in the plane of the same length L, determine that one which encloses the maximum area—the solution is the circle. This result can be expressed algebraically by the following isoperimetric *inequality* for any plane closed curve with area A: namely, $A \leq L^2/4\pi$ (the right member gives the area of the circle, since $L = 2\pi r$ for a circle). This inequality relates the area of a general enclosed plane region to the length of its boundary.

A like inequality holds in space between the volume V of any closed surface and its area A; namely, $V^2 \leq A^3/36\pi$; equality is realized for a sphere ($V = \frac{4}{3}\pi r^3$, $A = 4\pi r^2$). Hence the sphere encloses maximum volume V for constant surface area A. Isoperimetric problems are studied in the **calculus of variations**, where "isoperimetric" is allowed a more general meaning.

Ref. [28, 74].

Isosceles   In geometry, having at least two equal sides. An important case is the *isosceles triangle;* here, the angle included between equal sides is the *vertex,* or *summit angle,* the side opposite it the *base,* and the angles opposite the equal sides the *base angles.* These base angles are equal

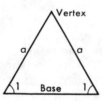

[this is suposed to be one of the first statements of mathematics for which a general proof was given (Thales, sixth century B.C.)]. Conversely, if two angles of a triangle are equal, then the triangle is isosceles. Another condition for a triangle to be isosceles is that two angle bisectors be equal (terminating at the sides of the

triangle); this theorem is surprisingly difficult to prove.

An *isosceles trapezoid* is a trapezoid whose nonparallel sides are equal. In solid geometry, an *isosceles spherical triangle* is a spherical triangle with at least two sides equal.

Iterated Integral   An expression indicating successive integrations involving one variable at a time; this is the usual method of evaluating a **double integral** (or multiple integral). Integration is first carried out with respect to one variable, regarding the other variables as constants; then integration is carried out with respect to a second variable, regarding the remaining ones as constants; and so on. For example, let

$$\iint_R xy \, dx \, dy$$

be a double integral over the triangular region R bounded by the line $y = x$, the x-axis, and the vertical line through $x = 1$. This is equal to the iterated integral

$$\int_0^1 x \left\{ \int_0^x y \, dy \right\} dx = \int_0^1 x[x^2/2]dx$$
$$= \frac{1}{2}\int_0^1 x^3 dx = \frac{1}{8}.$$

More generally, let R be the region included between the curves $y = g(x)$ and $y = h(x)$ where $g(x) \leq h(x)$, with x ranging from a to b; then

$$\iint_R f(x,y)dx\,dy = \int_a^b \left\{ \int_{g(x)}^{h(x)} f(x,y)dy \right\} dx$$

(here, the left side is a double integral, and the right side is an iterated integral). Under general assumptions, a double (or multiple) integral can be evaluated integrating out the variables in any order.

Iterative Method   A method of calculation which consists of the repetition of an underlying process. Long division is an iterative method;

methods of successive **approximation** are usually iterative.

J

Joint Variation   A **variation** in which the values of one variable depend upon those of several other variables, as in $z = kxy$.

Jordan Curve Theorem   See **Interior of closed curve**.

K

Kilo   One thousand, used as a prefix. For example, a kilometer is 1,000 meters; in less scientific terminology, a kilobuck is 1,000 dollars.

Königsberg Bridge Problem   A famous problem in the history of mathematics concerning the seven bridges of the town of Königsberg and the question of traversing these bridges in one continuous walk without recrossing any bridge (see figure). The impossibility of such a path was demonstrated by Euler in the first half of the eighteenth century; this was one of the early results in the field of topology.

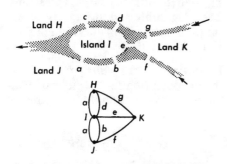

To analyze the problem, the geographical picture is replaced by a schematic representation in which the four separate portions of land are represented by vertices (H, I, J, K), and the seven bridges by segments joining the vertices. The re-

sulting figure is called a "graph" (in a special sense of topology). The problem is now the following: Beginning at any vertex of the graph, draw a continuous path which traverses every segment (exactly) once. The impossibility of such a path in this configuration is a special case of a general proposition concerning graphs of any number of segments and vertices. Let an *even* (*odd*) *vertex* be one that belongs to an even (odd) number of segments (for example, in the figure, each vertex is odd, belonging to 3 or 5 segments). The general proposition states: **(1)** if every vertex is even, then there is a path returning to its starting point and traversing each segment once; **(2)** if the graph has either one or two odd vertices, there is a path that traverses every segment once, but it begins at one vertex and ends at another; **(3)** if the graph has more than two odd vertices, there is no path that traverses every segment once. The Königsberg configuration corresponds to the third situation.

Ref. [6, 73, 100].

L

Lateral Area   Area of surface exclusive of bases, as in a cone or cylinder.

Lateral Edge or Face   An edge or face of a **prism** or **pyramid** which is not a part of a base.

Latin Square   A square array of n^2 entries built out of n different symbols, and having the following prop-

Order 3		
2	0	1
1	2	0
0	1	2

Order 4			
1	2	3	0
2	3	0	1
3	0	1	2
0	1	2	3

erty: each row and each column consists of the n symbols in some arrangement. The number of possible latin squares increases rapidly with its *order n*. For example, there are two squares of order two, 12 of order three, 576 of order four, 161,280 of order five, and 81,851,200 of order six. These arrays are used in statistics, for example, in designing experiments. Ref. [6].

Latitude See **Spherical coordinates**.

Latus Rectum A chord of a conic which passes through a focus and is perpendicular to the axis of the conic. See **Ellipse, Hyperbola, Parabola**.

Law A statement of a general relationship, such as the law of cosines in trigonometry. See **Formula**.

Law of Contradiction and Excluded Middle Two principles of logic: **(1)** the *law of contradiction* asserts that a proposition and its denial cannot both be true, and **(2)** the *law of the excluded middle* asserts of a proposition and its denial that at least one must be true. From these two, it follows that of two propositions "*P*," and "not *P*," one is true and the other is false; for example, one of the statements "There is life on Mars" and "There is no life on Mars" is true and the other is false. As general principles of logic, these do not deal with the meanings of statements but with the forms of statements to which they are applied; they are the basis of the commonly used proof by contradiction. In the **algebra of propositions**, the law of excluded middle and the law of contradition are expressed by the logical validity, respectively, of "$P \lor (\sim P)$" and "$\sim[P \land (\sim P)]$." The universal applicability of the law of excluded middle is rejected in a special view of mathematics called **intuitionism**.

Law of Cosines In *plane trigonometry,* the following relation, expressing a side of a triangle in terms of the other two sides and the cosine of the opposite angle:

$$c^2 = a^2 + b^2 - 2ab \cos C,$$

where a, b, c are the sides and A, B, C are their opposite angles. The law of cosines can be used for the solution of the triangle in the plane when three sides, or two sides and the included angle are given.

In *spherical trigonometry,* there are two analogous relations:

$$\cos c = \cos a \cos b + \sin a \sin b \cos C$$
$$\cos C = -\cos A \cos B + \sin A \sin B \cos c.$$

These equations can be used for the solution of the oblique spherical triangle when two sides (angles) and the included angle (side) are given.

Law of Quadrants For a spherical right triangle, a relationship concerning the relative sizes of its sides and angles. See **Species**.

Law of Signs In algebra, rules for carrying out arithmetic operations on signed numbers or expressions. See **Algebraic addition, Algebraic multiplication, Division, Sign of fraction, Subtraction**.

Law of Sines In *plane trigonometry,* the proposition that the sides of a triangle are proportional to the sines of the opposite angles; that is,

$$\frac{a}{\sin A} = \frac{b}{\sin B} = \frac{c}{\sin C}.$$

It is useful in the solution of the triangle in the plane when two angles and the included side, or two angles and the side opposite one of them, are given.

In *spherical trigonometry,* the corresponding formula is that the ratio of the sines of the sides of a spherical triangle are proportional to the sines of the opposite angle; that is,

$$\frac{\sin a}{\sin A} = \frac{\sin b}{\sin B} = \frac{\sin c}{\sin C}.$$

It is useful for the solution of the oblique spherical triangle when two sides (angles) and the angle (side) opposite one of them are given.

Law of Tangents In plane trigonometry, the relationship

$$\frac{a - b}{a + b} = \frac{\tan \frac{1}{2}(A - B)}{\tan \frac{1}{2}(A + B)}$$

among any two sides a, b and the respective opposite angles A, B of a plane triangle. It is applied to the solution of the triangle in the plane when two sides and the included angle are given, and logarithmic computation is used.

Laws of Equality See **Equality**.

Laws of Exponents See **Exponent**.

Laws of Inequality See **Inequality** relation.

Laws of Inference See **Inference**.

Laws of Logarithms See **Logarithm**.

Leading Coefficient Of a polynomial, the coefficient of the term with highest exponent; for example, the leading coefficient of $3x^2 - 2x + 7$ is 3.

Least Common Denominator See **Common denominator**.

Least Common Multiple See **Common multiple**.

Least Squares In statistics, the method of least squares is a principle applied to such problems as finding the line or curve which "best" fits a given set of data. It may be used to "smooth out" irregular data; for example, suppose (x_1, y_1), (x_2, y_2), ..., represent observed data [say, one pair (x, y) for each of a given group of individuals]. Let the data be plotted as points in a rectangular coordinate system; suppose it is desired to estimate a linear relationship $y = mx + b$ between the values of y and x. A particular relationship is determined by specifying the numbers m and b. The method of least squares would specify as the "best" values of m and b, those for which the sum of the squares

$$[y_1 - (mx_1 + b)]^2$$
$$+ [y_2 - (mx_2 + b)]^2 + \cdots$$

is the least (this sum is a measure of the vertical deviation of the plotted data from a line). The same method can be used to fit curves other than lines; in statistics, it is shown in what sense the method is "best." It is a common method in applied mathematics; it was first used about 1800 by Gauss in connection with errors in astronomical observations.

Least Upper Bound See **Bound**.

Leg Of a right triangle, either of the sides that includes the right angle.

Leibniz' Theorem (Syn.: Leibniz' formula) In the calculus, a formula for the derivative of any order, of a product of functions $f(x) \cdot g(x)$; it is expressed in terms of the derivatives of $f(x)$ and of $g(x)$ as follows:

$$D^n(f \cdot g) = (D^n f) \cdot g + n D^{n-1} f \cdot Dg$$
$$+ \frac{n(n-1)}{2} \cdot D^{n-2} f \cdot D^2 g + \cdots + f \cdot D^n g.$$

The coefficients of the right member are the same as the binomial coefficients in the expansion of $(x + y)^n$. See **Binomial theorem**.

Lemma A proved proposition which is useful mainly as a preliminary to the proof of a **theorem**.

Lemniscate A closed curve given by an equation $r^2 = a^2 \cos 2\theta$ in polar coordinates (r, θ). It consists of two symmetrical loops meeting at a "node." The lemniscate is related to the *rectangular hyperbola* in the manner indicated in the figure: if a

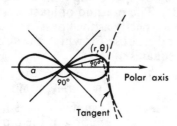

tangent line *l* is drawn at any point of the hyperbola, then the perpendicular from the origin to the tangent line will intersect *l* at a point on the lemniscate. This property may be used as a definition of the lemniscate.

Length A numerical measure expressing one-dimensional extent. When a unit length is fixed, the length of a one-dimensional figure may then be thought of as the number of unit lengths it contains [this number is not necessarily a whole number or even a rational number (fraction)].

A precise notion of length can be based on the length of a line segment. Thus, the length of a polygon or of a broken line is the sum of the lengths of its segments. The length of a *curve,* in general, is approximated by the length of an inscribed broken line; the exact length is taken as the *limit* of the lengths of an infinite sequence of inscribed broken lines, which approach the curve as their limiting figure. In the figure, the inscribed broken line *PQRST* approximates the curve; a more refined approximation is the broken line *PP'QQ'RR'SS'T*; suc-

cessive refinements produce closer

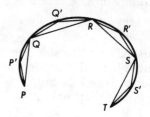

approximations. For example, the length of a circle, $2\pi r$, can be obtained as the limit of a sequence of inscribed regular polygons. The length of a closed curve in the plane is called its *perimeter* (see **Isoperimetric**). A useful fact is that the lengths of similar figures are in the ratio of the lengths of any corresponding segments (for example, doubling the radius of a circle, doubles its length; halving the side of a square, halves its perimeter).

In the calculus, the following formula occurs for the length of a curve $y = f(x)$ from $x = a$ to $x = b$:

$$\int_a^b \left\{ 1 + \left(\frac{df}{dx}\right)^2 \right\}^{1/2} dx.$$

When the curve is given by parametric equations $x = g(t)$, $y = h(t)$ the formula for the length from t_1 to t_2 is

$$\int_{t_1}^{t_2} \left\{ \left(\frac{dg}{dt}\right)^2 + \left(\frac{dh}{dt}\right)^2 \right\}^{1/2} dt.$$

See **Element of arc length**. Ref. [73].

Length of Tangent Of a circle, a

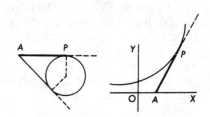

segment of a tangent line between the point of contact P and an external point A. The same definition applies to a sphere and a point outside it. In analytic geometry, the length of a tangent line to a curve is the segment from a point of tangency P to the point of intersection A of the tangent line with the x-axis.

Less Than　See **Inequality relation**.

L'Hospital's Rule　A procedure of the calculus to evaluate **indeterminate forms** such as $\frac{0}{0}$ and $\frac{\infty}{\infty}$; it relates a limit of a ratio $F(x)/G(x)$ to the limit of the ratio $f(x)/g(x)$ of the separate derivatives $f(x) = dF(x)/dx$ and $g(x) = dG(x)/dx$. Specifically, if $F(a)/G(a)$ is indeterminate but $f(a)/g(a)$ is well defined, then (under appropriate assumptions) the limit of $F(x)/G(x)$ as x approaches a exists and equals $f(a)/g(a)$. For example, $(\sin x)/x$ is indeterminate at $x = 0$; however, its limit is 1, which can be obtained by evaluating the ratio of derivatives, $(\cos x)/1$, at $x = 0$.

If the ratio $f(x)/g(x)$ should also be indeterminate, then the same procedure is applied to it. This is continued until a ratio is reached which is not indeterminate; if the final ratio is well defined at $x = a$, then (under appropriate assumptions) this value will equal the limit of the original ratio $F(x)/G(x)$ as x approaches a.

Like Terms　See **Similar terms** (syn.).

Limit　The fundamental concept of the calculus expressing the notion of tending to, or approaching, an ultimate value.

More precisely, an unending (infinite) *sequence* of numbers $a_1, a_2, a_3, \ldots, a_n, \ldots$ has the limit A (or approaches A) in case the following condition holds: whatever interval on the line is chosen with A as center,

all the terms of the sequence except for a finite number of values of n will fall inside that interval (the number of excluded values of n, say p, may depend on the size of the interval—the smaller the interval, the larger p). This condition is abbreviated

$$\lim_{n \to \infty} a_n = A.$$

For example, the sequence $1, -\frac{1}{2}, \frac{1}{4}, -\frac{1}{8}, \frac{1}{16}, \ldots$ of powers of $\frac{1}{2}$ with alternating signs has the limit 0; if the interval from -0.15 to $+0.15$ about 0

is picked, then all members of the sequence after $\frac{1}{4}$ lie in the interval; if the interval from -0.01 to $+0.01$ is picked, then all terms after $\frac{1}{64}$ lie in the interval.　See **Sequence, Series**.

A *function* $f(x)$ has the limit L (or approaches L) when x equals a (or approaches a) in case the following condition holds: for any sequence $a_1, a_2, a_3, \ldots$ approaching a, the corresponding sequence of functional values $f(a_1), f(a_2), f(a_3), \ldots$ approaches L. This condition is abbreviated

$$\lim_{x=a} f(x) = L.$$

As an illustration, consider $f(x) = (x - 1)/(\sqrt{x} - 1)$. When $x = 1$, direct substitution gives the indeterminant form $\frac{0}{0}$. However, $f(x)$ has the limit 2 when $x = 1$; this is made plausible by writing

$$f(x) = \frac{(x - 1)(\sqrt{x} + 1)}{(\sqrt{x} - 1)(\sqrt{x} + 1)}$$
$$= \frac{(x - 1)(\sqrt{x} + 1)}{x - 1} = \sqrt{x} + 1,$$

and evaluating the last expression at $x = 1$.　See **Continuous function, Infinity**.

155

The limit of certain combinations of functions can be expressed in terms of the limits of the functions themselves. Let $f(x)$, $g(x)$ have the respective limits L, M as x approaches a; then the following equations express so-called *fundamental theorems* on limits:

$$\lim[kf(x)] = kL \quad (k = \text{constant})$$
$$\lim[f(x) + g(x)] = L + M$$
$$\lim[f(x) \cdot g(x)] = L \cdot M$$
$$\lim\frac{f(x)}{g(x)} = \frac{L}{M} \quad (\text{when } M \neq 0).$$

Here, the limit is understood to be that as x approaches a. These rules simplify the calculation of limits of functions; similar ones hold for sequences.

Ref. [2, 96].

Line (Syn.: Straight line)   In Euclidean geometry, an undefined entity expressing the notion of an unturning path, indefinitely extended in both directions. Its assumed properties are given by postulates of Euclidean geometry. (Sometimes "line" means any path, or curve; in this case, "straight line" is used for the present line.) A *half-line*, or *ray,* is either one of the two portions into which a single point on a line divides a line, including the point itself, usually. A *line segment* is the portion of a line between two of its points, including the two points, usually; ("line" sometimes means line segment, as well as line). A *directed line* (or line segment) is one with a selected direction along it (see **Vector**).

In the plane, several relations between lines occur. Two lines are either *parallel* (no points in common), *intersect* in one point, or are *coincident.* When they intersect at right angles, they are *perpendicular.* *Concurrent lines* are three or more lines with a common point; all the lines through a point constitute a *pencil of lines*. In space, lines that do not meet and do not lie in a single plane are called *skew* (parallel lines are understood to lie in a plane).

In *plane analytic geometry* the line is studied algebraically within a rectangular coordinate system. The orientation of a line is described by its *inclination,* the counterclockwise angle of rotation from the positive x-axis to the line. The *slope* of the line is the tangent function of the inclination; it also equals the ratio

$$\frac{(y_2 - y_1)}{(x_2 - x_1)},$$

where (x_1, y_1) and (x_2, y_2) are two distinct points on the line. Distinct lines are parallel if their slopes are equal; lines are perpendicular if the product of their slopes is -1.

Lines in the *plane* are represented by (linear) equations $ax + by + c = 0$. There are several *standard forms of the equation of a line*. The *slope-intercept* form is $y = mx + b$, where m is the slope and b is the y-intercept. The *point-slope* form is $y - y_1 = m(x - x_1)$ where (x_1, y_1) is a fixed point on the line. The *two-point* form is

$$y - y_1 = [(y_2 - y_1)/(x_2 - x_1)](x - x_1)$$

where (x_1, y_1), (x_2, y_2) are two fixed points on the line. The *intercept* form is $x/a + y/b = 1$, where a is the x-intercept and b is the y-intercept. A linear equation $y = k$ ($x = k$) is a line parallel to the x-axis (y-axis) and

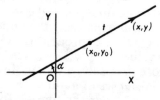

k units from the axis. *Parametric equations* of a line are given by

$$x = x_0 + t \cos \alpha, \quad y = y_0 + t \sin \alpha$$

[α is the inclination of the line, and the parameter t is the directed distance from a fixed point (x_0, y_0) to any other point (x, y) on the line].

See **Determinant**, **Normal form**, and **Polar equation** for other types of equations of lines.

In *solid analytic geometry,* the orientation of a line is described by its *direction cosines l, m, n,* or *direction numbers a, b, c.* Standard equations of a line include the following:

(1) the *two-point form*

$$\frac{x - x_1}{x_2 - x_1} = \frac{y - y_1}{y_2 - y_1} = \frac{z - z_1}{z_2 - z_1},$$

where (x_1, y_1, z_1), (x_2, y_2, z_2) are fixed points on the line;

(2) the *symmetric form*

$$\frac{x - x_1}{a} = \frac{y - y_1}{b} = \frac{z - z_1}{c};$$

(3) *parametric equations*

$$x = x_1 + lt, \; y = y_1 + mt, \; z = z_1 + nt,$$

where the parameter t is the (directed) distance from (x_1, y_1, z_1) to any point (x, y, z) on the line. A line can also be represented by two simultaneous linear equations in x, y, z, these being the equations of two planes intersecting in the given line. Distinct lines in space are *parallel* if their direction cosines are equal, that is, $l = l'$, $m = m'$, $n = n'$; they are *perpendicular* in case $ll' + mm' + nn'$ equals zero.

The "line" as described above is that of ordinary Euclidean geometry, where it is conceived as "straight" and "unlimited in extent." With the rise of **non-Euclidean geometry** the notion of line was generalized and these limitations removed.

Line at Infinity See **Projective geometry**.

Line Segment The portion of a line between two of its points.

Line, Tangent See **Tangent line to curve**.

Linear In *geometry,* pertaining to the line, as in "linear coordinates"; in *algebra,* of the first degree, as in the "linear equation" $ax + by + c = 0$.

Linear Combination Of two expressions U and V, a sum of the form $aU + bV$; a and b are the *coefficients* of the linear combination. For example, if U is $x^2 - 3y$ and V is $3x + 2y^2$, then $2(x^2 - 3y) + 3(3x + 2y^2)$ is a linear combination of these with coefficients 2 and 3. The notion of linear combination applies to three terms, $aU + bV + cW$, or any number of terms. Expressions are *linearly dependent* if some linear combination, with at least one coefficient not zero, is identically 0; otherwise they are *linearly independent*. For example, $5x - 10y$ and $3x - 6y$ are linearly dependent because with coefficients 3 and -5,

$$3(5x - 10y) - 5(3x - 6y) = 0.$$

Linear combinations are used in the solution of simultaneous equations. By a linear combination of given *equations* is meant a derived equation whose left and right members are linear combinations (with the same coefficients) of the corresponding members of the given equations. As an example, consider the equations $x - 3y = 2$ and $3x + 2y = 1$; the linear combination with the coefficients 2 and 3 is the equation

$$2(x - 3y) + 3(3x + 2y) = 2 \cdot 2 + 3 \cdot 1,$$

or $11x = 7$. This illustrates how linear combinations may achieve the elimination of variables.

A given equation is linearly dependent on several others in case it is a linear combination of them; otherwise, the equation is linearly independent of them. For example, $5x - 4y^2 = 7$ is linearly dependent

157

on $x - 3y^2 = 1$ and $3x + 2y^2 = 5$; it can be derived as a linear combination with coefficients 2 and 1, respectively. These notions have immediate geometric significance for linear equations, which represent lines and planes in analytic geometry.

See **Dependent linear equation, Independent linear equation** (in the terminology there, "dependent" and "independent" correspond to "linearly dependent" and "linearly independent"); also, see **Partial fractions** and **Vector** for linear combinations in these cases.

Linear Coordinates The standard method of matching points on a line with real numbers. A *zero* point, or *origin,* and *unit* point are first selected; this determines a positive direction (origin to unit point) and a negative (opposite) direction. Then any real number is marked off at a distance from the origin equal to its magnitude, with positive numbers in the positive direction and negative numbers in the negative direction.

The *coordinate* of a point P is the unique number p matched with it in this correspondence. On this *linear scale,* or *uniform scale,* the (positive) distance between any two points is the absolute value of the difference of their coordinates; that is, if points P, Q have coordinates p, q, respectively, then the distance between P and Q equals $|p - q|$. The directed distance from P to Q is $q - p$ (positive if the direction from P to Q is positive, and negative otherwise). The linear scale is used as a ruler for ordinary measurement. Other scales,

as in **logarithmic coordinates**, are also useful. See **Nomograph**.

Linear Equation In *one variable,* say x, an equation equivalent to one of the form $ax + b = 0$; in *two, three,* etc., *variables,* an equation equivalent to one of the form $ax + by + c = 0$, $ax + by + cz + d = 0$, etc. Examples are $2x - 1 = 0$ and $x - 3y + 5 = 0$. Linear equations are algebraic equations of the first degree; a *homogeneous linear equation* is one with constant term equal to 0, as in $ax = 0$ and $ax + by = 0$.

The linear equation $ax + b = 0$ in one variable (with $a \neq 0$) is satisfied by a single value of the unknown x; the solution is $x = -b/a$. The linear equation $ax + by + c = 0$ is satisfied by infinitely many pairs (x, y); together they comprise a **line** (the graph of the equation). Similarly the solutions (x, y, z) of a linear equation $ax + by + cz + d = 0$ comprise a **plane**. See **Simultaneous equations**.

Linear Function Of one or more variables, a function of the form $ax + b, ax + by + c, ax + by + cz + d$, etc.

Linear Inequality In *one variable,* an inequality equivalent to one of the form $ax + b < 0$ (or the same with $>$, $\leq$, or $\geq$). The inequality $ax + by + c < 0$ is a linear inequality in *two variables;* and so on, for more variables. The set of solutions of an inequality in one variable is a half-line; for two variables (three variables), the set of solutions is a half-plane (a half-space). Linear **simultaneous inequalities** can be used to represent regions such as the interior of polygons in the plane or of polyhedrons in space. See **Solution of inequality, Graph of inequality**.

Linear Interpolation The common method of interpolation which assumes a direct proportion between differences of functional values and differences of argument values. As an

$$a_1 \rightarrow f(a_1)$$
$$x \rightarrow f(x) = ? \quad \frac{f(x) - f(a_1)}{f(a_2) - f(a_1)} = \frac{x - a_1}{a_2 - a_1}$$
$$a_2 \rightarrow f(a_2)$$

example, suppose log 1.6514 is to be evaluated. A five-place table of common logarithms gives log 1.651 = 0.21775 and log 1.652 = 0.21801 for successive argument values; the following proportion is assumed,

$$\frac{\log 1.6514 - \log 1.651}{\log 1.652 \ - \log 1.651}$$
$$= \frac{1.6514 - 1.6510}{1.6520 - 1.6510},$$

which simplifies to

(log 1.6514 − 0.21775)/.00026 = 4/10;

this yields the estimate log 1.6514 = 0.21785. Tables of functional values usually carry values of *proportional parts* which give decimal fractions of tabular differences to aid in linear interpolation [for instance, the relation (.4)(26) = 10.4, of use in this example, would appear].

Linear Programming See **Mathematical programming**.

Linear Scale See **Linear coordinates**.

Linear Transformation or Functional See **Transformation** and **Functional**.

Linearly Dependent (Independent) See **Linear combination**.

Linearly Ordered See **Ordered set**.

Lituus A plane curve given by an equation $r^2 = a/\theta$ in polar coordinates (r, θ); it is a trumpet-shaped spiral (see figure). On the right it ap-

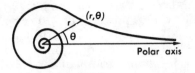

proaches closer and closer to the polar axis; on the left, it winds more and more closely about the origin, without end.

Locus The configuration, or set, of all points satisfying a given geometric condition. For example, in the plane, the locus of points for which the sum of the distances from two fixed points is a constant, is an ellipse (with the given points as foci); in space, the locus of points at a given distance from a given point is a sphere. An *equation* of a locus is an equation satisfied by the (coordinates of) points belonging to the locus and by no other points. See **Graph of equation**.

Logarithm The logarithm of a number N is the exponent when N is represented as a power of a fixed number, the *base*. This notion is used in simplification of arithmetical computation; it also has considerable theoretical importance. The idea of the logarithm is credited to Napier, in the early part of the seventeenth century; his approach was not through exponents, which were not then in common use. See **Computation with logarithms, Logarithmic function**.

"Logarithm," without qualification, usually means the *common logarithm* (or *Briggs' logarithm*) with base 10, which is used in computation. In this case, a positive number N is expressed as 10^u, and the logarithm of N is the exponent u, denoted by log N. For example, log 10 = 1, **159**

$\log 100 = 2, \log 10^n = n, \log 1 = 0,$ $\log \frac{1}{10} = -1, \log \frac{1}{100} = -2$. When numbers are arranged on a *logarithmic scale,* powers of 10 appear equally spaced (see **Logarithmic coordinates**). In the relation $N = 10^u$, N is the *antilogarithm* of u (or *inverse logarithm* of u), and denoted by *antilog u*; that is, antilog u is the number whose logarithm is u (for example, antilog $2 = 100$).

When the base is b (any positive number different from 1), a positive number N is expressed as b^u, and u is the logarithm of N to the base b, denoted by $log_b N$; the number N is the antilogarithm of u to the base b, denoted by antilog$_b u$. (In this notation, the common logarithm would be written $\log_{10} N$.) In theoretical work, the *natural logarithm (Napierian logarithm)* is used, where the base is $e(= 2.71828 \ldots)$. The change between common and natural logarithms is effected by the formula

$$\log N = (\log e)\log_e N;$$

the coefficient $\log e$ (approximately, .43429) is the *modulus* of common logarithms.

The following *laws of logarithms* hold (for any base): $\log(A \cdot B) = \log A + \log B, \log(A/B) = \log A - \log B, \log(A^n) = n \log A, \log \sqrt[n]{A} = (1/n) \log A$. There is no like simple expression for $\log(A + B)$ in terms of $\log A$ and $\log B$; for this reason logarithms are not convenient for computing sums.

The logarithm of a *negative number* can be defined by means of complex numbers. See **Logarithm of complex number**.

Ref. [28, 120].

Logarithm Function　Of real numbers x, the function whose value is $log_b x$ (with b a fixed base); the function is defined for positive numbers x, and its graph $y = log_b x$ is the *logarithmic curve.* Each value of the parameter b determines a different graph. When b is greater than 1, the

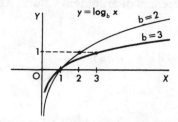

graph is increasing (rising more and more slowly with increasing x). When b is between 0 and 1, it is decreasing. Since $log_b 1 = 0$ for any b, all the graphs cross the x-axis at 1. The logarithm function $log_b x$ is the inverse function of the exponential function b^x; this is expressed by the equations $log_b(b^x) = x$ and $b^{log_b x} = x$. When b is 10, $log_b x$ is the common logarithm and is written $\log x$. Any function $log_b x$ can be expressed in terms of $\log x$ by the equation $log_b x = k \log x$; here, k is the constant $1/\log b$, or $log_b 10$.

The natural logarithm function $log_e x$ is principally used in theoretical work, and is a basic transcendental function of mathematics; from the laws of logarithms, it satisfies the *functional equation* $f(A \cdot B) = f(A) + f(B)$. (It can be proved that the logarithm functions $log_b x$ are the only continuous functions that satisfy this equation.) The derivative of $log_e x$ is $1/x$; hence, one way to define this function is as an indefinite integral of $1/x$. See **Logarithmic series**.

Ref. [2].

Logarithm of Complex Number　The logarithm (to the base e) of a complex number $x + iy$ is defined by the formula

$$\log_e(x + iy) = \log_e r + i\theta;$$

here, r is the absolute value and θ is the amplitude (in radians) of $x + iy$. This is an extension of the natural logarithm $\log_e x$ for x a positive, real number.

The formula allows a value (complex) to be assigned to the logarithm of a *negative real number;* namely, $\log_e(-A) = \log_e A + i\pi$. For example, $\log_e(-1) = i\pi$, $\log_e(-3) = \log_e 3 + i\pi$. Other interesting cases are logarithms of pure imaginary numbers, such as $\log_e i = i(\pi/2)$, $\log_e 3i = \log_e 3 + i(\pi/2)$. Actually, $\log_e(x + iy)$ is many-valued because the amplitude θ of $x + iy$ is fixed only to an integral multiple of 2π radians. Hence, in any of the preceding examples, the logarithm value may be modified by such a multiple; e.g., $\log_e(-1) = \pi i,\ 3\pi i,\ -\pi i$, etc., and $\log_e i = (\pi/2)i,\ (5\pi/2)i,\ -(3\pi/2)i$, etc.

The function defined by $\log_e z$, where z is complex, is one of the basic *functions of a complex variable.* See **Power series**.

Logarithmic Computation See **Computation by logarithms** (syn.).

Logarithmic Coordinates The method of matching points on a line with positive real numbers so that the distance between two points is the difference of the logarithms of the

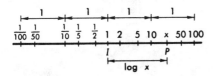

numbers. Such a *logarithmic scale* is determined by choosing a point I marked 1, and labeling the point P at a distance $\log x$ from I with the number x; x is then the *logarithmic coordinate* of P on the line. For example, 10 is located at a distance $\log 10$,

or 1 from I, and $\frac{1}{100}$ is located at a distance $\log \frac{1}{100}$, or -2 from I. On a logarithmic scale two numbers are a unit distance apart if their quotient is 10.

Logarithmic coordinates in the *plane* are defined by two rectangular axes, each marked with logarithmic scales; each pair of positive numbers (x, y) is matched with the point P in the plane having x, y as its logarithmic coordinates. The *logarithmic graph* of an equation in x and y is the set of its solutions (x, y) plotted in this logarithmic coordinate system.

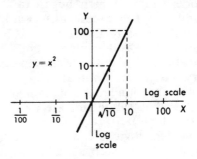

For example, the logarithmic graph of the equation $y = x^2$ is a line; more generally, the logarithmic graph of any equation $y = ax^n$ is a line.

The *semilogarithmic graph* of an equation is one with a uniform scale on one axis and a logarithmic scale on the other. These graphs are useful for equations of the form

$$y = k \cdot b^x;$$

the graphs of such equations appear as lines when the logarithmic scale is used along the y-axis.

Logarithmic Equation An equation containing a logarithm whose argument involves a variable, such as $x - \log x = 2$.

Logarithmic Series The power series expansion

$$\log_e(1 + x) = x - \frac{x^2}{2} + \frac{x^3}{3} - \frac{x^4}{4} + \cdots;$$

it converges to the logarithm value on the left for x between -1 and 1 (excluding -1, but including 1).

Logarithmic Spiral   See **Spiral**.

Logic   The study of the structure of statements and the formal laws of reasoning. Logic had its origins in the traditional syllogisms of the Greek philosopher Aristotle (fourth century B.C). Leibniz, in the seventeenth century, was a forerunner of modern logic, which began in the middle of the nineteenth century with the work of Boole, in what became known as Boolean algebra. The growth of logic in the twentieth century was greatly stimulated by problems in the foundations of mathematics. (Today, syllogisms are a minor part of logic).

Modern logic is characterized by its use of the algebraic and formal methods of mathematics; for this reason it is often referred to as "symbolic logic," or "mathematical logic." Subjects treated in this field include the algebra of propositions, quantifiers, sets, relations, and equality. Logical valudity (validity based on formal structure) is a prime aspect of logic. Modern logic also deals with the principles and methods of **deductive theory**; in this aspect it is referred to as *meta-mathematics*.

Ref. [89, 94, 115, 143].

Long Division and Multiplication Methods for carrying out these arithmetic operations in the decimal number system. Long division, for example, is a computational procedure in which the quotient is built up by a repetition of steps; in short division, this procedure is abbreviated, because of the simplicity of the divisor.

Longitude   See **Spherical coordinates**.

Lower Bound   See **Bound**.

Lowest Common Multiple   See **Common multiple**.

Lowest Terms   A fraction is in lowest terms in case its numerator and denominator are integers or polynomials which contain no common factors (other than ± 1).

Loxodromic Spiral (Syn.: Loxodrome; Rhumb line; Spherical helix) A curve on a sphere which cuts the meridians at a constant angle. A *complete loxodrome* is a double spiral with each pole of the meridians as a point which is endlessly encircled by the spiral. This curve is important in the history of navigation; in the sixteenth century it was erroneously believed that an arc of a loxodrome was the shortest distance between two points on the sphere (an arc of a great circle gives the least distance).

Lune   The portion of a sphere enclosed between two great semicircles having common endpoints, including the semicircles. The angle of the lune is the spherical angle formed by the

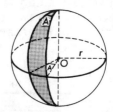

semicircles at a common endpoint. Its area equals $4\pi r^2 A/360$, where A is the degree measure of its angle, and r is the radius of the sphere.

M

Machine Intelligence (computer)

The performance of certain tasks by a computer ordinarily associated with human intelligence; also referred to as *artificial intelligence.* Typically, an important aspect of such use of a computer is to program in the feature of "learning"; that is, modifying and improving future performance on the basis of past experience. In this case, the programmed computer is often termed a *self-organizing,* or *self-adapting, system.* See **Computer program, Computer programming language**.

The following computer applications may be cited as examples of machine intelligence: (1) *pattern recognition,* such as the recognition of alphabetical characters and spoken language; (2) *machine translation of languages,* that is, the translation of written material in one language (say, Russian) into that in another language (say, English) without significant change of meaning; (3) *information retrieval,* that is, the automatic indexing, abstracting, and storage of written documents; (4) *real-time control,* in which the computer is programmed to control a system operating continuously in the real world, such as an air traffic system; (5) *problem-solving, game-playing,* and related activities, such as playing checkers or chess, proving theorems in geometry or logic, composing music, etc. See **Simulation**.
Ref. [91, 133, 146].

Maclaurin Series See **Taylor's theorem**.

Magic Square An *n*-by-*n* arrangement of the integers 1 through n^2 with the following property: the sum of the integers in any row, column, or diagonal is the same. The figure shows magic squares of orders 4 and 5, the order being the number of entries in a row or column. The subject of magic squares, as the name im-

12	7	9	6
13	2	16	3
8	11	5	10
1	14	4	15

9	2	25	18	11
3	21	19	12	10
22	20	13	6	4
16	14	7	5	23
15	8	1	24	17

plies, is a mathematical curiosity with many surprising features; they are supposed to have occurred more than 4,000 years ago in China. An unsolved problem concerns the number of possible squares of a given order. Apart from variations arising from rotations and reflections, there is one type of square of order 3, and 880 of order 4; the number of types of order 5 is unknown. Ref. [6, 12 46].

Magnitude Of a number or vector, its **absolute value**.

Major Arc Of a circle, the longer of two arcs which together make up the whole circle; the shorter is the *minor arc,* or *short arc.*

Major Axis of Ellipse The longer of its two perpendicular axes; usually denoted by *a*. The shorter is the minor axis; usually denoted by *b*. See **Ellipse**.

Major Axis of Ellipsoid The largest of its three axes, usually denoted by *a*. The intermediate axis is the *mean axis* and the smallest axis is the *minor axis,* usually denoted by *b* and *c*, respectively. See **Ellipsoid**.

Major Segment Of a circle, the larger of two segments that together comprise the entire region inside the circle; the smaller is the *minor segment.* See **Segment of circle**.

Mantissa of Logarithm The positive

decimal part of the common logarithm; the integral part is the *characteristic*. See **Computation by logarithms**.

Many-valued Function (Syn.: Multiple-valued function) A **correspondence** from a set *A* to a set *B* in which at least one member of *A* is matched with more than one member of *B*. An example is the correspondence $y^2 = x$ from numbers *x* to numbers *y*; another is the correspondence $y = $ arc tan *x*. The many-valued function stands in contrast to the single-valued function (or, simply, function). These correspondences can be distinguished by their graphs—the graph of a (single-valued) function has at most one point lying above each *x*-coordinate, while the graph of the many-valued function has at least two points above some *x*-coordinate. Sometimes the term "function" is used to include both the single-valued and many-valued function; in this case, "function" is synonymous with "correspondence." See **Implicit function, Inverse of function**.

Map or Mapping See **Function** (syn.).

Markoff Process Consider a chance process, or behavior, which is described by "states" at successive times 1, 2, 3, etc.; it is a *Markoff chain* in case (1) the change of state from one time to the next depends upon chance elements, and (2) the state at the "present" time, *n*, influences future states, but the particular steps by which the present state was reached does not influence future states. As an example, consider the behavior of a given stock in the market; the state is taken as its daily closing price. Item (1) above applies

since this price depends upon chance elements. However, the sequence of prices day after day will form a Markoff chain in case the price for any given day depends only on the price of the previous day, as far as the history of prices is concerned; if it depends upon whether the price has been falling or rising, for instance, then condition (2) above fails.

By a *Markoff process* is often meant a process in which the states unfold either *continuously,* or in discrete steps, as above; here again, future states depend upon the present state but not upon how it was attained. Briefly, a Markoff process is a **stochastic process** with no "memory." Markoff processes occur, for example, in the description of physical systems and genetic processes.

Mathematical Expectation See **Expected value** (syn.).

Mathematical Induction A principle for proving a proposition P(*n*) concerning an arbitrary natural number *n*, described by the following two steps: **(1)** prove P(1), that is, the proposition when $n = 1$; **(2)** prove that for any natural number *k*, the hypothesis P(*k*) implies the conclusion P($k + 1$). The verification of steps **(1)** and **(2)** allows the assertion that every proposition in the infinite chain P(1), P(2), P(3), ... holds; the justification for this is the so-called *axiom of induction* concerning the **natural numbers**. An informal justification is the following: P(1) holds by step **(1)**; since P(1) holds, P(2) holds by step **(2)**; since P(2) holds, P(3) holds by step **(2)** also; and so on to any particular proposition in the chain.

As an example, consider the following proposition P(*n*), "The sum of the angles of a (convex) polygon of $n + 2$ sides is $n \cdot 180°$." That is, P(1) states that the sum of the angles of a triangle is 180°, P(2) that the sum of the angles of a quadrilateral is 360°, and so on. The proof of P(n) for every n, by mathematical induction, has as its first step the proof of P(1); suppose this to be done. The

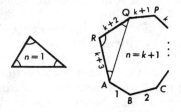

second step is to show that the proposition holds for $k + 3$ sides ($n = k + 1$) provided it holds for $k + 2$ sides ($n = k$). To do this consider the construction in the figure: regard the $(k + 3)$-sided polygon $AB \cdots PQRA$, as the $(k + 2)$-sided polygon $AB \cdots PQA$ with one more triangle QRA attached. By assumption, the proposition holds for the latter polygon, and so its angles add up to $k \cdot 180°$. From the first step, the angles of QRA add up to 180°; hence, the sum of the angles of the larger polygon is 180° $+ k \cdot 180°$, or $(k + 1) \cdot 180°$. This completes the second step of the proof, and hence the entire proof.

Both steps of mathematical induction are essential. For example, omission of the first step permits a "proof" of the false proposition that $n = n + 1$, for every natural number n. Proof: Assume the proposition when n is k, that is, $k = k + 1$; add 1 to both sides, obtaining $k + 1 = k + 2$; but this is the proposition when n is $k + 1$—completing the proof (without the first step). In a proof by induction, the first step is necessary to give a starting point for the chain process established by the second step.

Mathematical Programming

Mathematical induction need not begin with $n = 1$; if step (1) uses some other whole number, say r, the entire proof will establish the chain of statements beginning with P(r). Another variation is this: it is legitimate to assume not only P(k) in step (2) but any preceding proposition P($k - 1$), P($k - 2$), . . . , that might be useful [with the precaution that P(s) must not be assumed for s below the initial value r].

Mathematical induction provides the mathematician with his underlying hold on "infinity"; it is a "finite" technique for managing an infinite number of cases. An early statement of the principle occurs in the work of Pascal in the middle of the seventeenth century. Induction can be extended to transfinite induction, which reaches out to the transfinite numbers beyond the collection of natural numbers.

Ref. [29, 120].

Mathematical Programming The theory and technique of finding an *optimum* (maximum or minimum) *value* of a function of many variables, with the variables subject to restraints, usually in the form of equations or inequalities. Problems of this type arise in the field of **operations research**; they may involve a large number of variables, and frequently require the computational power of the electronic digital computer for their solution.

Linear programming deals with functions and conditions which are linear in the variables. An example is the problem of maximizing the function $x + y$, subject to the restraints (conditions) $x \geq 0$, $y \geq 0$, $x - 2y \leq 1$, $x + 2y \leq 4$. These limit (x, y) within or on the polygon bounded by the coordinate axes and the lines $x - 2y = 1$ and $x + 2y = 4$; the problem can be phrased as

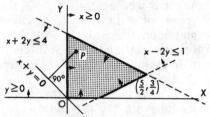

that of finding among all points P in this region, the one whose (perpendicular) distance from the line $x + y = 0$ is a maximum. The solution is the vertex $(\frac{5}{2}, \frac{3}{4})$. The occurrence of the optimum value at a vertex is typical of linear programming; this example also illustrates the common appearance of simultaneous inequalities in mathematical programming. Algorithms have been developed to solve any linear programming problem. The *simplex method* is such an algorithm; it shows how to proceed systematically from vertex to vertex until an optimum is reached in a finite number of steps.

Dynamic programming deals with optimization problems that involve sequential processes; it develops algorithms in situations, for example, where the variables x_1, x_2, x_3, etc. appear in a time sequence.

Ref. [26, 50, 75, 130].

Mathematical System   Broadly, a collection of concepts and assumptions that deal with a unified aspect of mathematics; more specifically, one or more sets of entities and a number of operations and relations involving them. For example, the points and lines of the plane and the relations expressed in the axioms and postulates of ordinary plane geometry constitute one mathematical system; the real numbers and the properties that characterize them make up another mathematical system; the **group** is a mathematical system, as is the **field**. Two mathematical systems which describe the same underlying system in different forms are called **isomorphic**.

A mathematical system is generally expressed as a **deductive theory**; the study of the foundations of geometry by Hilbert (about 1900) was a major factor in establishing this approach in the twentieth century. Today, the mathematician recognizes a mathematical system as a construction of the mind whose assumptions can be varied as he chooses; this modern view differs from centuries of previous thinking in which mathematics was seen as an attempt to uncover true relationships as they existed in some external sense.

Mathematics   The investigation of number, space, and the many generalizations of these concepts created by the intellectual genius of man. Two aspects of mathematics show the dual role of the mathematician as artist and artisan. One is *pure,* or *abstract, mathematics,* which has as its general purpose the advance of mathematical knowledge for its own sake; this search for new and significant relationships is guided by the state of the field and the mathematical culture at a given point in history. The other is *applied mathematics,* which is the "useful" face of mathematics; it is concerned with the development of mathematical tools for the solution of problems in physics, chemistry, astronomy, and the many fields of knowledge that depend upon mathematics. The problems of applied mathematics often motivate the abstract research of pure mathematics; in turn, theories of pure mathematics often find application in unexpected ways many years after their appearance. These two aspects began to first appear with the fundamental work of Newton on gravitation and motion in the seventeenth century.

Within mathematics as a whole, three major branches are often distinguished—*geometry, algebra,* and *analysis.* Very broadly, **geometry** is concerned with space, **algebra** with numbers and their abstractions, and analysis with continuity and limits. A distinction sometimes made between algebra and analysis is that the former deals with "finite" processes and the latter with "infinite" processes. It is generally agreed that mathematics as a deductive science was born with Greek geometry more than 2,000 years ago; since then, geometry has continued to be a prime field of mathematical invention. Analysis began with the invention of the **calculus** during the seventeenth century, which marked the beginning of modern mathematics; analysis includes many subbranches that grew out of the calculus. Algebra has an ancient history, but as it would be recognized today, algebra evolved in the sixteenth and seventeenth centuries. Contrary to popular ideas, the invention of new mathematics is going on today at a greater rate and in a wider range of subjects than ever before. Characteristic of modern mathematics is the intermingling of its various branches; for example, geometry is typically studied by algebraic-analytic methods. To the practicing mathematician, both pure and applied, the classifications are largely a philosophical and historical matter.

[*Biography* 1, 10, 30, 58, 59, 62, 68, 76, 85, 93, 116, 123].
[*General* 2, 8, 11, 15, 25, 28, 34, 42, 44, 56, 64, 69, 73, 78, 79, 94,

100, 109, 117, 126, 134, 135, 136, 137, 138, 139, 148].
[*History* 9, 17, 24, 39, 40, 43, 67, 71, 86, 132].

Matrix A square matrix of numbers is represented by an array such as
$$\begin{pmatrix} a & b \\ c & d \end{pmatrix} \text{ or } \left\| \begin{matrix} a & b \\ c & d \end{matrix} \right\|$$

This is a two-by-two matrix, or matrix of *order two;* the entries a, b, c, d are the *elements* of this matrix. A square matrix of *order n* is represented by an *n*-by-*n* array with n^2 elements. Square matrices may be viewed as a generalization of ordinary numbers (or square matrices of order one); they are subject to operations of "addition" and "multiplication" which are generalizations of those on numbers. For 2-by-2 matrices, the operations are the following:
$$\begin{pmatrix} a & b \\ c & d \end{pmatrix} + \begin{pmatrix} e & f \\ g & h \end{pmatrix}$$
$$= \begin{pmatrix} a+e & b+f \\ c+g & d+h \end{pmatrix}$$
$$\begin{pmatrix} a & b \\ c & d \end{pmatrix} \times \begin{pmatrix} e & f \\ g & h \end{pmatrix}$$
$$= \begin{pmatrix} ae+bg & af+bh \\ ce+dg & cf+dh \end{pmatrix}$$

Similar definitions apply to *n*-by-*n* matrices. See **Algebra of matrices, Determinant.**

A *rectangular matrix* is represented by an *m*-by-*n* array of $m \cdot n$ elements. Matrices, both square and rectangular may be interpreted in many useful ways. They symbolize *transformations* of a space (for example, the coefficients in a transformation of coordinates); they represent a set of *vectors* (the row, or column, vectors); etc. They are also important in the study of simultaneous linear equations.

Ref. [26, 32, 75, 127].

Matrix of Coefficients Of a set of simultaneous linear equations, the matrix represented by the coefficients of the variables, in an appropriate arrangement. For example, the set of equations

$$3x - 2y + z = 1$$
$$x + y - z = 2$$
$$x + 5y + 2z = -3$$

has the matrix of coefficients

$$\begin{pmatrix} 3 & -2 & 1 \\ 1 & 1 & -1 \\ 1 & 5 & 2 \end{pmatrix}$$

A similar description applies to any number of linear equations in any number of unknowns. See **Cramer's rule**.

Maximum A *relative maximum* (or, simply, *maximum*) of a **function of a real variable** is a value $f(a)$ of the function which is greater than values $f(x)$ for x in some interval about a, $x \neq a$ (often called *proper* maximum). $f(a)$ is an *absolute maximum* in case it is greater than or equal to $f(x)$ for all values of x. (Similar definitions apply to "minimum," with "greater than" replaced by "less than.") These notions apply, also, to functions of any number of variables; in general, a maximum (minimum) is a largest (smallest) value of some class of values to which it belongs.

For a function $f(x)$, a necessary condition for a (relative) maximum or minimum at $x = a$ is that the derivative of $f(x)$ vanish there. Similarly, a necessary condition for a function $f(x, y)$ of two variables to have a maximum or minimum at (a, b) is for both its partial derivatives to vanish there (an analogous statement applies for any number of variables). These are the conditions ordinarily used in the calculus to find maxima and minima.

Mean (Syn.: Average) For *two numbers, a* and *b,* the *arithmetic mean m,* the *geometric mean g,* and the *harmonic mean h* are defined, respectively, by the equations

$$m = \frac{(a + b)}{2}; \ g = \sqrt{ab}; \ \frac{1}{h} = \frac{1}{2}\left(\frac{1}{a} + \frac{1}{b}\right).$$

(The term "mean" or "average" is often used for the arithmetic mean.) For positive numbers a and b the arithmetic mean is never less than the geometric mean, which in turn is never less than the harmonic mean. For example, when a, b are 3, 12, these means, in turn, are 7.5, 6, and 5.8. An arithmetic progression is a progression in which any term is the arithmetic mean of its two neighbors; similarly, a geometric progression (harmonic progression) is one in which any term is the geometric (harmonic) mean of its neighbors.

For *n numbers, a_1, a_2, ... a_n,* the definitions of the three means are the following:

$$m = \frac{1}{n}(a_1 + a_2 + \cdots + a_n),$$
$$g = \sqrt[n]{a_1 a_2 \cdots a_n},$$
$$\frac{1}{h} = \frac{1}{n}\left(\frac{1}{a_1} + \frac{1}{a_2} + \cdots + \frac{1}{a_n}\right)$$

The same inequality relationships among the three means hold as before, when the a's are positive numbers. An interesting feature of the arithmetic mean m is the following "minimal" property: suppose the number

$$(a_1 - x)^2 + (a_2 - x)^2 + \cdots + (a_n - x)^2$$

is used as a measure of the deviation of the a's from the single number x; then this deviation has its smallest value when x is the arithmetic mean of the a's. Other types of means are also used; in general, a mean is a measure of the "central tendency" of a set of numbers. See **Mean** (statistics), **Mean value of function**.

Ref. [42, 44].

Mean Axis   See **Major axis**.

Mean Proportional   Of two numbers a and b, the number x that satisfies the proportion $a/x = x/b$; the solution is the geometric mean $\sqrt{ab}$. The mean proportional occurs in plane geometry; for example, a half-chord x of a circle is the mean

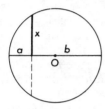

proportional of the two segments a and b into which it divides the perpendicular diameter.

Mean (statistics)   Of a set of data or measurements, its *arithmetic mean;* more specifically, if measurement a_1 occurs f_1 times, a_2 occurs f_2 times, etc., the (statistical) mean is $(1/n)(f_1 \cdot a_1 + f_2 \cdot a_2 + \cdots)$, where n, the total number of measurements, equals $f_1 + f_2 + \cdots$. For example, suppose the following measurements are obtained for the height of 10 individuals (in inches): three with height 69, two with height 70, and five with height 71. Then the mean height is

$$\frac{(3 \cdot 69 + 2 \cdot 70 + 5 \cdot 71)}{10} = 70.2.$$

Other estimates of the central tendency of data are the *median* and the *mode,* the first being the middle value and the second the most frequent value. In the example, 70 is the median and 71 the mode.   See **Expected value, Standard deviation**.

Mean Terms of Proportion   The second and third terms of a proportion; hence, in $a/b = c/d$, the terms b and c (a and d are the *extreme terms*).

Mean Value of Function (Syn.: Mean ordinate of function)   A generalization of the arithmetic average of a finite set of numbers to that of a continuous set of functional values $f(x)$. Geometrically, the mean value of $f(x)$ on the interval from $x = a$ to $x = b$ is that ordinate value m for which the rectangular area $m(b - a)$ equals the area bounded by the

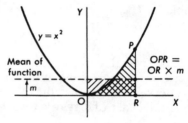

graph of $y = f(x)$, the x-axis, and the two vertical lines through $x = a$ and $x = b$ (see figure, where $a = 0, b = R$). In the calculus, this mean value is given in terms of the integral of $f(x)$ as follows:

$$m = \frac{1}{(b - a)} \int_a^b f(x)dx.$$

For example, when $f(x) = x^2$, and the interval is $x = 0$ to $x = 1$, the mean value equals $\frac{1}{3}$.

Mean Value Theorem (differential calculus)   For a function $f(x)$, the following assertion: if P and Q are two points on the graph of $y = f(x)$ and l is the line through P and Q, then at some point R on the graph between P and Q the tangent line is parallel to l. Put otherwise, if $a < b$, then there is a value c between a and

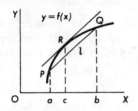

b ($a < c < b$) such that

$$f(b) - f(a) = (b - a)f'(c)$$

[here $f'(x)$ is the derivative of $f(x)$]. This formula is also called the *first law of the mean* for derivatives. It is valid under the assumption, for instance, that $f(x)$ and $f'(x)$ are defined (finite) at every point on the closed interval from a to b. As an example, let $f(x) = x^2$; then $f'(x) = 2x$ and, for given a and b,

$$b^2 - a^2 = (b - a)(2c).$$

In this special case, solving for c gives $c = (a + b)/2$, the midpoint of the interval. The mean value theorem is a special case of **Taylor's theorem.**

Mean Value Theorem (integral calculus) For a function $f(x)$, the following assertion: the area under the graph of $y = f(x)$ over an interval of the x-axis equals the length of this interval times some ordinate value $f(c)$, with c in the given interval. More precisely, if $a < b$, then there is a value c lying in the interval from a to b ($a \leq c \leq b$) such that

$$\int_a^b f(x)dx = (b - a)f(c).$$

This formula is also called the *first law of the mean* for integrals; the value $f(c)$ is the *mean value* of the function over the interval from a to b. It is valid under the assumption, for example, that $f(x)$ is continuous in the closed interval. As an example, let $f(x) = x^2$, $a = 0$; then

$$\int_0^b x^2 dx = b \cdot c^2.$$

Evaluating the left side directly gives $b^3/3$; then solving for c gives $c = b/\sqrt{3}$. In practice, the formula may be used to estimate a definite integral without the need of evaluating it (which may be difficult).

Measure Of a geometric, or other, entity, a number which makes precise some concept of the "size" of the entity. Particular examples of measures of geometric objects are *length, area, volume, degree of angle, radian,* and *steradian.* A specific numerical measure depends upon the selection of a *unit of measurement;* the measure of an object can then be thought of as the number of times it contains an object of unit measure; for example, the area of a plane figure is the number of times it contains a unit square.

Linear measure means length, *square measure* means area, *cubic measure* means volume. *Angular,* or *circular, measure* means the measure of angles. In elementary geometry the "measure" of a solid means its volume, the "measure" of a two-dimensional figure means its area, and the "measure" of a line segment or curve means its length.

Measurement The act or result of determining the measure of an entity. Physical measurement, as of a length with a ruler, generally gives an **approximate number**, or estimate. The *precision* of a measurement expressed in decimal form is the unit value of the last decimal place; for example, if a length is given as 1.72 inches, the precision is $\frac{1}{100}$ of an inch, while if the length is given as 1.7236, the precision is $\frac{1}{10,000}$ of an inch. The **error** of a measurement is the difference between it and the true value; the *accuracy* of a measurement is usually expressed in terms of the error, in some form such as the relative error.

Median (geometry)   Of a *triangle,* a line segment from a vertex to the midpoint of the opposite side. The three medians of a triangle meet in a single point; this is the median point, or **centroid of the plane figure**, and it is two-thirds of the way from the vertex along any median.

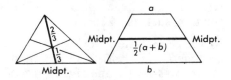

For a trapezoid, the median, or *midline,* is the line segment joining the midpoints of the nonparallel sides. It is parallel to the bases, and its length is the arithmetic average of the lengths of the bases. The area of a trapezoid is the height times the length of the median.

Median (statistics)   Of an odd number of increasing numerical values, the middle value; for example, the set {2, 11, 12, 14, 23} has 12 as its median. For an even number of values, the median is sometimes taken as the average of the two middle values.   See **Mean** (statistics).

Mega-   One million, used as a prefix; for example, a hydrogen bomb of 6 megatons is one with the explosive power of 6,000,000 tons of TNT.

Member of Equation   The expression on either side of the equality sign " $=$ " of an equation. For example, in $2x - 1 = 4x^2 + 3$, $2x - 1$ is the left, or first, member and $4x^2 + 3$ is the right, or second, member.

Member of Set (Syn.: Element of set) Any one of the individual things belonging to a **set**; the symbolic expression " $a \, \varepsilon \, A$ " denotes that a is a member of the set A. (" ε " is the Greek letter "epsilon"). For example, if A is the set of perfect squares, then $9 \, \varepsilon \, a$, but $8 \, \xi \, A$ (that is, 8 is not a member of A).

Meridian of Sphere   Any great circle which passes through a point on the sphere designated as a *pole*.

Meridian Section   See **Surface of revolution**.

Mersenne Number   A positive integer of the form $2^p - 1$, where p is a prime number (named after the seventeenth century French mathematician and priest Mersenne). A question in the theory of numbers is the determination of the values of p for which $2^p - 1$ is itself a prime number; for example, when p is 2, 3, 5, 7, or 13 the Mersenne number is prime, while when p is 11, 23 or 29, it is not; other such results are known. See **Perfect number**.
  Ref. [6].

Meta-Mathematics   The study of the principles of deductive theory as applied to theories of logic and mathematics; it belongs to the field of logic itself.   Ref. [41].

Metric Space   The following abstraction of ordinary space and the notion of **distance**. Let A be a set of entities, or "points," and suppose that for every pair of points P, Q of A there is defined a nonnegative number $d(P, Q)$, called the "distance" from P to Q; then A is a metric space with distance d in case the following *axioms* hold: **(1)** $d(P, Q) = 0$ if, and only if, P and Q are identical; **(2)** $d(P, Q) = d(Q, P)$ (the distance from P to Q equals the distance from Q to P); and **(3)** $d(P, Q) + d(Q, R) \geq$

$d(P, R)$ (the *triangle inequality*). These axioms provide a basis for the study of distance in abstract spaces.

Metric System The decimal system of measure of lengths and weights, based upon the meter and gram as the units of length and weight, respectively. It was established about 1800, and is used in scientific work.
Ref. [118, 129].

Micro- One millionth, used as a prefix; for example, a microsecond is a millionth of a second.

Midline of Trapezoid See **Median** (geometry).

Midpoint of Line Segment The point on a segment which divides it into two equal segments. On a linear scale, the midpoint between x_1 and x_2 is $\frac{1}{2}(x_1 + x_2)$. In the plane with rectangular coordinates, the midpoint $(\bar{x}, \bar{y})$ between (x_1, y_1) and (x_2, y_2) is given by

$$\bar{x} = \frac{(x_1 + x_2)}{2}$$

$$\bar{y} = \frac{(y_1 + y_2)}{2}.$$

See **Division of line segment**.

Milli- One thousandth, used as a prefix; for example, a millimeter is a thousandth of a meter.

Minimal Surface See **Surface**.

Minimax Principle See **Theory of games**.

Minimum See **Maximum**.

Minor See **Major**.

Minuend In the difference $a - b$, a is the minuend and b is the *subtrahend*. See **Subtraction**.

Minus Sign (Syn.: Negative sign) In arithmetic, the symbol " $-$," denoting the operation of subtraction as in

$8 - 5$, or $a - b$. It is also used to denote the negative of a number; as in -3 or $-a$. Both uses occur in the formula $0 - a = -a$, for example. The symbol was introduced about 1500.

Minute In degree measure, one-sixtieth of a degree of angle.

Mixed Decimal In the decimal number system, a string of digits representing an integer plus a decimal fraction, such as 14.85.

Mixed Expression or Number In arithmetic (algebra), a mixed number (expression) is one of the form of an integer (polynomial) plus a proper fraction. Examples are $2 + \frac{3}{5}$ (abbreviated $2\frac{3}{5}$) and

$$2x^2 + 2x - 1 + \frac{x + 2}{x^2 - x + 3}.$$

An improper fraction can always be reduced to a mixed expression by division   (see **Division of whole numbers**, **Division of polynomials**).

Möbius Strip (Syn.: Möbius band) A twisted surface in space formed by turning one side of a rectangle through 180° (relative to the opposite side) and joining it to the opposite side; it is named after the nineteenth century German mathematician Möbius. A cylinder, by contrast, is formed by joining the sides without turning. The Möbius strip

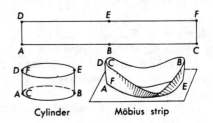

Cylinder   Möbius strip

has unusual properties. For one thing, it is a *one-sided surface;* that is, any point P on it can be joined to its "opposite" P' (or to any point) by a path that does not cross the edge of the surface. (This is in striking contrast to the ordinary surface in space, which is a *two-sided surface*.) For another thing, when the Möbius strip is cut along the center line of the strip it does not fall into two parts; it changes to a single two-sided surface. The study of such properties of figures belongs to the field of topology. Ref. [28,88].

Mode   In statistics, the most frequent value of a set of observations. See **Mean** (statistics).

Model   In applied mathematics, the representation of a real system in terms of mathematical relations. The mathematical expression of real behavior allows the methods and logic of mathematics to be applied to the phenomena of the physical world. The scientific advance of a subject is often closely connected with the increased use of mathematical methods. The modern digital computer is playing an important role in the wider use of mathematical models; the reason is that it permits the consideration of theoretical models which would otherwise be too involved for practical computation. See **Simulation**.

The term "model" also means an interpretation of an abstract deductive theory which satisfies the axioms of the theory. For example, the integers under the operation of addition comprise a model of the *group*.

Modulus of Common Logarithm
The logarithm of the number e to the base 10; it has the approximate value .43429. It appears in the following formula for converting natural loga-

rithms into common logarithms:

$$\log N = .43429 \log_e N$$

Modulus of Complex Number   See **Absolute value of complex number** (syn.).

Modulus of Congruence   See **Congruent integers**.

Modus Ponens   See **Inference**.

Monomial   An algebraic expression which is a product of constants and variables, such as $5ax^2$. When $4a^2 - 2ax + 6ax^2$ is factored as $2a(2a - x + 3x^2)$, the factor $2a$ is a *monomial factor*.

Monotonic   Always increasing, or always decreasing; see **Sequence**, **Function of a real variable**.

Monte Carlo Method   As a method of numerical solution, broadly, one which involves chance, or random, elements and continued sampling of values of these elements. The solution x of a problem may be obtained by this method by setting up mathematical relationships describing a **stochastic process** (chance process) and using it as follows; obtain a series of estimates of x by repeated runs through the process (because of the chance elements, these estimates will generally vary from run to run); approximate the solution x as the average value of these estimates. The stochastic process may correspond directly to the physical process of the problem, or it may be an artificial device. The computations often require a high-speed, automatic computer and the use of **random numbers**.   See **Simulation**.

Multinomial   An algebraic expression which is the sum of two or more monomials (terms). The *multinomial theorem* is the generalization of the *binomial theorem* to the expansion of

173

$(x_1 + x_2 + \cdots + x_p)^n$.

Multiple Of an integer (polynomial), an integer (polynomial) which has the given one as a **factor**. For example, 18 is a multiple of 3, and $x^2 - 1$ is a multiple of $x + 1$. Thus, a multiple is a product of the given integer (polynomial) with another. See **Common multiple**.

Multiple Integral The **double integral** as well as integrals over three-dimensional and higher-dimensional regions.

Multiple Root (Syn.: Repeated root) Of an equation, a root which occurs more than once; more precisely, r is a *root of order n* of the polynomial equation $p(x) = 0$ in case $(x - r)^n$ is a factor of $p(x)$—this being the highest power which is a factor. For example, the cubic equation $x^3 - 3x^2 + 4 = 0$ can be written $(x - 2)^2(x + 1) = 0$; hence, it has 2 as a double root, or root of order 2; the other root, -1, is a *simple root*. Also, in the equation

$$(x - 5)^4(x + 6)^3(x - 3) = 0,$$

5 is a root of order four, -6 a triple root, and 3 a simple root. The following general statement holds for multiple roots: Suppose r is a root of $p(x) = 0$; then it will be a root of order n if and only if it is a root of order $n - 1$ of $d[p(x)]/dx = 0$, where the left side is the *derivative* of $p(x)$. For example, $x^3 - 3x^2 + 4 = 0$ had 2 as a double root and -1 as a simple root; taking the derivative gives $3x^2 - 6x = 0$, or $3x(x - 2)$ which has 2 as a simple root and does not have -1 as a root at all ("root of order 0" is understood as no root). See **Discriminant**.

Multiple-Valued Function See **Many-valued function** (syn.).

Multiplicand When, in a product, one number is thought of as being "multiplied by" another, the first is called the *multiplicand* and the second the *multiplier;* the commutative law of multiplication guarantees that a multiplied by b equals b multiplied by a.

Multiplication Multiplication of numbers is one of the fundamental operations of arithmetic. The result of combining numbers a and b by this operation is the *product* of the numbers, and is denoted by $a \times b$, $a \cdot b$, or, most simply, ab (notation introduced in the seventeenth century). The product $m \cdot n$ of whole numbers m and n can be thought of as the sum $n + n + \cdots + n$ (n taken m times). As the concept of number is extended, so is the notion of multiplication. In arithmetic, methods are given for carrying out multiplication of numbers in various forms. For example, multiplication in the decimal number system is carried out by long multiplication. **Algebraic multiplication** shows how to multiply signed numbers; also, see **Fraction**, **Radical**.

Multiplication is an example of a *binary operation*; further, it is commutative, that is, $a \cdot b = b \cdot a$, and associative, that is, $(ab)c = a(bc)$. These properties ensure that a product of a finite number of factors is unaffected by the order of carrying out the individual products. For example, the product of 3, 4, and 5 can be written $(3 \cdot 4) \cdot 5$ to give $12 \cdot 5$, or 60; it can also be written $4 \cdot (5 \cdot 3)$ to give $4 \cdot 15$, or 60. The number 1 is the *identity element* of multiplication, that is, $1 \cdot a = a$. The number 0 also has a special role; it reduces any product to zero, that is, $0 \cdot a = 0$. The distributive law is the formula $a \cdot (x + y) = a \cdot x + a \cdot y$; it provides a connection between multiplication and addition; for example, this principle is the basis of long multiplication of decimal numbers, and of factoring and multiplying polynomials. See **Field**.

Multiplication by Logarithms See **Computation by logarithms**.

Multiplication of Complex Numbers See **Complex number**.

Multiplication of Matrices See **Matrix**.

Multiplication of Polynomials The product of two polynomials can be carried out by multiplying each term of one into each term of the other, and then adding similar terms. For example,

$$(x^2 + 2x - 1)(2x^2 - 3x + 4)$$
$$= x^2(2x^2 - 3x + 4) + 2x(2x^2 - 3x + 4)$$
$$\qquad - (2x^2 - 3x + 4)$$
$$= 2x^4 - 3x^3 + 4x^2 + 4x^3 - 6x^2$$
$$\qquad + 8x - 2x^2 + 3x - 4$$
$$= 2x^4 + x^3 - 4x^2 + 11x - 4.$$

Multiplication of Vectors See **Vector**.

Multiplier See **Multiplicand**.

Mutually Exclusive The several alternative outcomes of an *event* are mutually exclusive if the occurrence of one excludes the occurrence of any of the others; for example, the appearance of a seven, eight, or nine, are three mutually exclusive outcomes in throwing two dice. Outcomes are *exhaustive* if they include all possible alternatives; thus, the outcomes 2, 3, 4, 5, 6, 7, 8, 9, 10, 11 or 12, are the eleven exhaustive alternatives in a throw of two dice.

Several *sets* are mutually exclusive if no two have members in common; they are exhaustive of a given set, if together they contain all members of the given set. For example, {0, 1, 3, 6}, {2, 4, 8}, {5, 7, 9} are mutually exclusive sets; they are also exhaustive of the integers 0 through 9. See **Partition, Probability**.

N

Napierian (or Naperian) Logarithm See **Natural logarithm** (syn.).

N

Napier's analogies (Syn.: Napier's formulas) In spherical trigonometry, the following relations among the sides a, b, c and the opposite angles A, B, C of a spherical triangle:

$$\frac{\sin \tfrac{1}{2}(A - B)}{\sin \tfrac{1}{2}(A + B)} = \frac{\tan \tfrac{1}{2}(a - b)}{\tan \tfrac{1}{2}c}$$

$$\frac{\cos \tfrac{1}{2}(A - B)}{\cos \tfrac{1}{2}(A + B)} = \frac{\tan \tfrac{1}{2}(a + b)}{\tan \tfrac{1}{2}c}$$

$$\frac{\sin \tfrac{1}{2}(a - b)}{\sin \tfrac{1}{2}(a + b)} = \frac{\tan \tfrac{1}{2}(A - B)}{\cot \tfrac{1}{2}C}$$

$$\frac{\cos \tfrac{1}{2}(a - b)}{\cos \tfrac{1}{2}(a + b)} = \frac{\tan \tfrac{1}{2}(A + B)}{\cot \tfrac{1}{2}C}$$

These formulas are useful for the **solution of an oblique spherical triangle** when two sides (angles) and the included angle (side) are given. The Scotsman Napier is best known as the inventor of logarithms in the early part of the seventeenth century.

Napier's Rules of Circular Parts A device for recalling the formulas used in the solution of the right spherical triangle. Let A, B, C be the angles with C as right angle, and let

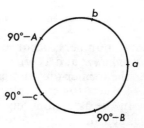

a, b, c be the opposite sides. Arrange a, b and the complements $90° - A$,

90° − *c*, 90° − *B* on a circle as shown. Each of these is termed a *circular part;* each circular part has two adjacent parts and two opposite parts. Napier's rules are the following: **(1)** the sine of any circular part equals the product of the tangents of the adjacent parts; **(2)** the sine of any circular part equals the product of the cosines of the opposite parts. This leads to ten relations; for example, rule **(2)** yields sin *a* = cos (90° − *A*) cos (90° − *c*), or

$$\sin a = \sin A \sin c.$$

Nappe   Either of the two portions of a **conical surface** or **pyramidal surface** entirely on one side of the vertex.

Natural Logarithm (Syn.: Napierian logarithm)   The logarithm to the base *e*; it is used principally in theoretical work, whereas the common logarithm (base 10) is used in computation.

Natural Number (Syn.: Whole number)   Any one of the numbers 1, 2, 3, ... The natural numbers are the basis for all ordinary **numbers** (integers, rational numbers, real numbers) in that the latter can be constructed out of the natural numbers by mathematical processes. The principle that the natural numbers form an unending sequence is sometimes referred to as the *axiom of infinity.*

Natural numbers occur both as *cardinal numbers* and as *ordinal numbers.* As the former they indicate the "size" of a set; for example, this is the use in the assertion "eight people attended the party." As ordinal numbers they indicate position in an ordered sequence; for example, this is the use in the assertion "he is the

eighth person to come." In English, ordinal numbers are expressed as *first, second, third, fourth,* and so on. The (finite) natural numbers and the arithmetic of such numbers can be extended to *transfinite numbers,* which measure or order infinite sets.

It is possible to describe the natural numbers as a deductive system based on axioms, although this is not commonly done in elementary mathematics. In the *Peano postulates,* the terms *natural number,* and *successor* are taken as primitive, or undefined, and the following four postulates are assumed. **(1)** Every natural number has a successor, which is another natural number. **(2)** There is a unique natural number, called "1," which is the successor of no natural number. **(3)** Different natural numbers have different successors. **(4)** Any collection of natural numbers which contains 1 and which contains the successor of every one of its members, is the set of all natural numbers. The first three postulates state that the successor relation is a one-to-one correspondence from the set of natural numbers to the set of natural numbers with 1 omitted. The last postulate is the axiom of induction, which is the basis of **mathematical induction**.

From these postulates the individual natural numbers 1, 2, 3, etc., can be described, the operations of addition and multiplication defined, and all the rules of arithmetic deduced. For example, the number 2 is given as the successor of 1, the number 3 as the successor of 2, and so on. Addition, for example, is defined as follows: *n* + 1 is defined as the successor of *n*, *n* + 2 as the successor of *n* + 1, *n* + 3 as the successor of *n* + 2, and so on, to any sum *n* + *m*. This deductive approach was formulated by the Italian mathematician and logician Peano near the end of the nineteenth century.

Ref. [44, 76, 134].

Necessary Condition   One **condition** P is necessary for another Q in case P holds whenever Q holds; that is, Q implies P.

Negation   See **Denial** (syn.).

Negative   A *negative number* is a number less than 0. The negative numbers lie to the left of 0 on a linear scale, the *positive numbers* to the right of 0. The sum of negative numbers is negative, while the product or quotient of negative numbers is a positive number.

The *negative of a number b*, denoted by $-b$, is the number which, added to b, yields the sum 0. (It is the "inverse" of b with respect to additions). For example, the negative of 3 is -3, of -5 is 5, of 0 is 0. (Notice that $-b$ is not necessarily a negative number; this is so only when b is positive.) Some properties are the following:

$$-0 = 0,$$
$$-(-a) = a,$$
$$a + (-b) = a - b,$$
$$-(a + b) = -a - b = (-a) + (-b),$$
$$-(a - b) = (-a) + b.$$

These rules show that in taking the negative of a sum or a difference the negative sign is carried to the individual terms; for example,

$$-(a - b + c) = -a + b - c,$$
$$-(-2x^2 + 3x - 7) = 2x^2 - 3x + 7.$$

In the early history of mathematics negative numbers were at first regarded as meaningless or mysterious entities, much as complex numbers were later. By the middle of the seventeenth century, operations with them were well accepted, although a rigorous logical basis had to wait until the beginning of the nineteenth century.

Negative Angle   An **angle** as a clockwise rotation.

Negative Exponent   In arithmetic, a^{-p} is defined as $1/a^p$, with p positive. See **Exponent**.

Negative Sign   See **Minus sign** (syn.).

Newton's Method   A method of successive approximations for finding roots of an equation $f(x) = 0$; it is based upon replacing a piece of a curve by a portion of a tangent line to the curve. If x_0 is a first estimate of a root, the next estimate x_1 is given by

$$x_1 = x_0 - \frac{f(x_0)}{f'(x_0)}$$

[here, $f'(x)$ is the derivative of $f(x)$]. This process is repeated beginning with x_1, and so on; in general, the formula

$$x_{n+1} = x_n - \frac{f(x_n)}{f'(x_n)}$$

shows how to calculate the next estimate x_{n+1} from the present one x_n. Under general conditions, the sequence $x_0, x_1, x_2, \ldots$ will converge to a root of $f(x) = 0$; an approximate root is obtained by terminating the process at some stage. This method can be generalized to the solution of simultaneous equations in several unknowns.

Nomograph   Any graphical method of computation which uses a straight edge and several scales of numbers. For example, the figure shows a nomograph for addition of numbers (the second scale is midway between the outer scales, and has its unit

length half of theirs); the sum of two

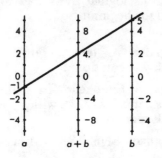

numbers a and b is found by joining a (first scale) with b (third scale) by a straight edge, and reading the sum $a + b$ off the middle scale. The typical nomograph is more complicated, using nonuniform and even curved scales to calculate more involved expressions. Ref. [70, 107].

Non-Euclidean Geometry (Syn.: Non-Euclidean space)   A geometry in which the parallel postulate of Euclidean geometry does not hold (that a given line has exactly one parallel through a point external to it).

Two general types of non-Euclidean geometries (or spaces) are the *hyperbolic* and *elliptic*—in the first, a line has an infinite number of parallels through a point; in the second, a line has no parallel through a point. The Euclidean space, with one parallel through a point, is called *parabolic*. The first figure shows an hyperbolic space. The entire "space"

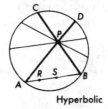

Hyperbolic

is the interior of the circle, and an

(entire) "line" is a chord of the circle (excluding its endpoints). As in Euclidean geometry, two points in this space determine a unique "line" (for example, R and S). However, the parallel postulate fails; any one of the infinite number of "lines" through P lying between AD and CB is "parallel" to AB ("parallel" in the sense of having no point in common with AB). A "line segment" is a portion of a "line"; in this geometry, the sum of the "angles" of a triangle is less than 180° ("angle" being appropriately understood). The hyperbolic geometries of Bolyai and Lobachevsky in the first half of the nineteenth century were the first published examples of non-Euclidean geometries.

The second figure shows an elliptic space. The "space" is the entire surface of the sphere, and a "line" is a great circle of a sphere. Two points determine a unique "line," as in Eu-

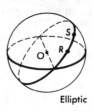

Elliptic

clidean geometry. However, there are no parallel lines (any two great circles intersect). Other features of Euclidean geometry must also be changed here, such as the notion of "betweenness" (because of the closed nature of the space). A "line segment" is an arc of a great circle, and a "triangle" is an ordinary spherical triangle; the sum of the angles of a "triangle" is greater than 180° ("angle" being the ordinary spherical angle). Riemann introduced the elliptic type of geometry in the middle of the nineteenth century.

In this example of an elliptic geometry, the "distance" between two points R and S is the length of the shorter spherical arc connecting them; in the example of the hyperbolic geometry, the "distance" between two points R and S is so defined that when either point approaches the end of the chord the "distance" grows infinitely large. In either geometry a "line segment" between two points is the path of shortest length joining them (in terms of "distance" in that space).

This general view of a "line segment," as the path of least distance in a space, is used in modern advanced geometry: a "space" is defined by specifying what is meant by the "length" of a path; then a "line segment" or *geodesic,* is taken as the path of least length between two points. This unifying approach to general geometry was created by Riemann; it leads to so-called Riemannian geometries, or spaces.

Non-Euclidean geometries were invented in the first half of the nineteenth century after various attempts to show the independence of the parallel postulate of Euclidean geometry failed. These geometries broke with the thinking of centuries in rejecting the Euclidean notion of a line as "straight" and "unlimited" in extent. This opened a new and richer concept of geometry which had a profound effect on mathematics and notions of space. The non-Euclidean geometry which has probably received the greatest public attention is the **four-dimensional space** of relativity theory.

Ref. [41, 48, 52, 53, 101].

Normal   See **Perpendicular** (syn.). Also see **Normal to surface, Plane**.

Normal Form   In the *plane,* the following form of the *equation of a line:* let p be the length of the perpendicular segment from the origin to the line, and let θ be the angle from the positive x-axis to this segment; then

$$x \cos \theta + y \sin \theta - p = 0$$

is the normal form of the equation. A linear equation $ax + by - p = 0$ can be recognized as having this form when $a^2 + b^2 = 1$ (and p is positive). For example, consider the equation $3x - 4y + 8 = 0$; divide by -5 to obtain $-\frac{3}{5}x + \frac{4}{5}y - \frac{8}{5} = 0$; since $(-\frac{3}{5})^2 + (\frac{4}{5})^2 = 1$, this is the normal form. The example illustrates how to change any linear equation $Ax + By + C = 0$ to normal form; namely, divide by $\pm\sqrt{A^2 + B^2}$, using the sign opposite to that of C. The normal form provides an immediate formula for the distance between the

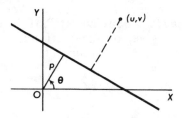

line and any point (u, v): this distance is the numerical value of $au + bv - p$ (where $ax + by - p = 0$ is the normal form). For example, to find the distance between the line $3x - 4y + 8 = 0$ and the point $(-5, 2)$, substitute the latter into the left side of the normal form above; this gives $(-\frac{3}{5})(-5) + (\frac{4}{5})(2) - \frac{8}{5}$, or 3.

In *space,* the normal form of the *equation of a plane* is $lx + my + nz - p = 0$, where p is the length of the perpendicular segment from the origin to the plane, and $l, m, n,$ are the direction cosines of this segment. As above, to change $Ax + By + Cz + D = 0$ to normal form divide by $\pm\sqrt{A^2 + B^2 + C^2}$; the distance be-

179

tween the plane and any point (u, v, w) is the numerical value of $lu + mv + nw - p$. As an example, consider the plane $2x - y + z - 10 = 0$; dividing by $\sqrt{4 + 1 + 1}$, or $\sqrt{6}$, gives

$$(2/\sqrt{6})x - (1/\sqrt{6})y + (1/\sqrt{6})z - (10/\sqrt{6}) = 0;$$

hence the plane is $10/\sqrt{6}$ units from the origin and the direction cosines of the perpendicular to the plane are the three coefficients of x, y, z. The distance between $(6, -2, 2)$ and the plane equals

$$(12/\sqrt{6}) + (2/\sqrt{6}) + (2/\sqrt{6}) - (10/\sqrt{6}),$$

or $\sqrt{6}$.

Normal to Surface The line perpendicular to the surface at a given point P; the normal l is perpendicular to any curve on the surface lying in a plane through l. The normal is also perpendicular to the *tangent plane* to the surface at P. If the surface is given by an equation $z = f(x, y)$, then *direction numbers* of the normal are

$$\frac{\partial f}{\partial x}, \frac{\partial f}{\partial y}, -1,$$

in terms of the partial derivatives of $f(x, y)$. If the surface is given by $F(x, y, z) = 0$, direction numbers of the normal are

$$\frac{\partial F}{\partial x}, \frac{\partial F}{\partial y}, \frac{\partial F}{\partial z}.$$

The **tangent plane to the surface** at (x_0, y_0, z_0) is given by

$$a(x - x_0) + b(y - y_0) + c(z - z_0) = 0,$$

where a, b, c, are direction numbers of the normal at (x_0, y_0, z_0); these are determined by the partial derivatives, as above.

Null Set See **Empty set** (syn.).

Number A real number, as ordi-

narily understood (sometimes, a whole number).

The *natural numbers,* or whole numbers, are the numbers 1, 2, 3, 4, ... These are the simplest numbers, and they continue without end. They suffice for ordinary counting and specifying the size of finite collections of things, and they are the basis for building up other types of numbers. The whole numbers are closed under addition and multiplication; that is, the sum or product of whole numbers is a whole number. However, these numbers are inadequate for subtraction—the difference of whole numbers, for example, $3 - 5$, is not always a whole number. This shortcoming is eliminated by inventing the *integers,* which include the *positive integers* (these being the whole numbers), *zero,* and the *negative integers* -1, -2, -3, ... The integers are closed under addition, multiplication, and subtraction, that is, the sum, product, or difference of two integers is an integer. The integers suffer, however, by not being closed under division; for example, $5 \div 3$ is not an integer. Another version of this shortcoming is that an equation of the form $nx = m$, where m and n are integers, is not always solvable when the unknown x is required to be an integer. The invention of *rational numbers* (fractions) resolves this difficulty. A rational number is a number of the form m/n, where m and n are integers and n is not 0; the integers are included as rational numbers with denominator n equal to 1. The rational numbers are closed under the four fundamental operations of arithmetic, addition, subtraction, multiplication, and division, and permit the solution of any linear equation $ax = b$ where a and b are rational numbers and a

is not 0. The rational numbers represent a major point in the extension of the number concept. They constitute a **number field**, and are adequate for many purposes.

A difficulty arises with the rational numbers in the measurement of lengths. There are line segments whose lengths cannot be expressed as fractions, for example, the hypotenuse of a right triangle with legs of unit length. Another form of this difficulty is that equations such as $x^2 = 2$, $x^2 = 3$, $x^2 = 5$ have no solution when the unknown x must be a rational number. This difficulty is overcome by inventing the *real numbers*. These numbers include the rational numbers and the irrational numbers, such as $\sqrt{2}$. Like the rational numbers, they are closed under the fundamental operations of arithmetic. But when they are spread out on a line in a uniform scale they cover every point, thereby providing a measurement of any length. This property is the axiom of continuity, and the ordered set of real numbers is called a *continuum*.

The **decimal number system** is commonly used to represent real numbers, it being necessary to permit unending decimals to capture all real numbers. The rational numbers appear in decimal form as either finite or repeating decimals. Beyond the rational numbers, two other types of real numbers are distinguished, these being the *algebraic number* and the *transcendental number*. The former is one which is a solution of a polynomial equation (with rational coefficients); an example is the number $\sqrt{2}$, which is a solution of $x^2 = 2$; another is the number $\sqrt[3]{5}$, which is a solution of $x^3 - 5 = 0$. A transcendental number is one which is not algebraic; outstanding examples are the numbers π, and e (the base of natural logarithms). It is usually a difficult and advanced enterprise to prove that a given real number is transcendental.

There is no need to extend the real numbers for many parts of mathematics. However, an algebraic shortcoming of the real numbers is that certain equations, like $x^2 = -1$, have no solutions in real numbers; hence, it is useful to make a further extension to *complex numbers*. The complex numbers allow the solution of these equations; in fact, any algebraic equation has a solution in complex numbers. While the real numbers are visualized as spread out over a line, the complex numbers are visualized as spread out over a plane, with any complex number being represented by rectangular coordinates. A price is paid for the algebraic advantage of the complex number; the linear ordering which is an inherent feature of ordinary numbers is lost with the complex numbers.

Further important extensions beyond the complex numbers of a more advanced mathematical nature exist, but such numbers are not in common use. (The above description is not in historical order; for example, negative numbers came much later than positive rational numbers). There is another direction of generalization of the number concept, beginning with natural numbers. This is the extension to *transfinite numbers* (infinite cardinal and ordinal numbers) and transfinite arithmetic. This path leads to problems associated with logic and the foundations of mathematics.

Ref. [29, 43, 67, 94, 132].

Number Field   A set of numbers

which is *arithmetically closed,* in the sense that the application of the ordinary operations of addition, multiplication, subtraction, and (non-zero) division to its members always results in a member of that set. The set of rational numbers and the set of real numbers are examples of number fields.

Many other number fields occur in modern higher algebra. An example is the set of all numbers $a + b\sqrt{2}$, where a and b are any rational numbers (examples of its members are $3 + 5\sqrt{2}$, $1 - \sqrt{2}$, $\frac{2}{3}$, $\sqrt{2}/3$). To verify that these numbers comprise a number field it is to be proved that the sum, product, difference, and quotient of two such numbers, $a + b\sqrt{2}$ and $c + d\sqrt{2}$, is again a number of the form $p + q\sqrt{2}$ (verification for the quotient uses rationalization of the denominator). This number field is constructed out of the rational numbers as a "ground" field by "adjoining" to them a solution of the algebraic equation $x^2 - 2 = 0$. Similarly, any algebraic equation (with rational coefficients) can be used to generate such an *algebraic number field* over the rational numbers by adjoining a solution of that equation. This approach to numbers and equations is typical of modern higher algebra. The significance of this algebraic type of number construction can be recognized from the important example of complex numbers; these use the real numbers as a ground field and adjoin the imaginary unit i, namely, a solution $x^2 + 1 = 0$. See **Conjugate radicals**.

A number field is a field in the technical sense of satisfying the axioms of the *field.* Any algebraic number field built on the rational or real numbers is a subcollection of the complex numbers.

Ref. [28, 44].

Number System　In one meaning, a method of notation for real numbers and the rules for arithmetic computation in that notation; by far the most common is the *decimal number system.* The *binary number system* is also used, particularly in connection with the electronic digital computer. Both of these are *place value* systems, the first having the base ten, the second the base two. The duodecimal and ternary systems use the base twelve and three, respectively. The adoption of the Hindu-Arab place value decimal system, which began in Europe after 1000 A.D., was a major advance in Western culture.

As used in "real number system" or "complex number system," the term "number system" denotes a *mathematical system* (not a system of notation, as above). In this sense it might refer to a system which is a generalization of ordinary numbers, such as matrices.

Ref. [28, 44, 94].

Numbers π and e　See **Pi**, π, and e.

Numbers, Theory of　See **Theory of Numbers**.

Numerals　Any system of marks for denoting numbers. In *Roman numerals* the symbol I is used for one, V for five, X for ten, and so on. The *Arabic numerals* are the symbols (digits) 0, 1, 2, 3, 4, 5, 6, 7, 8, 9; these are used in the decimal number system.　Ref. [29, 67, 100].

Numerator　Of a fraction A/B, the expression (represented by) A; the *denominator* is B.

Numerical　Referring to constants, such as 2 or 5, rather than to literal symbols or variables. For example, $3x^2 - 2x + 5 = 0$ is called a "numerical" equation because the coefficients are numerical; in contrast, $ax^2 + bx + c = 0$ is called a "literal" equation.

Numerical Analysis The general study of methods of approximation for the solution of various classes of mathematical problems. The increased use of the high-speed computer has greatly stimulated the growth of this field. Ref. [80].

Numerical Value See **Absolute value** (syn.).

O

Oblate Ellipsoid (Syn.: Oblate spheroid) An **ellipsoid** produced by rotating an ellipse through 360° about its shorter axis.

Oblique Neither parallel nor perpendicular, generally. For example, an oblique angle is an angle which is not a multiple of 90°; an oblique triangle is a triangle with no right angle; an oblique circular cone is a circular cone whose axis is not perpendicular to the base.

Oblique Coordinates Cartesian coordinates in the plane (or in space) where the axes are not at right angles.

Obtuse An *obtuse angle* is one which lies between 90° and 180°; an *obtuse triangle* is one which contains an obtuse angle.

Octagon A polygon with eight sides; it is a regular octagon if all its sides are equal and all its angles are equal.

Octahedron A polyhedron with eight faces. A regular octahedron is a **regular polyhedron** with eight faces; its faces are equilateral triangles.

Octant Any one of the eight portions of space determined by the three coordinate planes of **Cartesian coordinates in space**. An octant consists of all points lying on selected sides of the three coordinate planes; each of the coordinates x, y, z has a fixed sign in a given octant. For example, all points with x and y positive, and z negative form one octant.

Odd See **Even**.

Omega, ω The least (infinite) **ordinal number** after the natural numbers 1, 2, 3, ...

One In arithmetic, the number denoted by "1"; it is the "identity element" of multiplication, that is, $x \cdot 1 = 1 \cdot x = x$, for any number x.

"One" may be thought of as the cardinal number of a set with a single member. The symbol "1" is also used to denote the *universe* in the algebra of sets.

One-Dimensional See **Dimension**.

One-To-One Correspondence (Syn.: One-to-one function) A **correspondence** between two collections of numbers or things in which a member of either collection is paired with exactly one member of the other. For example, in a monogomous society, the marriage relation specifies a one-to-one correspondence between the set of married men and the set of married women.

Operation An operation in a set A is any process that combines two or more members of a set A into a single member of A (also, one that converts a single member of A into a member of A). It is a *binary operation* if it combines pairs of members, *ternary* if it combines triples, etc. For example, ordinary addition and multiplication are binary operations (where the set A is the set of real numbers); the extraction of the square root is an example of an

O

operation on single (positive) numbers. Associated with a binary operation is its *inverse operation;* for example, subtraction is inverse to addition, and raising to a power is inverse to root extraction.

The *fundamental operations of arithmetic* are addition, multiplication, and their inverses, subtraction and division. These, together with root extraction make up the *algebraic operations.* A *transcendental operation* on numbers is one that is not algebraic (an example is taking the logarithm of a number); such operations use the limit concept of the calculus for complete definition.

Operations on Sets   See **Algebra of sets**.

Operations Research   The application of mathematical and scientific methods to problems of military, business, and man-machine systems with a view toward improving the over-all performance of such systems by analyzing the interaction of its various parts. This field grew out of activities in World War II when groups made up of research experts from various scientific fields worked together with military personnel on the improvement of war time operations. Since then, the field has grown steadily, extending into a variety of business and government operations, and other areas. Examples of techniques of operations research are **mathematical programming**, and **simulation**.

Ref. [63, 90, 112].

Opposite   In a *triangle,* a side and angle are opposite if the angle is included between the remaining two sides (such as angle A and side a). In a *quadrilateral,* sides are opposite if they have no common vertex, and

angles are opposite if they have no

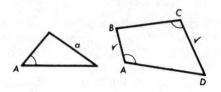

common side (such as angles A and C, sides AB and CD).

Opposite Angles   See **Vertical angles** (syn.).

Order of Radical (Syn.: Index of radical)   The whole number n in the expression $\sqrt[n]{a}$ for a radical; for example, the order of $\sqrt{3}$ (that is, $\sqrt[2]{3}$) is 2.

Order of Root   See **Multiple root**.

Order Relation   For numbers, the *inequality relation;* more generally, and informally, a relation among things which in some sense "orders" them (and not necessarily in the same way that points are ordered on a line).   See **Ordered set**.

Ordered Pair, Triple, n-Tuple   An ordered pair (or triple) consists of things in the order of the natural numbers 1, 2 (or 1, 2, 3); an ordered n-tuple consists of things in the order 1, 2, 3, . . . , n. These are denoted by (x, y), (x, y, z), and $(x_1, x_2, . . . , x_n)$, respectively (the things x, y, etc., need not be distinct). The ordered pair of numbers (x, y) represents a point in plane rectangular coordinates [the order is important since, for example, (3, 5) represents a different point than (5, 3) does]. Similarly, an ordered triple or n-tuple of numbers represent points in three-dimensional or n-dimensional space, respectively. Formally, an ordered n-tuple is a *function* from the set {1, 2,

..., n} to a set of numbers (or other things).

Ordered Set Consider any set A and a relation between members of A, denoted by "x precedes y." Then the set A is said to be *linearly,* or *simply, ordered* by the relation in case the following two properties hold: **(1)** for any members x, y of A, one and only one of the statements "x precedes y," "x equals y," "y precedes x" holds (*trichotomy* property); **(2)** if x precedes y and y precedes z, then x precedes z (*transitive* property). This is a generalization of the ordering of the real numbers by the usual inequality relation $x < y$ (x is less than y). This inequality relation is ordinarily visualized as that of points on a line; similarly, any simply ordered set A can be visualized as spread out along a line, with "x precedes y" meaning that x lies to the left of y.

A more general situation is that of *partial ordering.* The set A is said to be *partially ordered* by a relation "x precedes y" in case the following two properties hold: **(1)** for any x, y, the statements "x precedes y" and "y precedes x" do not hold simultaneously; **(2)** the relation is transitive. The essential difference between simple and partial order is that in the latter case it may occur that some distinct elements a, b are not "comparable" (that is, neither a precedes b nor b precedes a). The relation "a is a descendant of b" (between people) is an illustration; the relation is transitive, but it does not have the trichotomy property (since of two different people, neither need be a descendant of the other). Although a partial ordering cannot be visualized along a line, it can be helpfully pictured by means of a branching arrangement. To illustrate, let the rela-

tion "m precedes n" between whole numbers m, n stand for "m is an exact

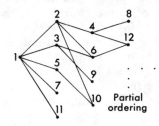

Partial ordering

divisor of n and $m \neq n$"; this satisfies properties **(1)** and **(2)**. The figure gives a geometric representation of this relation (m is in the given relation to n in case there is a connected chain of segments from m to n, going left to right).

A *well-ordered set A* is a simply ordered set with the property that within any subset B of A there is an element which precedes all other elements of B. For example, the real numbers are not well ordered, since, for example, the subset B of numbers (strictly) greater than 2 is preceded only by 2 or any number less than 2, and B contains none of these. The natural numbers are well-ordered; so are all the *ordinals* from, say, 1 up to any transfinite ordinal. A proposition related to the fundamental concepts of the theory of sets is the following: any set can be well-ordered, provided the **axiom of choice** is allowed.

Ref. [81, 134].

Ordinal Number A *finite ordinal number* is a whole number considered as a place in the ordered sequence of whole numbers (as in the counting

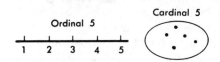

process *first, second, third,* etc.).

When used to specify how many objects are in a set, a whole number is termed a *cardinal number.* The sequence of whole numbers can be extended to *infinite,* or *transfinite, ordinals.* The first such ordinal greater than the whole numbers is designated by "ω" (Greek letter "omega"); the transfinite ordinals beyond ω continue in an unending chain

$$1 < 2 < 3 < \cdots < \omega < \omega + 1 < \omega + 2$$
$$< \cdots < 2\omega < 2\omega + 1 \cdots.$$

In the finite case, ordinals and cardinals are in one-to-one correspondence—they appear to be different ways of representing the same thing. In the infinite case (transfinite numbers) ordinals and cardinals are quite different; for example ω and 2ω are distinct ordinal numbers but they represent the same cardinal number, aleph-null. The theory of transfinite ordinals was created by G. Cantor in the latter half of the nineteenth century.

Ref. [29, 149].

Ordinate The second or vertical, coordinate, *y*, of a pair (x, y) of **Cartesian coordinates in the plane**; the first, *x*, is the *abscissa.*

Orientation See **Rigid motion, Trihedral**.

Origin of Coordinate System The point of intersection of the axes in a system of Cartesian coordinates; it has coordinates (0, 0) in the plane, and (0, 0, 0) in space.

Orthocenter of Triangle The common point of intersection O of the altitudes of a triangle. For an acute triangle *ABC*, the feet of the altitudes are the vertices of an inscribed triangle $A'B'C'$; the altitudes of *ABC* are the angle bisectors of this triangle. Triangle $A'B'C'$ is a type of in-

scribed triangle known as a *pedal tri-*

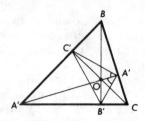

angle. This triangle has an interesting relationship to the given triangle; of all triangles inscribed in *ABC*, triangle $A'B'C'$ has the least area.

Orthogonal See **Perpendicular** (syn.).

Orthonormal See **Basis vector**.

Overlapping Sets Sets which have at least one member in common; otherwise the sets are *disjoint*, that is, have no members in common. For example, the set of odd numbers $\{1, 3, 5, 7, \dots\}$ and the set of perfect squares $\{1, 4, 9, 16, 25, \dots\}$ are overlapping, having 1, 9, 25, 49, etc., in common. See **Algebra of sets**.

P

Pair See **Ordered pair**.

Pappus See **Theorem of Pappus**.

Parabola A **conic** with eccentricity 1; it is defined as the locus of points *P* whose distance from a fixed point (the *focus*) is equal to its distance from a fixed line (the *directrix*). It occurs in nature as the path of a moving object in a vacuum acted on by the vertical pull of gravity, for example. The parabola is symmetrical about its *axis,* which is the line through the focus perpendicular to the directrix; the point of intersection of the axis with the curve is the *vertex V.* A line segment joining two points of the parabola is a *chord;* it is a *focal chord* if it passes through the focus. The focal chord which is perpendicular to the axis, is the *latus rectum.* A parabola is uniquely determined when its vertex and focus are given, or when the latus rectum is given (and the side V is on).

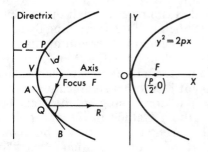

The parabola has the following *focal,* or *reflection property:* the focal chord to any point Q on the parabola, and the horizontal line QR make equal angles with the tangent line at Q (angle FQA = angle RQB in the figure). This means that light coming from a source at the focus will be reflected in parallel horizontal rays off the inside of the parabola.

In analytic geometry, the parabola is in standard position, when its vertex is at the origin and its focus is on the positive x-axis. Its *equation* is then $y^2 = 2px$, where $p/2$ is the distance between the vertex and the focus. The latus rectum is of length $2p$, and the directrix is at distance p from the focus.

Parabolic Cylinder   A **cylindrical surface** whose right sections are parabolas.

Parabolic Segment   The plane region bounded by a chord of a parabola perpendicular to the axis, and the arc of the parabola cut off by the chord. The chord is the *base* of the

parabolic segment, and the perpendicular segment from the vertex to the base (or its length) is the altitude.

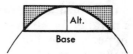

The area of a parabolic segment equals $(\frac{2}{3})ab$, where a is the altitude, and b the length of the base (this is two-thirds of the area of the rectangle of the same base and altitude).

Parabolic Spiral   See **Spiral**.

Paraboloid   A *paraboloid of revolution* is a surface of revolution produced by rotating a parabola about its axis. When it is in standard position (vertex and axis of the parabola

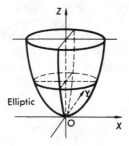

coincident with the origin and positive z-axis), the paraboloid has the *equation*

$$\frac{x^2}{a^2} + \frac{y^2}{a^2} = 2cz \qquad (c > 0).$$

The plane sections parallel to the xy-plane are circles, and those parallel to the other coordinate planes are parabolas. A more general surface is the *elliptic* paraboloid, which has the equation

$$\frac{x^2}{a^2} + \frac{y^2}{b^2} = 2cz;$$

plane sections parallel to the xy-plane are similar ellipses.

A *hyperbolic* paraboloid is a surface with the equation

$$\frac{x^2}{a^2} - \frac{y^2}{b^2} = 2cz \qquad (c > 0)$$

in the standard position shown; plane sections parallel to the *xy*-plane are similar hyperbolas, while plane sections parallel to the other coordinate

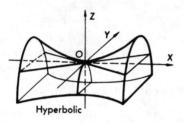

Hyperbolic

planes are parabolas. The origin is a *saddle point* of the surface; that is, it is the minimum point of the parabola above it (the plane section by the *xz*-plane), but the maximum point of the parabola below it (the plane section by the *yz*-plane).

The paraboloids belong to the class of *quadric surfaces*. The hyperbolic paraboloid (like the hyperboloid of one sheet) is a *doubly ruled surface*—that is, two distinct families of (straight) lines can be drawn on it, each family covering the surface completely.

Paradox (Syn.: Antinomy)   A contradiction between two equally reasonable conclusions, supported by an argument that appears to have no faults in it.

Perhaps the most familiar type of paradox is the *fallacy,* or "false proof." Examples are "proofs" of the propositions that $1 = 2$ and that every angle is a right angle. These are paradoxes only in a superficial sense; they are deliberate puzzles or instances of incorrect reasoning

which are settled by finding the hidden assumption or incorrect step.

A deeper type of paradox is *Zeno's paradox* of Greek antiquity, which concerns the continuity of motion. One form of the paradox is this: suppose an object moves with constant speed along a straight line from the point 0 toward the point 1; the object must first cover half the distance ($\frac{1}{2}$), then half the remaining distance ($\frac{1}{4}$), then half the remaining distance ($\frac{1}{8}$), and so on without end; conclusion: the object never reaches the point 1. Another significant paradox is one concerning infinite sets put forth by Galileo in the first half of the seventeenth century. This shows that the whole can equal a "part" of itself by noting that the unending sequence of positive integers 1, 2, 3, . . . can be put in one-to-one correspondence with the unending sequence of perfect squares $1^2, 2^2, 3^2, \ldots$. Both of these puzzling situations were satisfactorily resolved only by a clarification of basic mathematical concepts. The first found an answer in the rigorous concept of *limit* that emerged in the nineteenth century (out of the calculus of the seventeenth century), and the second in the concept of *cardinal number* of the theory of infinite sets in the latter half of the nineteenth century.

The theory of infinite sets is itself subject to deeper paradoxes which are related to the underlying logic of mathematical reasoning; these have led to extensive studies in the **foundations of mathematics** in this century. One paradox of this type which goes back to antiquity, is the following *dilemma of the crocodile:* a crocodile steals a child; he says that he will return the child if the father guesses correctly whether or not he will do so; the father guesses he will not return the child; what should an honest crocodile do? One of the better-known logical paradoxes of our time is the *Russell paradox*. This can be expressed in the formalism of logic, but in popular language it can be explained as follows. Consider all books which are catalogs, or listings of titles, of books. Classify them into two types: type 1 is a catalog that does not list its own name, and type 2 is a catalog that does. It is desired to make up a catalog which lists the titles of all catalogs of type 1 (and none of type 2): should the new catalog list its own name? (Remember that the new catalog must now be counted among all catalogs.)

Paradoxes in the logical foundations of mathematics still exist, although they do not interfere to any serious extent with the work of the mathematician. It seems that a resolution of these problems will come only with a profound new insight into the nature of logical reasoning. Ref. [21, 103, 105, 114].

Parallel *Parallel lines* (*planes*) are lines (planes) lying in a plane (space) which have no common point no matter how far extended. The parallel postulate of Euclidean geometry states that through a point *P* not on a given line *l*, there is exactly one line parallel to *l*. The analogous statement holds for planes in space:

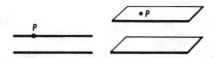

through a point *P* not on a given plane *p* there is exactly one plane parallel to *p*. Lines in space which have no common point but do not lie in a plane are *skew*. Distinct planes in space are parallel in case lines perpendicular to them are. In analytic geometry, parallelism is expressed

algebraically in terms of slopes and direction numbers; (distinct) lines are parallel in case their slopes are equal, and (distinct) planes are parallel in case their direction numbers are proportional (see **Line, Plane**).

Parallel Postulate of Euclidean Geometry The following famous postulate of plane geometry: Through a given point not on a given line there is exactly one line parallel to the given line. This postulate was stated by Euclid in the following form: If a straight line falling on two straight lines makes the angles, internal and on the same side, less than two right angles, the two straight lines, being produced indefinitely, meet on the side on which are the angles less than two right angles. This longer statement, taken together with the other postulates, is equivalent to the simpler form. A geometry in which the parallel postulate does not hold is a **non-Euclidean geometry**.

Parallelepiped A prism whose bases are parallelograms (as with any prism, the lateral faces are also parallelograms). A *diagonal* is a line segment joining two vertices not in the same face. There are four diagonals; they are concurrent and their common point of intersection is the *center* of the parallelepiped. The center bisects each diagonal.

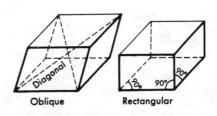

Oblique   Rectangular

Parallelepipeds are classified as follows. A *right parallelepiped* is one whose lateral edges are perpendicular to the bases; otherwise it is an *oblique parallelepiped.* A *rectangular parallelepiped* is a right parallelepiped whose bases are rectangles; it is frequently called a *rectangular solid.* A rectangular solid is determined by its three dimensions, namely, the lengths of three edges meeting at a vertex. When the three dimensions are equal, the rectangular parallelepiped is a *cube.*

The volume of a parallelepiped equals the area of the base times the altitude; for a rectangular parallelepiped this equals *abc,* the product of the three dimensions, and for a cube it equals a^3. The total area of a rectangular parallelepiped is $2(ab + ac + bc)$; for a cube, this equals $6a^2$.

Parallelogram A quadrilateral whose opposite sides are parallel. Any side can be taken as the *base;* then the *altitude* is a perpendicular line segment (or its length) between the lines through the bases. A *diagonal* is a line segment joining opposite vertices. Among the properties of parallelograms are the following: **(1)** the diagonals bisect each other; **(2)** opposite sides are equal; **(3)** opposite angles are equal. Conversely, if a quadrilateral has any one of these properties it is a parallelogram. Also, if a quadrilateral has one pair of opposite sides parallel and equal, then it is a parallelogram.

Rhombus

Parallelograms are classified as follows. A *rhombus* is one with a pair of adjacent sides equal (hence, all sides equal). A *rectangle* has adjacent sides perpendicular; the *square* has adjacent sides both equal and perpendicular.

The area of a parallelogram equals the length of the base times the altitude; for a rectangle this equals *ab,* where *a* and *b* are the lengths of adjacent sides (the *dimensions* of the rectangle).

Parallelogram Law The geometric rule for the **addition of vectors**.

Parameter Generally, a **variable** used as an arbitrary constant. One common use is to describe a *family* of functions or graphs; for example, the equation $y = 3x + b$ containing the parameter "*b*," represents the family of parallel lines in the plane with slope 3 (the parameter is the *y*-intercept). Another use of the parameter is as the auxiliary variable in *parametric equations* for a curve.

Parametric Equations In analytic geometry, parametric equations of a *plane curve* are two equations which express the coordinates *x* and *y* of points on the curve as separate functions of a common variable, called the *parameter.* For example, the circle with center at (0, 0) and radius 3, can be represented by the parametric equations $x = 3 \cos \theta, y = 3 \sin \theta$, where θ is the angle of rotation of the positive *x*-axis into the point (x, y) on the circle; each value of θ determines a particular point on the circle, and as θ goes from 0° to 360°, the entire circle is swept out. In general, parametric equations $x = f(t), y = g(t)$ of a plane curve give one point of the curve for each value of the parameter *t*, and describe the whole curve for the full range of *t*; the parameter often has a direct geometric or physical interpretation, although it need not (see particular plane curves **Cycloid, Ellipse**, etc.). In the study of motion, a common parameter is time; the values of *x* and *y* at any in-stant t specify the position of the particle at that time.

In three-dimensional *space*, a curve has the parametric form $x = f(t)$, $y = g(t)$, $z = h(t)$; in a space of n dimensions, this becomes $x_1 = f_1(t)$, $x_2 = f_2(t), \ldots, x_n = f_n(t)$.

Parentheses   The marks "( )," used to indicate that the enclosed expression is to be regarded as an individual part of a larger expression containing it. For example, in "$a(b + c)$" the form "aB" is understood, with "$b + c$" in place of "B"; without parentheses, it would read "$ab + c$" which has the different form "$A + c$." Varieties of parentheses are *braces* "{ }" and *brackets* "[ ]"; these are used to avoid ambiguity in more complicated expressions. An example is

"$(x - y)[x + 5\{(x + y)(2x - y) + 1\}]$";

working from the outside in, this is, first of all, a product "$(x - y)[\cdots]$"; within the bracket it is a sum "$x + 5\{\cdots\}$"; within the brace it is a sum "$(\cdots)(\cdots) + 1$"; and within each pair of parentheses it is a sum or difference. A less frequently used symbol is the raised horizontal line, or *vinculum*, as in "$\overline{a + b}$." Parentheses and such variations are called *signs of aggregation*.

Parity   Evenness or oddness. Two integers have the *same parity* if they are both even or both odd; otherwise they have *opposite parity*. Thus, 3 and 5 have the same parity, 3 and 4 have opposite parity.

Partial Derivative of Function   An ordinary derivative of a function of two or more variables with respect to a selected variable, with the remaining variables held constant. For instance, a function $f(x, y)$ of two

variables has two partial derivatives: the partial derivative with respect to the first variable, x, is denoted variously by

$$\frac{\partial f}{\partial x}, \; f_x, \; D_x f;$$

the partial derivative with respect to the second variable, y, is denoted similarly. For example, let

$$f(x, y) = x^2 - 3xy + 2y^2 + x;$$

then $\partial f/\partial x = 2x - 3y + 1$ and $\partial f/\partial y = -3x + 4y$. A function $F(x, y, z)$ has three partial derivatives, $\partial F/\partial x, \partial F/\partial y, \partial F/\partial z$; and so on, to functions of any number of variables.   See **Normal to surface** for a geometric interpretation of partial derivatives.

Partial Fractions   Proper fractions of the form

$$\frac{A}{(ax + b)}, \quad \frac{(Ax + B)}{(ax^2 + bx + c)}$$

and, more generally, of the form

$$\frac{A}{(ax + b)^n}, \quad \frac{(Ax + B)}{(ax^2 + bx + c)^n}$$

with n a positive integer. The reason for the designation "partial" is that any proper fraction can be decomposed into a sum of fractions of these types; the denominators are linear and quadratic factors of the denominator of the given fraction. For example,

$$(5x - 7)/(x - 1)(2x - 3)$$

can be written

$$2/(x - 1) + 1/(2x - 3);$$

another example is

$$\frac{2x^2 - 6x + 7}{(x + 2)(x^2 - x + 3)}$$
$$= \frac{3}{x + 2} - \frac{x + 1}{x^2 - x + 3}.$$

Such a decomposition can be viewed as the reverse of adding fractions; it is useful, for instance, in the calculus for the integration of rational functions.

Partial Product In long multiplication of decimal numbers, the product of a single digit of the multiplier with the multiplicand; the complete product is the sum of (shifted) partial products.

Partial Sum Of an infinite **series** $a_1 + a_2 + a_3 + \cdots$, the sum of a finite number of consecutive terms, beginning with a_1.

Partition To partition a *positive integer* is to write it as a sum of a given number of positive integers; for example, the square 25 can be partitioned into a sum of two squares, $9 + 16$. The theory of numbers deals with various questions on the partition of numbers; a famous unsolved one is the Goldbach conjecture that every even positive integer (except 2) is the sum of the two primes.

To partition a *set* of things, is to separate it into mutually exclusive sets which exhaust the given set. For example, the separation into even numbers and odd numbers is a partition of the set of natural numbers; also, the unit segment from 0 to 1 is partitioned into ten subintervals by the intermediate points $0.1, 0.2, \ldots,$ 0.9 (to be precise, each intermediate point may be assigned to its left subinterval). Any **equivalence relation** among members of a set produces a partition of that set.

Pascal's Theorem See **Hexagon**.

Pascal's Triangle The triangular array of the **binomial coefficients**.

Peano's Postulates Postulates for the **natural numbers**.

Pedal Triangle A triangle inscribed in a given triangle in the following manner: its vertices are the feet of

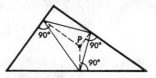

the three perpendiculars to the sides from some point inside the given triangle. See **Orthocenter of triangle**.

Pencil In the *plane*, a *pencil of lines* is the collection of all lines passing through a fixed point, or all lines parallel to a given line (in the latter case, the fixed point can be thought of as a "point at infinity"). If $L_1 = 0, L_2 = 0$ are the equations of two lines intersecting at P, then the pencil through P is represented by $hL_1 + kL_2 = 0$ where h and k are arbitrary constants (that is, any line through P has an equation of this form). A *pencil of circles* in the plane is the collection of all circles passing through two fixed points; the line joining the points is the *radical axis* of the pencil. If $C_1 = 0, C_2 = 0$ are the equations of two circles intersecting in P and Q, then the pencil of circles through P and Q is given by $hC_1 + kC_2 = 0$.

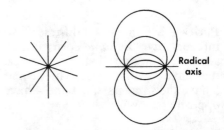

Radical axis

In *space,* the collection of all planes containing a fixed line (the axis) form a *pencil of planes* (see **Collinear**); the collection of all spheres passing through a given circle form a *pencil* *of spheres,* the plane of the circle being the *radical plane* of the pencil.

Pentadecagon   A polygon with fifteen sides.

Pentagon   A polygon with five sides; it is a regular pentagon if all sides are equal and all its angles are equal.

Pentahedron   A polyhedron with five faces.

Per cent   The unit $\frac{1}{100}$ for expressing numbers, denoted by "%"; thus, $x\%$ stands for $x/100$. For example 12% equals $\frac{12}{100}$, or .12, and 6.8% equals 6.8/100 or .068. In general, to change from percent to ordinary units, divide by 100 (or shift the decimal point two places left). Conversely, to convert a number to percent, multiply by 100 (or shift the decimal point two places right); for example, .25 equals 25%, and .036 equals 3.6%.

Percent Error   The relative error expressed in percent.

Perfect Number   A whole number which equals the sum of its divisors (including 1, but excluding itself, as divisors). A number is *defective* (or *deficient*) if the sum of divisors is less than the number; it is *redundant* (or *abundant*) if the sum is greater than the number. For example, 28 is a perfect number because $28 = 1 + 2 + 4 + 7 + 14$; also, 9 is defective, but 12 is redundant. The first five perfect numbers are 6, 28, 496, 8128, and 33550336; the perfect numbers grow very rapidly in size and only a few are known (the larger ones through computation on high speed computers).

A number of the form $2^{p-1}(2^p - 1)$, with p a prime number, is a perfect number in case $2^p - 1$ is itself a prime number; the five examples cited above correspond to the values

for p of 2, 3, 5, 7, 13. The study of perfect numbers goes back to early Greek mathematics.   Ref. [6, 8, 13].

Perfect Power   In arithmetic and algebra, an integer (polynomial) which is a square, cube, ..., or n^{th} power of an integer (polynomial). For example 25 is a perfect square ($=5^2$), 64 is a perfect cube ($=4^3$), and $x^2 + 2x + 1$ is a perfect (trinomial) square $[=(x + 1)^2]$.

The following formula expresses a perfect square integer as a sum of consecutive odd integers:

$$n^2 = 1 + 3 + 5 + \cdots + (2n - 1);$$

for example, when $n = 6$ this gives

$$6^2 = 1 + 3 + 5 + 7 + 9 + 11.$$

There is also a formula that expresses a perfect square of an odd number as a sum of consecutive integers, namely,

$$(2n + 1)^2 = (n + 1) + (n + 2) + \cdots + (3n + 1);$$

for example, when $n = 3$ this gives

$$7^2 = 4 + 5 + 6 + 7 + 8 + 9 + 10.$$

See **Sum of perfect powers of integers**.

In algebra, the following formulas for the square and cube of a binomial $x + a$ are useful for factoring:

$$(x + a)^2 = x^2 + 2ax + a^2,$$
$$(x + a)^3 = x^3 + 3ax^2 + 3a^2x + a^3.$$

These are particular cases of the **binomial theorem**.

Perigon   An angle of 360°, that is, one complete revolution; seldom used.

Perimeter   The perimeter of a *closed curve* is its length; the perimeter of a two-dimensional region is the length of its boundary (or, sometimes, the boundary itself). The perimeter of a *circle* is called its circumference.

193

Figures with the same perimeter are called **isoperimetric**; they occur in various interesting problems of geometry and calculus.

Period of Function See **Periodic function**.

Periodic Decimal See **Repeating decimal** (syn.).

Periodic Function A function of a real variable is periodic if it duplicates its values over succesive intervals of fixed length (its period); more precisely, $f(x)$ is periodic of *period p* in case $f(x + p) = f(x)$ for every x (p the least positive number for which this holds). The graph of $f(x)$ is a *periodic curve*. The *amplitude* is the largest absolute value of $f(x)$; the *frequency* is $1/p$, the reciprocal of the period (this is the number of repetitions of the graph per unit length). Such functions arise in the study of sound, light, electricity, and other vibrational and wave phenomena.

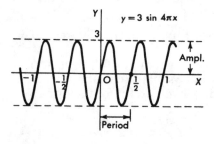

The simplest periodic functions are the trigonometric functions, sine and cosine. For example, $\cos x$ is periodic of period 2π radians (360°); its amplitude is 1 and its frequency $1/2\pi$. The function $3 \sin 4\pi x$ is a periodic function of period $1/2$, amplitude 3 and frequency 2. More generally, $A \sin (2\pi x/k)$ or $A \cos (2\pi x/k)$ is a periodic function of period k and amplitude A; these are the *simple harmonic functions*.

Periodic functions can have complicated graphs. The analysis of such

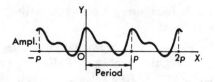

functions in terms of the simpler sine and cosine types is significant in mathematics and physics (see **Trigonometric series**).

Ref. [11, 148].

Permutation An arrangement of a set of objects in a particular order. For example, the three letters a, b, c permit the following six permutations: abc, acb, bac, bca, cab, cba. In this case of 3 objects, there are 6, or $3 \cdot 2 \cdot 1$ permutations. With n objects there are $n(n - 1) \cdots 2 \cdot 1$, or $n!$ (n factorial) permutations. More generally, the number of permutations of n things taken r at a time is

$$n(n - 1)(n - 2) \ldots (n - r + 1),$$

or

$$\frac{n!}{(n - r)!},$$

this is abbreviated $P(n, r)$. For example, the various permutations of two objects ($r = 2$) taken from four objects a, b, c, d ($n = 4$) are ab, ba, ac, ca, ad, da, bc, cb, bd, db, cd, dc; in this case $P(4, 2) = 4 \cdot 3 = 12$. The number of permutations of n things taken r at a time, with repetitions allowed, is n^r.

In studying relations among permutations, any permutation may be thought of as a rearrangement of a given one; for example, $dabc$ is a permutation of $abcd$. A *cyclic permutation*, is one produced by advancing the letters of a given arrangement one place to the right (putting the last letter in the first position); the last example is cyclic. A *transposition* is a permutation in which two places are interchanged, for example, *bac* is a transposition of *abc* (interchange *a* and *b*). Any permutation may be realized by a sequence of transpositions; for example, *bcad* can be obtained from *abcd* by interchanging *a* and *c* (to obtain *cbad*), and then interchanging *b* and *c*. A permutation is *even* (*odd*) if it can be realized by an even (odd) number of transpositions (the same permutation may be obtained by different sequences of transpositions, starting with the same initial arrangement, but they will all be even or all be odd).

Two permutations in a given order can be combined by performing the first and following it by the second; this defines a *binary operation* among permutations, which is of importance in the theory of permutations. The study of permutations is closely related to the study of finite groups and, in particular, to the study of symmetry of figures (see **Group of symmetries**). Permutations arise in the theory of equations, and in many parts of higher algebra.

Ref. [102, 108, 120].

Perpendicular (Syn.: Normal; Orthogonal) In general terms, two geometric figures are perpendicular in case they are at right angles.

In the *plane,* perpendicular lines are lines which intersect at right angles; either line is called a "*perpendicular*" to the other. A line is

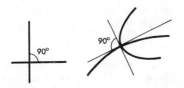

perpendicular to a curve at a point of intersection *P* in case it is perpen-dicular to the tangent line at *P*; similarly, two curves are perpendicular if their tangent lines are. Through a point in the plane, there is a unique perpendicular line to a given line. Also, a line perpendicular to a circle always passes through the center of the circle.

In *space,* a line is perpendicular to a plane in case it is perpendicular to every line in the plane passing through the *foot* of the perpendicular (that is, through the point of intersection with the plane). If the line is perpendicular to just two lines of the plane it will be perpendicular to the rest. Through any point in space there is exactly one perpendicular to a given plane. Two planes are perpendicular if they form a right

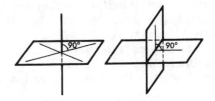

dihedral angle; through any line not perpendicular to a plane, there is exactly one plane perpendicular to the given plane. Two lines in space are perpendicular in case they are so after being moved parallel to themselves to a common point of intersection.

In analytic geometry perpendicularity is expressed in terms of slopes and direction numbers; for example, in the plane, two lines are perpendicular in case the product of their slopes is −1. See **Line, Normal to surface, Plane**.

Perpendicular Bisector Of a line segment in the plane (space); the line (plane) which is perpendicular to it and bisects it; it consists of all points

195

P equidistant from the end points of the segment.

Phase of Complex Number See **Amplitude of complex number** (syn.).

Pi, π A fundamental number of mathematics defined as the ratio of the circumference of a circle to its diameter. (The notation "π" was introduced by English mathematicians near the beginning of the eighteenth century.) A rational approximation to π is $\frac{22}{7}$, which is adequate for many applications; a closer approximation is $\frac{355}{113}$. The number π itself is not a rational number; a proof of this difficult proposition was not found until the middle of the eighteenth century (by the German mathematician Lambert). Even more, π is a transcendental number, a fact not proved until the latter half of the nineteenth century (by the German mathematician Lindemann).

The attempts to evaluate π make an interesting story in the history of mathematics. Some formulas for π are the following:

$$\frac{\pi}{4} = 1 - \frac{1}{3} + \frac{1}{5} - \frac{1}{7} + \frac{1}{9} - \frac{1}{11} + \cdots$$

$$\frac{\pi^2}{6} = \frac{1}{1^2} + \frac{1}{2^2} + \frac{1}{3^2} + \frac{1}{4^2} + \cdots$$

$$\frac{\pi}{2} = \left(\frac{2}{1} \cdot \frac{2}{3}\right) \cdot \left(\frac{4}{3} \cdot \frac{4}{5}\right) \cdot \left(\frac{6}{5} \cdot \frac{6}{7}\right)$$
$$\cdot \left(\frac{8}{7} \cdot \frac{8}{9}\right) \cdots$$

(The latter is known as *Wallis' product* for π.) Other formulas have been developed which are more suited to the numerical evaluation of π.
Ref. [9, 28, 140].

Place Value The principle of notation for numbers in which the value assigned to an individual digit depends upon its place in a string of digits. This is the principle used in the **decimal number system**; for ex-

ample, in 527.836 the (place) values of the digits to the right of the decimal point are $8/10$, $3/10^2$, $6/10^3$ respectively, while the (place) values of the digits to the left are $7 \cdot 1$, $2 \cdot 10$, $5 \cdot 10^2$, respectively. In general, in this system, the unit value of the kth place to the left (to the right) of the decimal point is 10^{k-1} $(1/10^k)$. In the **binary number system** the base is 2 and the unit value of a place is a power of 2.

The Hindus are generally credited with the development of the place value notation, and the Arabs with its popularization in Europe after 1000 A.D. Particularly significant was the Hindu invention of using the digit 0 as a "no value" mark. Arithmetical facility with the decimal system of place values eventually became a common skill.   Ref. [44].

Plane A basic configuration of solid geometry which, informally, is a surface that is everywhere flat; more precisely, it is a two-dimensional figure with the following property: it contains the entire line through any two of its points (and it contains at least three points not on a line). By definition, a plane extends indefinitely in all directions on it; the term "plane" or "plane surface" is often used to denote any two-dimensional, connected portion of a plane. A *half-plane* is either one of the two portions entirely on one side of a line in the plane (including or excluding the line itself).

A plane is determined by any one of the following conditions: **(1)** three points *P*, *Q*, *R* not on a line; **(2)** a line *l* and a point *P* not on it; **(3)** two

intersecting lines; **(4)** two parallel

lines. Two lines in space need not lie in a plane—such lines are skew lines.

Two distinct planes in space either intersect in a line, or they do not intersect at all; in the latter case they are *parallel*. If they intersect at right angles, they are *perpendicular*. A line

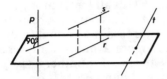

in space has one of the following relations to a plane: **(1)** it can lie entirely in the plane (line *r* in figure), **(2)** it can intersect the plane in one point (line *t* and perpendicular line *p*); **(3)** it can be parallel to the plane, that is, have no common point with the plane (line *s*). The distance from a point to a plane is the length of the shortest line segment from the point to the plane; this is a perpendicular segment. Three or more planes which meet in a common line are called collinear; all the (collinear) planes through a common line form a *pencil of planes*.

In analytic geometry, a plane is represented as the graph of a linear equation $Ax + By + Cz + D = 0$. If the coefficient of one of the variables is zero, the plane is parallel to (or contains) one of the axes; for example, $x + 2y - 4 = 0$ is the equation of a plane parallel to the z-axis; this plane intersects the xy-plane in the line with the same equation (as an equation in the xy-plane). If the coefficients of two of the variables are zero, the plane is parallel to one of the coordinate planes; for example, $z = 6$ is a plane parallel to the xy-plane and 6 units above it.

There are several standard forms of the *equation of a plane*. One is the

intercept form:

$$\frac{x}{a} + \frac{y}{b} + \frac{z}{c} = 1,$$

where a, b, and c are the $x -$, $y -$, and $z -$ intercepts, respectively. Another is the **normal form**. The direc-

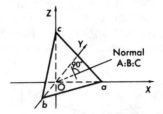

tion numbers of a perpendicular, or normal, to a plane are used to specify its orientation; the equation of the plane with direction numbers A, B, C and passing through the point (x_0, y_0, z_0) is

$$A(x - x_0) + B(y - y_0) + C(z - z_0) = 0.$$

In any linear equation $Ax + By + Cz + D = 0$, the coefficients A, B, C are the direction numbers of a normal to the plane of the equation. A second plane, $A_1x + B_1y + C_1z + D_1 = 0$, will be perpendicular to this plane in case $AA_1 + BB_1 + CC_1$ equals 0; it will be parallel in case A, B, C is proportional to A_1, B_1, C_1.

Plane coordinates   Any of several methods for locating a point in the plane by means of a pair of numbers. See **Cartesian coordinates in plane**, **Polar coordinates in plane**.

Plane Curve or Figure   A curve or figure which lies entirely in a plane.

Plane Geometry   The study of geometric figures in the plane; usually, the elementary aspects of the subject concerned with lines, angles, triangles, quadrilaterals, polygons, and circles. Plane analytic geometry is the study of plane figures through the

197

use of a coordinate system and the methods of algebra; it includes the conic as a principal topic. See **Euclidean geometry**.

Plane Section (Syn.: Section) Of a solid, its intersection with a plane. (In the figure, *ABC* is the plane section of the solid by the plane *p*). A plane section of a sphere is a circle; a plane section of a right circular cone is a conic; a plane section of a

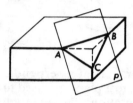

polyhedron is a polygon. See **Section of solid**, **Trace of surface**.

Plane Surface A two-dimensional, connected portion of a plane; for example, the face of a polyhedron is a plane surface. See **Surface**.

Plotting The marking of points in a coordinate system; also, drawing a graph by this means. See **Graphing**.

Plus Sign In arithmetic, the symbol "+," denoting the operation of addition, as in $8 + 5$, or $a + b$. It is also used to denote a positive number, such as $+5$ (in contrast to a negative number). The symbol was introduced about 1500.

Point In geometry, an undefined entity expressing the notion of an object with position but no dimensions. Geometric figures (line, circle, plane, sphere, etc.) can be thought of as sets of points. In the plane, two distinct points determine a line, that is, given two points there is exactly one line containing them. Three distinct points which belong to a single line are *collinear;* if they are not collinear,

they determine a unique circle and a unique triangle. In space, three non-collinear points determine a plane.

In a Cartesian coordinate system in the *plane* a point is represented by a pair of numbers, or coordinates, (x, y); the coordinate system matches all points of the plane in a one-to-one manner with all (real) number pairs (x, y). In a Cartesian coordinate system in three-dimensional (*n*-dimensional) *space* a point is represented by a triple of numbers (x, y, z), [*n*-tuple of numbers $(x_1, x_2, \ldots, x_n)$]; the coordinate system matches all points of the space in a one-to-one manner with all number triples (*n*-tuples).

Point at Infinity In **projective geometry**, an "ideal point" attached to an ordinary line; in this geometry, (ordinary) parallel lines share a common point at infinity.

Point of Division Of a line segment, a point which divides the segment in a given ratio. See **Division of line segment**.

Point of Inflection Of a plane curve, a point *P* where the tangent line reverses its sense of rotation (it is *S*-shaped at *P*). A point of inflection of a *function of a real variable*

$f(x)$ is an inflection point of its graph $y = f(x)$; if the second derivative of $f(x)$ vanishes at $x = a$ (and also changes sign there), then $f(x)$ has an inflection point there.

Point of Tangency (Syn.: Point of

contact) See **Tangent line to curve, Tangent plane to surface**.

Point-Slope or Two-Point Equation of Line See **Line**.

Poisson Distribution
Let X be a **random variable** taking on the integral values $p = 0, 1, 2, \ldots$; then X is said to have a Poisson distribution in case the probability of the value p is $m^p e^{-m}/p!$. The mean and variance of X have the common value m.

Polar Angle and Axis See **Polar coordinates in plane, Spherical coordinates**.

Polar Coordinates in Plane
A method of locating a point in the plane by its distance from a fixed point (the *pole*) and its orientation with respect to a half-line having the pole as its initial point (the *polar axis*). Given a point P, the line segment from the pole to P is the *radius vector* to P; the point P is located by

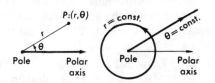

the length r of the radius vector and the angle of rotation θ from the polar axis to the radius vector. The values (r, θ) are the *polar coordinates* of P; θ is the *polar angle* (also, *vectorial angle, amplitude, anomaly,* or *azimuth*). For example, the point $(2, 30°)$ is 2 units from the pole and has a polar angle of $30°$; the point $(a, 0°)$ is on the polar axis at a distance a from the pole; the pole itself has polar coordinates $(0, \theta)$, θ being any angle. When r is held constant (and θ goes from $0°$ to $360°$), P sweeps out a circle of radius r. When θ is held constant (and

r increases from 0), P traces out a half-line at an angle θ with the polar axis. Polar coordinates are also given meaning when r is negative; in this case the radius vector is measured off in the reverse direction. For example, $(-3, 45°)$ is located three units from the pole in a direction opposite to that of the $45°$ half-line; this same point has other coordinate pairs, for instance, $(3, 225°)$ and $(3, -135°)$. In general, one point has many pairs of polar coordinates—by restricting θ to lie between $0°$ and $360°$ (excluding $360°$) and restricting r to be nonnegative, unique polar coordinates are assigned to each point (except the pole).

Suppose a rectangular coordinate system is superimposed on a polar coordinate system so that the origin and pole coincide, the positive x-axis and the polar axis coincide, and the y-axis is at a polar angle of $90°$.

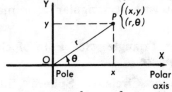

The *equations of transformation* expressing (x, y) in terms of (r, θ) are $x = r \cos \theta, y = r \sin \theta$. Those expressing (r, θ) in terms of (x, y) are $r^2 = x^2 + y^2, \tan \theta = y/x$.

Polar Cordinates in Space See **Spherical coordinates** (syn.).

Polar Distance See **Pole of circle on sphere**.

Polar Equation Of a curve in the

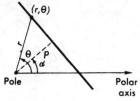

plane, an equation in polar coordinates (r, θ) which is satisfied by just those points which belong to the curve. The polar equation of a *line* has the general form $r = p \sec(\theta - \alpha)$, where p is the length of the perpendicular segment from the pole to the line, and α is the angle from the polar axis to this segment. For example, the equation $r = 3 \sec(\theta - 45°)$ is the polar equation of the line at a distance 3 from the pole whose perpendicular from the pole is inclined 45° to the polar axis. The polar equation is particularly convenient for representing such curves as **spirals**, the **lemniscate**, etc; also, see **Conic**.

Polar Form of Complex Number (Syn.: Trigonometric form of complex number)   The expression

$$r(\cos \theta + i \sin \theta)$$

for a complex number $x + iy$; here, (r, θ) are the polar coordinates of the point with rectangular coordinates (x, y).

Polar Triangle   See **Pole of circle on sphere**.

Pole of Circle of Sphere   Either point in which the diameter of the sphere which is perpendicular to the plane of the circle meets the sphere; the diameter is the *axis* of the circle. (The *poles* of a circular arc on the sphere are taken to be those of the circle containing the arc.) The polar distance of the circle is the spherical (great circle) distance from the nearer pole to any point on the circle(in the

figure PA and PB are polar distances).

Each spherical triangle is mated with another triangle on the sphere called its *polar triangle,* and defined as follows. Let ABC be the given spherical triangle. Opposite the vertex A is the circular arc BC; this arc has two poles; let A' be that one of its poles which is nearer A. Similarly, B determines a point B' which is the nearer pole of AC, and C determines C' which is the nearer pole of AB. The triangle $A'B'C'$ is defined as the polar triangle of ABC. This relationship is symmetric; that is, ABC is the polar triangle of $A'B'C'$. The following holds between a spherical triangle and its polar triangle—an angle (side) of a given spherical triangle equals the supplement of that side (angle) of the polar triangle which is opposite it (for example, the angle A equals 180° minus the arc $B'C'$). See **Solution of the oblique spherical triangle**.

Pole of Coordinate System   The point from which radial distances are measured in a system of **polar coordinates**.

Pole of Ellipsoid of Revolution   The endpoints of the axis of revolution of the **ellipsoid**.

Polygon   A closed path of connected line segments AB, BC, . . . , PQ, QA in the plane which does not cut across itself. The defining points $A, B, C, \ldots, P, Q$ are the *vertices,* and the connecting segments the *sides* of the polygon. Polygons are named according to the number of sides (or vertices); a *triangle* has three sides (the fewest possible), a *quadrilateral* four sides, a *pentagon* five sides, . . . , an *n-gon, n* sides.

In elementary geometry, "polygon" usually means *convex* polygon; this is a polygon for which any line

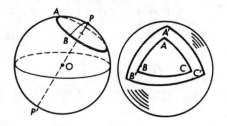

drawn through a side does not cut across the polygon. Another descrip-

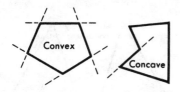

tion of a convex polygon is this: the line segment joining two points interior to the polygon never meets a side of the polygon. A polygon is *concave* in case it is not convex (this is a polygon that "cuts into itself").

A *diagonal* of a polygon is a line segment between nonadjacent vertices (a polygon can be subdivided into triangles by means of diagonals). An *angle* (or *interior angle*) of a polygon is an angle formed by adjacent

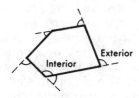

sides (and whose interior lies inside the polygon near the vertex); an *exterior angle* is an angle at a vertex of the polygon which is formed by a side and the extension of an adjacent side (and whose interior lies outside the polygon, near the vertex). The sum of the (interior) angles of an n-sided convex polygon is $(n - 2) \cdot 180°$; the sum of the exterior angles is $360°$, regardless of the number of sides (counting one exterior angle at each vertex).

A polygon is *equilateral* if all its sides are equal, *equiangular* if all its angles are equal. A *regular polygon* is one which is both equilateral and equiangular. Two polygons are *similar* if the vertices of one, $ABC \cdots$,

can be paired with the vertices, $A'B'C' \cdots$, of the other so that **(1)** corre-

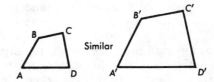

sponding angles are equal, and **(2)** corresponding sides are proportional; the *ratio of similitude* is the ratio of any pair of corresponding sides. For triangles, either of the conditions **(1)** and **(2)** implies the other, that is, either one is sufficient for similarity; the same does not hold for polygons of four or more sides. The polygons are **congruent figures in the plane** in case they are similar and corresponding sides are equal, that is, the ratio of similitude is 1. Of two congruent polygons, either can be brought into coincidence with the other by a rigid motion in space. Perimeters of similar polygons are proportional to corresponding sides, and areas are proportional to the squares of corresponding sides.

See **Circumscribed polygon, Inscribed polygon, Spherical polygon**. Ref. [110].

Polyhedral Angle In solid geometry, a configuration made up of three or more (distinct) rays (half-lines) emerging from a common point and the planar faces between them. More precisely, let $abc \cdots pq$

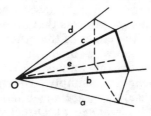

be an arrangement of three or more

rays with a common initial point O; the plane surfaces aOb, bOc, $\cdots$, pOq, qOa make up a polyhedral angle provided none of the plane surfaces intersect (except successive surfaces along a common ray). The common point is the *vertex,* the rays are the *edges,* and the planar surfaces are the *faces* of the polyhedral angle. A polyhedral angle divides space into two separate portions, one of which is designated as the *interior* of the polyhedral angle. An angle formed by successive rays (faces) is a *face angle* (*dihedral angle*) of the polyhedral angle. Polyhedral angles are named according to the number of faces (or edges); a *trihedral* angle has three faces, a *tetrahedral* angle four faces, a *pentahedral* angle five faces, and so on.

A *section* of a polyhedral angle is the polygon formed by a plane (not through the vertex) which cuts all its edges. If a section is a convex (concave) polygon, the polyhedral angle is *convex* (*concave*). The sum of the face angles of a convex polyhedral angle is less than 360°, regardless of the number of edges. *Opposite polyhedral angles* are angles with a common vertex in which the edges of one are the extensions of the edges of the other.

Suppose two polyhedral angles have their edges matched so that **(1)** corresponding face angles are equal, and **(2)** corresponding dihedral angles are equal. Now if the rotational arrangement of the edges in one polyhedral angle (as viewed from the vertex) is the same as that of the corresponding edges of the other angle (both clockwise or both counterclockwise), the angles are *directly congruent* (or, simply, *congruent*); otherwise, they are *oppositely congruent* (or *symmetric*). Directly congruent polyhedral angles can be made

to coincide by a rigid motion in space, oppositely congruent ones

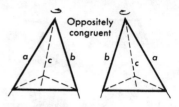

cannot. Opposite polyhedral angles are oppositely congruent. See **Solid angle, Spherical polygon, Trihedral angle**.

Polyhedron   In solid geometry, a closed surface made up of a finite number of planar surfaces, or *faces;* it divides space into two connected portions, its *interior* and its *exterior,* of which it is the common boundary. The faces meet along line segments, called *edges,* and the edges meet at endpoints, called *vertices.* The faces are plane polygons (plus interiors). A *polyhedral angle* of a polyhedron is one made up of the edges meeting at a vertex. A *diagonal* is a line segment joining two vertices not in the same face. Polyhedrons are named according to the number of faces; a *tetrahedron* has four faces (the fewest possible), a *pentahedron* five faces, a

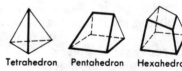

Tetrahedron   Pentahedron   Hexahedron

hexahedron six faces, and so on. Euler's theorem on polyhedrons is the general relationship $E = F + V - 2$ among the number of faces F, the number of edges E, and the number of vertices V of any polyhedron.

A polyhedron is *convex* in case it lies entirely on one side of any plane containing a face; otherwise, it is *concave*. Elementary solid geometry is usually restricted to convex polyhedrons. A plane section of a convex polyhedron is a convex polygon. A **regular polyhedron** is one all of whose faces are congruent polygons and all of whose polyhedral angles are congruent.

Two polyhedrons are *directly congruent* (or, simply, *congruent*) in case one can be brought into coincidence with the other by a rigid motion; they are *oppositely congruent* (or *symmetric*) in case one is congruent to the reflection of the other in a plane. Two polyhedrons are *similar* in case their vertices can be put into one-to-one correspondence in such a way that i) corresponding polyhedral angles are congruent, and ii) corresponding faces are similar polygons (and have the same relative position with respect to the whole polyhedron). See **Congruent figures in space**, **Similar** (geometry).

Ref. [6, 110].

Polyhedron, Circumscribed or Inscribed See **Circumscribed polyhedron, Inscribed polyhedron**.

Polyhedron, Regular See **Regular polyhedron**.

Polynomial A polynomial in one variable, x, is a sum of terms Ax^k, where A is a constant and k is a whole number or 0; e.g., $2x^2 - x + 7$. They are basic in ordinary and higher algebra; in ordinary algebra, the constants A are generally understood to be rational numbers. The *degree* of a polynomial is the exponent of the highest power; the *leading coefficient* is the coefficient of this term, while the *constant term* is the term in which x is missing (that is, the coefficient of x^0). For example, in $3x^2 + 2x - 5$, the degree is 2, the leading coefficient is 3, and the constant term is -5; in $x^4 - 7x^3 - x^2 + x$, the degree is four, the leading coefficient is 1, and the constant term is 0. The *general form,* or *standard form,* of a polynomial of degree n is

$$a_0x^n + a_1x^{n-1} + \cdots + a_{n-1}x + a_n,$$

the leading coefficient being a_0 (different from zero), and the constant term a_n; there are $n + 1$ terms in the general form but in any particular polynomial some of the coefficients a_k may be zero. A polynomial is also called a *rational integral* algebraic expression (because among fractional (rational) algebraic expressions, it is analogous to the ordinary integer among fractional (rational) numbers). Polynomials are classified according to their degree: a first degree polynomial, $a_0x + a_1$, is *linear,* a second degree polynomial, $a_0x^2 + a_1x + a_2$, is *quadratic,* and so on, through *cubic, quartic, quintic,* etc. For example, the polynomial $3x + 1$ is linear, the polynomials $x^2 - 2x + 3$, $x^2 + 4x$ are quadratic, and the polynomial $x^3 + 2x^2 - 3x$ is cubic.

Polynomials can be added and subtracted, multiplied and divided; the rules and techniques for carrying out these operations are studied in elementary algebra (see **Division of polynomials, Multiplication of polynomials**). A polynomial $P(x)$ has the polynomial $p(x)$ as a *factor* in case $P(x)$ is the product of $p(x)$ with some polynomial $q(x)$; that is, $P(x) = p(x) \cdot q(x)$ [the factor $p(x)$ is also called a *divisor* of $P(x)$]. For example, $x - 2$ is a factor of $x^2 - 3x + 2$ because

$$x^2 - 3x + 2 = (x - 2) \cdot (x - 1).$$

An *irreducible,* or *prime, polynomial,* is one that has no factors of lower

203

degree (other than a constant). The factoring of polynomials is a main topic in algebra. Any polynomial is a product of irreducible polynomials (just as every integer is a product of prime numbers). See **Factor of polynomial**.

A polynomial in *two variables, x* and *y*, is a sum of terms of the form Ax^jy^k, with A being a constant and j, k nonnegative integers; for example,

$$x^2y - 2xy^2 + xy + 4x^2 - 6y + 7$$

is a polynomial in x and y. The degree of a term Ax^jy^k is $j + k$; the *degree* of the polynomial is the highest degree among its terms (in the last example, the degree is 3, and there are two terms of this degree). Polynomials in any number of variables are similarly defined. The term "polynomial," without qualification, usually means a polynomial in one variable.

Ref. [18, 81, 120].

Polynomial Equation   An equation which is equivalent to one of the form $P = 0$, with P a polynomial. For example, $3x^2 - x = x - 5$ is a polynomial equation; it is equivalent to $3x^2 - 2x + 5 = 0$. A polynomial equation $P = 0$ is *linear, quadratic,* etc., according as the polynomial P is linear, quadratic, etc. A principal question of algebra and the theory of equations is the solution of polynomial equations.   See **Roots of polynomial equation**.

Polynomial Function   A function whose values are given by a polynomial. The function is *linear, quadratic, cubic,* etc., according as the polynomial is. The graph of a linear function (in one variable) is a line, and of a quadratic polynomial is a parabola. The graphs of the "pure" polynomial

functions, $y = x^n$, for $n = 1, 2, 3, 4,$ are shown in the figure. In general,

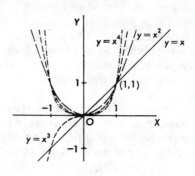

the graph of a polynomial function $p(x)$ may contain several peaks and troughs (maxima and minima), but the largest possible number of these is the one less than the degree.

A **power series** can be thought of as a generalization of a polynomial function of finite degree to one of "infinite" degree.

Positive Angle   An **angle** as a counterclockwise rotation.

Positive Number   A number greater than zero. The positive numbers are those that lie to the right of zero on a number scale; the negative numbers lie to the left. The sum, product, or quotient of positive numbers is a positive number.   See **Inequality relation**.

Positive sign   See **Plus sign**.

Postulate   See **Axiom**.

Postulates of Euclid   Basic assumptions of Euclid's geometry that concern properties of lines, points, circles, and so on. Euclid separated these geometric assumptions from general assumptions about equality, which he called "common notions." An example of a postulate of Euclid is that two distinct points determine a line.   See **Axioms of Euclid, Parallel postulate of Euclidean geometry**.

Power The first power of a is a^1 ($= a$); the second power, or *square*, of a is a^2 ($= a \times a$); etc. In general, a^p is called a power of a (the pth power), whether or not p is a positive integer; sometimes the term "power" is used for the **exponent p** itself.

Power of Complex Number The complex number $(x + iy)^n$ is the nth power of $x + iy$. It can be calculated by means of DeMoivre's theorem, when the complex number is written in its polar form $r(\cos\theta + i\sin\theta)$; the formula is

$$[r(\cos\theta + i\sin\theta)]^n = r^n(\cos n\theta + i\sin n\theta).$$

This applies as well when n is a rational number; the formula can be used therefore to calculate a **root of a complex number**.

Power of Set The **cardinal number** of a set.

Power Series In one variable, an infinite series in which successive terms are of the form of constants times successive integral powers of the variable; that is, it has the form

$$a_0 + a_1 x + a_2 x^2 + a_3 x^3 + \cdots.$$

The power series is a fundamental tool of mathematical analysis. Every power series in a real variable x has an *interval of convergence;* for x interior to this interval, say I, the series has a finite sum (converges), while exterior to I, it does not (this "interval" can be a point or the whole line). An example is the unending geometric series.

$$1 + x + x^2 + \cdots;$$

this series converges when x is inside the interval from -1 to 1, but not outside. When it converges, it has the value $1/(1 - x)$; for example, when x is $1/2$, $1/(1 - x) = 2$, so that

$$2 = 1 + \frac{1}{2} + \frac{1}{4} + \frac{1}{8} + \cdots.$$

A *binomial series* is a power series converging to $(a + x)^r$, where r is a rational number other than a nonnegative integer; examples are

$$(1 + x)^{-1} = 1 - x + x^2 - x^3 + \cdots$$
$$(1 + x)^{-2} = 1 - 2x + 3x^2 - 4x^3 + \cdots$$
$$(1 + x)^{1/2} = 1 + \tfrac{1}{2}x - \left(\frac{1}{2^2 \cdot 2!}\right) x^2$$
$$+ \left(\frac{1 \cdot 3}{2^3 \cdot 3!}\right) x^3 - \left(\frac{1 \cdot 3 \cdot 5}{2^4 \cdot 4!}\right) x^4 + \cdots.$$

The interval of convergence of these series is the interval from -1 to 1, and the equations hold inside this. These expansions, or of any power $(a + x)^r$, are obtained by the same procedure that gives the term-by-term (finite) expansion of $(1 + x)^n$, according to the **binomial theorem**, when n is a positive integer; the binomial series for $(a + x)^r$ converges to $(a + x)^r$ for x between $-a$ and a, which is its interval of convergence.

Power series provide an important way to represent functions of mathematics; such representations have many uses, one of these being a means of computing (approximate) values of the function. The following *sine series, cosine series,* and *exponential series* are examples.

$$\sin x = x - \frac{x^3}{3!} + \frac{x^5}{5!} - \frac{x^7}{7!} + \cdots$$
$$\cos x = 1 - \frac{x^2}{2!} + \frac{x^4}{4!} - \frac{x^6}{6!} + \cdots$$
$$e^x = 1 + x + \frac{x^2}{2!} + \frac{x^3}{3!} + \frac{x^4}{4!} + \cdots$$

These series converge for all values of x. The (natural) logarithm function is represented by the following *logarithmic series*

$$\log_e(1 + x) = x - \frac{x^2}{2} + \frac{x^3}{3} - \frac{x^4}{4} + \cdots;$$

it converges for x between -1 and

+1 (including +1, but excluding −1). **Taylor's theorem** gives a general method for expanding functions in power series.

If the variable x in a power series is replaced by a variable z standing for a complex number, the series still has meaning in terms of operations on complex numbers. Such functions as trigonometric functions, exponential functions, logarithmic functions, can then be generalized to *functions of a complex variable* by taking these power series in z as definitions of the functions. The study of these functions is carried out in advanced calculus.

Precision The smallest unit measurement in terms of which an **approximate number** or measurement is expressed; for example, if a measurement is determined as 4.136 then its precision is .001 (one-thousandth), the unit of the last place. A distinction is to be made between the precision of an approximation and its relative accuracy; the latter is commonly expressed in terms of the relative **error**. For example, if .0015 is an approximate number for .00148 and 326 is an approximate number for 325.6, the first has higher precision, but the second has higher relative accuracy.

Prime Factor In arithmetic (algebra), a factor which is a prime number (prime polynomial). See **Factor of integer**, **Factor of polynomial**.

Prime Number (Syn.: Prime) An integer p which has no factors other than ± 1 and $\pm p$; the low positive primes are

$$2, 3, 5, 7, 11, 13, 17, \cdots$$

(1 is usually excluded). The only even positive prime is 2; there are in-

finitely many primes, but there is no general formula for all primes. (Euclid gave the first known general proof of the infinitude of primes). See **Arithmetic progression**.

The prime numbers are the building blocks for all natural numbers in the sense that every natural number can be written as a product of unique positive primes; this is the **unique factorization theorem** of arithmetic. Two integers are *relatively prime* in case they have no prime factor in common (hence no positive factor other than 1 in common); for example, 50 and 63 are relatively prime (the first equals $2 \cdot 5 \cdot 5$, the second, $3 \cdot 3 \cdot 7$).

Prime numbers have fascinated serious mathematicians and amateurs for centuries; their study is an important part of the **theory of numbers**. Various conjectures concerning prime numbers, centuries old, still remain unanswered. One of these is the following problem of *twin primes* (or *prime pairs*): in the unending series of primes there occasionally occur odd consecutive pairs such as (11, 13), (17, 19), and (59, 61); it is unknown whether there are infinitely many such twin primes.

Ref. [11, 29, 84, 137].

Prime Number Theorem The following famous theorem of the theory of numbers concerning the "distribution," or "density," of prime numbers among all positive integers. Let $P(n)$ equal the number of primes from 1 to n [for example, $P(10)$ equals 4, since 2, 3, 5, 7, are the primes from 1 to 10]; the proportion of primes to all the integers from 1 to n is then the ratio $P(n)/n$. The theorem asserts that the ratio $P(n)/n$ divided by $1/\log n$ has the limit 1 as n increases without bound (here, $\log n$ is the natural logarithm). Put otherwise, the ratio $P(n)/n$ is approximated by the ratio $1/\log n$ when n is large, the approximation improving with increasing n; for example, for n equal to a billion, $1/\log n$ is .05; hence about 5% of the positive integers up to one billion are primes. The prime number theorem was first proved about 1900. Ref. [29, 34, 132].

Prime Pair Two **prime numbers** which are consecutive odd integers, such as 11, 13.

Prime Polynomial See **Irreducible polynomial** (syn.).

Primitive of Function See **Indefinite integral of function** (syn.).

Primitive Term See **Undefined term** (syn.).

Principal Angle See **Principal value** (syn.).

Principal Parts of Triangle The sides and the (interior) angles of a triangle. Other parts, such as altitudes, medians, exterior angles, etc., are *secondary parts*.

Principal Root Of a *positive number,* that root which is positive; of an odd root of a *negative number,* the (unique) negative root. For example, the square roots of 64 are 8 and -8, of which 8 is the principal root; the principal root of $\sqrt[3]{64}$ is the (unique) root 4, and of $\sqrt[3]{-64}$ is the (unique) root -4. Sometimes the symbol $\sqrt[n]{a}$ denotes just the principal root; then $\sqrt{a}$ and $-\sqrt{a}$, for example, would denote the two square roots of the positive number a. See **Root of number**.

Principal Value (Syn.: Principal angle) The principal values of a (many-valued) *inverse trigonometric function* are those in a set of values restricting it to a single-valued func-

tion; principal values are shown in the table. For example $\cos^{-1}(\frac{1}{2})$ has the values $60°$, $-60°$, $300°$, $-300°$, or any angle coterminal with $60°$ or $300°$; but its principal value is $60°$, or $\pi/3$ radians. The principal value of each function is chosen in the first

Function	Principal value	
	Degrees	Radians
Sin^{-1}	$-90°$ to $90°$	$-\frac{\pi}{2}$ to $\frac{\pi}{2}$
Cos^{-1}	$0°$ to $180°$	0 to π
Tan^{-1}	$-90°$ to $90°$	$-\frac{\pi}{2}$ to $\frac{\pi}{2}$
Cot^{-1}	$0°$ to $180°$	0 to π
Sec^{-1}	$-270°$ to $-180°$ $0°$ to $90°$	$-\frac{3}{2}\pi$ to $-\pi$ 0 to $\frac{\pi}{2}$
Csc^{-1}	$-180°$ to $-90°$ $0°$ to $90°$	$-\pi$ to $-\frac{\pi}{2}$ 0 to $\frac{\pi}{2}$

quadrant when the argument of the function is positive; when the argument is negative, the choice shown in the table for $\sec^{-1}x$ and $\csc^{-1}x$ is often, but not universally, agreed upon. The principal value is sometimes denoted by a capital letter, as in $\mathrm{Cos}^{-1}x$, $\mathrm{Sin}^{-1}x$, etc.; for example, $\mathrm{Tan}^{-1}(-1) = -45°$.

Prism A polyhedron (closed surface with plane faces) defined by a polygon $ABC\cdots$ (the *directrix*) and a line segment l (not in the plane of the polygon) in the following manner. When l is moved parallel to itself with one endpoint tracing out the polygon $ABC\cdots$, it generates a *lateral surface,* as well as a duplicate $A'B'C'\cdots$ of the directrix at the other endpoint; a prism consists of this lateral surface and two congruent *bases,* made up of the polygons and their interiors (see **Cylinder**). The points A, B, C, ..., A', B', C',

... are the *vertices,* the line segments *AA', BB', CC',* ... are the *edges,* and the parallelograms *AA'B'B, BB'C'C,* ... are the *lateral faces* of the prism. (Put otherwise, a prism is a polyhedron with a pair of congruent and parallel faces (the bases), whose other faces (the lateral faces) are parallelograms determined by corresponding sides of the bases.) A

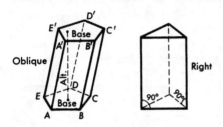

prism is *convex* in case the base is a convex polygon.

The *altitude* is a perpendicular line segment (or its length) between the planes of the bases; a *right section* is an intersection with a plane perpendicular to a lateral edge. The lateral area of a prism (the sum of the areas of the lateral faces) equals the length of a lateral edge times the perimeter of a right section. The volume of a prism equals the area of the base times the altitude.

Prisms are named according to the base; for example, a *triangular* prism has a triangle as base, a *quadrangular* prism a quadrilateral, and so on. Prisms are also classified as *right* and *oblique,* the former having its lateral

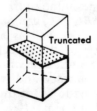

edges perpendicular to the bases and

the latter having them oblique to the bases. A *regular* prism is a right prism whose bases are regular polygons. For a right prism, the lateral area equals the altitude times the perimeter of the base. A *truncated* prism is a solid included between a base of a prism and a plane not parallel to the base (and intersecting all the edges).

Prismatic Surface In solid geometry, an indefinitely extended surface generated by a line (the *generator* or *generatrix*) as it moves parallel to itself, always passing through a fixed plane broken line (the *directrix*). The

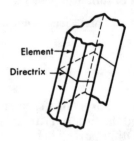

generator in any position is an *element.* If the broken line is a polygon, the prismatic surface is *closed;* if the broken line is open, the surface is *open.* A solid determined by two parallel planes intersecting all the edges of a closed prismatic surface is a **prism.** See **Cylindrical surface**.

Prismatoid A polyhedron whose vertices lie in two parallel planes; the

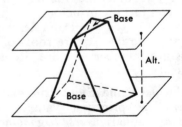

prism and pyramid are particular types of prismatoids. The *bases* are the faces in the parallel planes, and the *altitude* is a line segment (or its length) between these planes. The other faces are *lateral* faces; a lateral face is either a triangle, parallelogram, or trapezoid. A *midsection* is a plane section parallel to and midway between the bases. The volume V of a prismatoid is given by the *prismoidal formula*, $V = \frac{1}{6}h(B_1 + B_2 + 4B_m)$, where h is the altitude, B_1 and B_2 are the areas of the bases, and B_m is the area of the midsection. This formula gives the volumes of the prism and pyramid as special cases.

Prismoid A type of *prismatoid* in which the two bases are polygons with equal numbers of sides, and the lateral faces are quadrilaterals

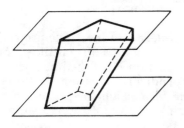

(necessarily trapezoids or parallelograms) formed by connecting corresponding vertices of the bases. A *prism* can be defined as a prismoid whose bases are congruent.

Probability Informally, a numerical value of the "chance" of occurrence of one of several possible outcomes of an unpredictable event. Suppose the event has n alternative outcomes A (mutually exclusive and exhaustive); then the probability of each alternative is a number $p(A)$ between 0 and 1. The sum of the $p(A)$ over all alternatives A equals 1. The number $p(A)$ can be interpreted as the fraction of times the alternative will occur, approximately, in a large num-

ber of trials, or, as the "limit" of this fraction as the number of trials increases without bound. For example, two outcomes can result from tossing a coin—heads or tails; the probability of heads is $\frac{1}{2}$ and the probability of tails is $\frac{1}{2}$. Eleven outcomes can occur for the sum of the faces that show in the event two dice are rolled—2, 3, 4, 5, 6, 7, 8, 9, 10, 11, 12; the probability of these outcomes are, respectively, $\frac{1}{36}, \frac{2}{36}, \frac{3}{36}, \frac{4}{36}, \frac{5}{36}, \frac{6}{36}, \frac{5}{36}, \frac{4}{36}, \frac{3}{36}, \frac{1}{36}$. (Thus, if two dice are rolled 1,000,000 times, it is expected that 7 will occur close to $\frac{1}{6}$ of the time). If a container holds B balls with w being white, b being black, and r being red, then the probability of blindly picking out a white ball is w/B, a black ball is b/B, and a red ball is r/B.

Suppose $A_1, A_2, \ldots$ are the alternatives for one random event and $B_1, B_2, \ldots$ are the alternatives for another random event; then the probability of the simultaneous occurrence of a pair of alternatives, such as $(A_1, B_1), (A_2, B_1), (A_1, B_2)$, and so on, can be considered. For *independent random events,* the probability of any pair is the product of the probabilities of the individual alternatives of the pair; for *dependent random events* this is not so, and the notion of the *conditional probability* of one alternative A given another B is used to describe the relationship between the random events. See **Expected value, Random variable.**

Ref. [31, 41, 86, 104, 144].

Probability Function See **Random variable.**

Probability in Repeated Trials The probability of a given number of successes in a certain number of trials, when the probability of success in a single trial is the same from trial to trial. More exactly, let the outcome

S ("success") in one trial occur with probability p; the probability, q, that S does not occur equals $1 - p$. (For example, if S is the occurrence of a seven in a single roll of two dice, then p is $\frac{1}{6}$ and q is $\frac{5}{6}$). Then the probability of *r successes in n repeated trials* (i.e., exactly r successes) equals

$$\frac{n!}{(n - r)!r!}\, p^r q^{n-r}$$

where $k!$, or k factorial, equals $1 \cdot 2 \cdot 3 \cdots (k - 1) \cdot k$. (For example, consider the probability of two sevens in three throws of the dice; here $p = \frac{1}{6}$, $q = \frac{5}{6}$, $n = 3$, $r = 2$, and the formula gives $(3!/1!2!)(1/6)^2(5/6)$ or $5/72$.) This formula is identical with the term containing the power $p^r q^{n-r}$ in the expansion of $(p + q)^n$ by the binomial theorem; the formula is called the *binomial distribution* (the terms of the expansion giving the probabilities of the various values of r, for a fixed n). Ref. [108].

Probability Theory The mathematical theory of the notions of chance, or random, phenomena; *statistics* is the application of this theory to questions that arise in real phenomena and the analysis of experimental data. Probability occurred in the writings of Fermat and Pascal in the middle of the seventeenth century; the classical work, however, was that of Laplace at the beginning of the nineteenth century.

Product In arithmetic, the result of the operation of **multiplication**; the product of a and b is denoted by $a \times b$, $a \cdot b$, or ab.

Product Formulas (trigonometry) The following trigonometric identities expressing the product of sines and cosines as sums of these functions.

$\sin A \cos B$
$\quad = \frac{1}{2}[\sin (A + B) + \sin (A - B)]$
$\cos A \sin B$
$\quad = \frac{1}{2}[\sin (A + B) - \sin (A - B)]$
$\cos A \cos B$
$\quad = \frac{1}{2}[\cos (A + B) + \cos (A - B)]$
$\sin A \sin B$
$\quad = \frac{1}{2}[\cos (A - B) - \cos (A + B)]$

Product of Sets See **Intersection of sets** (syn.).

Programming See **Computer program**, **Mathematical programming**.

Programming Language See **Computer programming language**.

Progression See **Arithmetic progression**, **Geometric progression**, **Harmonic progression**.

Projection on Line The projection of a *point P* on a line l is the point of intersection P' of the line l with the perpendicular through P; "projection" also means the process of generating P' from P. As an example,

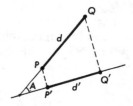

the projection of the point (x, y) on the x-axis is $(x, 0)$, the projection on the y-axis is $(0, y)$. The projection of a *line segment PQ* on the line l is the line segment $P'Q'$, where P' and Q' are the projections of P and Q respectively. The length d' of $P'Q'$ is given by $d' = d \cos A$, where d is the length of PQ and A is the angle between the lines.

Projection on Plane The projection of a *point P* on a plane p, is the point of intersection P' of the plane with the perpendicular line through P; "projection" also means the process of generating P' from P. For example, in a rectangular coordinate system in space, the projection of a point (x, y, z) on the xy-plane is $(x, y, 0)$; similarly, the projections on the xz-plane and yz-plane are $(x, 0, z)$ and $(0, y, z)$, respectively. The projection of a *line l* on the plane p is the

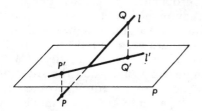

line l' consisting of the projections of the points of l (it is also the intersection of p with the perpendicular plane through l). In general, the projection of any *figure F* in space on a plane is the plane figure F' made up of the projections of the points of F. See **Projective Geometry**.

Projective Geometry Projective geometry of the plane is the study of those properties of plane figures that are retained under any central projection. A *central projection* of one plane p in space on another p', is a correspondence from the points P of p to the points P' of p' by means of a *center of projection O* not in either

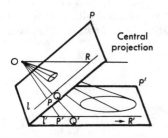

plane: here, the point P' corresponding to P is the point in which OP intersects p'. (The case of *parallel projection,* when lines PP' between corresponding points are all parallel to a fixed line, occurs when O is the "point at infinity.") Projective geometry in a space of any dimension is similarly defined (under an appropriate definition of "projection.") See **Geometry**.

Under central projection of a plane, every figure in the given plane is transformed into one in the other plane; lines go into lines, triangles into triangles, and polygons into polygons. However, most familiar properties, such as length of line segment, measure of angles, congruence of polygons, etc., are not preserved. Circles need not project into circles, nor need ellipses project into ellipses; however, every conic does project into a conic (not necessarily of the same type), and therefore the property of being a conic is preserved under central projection. Another preserved property is that expressed in **Desargues' theorem**—this is therefore a theorem of projective geometry; *Pascal's theorem* is likewise a theorem of projective geometry (see **Hexagon**). *Harmonic division* is another projective "invariant."

In projective geometry, an *ideal point,* or *point at infinity,* is adjoined to each line. This comes about in a natural way if a central projection is to establish a one-to-one correspondence between planes. In the figure showing l and its central projection l', the point R lying on l fails to project into a point R' of l' (because OR is parallel to the plane of l'). This difficulty is resolved by defining an "ideal point" R' which is assigned to the line l', and taken as the projection of R on the line l'. Under this concept, the projective plane consists of the ordinary plane together with an *ideal line,* or *line at infinity,* which contains all ideal points. Parallel lines have the same ideal point; that

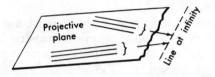

is, all parallel lines meet in a common point on the line at infinity. The concepts of ideal point and ideal line appear to be elusive only when they are described in the framework of ordinary Euclidean geometry; they are amenable to precise definition in a rigorous approach to projective geometry.

An important feature of projective geometry, which does not occur in ordinary geometry, is the principle of *duality;* this assures that for each relationship of plane projective geometry concerning points and lines, there is a "dual" relationship derived by interchanging the roles of "point" and "line" (e.g., the converse in Desargues' theorem is the dual of the given statement).

Analytic projective geometry is the study of projective geometry by algebraic methods based on "projective" coordinates, just as analytic geometry is the algebraic study of ordinary geometry by Cartesian coordinates. The invention of projective geometry is credited to Desargues' in the first half of the seventeenth century; however, his work went unnoticed until the revival of the subject in the early nineteenth century.

Ref. [28, 101].

Prolate Ellipsoid (Syn.: Prolate spheroid)   An **ellipsoid** produced by rotating an ellipse through a complete revolution about its longer axis.

Proof   A logical derivation of a

proposition from axioms, or explicit assumptions, and previously proved propositions. Mathematical proofs use the deductive method of reasoning, not the method of scientific induction in which general propositions are accepted on the basis of strong empirical or experimental evidence.   See **Deductive theory**.

One way of classifying proofs is as *direct* and *indirect.* A direct proof of a proposition typically begins by granting the hypothesis of the proposition and arguing to the conclusion. For example, a direct proof of the proposition "If two angles of a triangle are equal, then the sides opposite them are equal" would ordinarily begin by taking a triangle with two equal angles and attempting to argue logically that the opposite sides are equal. An indirect proof typically begins by denying the proposition to be proved and then attempts to deduce a contradiction; for example, an indirect proof of the proposition "There is no rational number whose square is 2" might begin by assuming there is a rational number whose square is 2, and showing that this leads to a logical contradiction. The indirect proof is sometimes called *proof by contradiction* or *reductio ad absurdum.*

An important type of proof in mathematics is **mathematical induction** or proof by induction. (This does not refer to the method of scientific induction). It is applied to propositions which hold for an arbitrary positive integer n; an example is the proposition

$$1^2 + 2^2 + 3^2 + \cdots + n^2 = n(n + 1)(2n + 1)/6.$$

In geometry, an *analytic proof* is one which uses the techniques of algebra rather than the methods of geometry; the latter is sometimes called a *synthetic proof.* An analytic proof uses a coordinate system to represent points as numbers, and treats lines, circles, etc., as equations in coordinate variables.

The study of the nature of mathematical proof is a part of modern logic; the logician has shown how proofs can be analyzed in terms of a few basic patterns of **inference**, or "rules of proof." Ref. [34, 131].

Proper Fraction In arithmetic (algebra), a ratio of positive integers (polynomials) in which the value (degree) of the numerator is less than that of the denominator. See **Fraction**, **Fraction** (algebra).

Proper Subset Of a set A, a subset of A which is not identical with A; that is, a subset which lacks one or more members of A.

Property Some characteristic of numbers or things, or some condition they satisfy. For example, any triangle has the property that the sum of its three angles equals a straight angle; a whole number whose decimal digits add up to a multiple of nine has the property of being a multiple of nine itself. A property is used to define a **set**, or collection, of things; for example, the property of being divisible by 2 defines the set of even whole numbers (within the class of all whole numbers).

Properties can be combined to produce other properties; from the property "is red" and the property "is new" one can construct the properties "is red or is new," "is red and is new," "is not red," etc. Combinations of properties are reflected in corresponding combinations of sets. For example, if A is the set of red things and B is the set of new things, then (1) the set of things which are red *or* new is the *union* of the sets A and B, (2) the set of things which are red *and* new is the *intersection* of the sets, and (3) the set of things which are not red is the *complement* of the set A. See **Algebra of sets**, **Quantifier**.

Proportion An equality of two ratios; hence, a relation of the form $a/b = c/d$, among a, b, c, and d (sometimes written $a:b = c:d$). Proportions arise frequently in mathematics; for example, segments cut out of two lines by three parallel lines satisfy such a relationship; so do two pairs of corresponding sides of similar triangles.

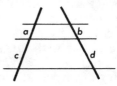

In the proportion $a/b = c/d$, a, b, c, and d are the *terms,* with a and d being the *extreme* terms and b and c the *mean terms.* In any proportion, the product of the means equals the product of the extremes, that is $ad = bc$; this is known as the *rule of three* (because it provides a convenient way to solve a ratio for one of the terms when the other three are given). A proportion $a/b = c/d$ is equivalent to two equalities, $a = kb$ and $c = kd$, where k is a common factor.

The following are some traditional rules for changing a given proportion $a/b = c/d$ into other proportions involving combinations or rearrangements of the terms: (1) *proportion by addition,*

$$(a + b/b = (c + d)/d;$$

(2) *proportion by subtraction,*

$$(a - b)/b = (c - d)d;$$

(3) *proportion by alternation,* $a/c = b/d$; **(4)** *proportion by inversion,* $b/a = d/c$. This terminology exists principally for historical reasons.

Proportion, Direct or Inverse See **Proportionality**.

Proportional In a proportion $a/b = c/x$, x is the *fourth proportional* to a, b, c. In $a/x = x/d$, the common value x is the *mean proportional* between a and d (the same as the geometric mean of a and d). In $a/b = b/x$, x is the *third proportional* to a and b. For the meaning of "y is proportional to x," and similar relationships, see **Proportionality**.

Proportional Parts (geometry) Parts of one geometric figure, with measures $a, b, c, \ldots$, are proportional to those of another with measures a', $b', c' \cdots$ in case $a/a' = b/b' = c/c' = \cdots$; for example, all sides (and other segments) of a polygon are proportional to the corresponding sides (and other segments) of a similar polygon.

Proportional Parts in Table Auxiliary lists accompanying a table of values of a function, which give the decimal fractions of differences of tabular values of the function. They are used in **linear interpolation**.

Proportionality A *direct proportionality* (or *direct proportion*) between y and x is a relation of the form $y = kx$; y is said to be directly proportional (or, more simply, proportional) to x, and k is the *factor* (or *constant*) *of proportionality*. (For example, the circumference C of a circle is proportional to its radius r, since $C = 2\pi r$; the factor of proportionality is 2π.) If y is proportional to x, then x is proportional to y [$y = kx$ implies $x =$

$(1/k)y$]. A direct proportion $y = kx$ is the simplest relationship between y and x. When y is plotted against x, the result is a line through the origin

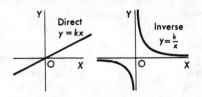

(with slope k). The equation $y = kx$ amounts to the proportion $y_1/x_1 = y_2/x_2$ for any pairs (x_1, y_1) and (x_2, y_2) that satisfy the equation; hence $y = kx$ represents an infinite number of ordinary proportions $a/b = c/d$. The notion of proportionality applies as well to finite *sets of numbers;* for example, the set of numbers $(2, 3, 4, 5)$ is said to be proportional to $(6, 9, 12, 15)$ because the relation $y = 3x$ holds for x in the first set and y the corresponding member in the second set.

An *inverse proportionality* (or *inverse proportion,* or *reciprocal proportion*) is a relation of the form $y = k/x$; y is said to be inversely proportional to x. (For example, given a fixed distance k, the time T to travel this distance is inversely proportional to the speed S, that is, $T = k/S$.) In an inverse proportion, $y = k/x$, with the constant k positive, y decreases as x increases; the graph is a hyperbola, as shown in the figure. If y is inversely proportional to x, then x is inversely proportional to y. See **Variation**.

Proposition A mathematical statement; usually a proved statement (hence, a theorem).

Propositional Algebra See **Algebra of propositions** (syn.).

Pseudo-Random Number See **Random number**.

Ptolemy's Theorem A theorem stating a condition on the sides of a quadrilateral in order for it to lie in a **circumscribed circle**.

Pure Imaginary Number A complex number of the form bi, with $b \neq 0$.

Pure Mathematics See **Mathematics**.

Pure Quadratic A quadratic equation of the form $ax^2 + c = 0$; that is, one with the term of the first degree missing.

Pyramid A polyhedron (closed surface with plane faces) defined by polygon $ABC \ldots$, (the *directrix*) and a point V (the *vertex*, or *apex*) outside the plane of the polygon; the pyramid consists of the *lateral faces* VAB, $VBC, \ldots$, and the *base*, which is the directrix and its interior (see **Cone**). The line segments VA, VB, $VC, \ldots$ are the *lateral edges* of the pyramid. The pyramid is *convex* in case the directrix is a convex polygon. The *alti-*

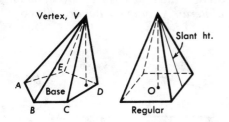

tude of a pyramid is the perpendicular segment (or its length) from the vertex to the plane of the base. By the lateral area is meant the sum of the areas of the lateral faces. The volume of a pyramid equals $(\frac{1}{3})hB$, where h is the altitude and B is the area of the base.

Pyramids are named according to the base. A *triangular* pyramid has a triangle as base, a *quadrangular* pyramid has a quadrilateral as base, and

so on. A *regular pyramid* is one whose base is a regular polygon and whose altitude passes through the center O of the base. The lateral faces of a regular pyramid are congruent isosceles triangles, and they form equal dihedral angles with the base plane; the *slant height s* is the altitude of any congruent face. The lateral area of a regular pyramid equals $(\frac{1}{2})sP$, where P is the perimeter of the base.

A *frustrum of a pyramid* is the solid between the base and a plane section parallel to the base (and intersecting all the lateral edges); its bases are given by the section and the original

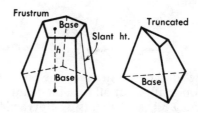

base, and the altitude h is the perpendicular distance between the planes of the bases. The volume of the frustrum equals $(\frac{1}{3})h(B_1 + B_2 + \sqrt{B_1 B_2})$, where B_1 and B_2 are the areas of the bases. The lateral faces of a frustrum are trapezoids; for a frustrum of a regular pyramid, these faces are congruent isosceles trapezoids and their common altitude is the slant height s of the frustrum. In the latter case, the lateral area, that is, the area exclusive of the bases, equals $(\frac{1}{2})s(P_1 + P_2)$, with P_1, P_2 being perimeters of the bases; hence, this area is the slant height times the perimeter of a parallel plane section midway between the bases. The solid between the base of a pyramid and a plane section not parallel to the base (and intersecting all the lateral edges) is a *truncated pyramid*.

215

Pyramidal Surface   In solid geometry, an indefinitely extended surface generated by a line (the *generator,* or *generatrix*), which is fixed at a point (the *vertex*), and moves so as to pass through a given broken line (the *directrix*). The generator in any position is an *element*. If the broken line is a polygon, the surface is *closed;* if the broken line is open, the surface is *open*. A pyramidal surface consists of two *nappes* which meet at a vertex.

The solid determined by the portion of one nappe cut off by a plane intersecting all its elements, is a **pyramid**. See **Conical surface**.

Pythagorean Identities   The following basic trigonometric identities: $\sin^2 x + \cos^2 x = 1$, $1 + \tan^2 x = \sec^2 x$, and $1 + \cot^2 x = \csc^2 x$; they are consequences of the theorem of Pythagoras and the definitions of the trigonometric functions.

Pythagorean Numbers   Any three positive integers which satisfy the equation $a^2 + b^2 = c^2$ (this is the relation of the theorem of Pythagoras).

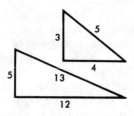

Such a triple of numbers describes a right triangle whose sides are all integers. Examples of Pythagorean numbers are 3, 4, 5 and 5, 12, 13. An unlimited number of such triples exist; they can all be generated by the formulas $m^2 - n^2$, $2mn$, $m^2 + n^2$, where m and n are integers (m greater than n); for example when m is 2 and n is 1 the formulas produce 3, 4, 5; when m is 3 and n is 2, it produces 5, 12, 13. The general formula was given by Euclid.   See **Fermat's last theorem**. Ref. [28].

Pythagorean Theorem   See **Theorem of Pythagoras** (syn.).

Q

Quadrangle   A *simple quadrangle* is a closed broken line in the plane consisting of four vertices A, B, C, D (no three on a line) in a given arrangement, and the four line segments AB, BC, CD, DA (obtained by joining them in order). These segments may or may not intersect; when they do not, the figure is a (simple) *quadrilateral*. A *complete quadrangle* consists of four vertices A, B, C, D and

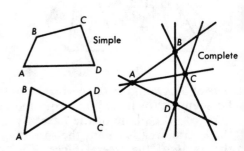

the six lines which they determine in all possible pairs; this configuration is important in projective geometry.

Quadrangular   Ordinarily, pertaining to the quadrilateral; quadrangular prisms and quadrangular pyramids are prisms and pyramids whose bases are quadrilaterals.

Quadrant Of a system of *Cartesian coordinates in the plane,* any one of the four portions into which the plane is divided by the two axes. A *quadrant of a circle* is a circular arc of 90° (or the sector determined by the arc).

Quadrant of an Angle The quadrant containing the terminal side of an angle of rotation (with initial side along the positive *x*-axis). If the terminal side coincides with an axis, then the angle is a *quadrantal angle,*

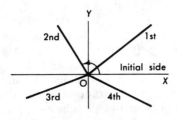

that is, a multiple of 90°.

Quadrantal Spherical Triangle A **spherical triangle** in which at least one side is a quarter of a great circle.

Quadratic Equation and Formula A quadratic equation (or, simply, *quadratic*) is a polynomial equation of degree two; it has the general form $ax^2 + bx + c = 0$. A *pure* quadratic has the form $ax^2 + c = 0$, such as $x^2 - 3 = 0$. The pure quadratic can be solved by square roots; for example, $3x^2 - 8 = 0$ is solved by the steps $x^2 = \frac{8}{3}, x = \pm 2\sqrt{2}/\sqrt{3}$, or $\pm 2\sqrt{6}/3$. Certain other quadratics can be solved by direct factoring; for example, $x^2 + x - 6 = 0$ can be written $(x - 2)(x + 3) = 0$, which gives $x - 2 = 0$ or $x + 3 = 0$, that is, $x = 2$ or -3. A general method for solving the quadratic is completing the

Quadratic Function and Polynomial

square; applied to the general quadratic equation $ax^2 + bx + c = 0$, it produces the *quadratic formula*

$$x = \frac{-b \pm \sqrt{b^2 - 4ac}}{2a}.$$

This gives the roots of any quadratic equation by substituting values for the coefficients a, b, c. For example, to solve $x^2 - 4x - 7 = 0$, substitute $a = 1, b = -4, c = -7$ to obtain

$$x = \frac{4 \pm \sqrt{44}}{2}, \text{ or } 2 \pm \sqrt{11}.$$

The *discriminant* is the expression $b^2 - 4ac$ under the radical sign in the quadratic formula; if the discriminant is positive the roots are real and distinct, if negative the roots are imaginary, and if zero the roots are real and equal. Two simple relationships, free of radicals, exist between the roots of a quadratic and its coefficients; namely, the sum of the roots is $-b/a$, and the product is c/a (this can be checked in $x^2 + x - 6 = 0$ whose roots were 2 and -3). These relationships generalize to the coefficients and **roots of a polynomial equation** of higher degree.

The rational numbers are not adequate for the solution of quadratic equations; that is, there are quadratic equations whose coefficients are rational numbers (in fact, integers) which have no rational number solution (an example is the equation $x^2 = 2$). This is a motivation for creating the irrational real number. Even so, it is necessary to extend the notion of number to the complex number to solve all quadratic equations; for example, the solutions of $x^2 + 4 = 0$ are the complex numbers $\pm 2i$. Ref. [81, 120].

Quadratic Function and Polynomial
A *quadratic polynomial* is a polynomial of the second degree; it has the

217

form $ax^2 + bx + c$. A *quadratic function* is a function whose value is given by a quadratic polynomial. The graph of the function is the graph of $y = ax^2 + bx + c$; it is a parabola with a vertical axis; the vertex is a low point or high point according to whether a is positive or negative. The solutions of the quadratic equation $ax^2 + bx + c = 0$ are called the *zeros* of the quadratic function; they specify the points of the graph where $y = 0$ (the intersection with the x-axis). The graph crosses the x-axis twice, once, or not at all

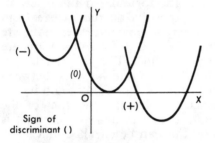

Sign of
discriminant ( )

according to whether the discriminant $b^2 - 4ac$ of the quadratic equation is positive, zero, or negative.

Quadratic Inequality   In one variable, an inequality which can be expressed in the form $ax^2 + bx + c < 0$ (or the same with $>$, $\leq$ or $\geq$ 0). A *solution* is any value of x for which the inequality holds. The solutions of the $ax^2 + bx + c < 0$ can be expressed in terms of the graph (parabola) of $y = ax^2 + bx + c$; they are

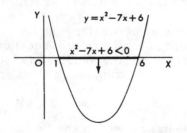

the values of x for which the graph lies below the x-axis (above the x-axis for the inequality "> 0").

The following properties of inequalities are useful in the solution of the quadratic inequality: **(1)** a product is positive just in case the factors are both positive or both negative, that is, $F \cdot G > 0$ just in case $F > 0$ and $G > 0$, or $F < 0$ and $G < 0$; **(2)** a product is negative just in case one factor is positive and the other is negative, that is, $F \cdot G < 0$ just in case $F < 0$ and $G > 0$, or, $F > 0$ and $G < 0$. These are applied to solve certain inequalities by *factoring*. For example, to solve $x^2 - 7x + 6 < 0$, write it as $(x - 1)(x - 6) < 0$. This leads to two cases: **(1)** $x - 1 < 0$ and $x - 6 > 0$, case **(2)** $x - 1 > 0$ and $x - 6 < 0$. Case **(1)** can be written $x < 1$ and $x > 6$; this has no solution because a number cannot be simultaneously less than 1 and greater than 6. Case **(2)** can be written $x > 1$ and $x < 6$; this is satisfied by any number between 1 and 6; hence the set of all solutions is (the interior of) the interval from 1 to 6.

Quadrature of Circle   See **Squaring the circle**.

Quadric Curve   The graph of a second degree equation in two variables,

$$ax^2 + bxy + cy^2 + dx + ey + f = 0;$$

such a curve is a *conic* (see **General equation**).

Quadric Surface (Syn.: Conicoid) The graph of a second degree equation in three variables. The quadric surfaces include the *ellipsoid, hyperboloid,* and *paraboloid;* because they have centers of symmetry, the former two are called *central quadrics*.

Quadrilateral   A polygon with four

sides. A scheme for classifying quadrilaterals is based on parallelism of sides: the figure is a trapezium, trapezoid, or parallelogram depending upon whether no, one, or two pairs of opposite sides are parallel, respectively. A rectangle is a parallelogram with all angles equal, and a square is a rectangle with all sides equal. (For a quadrilateral inscribed in a circle, see **Circumscribed circle**.)

The *complete quadrilateral* is a plane figure in projective geometry

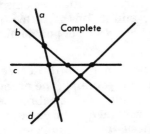

Complete

consisting of four lines *a, b, c, d* (no three concurrent) and the six points of intersection.

Quadruple Numbers or things in the order of the natural numbers 1, 2, 3, 4. A quadruple of numbers (x, y, z, w) represents a point in **four-dimensional space**.

Quantifier In logic, the propositional prefix "For every x" is a *universal quantifier;* it is written ($\forall x$), or (x). The propositional prefix "there exists an x," or "for some x" is an *existential quantifier;* it is written ($\exists x$). The study of quantifiers is a part of symbolic logic known as *quantification theory,* or *predicate calculus.*

To illustrate, consider the sentences "All men are good" and "Some man is good." To exhibit these explicitly as *quantified sentences,* they are rephrased as follows: "For every x, x is good" and "There exists an x such that x is good"; or, symbolically "($\forall x$)[x is good]" and "($\exists x$)[x is good]." The sentence "No man is good" can be written "There is no x such that x is good," which exhibits another type of quantifier. However, this prefix "there is no x" can be expressed as the negation of the existential quantifier; the given sentence is logically equivalent to the statement "It is false that ($\exists x$) [x is good]." The following mathematical statements are examples of quantified sentences: "There is exactly one line passing through two distinct points," and "Every whole number can be factored into a produce of primes."

A sentence such as "x is even" about an integer is neither true nor false as it stands; it expresses a *property* of x. Prefixing a quantifier converts it to a proposition which has a truth-value, true or false. For example, "For every x, x is even" (that is, "Every x is even") is false; on the other hand, "There exists an x such that x is even" (that is, "Some x is even") is true. Quantifiers are operators on sentences; they act on sentences to produce other sentences.

A sentence such as "x loves y" expresses a *relation* between two individuals x and y. This type of sentence may be prefixed by one quantifier or two quantifiers, corresponding to the separate variables. For convenience, let "xLy" stand for "x loves y." Prefixing one quantifier leads to four singly quantified sentences: **(1)** ($\forall x$)[xLy], standing for "Everybody loves y;" **(2)** ($\forall y$)[xLy] standing for "x loves everybody;" **(3)** ($\exists x$)[xLy] standing for "Someone loves y"; **(4)** ($\exists y$)[xLy] standing for "x loves someone." These examples show how a quantifier "binds" one variable, but leaves other variables "free" (in the first example, x is bound but y is free). Free variables are subject to further quantification; quantifying over the free variable in the examples leads to the following doubly quantified statements: **(1′)** $(\forall y)(\forall x)[xLy]$, or "Everybody loves everyone"; **(1″)** $(\exists y)(\forall x)[xLy]$, or "There is someone everybody loves"; **(2′)** $(\forall x)(\forall y)[xLy]$, or "Everyone loves everybody"; **(2″)** $(\exists x)(\forall y)[xLy]$, or "There is someone who loves everybody," or "Someone loves everybody"; **(3′)** $(\forall y)(\exists x)[xLy]$, or "For everyone, there is someone who loves that person," or "Everyone has someone who loves him"; **(3″)** $(\exists y)(\exists x)[xLy]$, or "Someone loves somebody"; **(4′)** $(\forall x)(\exists y)[xLy]$, or "Everybody has someone he loves," or "Everybody loves someone"; **(4″)** $(\exists x)(\exists y)[xLy]$, or "Somebody loves someone." Quantifiers of the same type "commute," that is, $(\exists x)(\exists y)$ expresses the same thing as $(\exists y)(\exists x)$, and $(\forall x)(\forall y)$ as $(\forall y)(\forall x)$ [see **(1′)**, **(2′)** and **(3″)**, **(4″)**]; quantifiers of different types, $\exists$ and $\forall$, do not commute in general [compare **(1″)** with **(4′)**, and **(2″)** with **(3′)**].

Two quantified sentences are *logically equivalent* in case they express the same thing in different logical forms. For example, the sentence "Every man is happy and married" is logically equivalent to the sentence "Every man is happy and every man is married;" that is, the logical form "$(\forall x)[P(x)$ and $Q(x)]$" is equivalent to the logical form "$(\forall x)[P(x)]$ and $(\forall x)[Q(x)]$" [in the example "$P(x)$," "$Q(x)$" stand for "x is happy," "x is married," respectively]. Also, the denial of the sentence "Every man is married" is logically equivalent to the sentence "Some man is not married;" that is, the logical form "not $(\forall x)[Q(x)]$" is equivalent to "$(\exists x)$

[not $Q(x)$]."

Ref. [89, 115].

Quantity   In a general way, a number, or other entity, denoted by an expression in constants and variables.

Quartic (Syn.: Biquadratic)   Of the fourth degree. The *quartic polynomial* has the general form $ax^4 + bx^3 + cx^3 + dx + e$. A *quartic equation* is one equivalent to a quartic polynomial equated to zero. An explicit formula for the solution of the general quartic equation was discovered in the middle of the sixteenth century.   See **Roots of polynomial equation**.

Quintic   Of the fifth degree, as in quintic polynomial. The proof of the impossibility of an algebraic solution of the general quintic equation was a milestone in the development of mathematics.   See **Roots of polynomial equation**.

Quotient   The result of the operation of *division;* the quotient of a by b is denoted by $a \div b$, or a/b. In the **division of whole numbers**, the term "quotient" has a modified meaning; it denotes the integral part of the result of division. A similar situation occurs in the **division of polynomials**.

R

Radian   The radian measure of an

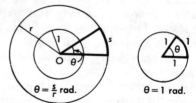

$$\theta = \frac{s}{r} \text{ rad.} \qquad \theta = 1 \text{ rad.}$$

angle is the length s of the arc intercepted by the angle as a central angle in a circle of radius 1. In the case of a circle of radius r, the radian measure θ of a central angle is s/r; this gives $s = r\theta$, which relates arc length, radius, and radian measure. A *unit angle,* in this measure, is one that intercepts an arc of length equal to the radius.

Radian measure π is the same as degree measure 180 (both measure a half-revolution). Similarly, $\pi/2$ radians is 90°, $\pi/3$ radians is 60°, and so

Degrees	Radians
1°	$0.01745\cdots$
30°	$\frac{1}{6}\pi$
45°	$\frac{1}{4}\pi$
57.295°$\cdots$	1
60°	$\frac{1}{3}\pi$
90°	$\frac{1}{2}\pi$
180°	π

on. An angle of 1° has radian measure $\pi/180$, or 0.01745 approximately; an angle of 1 radian has degree measure $180/\pi$, or 57.30 (57° 17′ 44″) approximately. In general, the relationship

$$180 \times \theta = \pi \times A$$

holds between radian measure θ and degree measure A; thus, to change radian measure to degree measure multiply by $180/\pi$, and to change degree measure to radian measure multiply by the reciprocal $\pi/180$.

Degree measure is common in trigonometry to solve triangles and calculate indirect measurements. Radian measure is preferred in a more theoretical study of trigonometric functions; for example, in the calculus, the expression "tan x" is used, with x standing for radian measure.

Radical In ordinary algebra, an expression for root extraction, such as $\sqrt{5}$, or $\sqrt[3]{x}$. The radical $\sqrt{A}$ has index two and denotes the square root of A; $\sqrt[3]{A}$ has index three and denotes the cube root, . . . , $\sqrt[n]{A}$ has index n and denotes the nth root. The mark "$\sqrt{}$" is the radical *sign* (introduced in the sixteenth century); the expression under the sign is the *radicand*. (A radical is sometimes called a *surd*.) A radical (or irrational) *expression* in a variable x is an algebraic expression that involves x in a radicand, such as $\sqrt{x^2 + 1}$, or $\sqrt{x} + \sqrt{x - 1}$. See **Root of Number**.

A radical may be simplified by removing a factor from the radicand which is a perfect power; for example, $\sqrt{12}$ can be written $\sqrt{3 \cdot 4}$, and simplified to $2\sqrt{3}$, since $\sqrt{4} = 2$. An *irreducible* radical is one that cannot be simplified to a rational expression. In general, a single radical is in *simplified form* if the radicand contains no denominator and no factors which are perfect powers; for example, $\sqrt{\frac{2}{3}}$ is not in simplified form. A method of simplification is **rationalization of the denominator**; for example, $\sqrt{\frac{2}{3}}$ is changed to $\sqrt{\frac{6}{9}}$, then $\sqrt{6}/3$, which is now in simplified form.

The following general formulas hold regarding operations with radicals (written for square roots but valid for radicals of any index): **(1)** $a\sqrt{x} + b\sqrt{x} = (a + b)\sqrt{x}$; **(2)** $\sqrt{x}\sqrt{y} = \sqrt{xy}$; **(3)** $\sqrt{x}/\sqrt{y} = \sqrt{x/y}$. [Notice that $\sqrt{x + y} \neq \sqrt{x} + \sqrt{y}$; in particular, $\sqrt{a^2 + b^2} \neq a + b$]. Rule **(1)** shows that radical expressions can be added if a common radical factor is present; for example $3\sqrt{3} - 2\sqrt{3} = \sqrt{3}$, $4\sqrt{xy} + \sqrt{xy} = 5\sqrt{xy}$ (the sum $3\sqrt{2} + 2\sqrt{3}$ cannot be so simplified). Rule **(2)** shows how to multiply radicals; for example, $\sqrt{3} \cdot \sqrt{6} = \sqrt{18} = 3\sqrt{2}$, and $\sqrt{x + 1} \cdot \sqrt{x - 1} =$ **221**

$\sqrt{x^2 - 1}$. Rule **(3)** shows how to divide radicals. Also, the formulas $(\sqrt[n]{A})^n = A$, $\sqrt[n]{A^n} = A$ are valid for a positive number or expression A.

Radical Axis and Plane See **Pencil**.

Radical Equation (Syn.: Irrational equation) An equation containing a radical expression involving the unknown, such as $3\sqrt{x} - \sqrt{x+1} = 2$. A method for solving such equations is **rationalization of the equation**.

Radicand The expression under a radical sign; for example, 3 is the radicand in $\sqrt{3}$, and $x + 1$ in $\sqrt[n]{x+1}$.

Radius Of a circle (sphere), a line segment, or its length, from the center to a point on the circle (sphere).

Radius of Curvature See **Curvature**.

Radius of Regular Polygon The *long* radius (*short* radius) of a regular polygon is the radius of the circumscribed (inscribed) circle. *Apothem* is used for "short radius."

Radius Vector In **polar coordinates** or **spherical coordinates**, a line segment from the pole, or origin, to any point.

Radix The radix of a *number system* using place values is its base; for example, ten is the radix of the decimal number system, and two is the radix of the binary number system. A *radix* fraction is a sum of fractions (positive and proper fractions) whose denominators are powers of a given base. For example,

$$\frac{3}{10} + \frac{1}{10^2} + \frac{5}{10^3}$$

is a radix fraction in the decimal system (written .315 in decimal notation). For the base b, a radix fraction

has the form $(A/b) + (B/b^2) + (C/b^3) + \cdots$, where A, B, C are digits from among $0, 1, 2, \cdots, b - 1$ (written $.ABC\cdots$, in notation with base b).

Random Event An event whose alternative outcomes occur with a certain **probability**. For example, the roll of two dice has eleven possible numerical outcomes for the sum of the faces that show; in particular, the alternative 2 occurs with probability $\frac{1}{36}$. See **Dependent random event, Independent random event, Random variable**.

Random Numbers A *table of random numbers* is a list in which the numbers are distributed as though by chance, in accordance with given (total) frequencies of occurrence. Of particular interest are *uniformly distributed* decimal numbers, where the given frequencies are the same for all values; in this case any one of the individual digits $0, 1, 2, \ldots, 9$ is equally likely to occur in any place in any one of the numbers. Algorithms have been devised for high speed computers to generate such lists, and for a method to be acceptable it must pass certain statistical tests; the numbers generated by such an algorithm are often called *pseudo-random numbers*. These numbers are used in numerical computations involving chance events (see **Monte Carlo method**).

Random Process See **Stochastic process** (syn.).

Random Variable (Syn.: Chance variable, Stochastic variable) A basic concept of probability theory which expresses the idea of a variable that takes on each of its values with a certain *probability*. When a random variable X is restricted to a finite set of values $a_1, a_2, a_3, \ldots, a_n$ (or a denumerably infinite set), it is a *discrete random variable*. For each value, there is probability $p_1, p_2, p_3,$

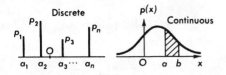

..., p_n between 0 and 1; these probabilities add up to 1, that is, $p_1 + p_2 + p_3 + \cdots + p_n = 1$. (For example, the outcomes for the sum of the faces that show of a roll of two dice describe a random variable; its values range through the integers 2 through 12, and each has a certain probability between 0 and 1.) The *expected value* $E(X)$ of X is the number $p_1a_1 + p_2a_2 + p_3a_3 + \cdots + p_na_n$; it can be thought of as the average of a large number of samples of X. The correspondence from values of X to their probabilities is the *frequency function*, or *probability function*, of the random variable; the binomial distribution is a well-known example (see **Probability in repeated trials**).

Two discrete random variables X and Y are *independent* in case the probability of any pair (a, b) is the product pq, where p is the probability that a will occur for X and q the probability that b will occur for Y; *dependent* variables are ones that are not independent. For example, successive rolls of two dice are independent events (the probability of a seven followed by an eleven, is just the probability of a seven times the probability of an eleven). See **Dependent random event**.

When a random variable X may assume any value on the line (or on a half-line, or interval) it is a *continuous random variable*. Such a random variable can be described by its *frequency function* $p(x)$ (also called its *probability density function*). This function has the following meaning:

the probability of X assuming a value within an arbitrary interval from a to b is the area under the graph of the function between a and b; in the notion of the integral calculus, this probability equals

$$\int_a^b p(x)dx.$$

The area under the whole graph is 1; the expected value $E(X)$ is given by the integral of the product $xp(x)$ over the full range of X. See **Distribution function, Standard deviation**.

Ref. [104, 144].

Range The *range of a variable* is its set of possible values; for example, a real variable is one whose range is all real numbers, and a complex variable is one whose range is all complex numbers. The *range of a function* is its set of functional values (see **Domain of function**). For example, the range of $f(x) = x^2 + 1$ is all real numbers greater than or equal to 1 (taking the range of x to be all real numbers).

Ratio The ratio of a to b is a/b (sometimes written $a:b$); "ratio" conveys the notion of relative magnitude. The terms "antecedent," for the numerator a, and "consequent," for the denominator b, are sometimes, but rarely, used. The *inverse ratio* of a to b is b/a; a *proportion* is an equality of two ratios.

Ratio of Division See **Division of line segment**.

Ratio of Geometric Progression The ratio of any term to the preceding term. See **Geometric progression**.

Ratio of Similitude In similar geometric figures, the ratio of length of

223

corresponding line segments. See **Similar** (geometry).

Ratio Test The following test for the *convergence* of an infinite series $a_1 + a_2 + a_3 + \cdots$ to a finite sum: the ratio of the numerical value of any term to that of the preceding term does not exceed a number less than 1, after a certain point on; that is, the inequality

$$\frac{|a_{n+1}|}{|a_n|} \leq q \quad (q < 1)$$

holds for n sufficiently large. This test is met, in particular, if the limit of the ratio exists as n approaches infinity and is less than 1 (the latter criterion is what is sometimes meant by the ratio test). For example, consider the series

$$\frac{1}{2} + \frac{2}{2^2} + \frac{3}{2^3} + \cdots + \frac{n}{2^n} + \cdots;$$

the ratio of successive terms is $(n + 1)/2^{n+1}$ divided by $n/2^n$, or

$$\frac{n + 1}{2n};$$

this has the limit $\frac{1}{2}$; hence the series converges. See **Comparison test**.

Rational Equation, Expression, Function A *rational expression* is an algebraic expression built out of variables and constants by use of the operations of addition, subtraction, multiplication, and division; examples are

$$\frac{1}{x} + 2x^2 + 3, \quad \frac{2x - y}{x^2 + 3y}.$$

When division (except division by constants) is excluded, the expression is a *rational integral expression,* or *polynomial.* A rational expression can always be expressed as a quotient of two polynomials. A *rational function* is a function whose value is given by a rational expression. Graphs of such functions present a great variety of curves in the plane;

the figure shows the case $y = 1 \div (x^2 - 1)$. A *rational equation* (or frac-

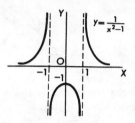

tional equation) is an equation whose members are rational expressions; such an equation can be reduced to a polynomial equation by "clearing of fractions." See **Fraction** (algebra).

Rational Number (Syn.: Fraction) A number which can be expressed in the form m/n, with m and n integers and n different from 0 (the term "rational" comes from "ratio"). The rational numbers are an extension of the integers permitting unrestricted use of the fundamental operations of arithmetic (except division by 0); that is, the system of rational numbers comprise a **number field**.

On an ordinary number scale, the *rational points* are the points matched with rational numbers. The following property of the *density of the rational numbers* holds: every segment of the line, no matter how small, contains a rational point (in fact, infinitely many). In spite of this, the rational points do not fill out the entire line (the extension to real numbers is required for this). What also seems surprising is that the rational numbers have the same cardinal number as the whole numbers (see **Enumeration of rational numbers**). In the decimal number system the rational numbers appear as the terminating and repeating decimals.

Rational Operations The operations

of addition and multiplication, and their inverse operations, subtraction and (nonzero) division.

Rationalization   Modification of radical expressions or equations to achieve removal of radicals.

Rationalization of Denominator Simplification of radical expressions to remove radical denominators or to eliminate denominators in a radicand. For example, $\sqrt{2}/\sqrt{3}$ is simplified by multiplying numerator and denominator by the "rationalizing factor" $\sqrt{3}$; this gives $(\sqrt{2} \cdot \sqrt{3})/(\sqrt{3} \cdot \sqrt{3})$, or $\sqrt{6}/3$. Another example is $2/(\sqrt{x} + 1)$; multiplying numerator and denominator by the rationalizing factor $\sqrt{x} - 1$ gives

$$2(\sqrt{x} + 1)/(\sqrt{x} + 1)(\sqrt{x} - 1),$$

or $(2\sqrt{x} - 2)/(x - 1)$. Rationalization is also used in the division of complex numbers.   See **Conjugate radicals**.

Rationalization of Equation   Elimination of radical expressions in the solution of equations. For example, to solve $\sqrt{3x + 2} - x = 1$, write it as $\sqrt{3x + 2} = x + 1$; then square both sides to obtain

$$3x + 2 = x^2 + 2x + 1,$$

which contains no radicals. This device will always work when one radical is present; when two or more radicals are present then it is used several times. For example, to solve $\sqrt{2x + 2} - \sqrt{x} = 1$, write it as $\sqrt{2x + 2} = \sqrt{x} + 1$; squaring gives $2x + 2 = x + 2\sqrt{x} + 1$, or $x + 1 = 2\sqrt{x}$; squaring again gives $x^2 + 2x + 1 = 4x$, as desired. The technique of rationalization may lead to a redundant equation with extraneous roots.

Ray   See **Half-line** (syn.).

Real Number

Real Axis   In general, the line taken together with a uniform scale of real numbers on it. In the **Argand diagram** for complex numbers $x + iy$, the real axis is the x-axis.

Real Number   A number which is a *rational number* or the limit of a sequence of rational numbers. It includes the *irrational* (nonrational) *number,* such as $\sqrt{2}$ or π. A concrete representation of real numbers is provided by the **decimal number system**; other number systems are possible, such as the binary number system. The real number is what is often understood by "number" in ordinary mathematics.

An important property of the set of real numbers is that it completely fills out the line in an ordinary number scale; this assures that real numbers are adequate for measurement of any length (this property is the *axiom of continuity*). From the point of view of the fundamental operations of arithmetic, the real numbers comprise a closed system of numbers, or **number field**. From the point of view of the relation of inequality the real numbers comprise a linearly, or, simply, **ordered set**.

The irrational real numbers fall into two categories, the *algebraic numbers* and the *transcendental numbers*. The first type is a number which satisfies some algebraic equation with rational coefficients; examples are $\sqrt{2}$, which satisfies $x^2 - 2 = 0$, and $1 + \sqrt[3]{5}$, which satisfies $x^3 - 3x^2 + 3x - 6 = 0$ [that is, $(x - 1)^3 = 5$]. The second type is a number which is not algebraic; examples are **pi**, π and e. In the decimal number system, the irrational number occurs as the nonrepeating, unending decimal; this reflects the fact that it is a limit of rational numbers. The Greek mathematicians of an-

225

tiquity gave considerable throught to the nature of irrational numbers; they were able to construct many special numbers by geometric methods, and Eudoxus developed a geometric theory of such numbers. It was not until the nineteenth century, however, that a rigorous and complete theory was finally established.

Real Variable   A variable which takes on only real numbers as a value. Commonly used letters for real variables are x, y, z, a, b, c; others are also used.

Reciprocal of Number (Syn.: Inverse of number)   The number 1 divided by the given number. The reciprocal of 2 is 1/2, of 2/3 is 3/2, of a/b is b/a. If one number is the reciprocal of another, then the second is also the reciprocal of the first. The product of reciprocals is 1; for example,

$$2 \cdot \frac{1}{2} = 1, \quad \frac{2}{3} \cdot \frac{3}{2} = 1, \quad \frac{a}{b} \cdot \frac{b}{a} = 1.$$

Reciprocal Proportion and Ratio (Syn.: Inverse proportion and ratio) The reciprocal *ratio* of a to b is the ratio of $1/a$ to $1/b$; it equals b/a. A reciprocal *proportion* is a relationship $y = k/x$ between x and y.   See **Proportionality**.

Reciprocal Spiral   See **Spiral**.

Rectangle   A quadrilateral whose angles are all right angles. Opposite sides of a rectangle are parallel and equal in length; it is a special type of

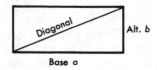

Base a

parallelogram. Any side may be considered the *base* (usually the longer one); an *altitude* is a perpendicular

segment (or its length) between the base and the opposite side. A *diagonal* is either of the two line segments joining opposite vertices. The dimensions of a rectangle are the lengths, a and b, of two perpendicular sides; the area equals ab, the perimeter equals $2(a + b)$, and the length of the diagonal equals $\sqrt{a^2 + b^2}$.

Rectangular   Pertaining to right angles. For example, a rectangular *coordinate system* is a Cartesian coordinate system in which the axes are at right angles; in this case, the axes and coordinates are called rectangular *axes* and rectangular *coordinates*.

Rectangular Hyperbola (Syn.: Equilateral or equiangular hyperbola) An hyperbola whose transverse and conjugate axes are equal in length.

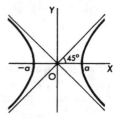

Its equation in standard form is $x^2 - y^2 = a^2$; its asymptotes are at right angles. The equation $xy = $ constant is also a rectangular hyperbola, but its asymptotes are the coordinate axes.

Rectangular Parallelepiped (Syn.: Rectangular solid)   A parallelepiped whose bases are rectangles and whose lateral edges are perpendicular to the bases. This solid has three dimensions a, b, and c, these being the lengths of three edges with a common vertex. Its volume equals abc, the total area of its six faces equals $2(ab + bc + ac)$; and the length of a diagonal equals $\sqrt{a^2 + b^2 + c^2}$.

Rectilinear Referring to lines or line segments. For example, a broken line or polygon is a rectilinear figure; this figure is used as a means of approximating general curves (for example, see **Length**).

Recurring Decimal See **Repeating decimal** (syn).

Reductio ad Absurdum The method of indirect **proof**.

Reduction of Algebraic Expression A modification of an algebraic expression to a simpler or more desirable form. For example, the expression $(x + 1)^2 - (x + 1)(x - 1)$ can be reduced to $2(x + 1)$. Reduction of a fraction to **lowest terms** involves the removal of all common factors of the numerator and denominator.

Reduction Formulas of Trigonometry Trigonometric identities which express a trigonometric function of any angle as a trigonometric function of an acute angle. These formulas are summarized in the table.

	$-A$	$90°±A$	$180°±A$	$270°±A$	$n(360°)±A$
sin	$-\sin A$	$\cos A$	$\mp\sin A$	$-\cos A$	$\pm\sin A$
cos	$\cos A$	$\mp\sin A$	$-\cos A$	$\pm\sin A$	$\cos A$
tan	$-\tan A$	$\mp\cot A$	$\pm\tan A$	$\mp\cot A$	$\pm\tan A$
cot	$-\cot A$	$\mp\tan A$	$\pm\cot A$	$\mp\tan A$	$\pm\cot A$
sec	$\sec A$	$\mp\csc A$	$-\sec A$	$\pm\csc A$	$\sec A$
csc	$-\csc A$	$\sec A$	$\mp\csc A$	$-\sec A$	$\pm\csc A$

To illustrate the table, consider the entry in the row headed "tan" and the column headed "180° ±A"; this entry stands for the identity

$$\tan (180° \pm A) = \pm \tan A.$$

Hence, $\tan 120° = \tan (180° - 60°) = -\tan 60°$; also $\cos 300° = \cos(270° + 30°) = \sin 30°$. Since tables of trigonometric functions generally list values for acute angles only, reduction formulas are needed

to compute trigonometric functions of other angles. See **Related angle**.

Redundancy of Information See **Information theory**.

Redundant Equation An equation which includes the roots of a given equation together with *extraneous roots*. Checking a presumed root in the original equation is a means of detecting extraneous roots. An equation which lacks some roots is a **defective equation**.

Some procedures that may lead to redundant equations are **(1)** multiplying or dividing both sides of an equation by an expression containing the variable, and **(2)** squaring both sides, as in the solution of radical equations. For example, solving $x(x - 1)/(x - 2) = 1 + 2/(x - 2)$ by multiplying both sides by $x - 2$ to clear the fractions, gives $x(x - 1) = (x - 2) + 2$, or $x^2 - 2x = 0$; the solutions of the last equation are 0 and 2, but checking in the original equation shows that 2 is an extraneous root.

Redundant Number (Syn.: Abundant number) A whole number which is less than the sum of its divisors (excluding itself, but including 1, as divisors). See **Perfect Number**.

Reflection in a Line The operation that replaces a point P by the point P', where PP' is perpendicular to

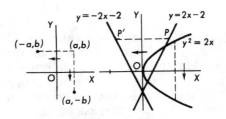

and bisected by the given line l; the point P' is called the reflection of P

227

Reflection in a Plane

(in l). If P is on l, then $P' = P$. The reflection in l of any figure F is the symmetrical figure F' made up of the reflections of the points of the given figure; in turn, the reflection of F' is the original figure F. The points of l itself are fixed under the reflection.

In rectangular plane coordinates, the reflection of the point (a, b) in the x-axis is $(a, -b)$, and in the y-axis is $(-a, b)$; for example $(2, 3)$ and $(-2, -3)$ are the reflections of $(2, -3)$ in the x- and y-axes. The reflection in the x-axis (y-axis) of the graph of an equation in x and y is the graph of the equation obtained by replacing y by $-y$ (x by $-x$). For example, the reflection of the line $y = 2x - 2$ in the y-axis is the line $y = -2x - 2$; the reflection of the parabola $y^2 = 2x$ in the x-axis is itself. See **Symmetry in plane, Symmetry in space**.

Reflection in a Plane In space, the operation that replaces a point P by the point P', where PP' is perpendicular to, and bisected by the given plane p; the point P' is called the reflection of P (in p). If P is on p, then $P' = P$. The reflection in p of any

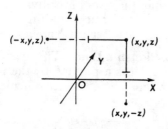

figure F is the symmetrical figure F' made up of the reflections of the points of the given figure; in turn, the reflection of F' is F. The points of p are fixed under the reflection. In terms of rectangular coordinates in space, the reflection of the point (x, y, z) in the yz-plane is $(-x, y, z)$, in the xz-plane is $(x, -y, z)$, and in the

228

xy-plane is $(x, y, -z)$; for example, $(-2, 4, -3)$ and $(2, 4, 3)$ are the reflections of $(2, 4, -3)$ in the yz- and xy-planes. See **Symmetry in space**.

Reflection in a Point The operation that replaces a point P by the point P', where PP' is bisected by the given point O; the point P' is called the reflection of P (in O) (the point O is its own reflection). The reflection in O of any figure F is the figure F' made up of the reflections of the points of the given figure; the reflection of F' is F itself.

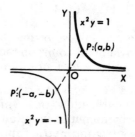

In plane rectangular coordinates, the reflection of the point (a, b) in the origin O is the point $(-a, -b)$; the reflection in O of the graph of an equation in x and y is the graph of the equation obtained by replacing x and y by $-x$ and $-y$. For example, $(2, -3)$ and $(-2, 3)$ are reflections of each other in the origin; also, the graphs of $x^2y = 1$ and $x^2y = -1$ are reflections of each other in the origin. See **Symmetry in plane, Symmetry in space**.

Reflection Property of Conic (Syn.: Focal property of conic) See conics **Ellipse, Hyperbola, Parabola**.

Reflex Angle An angle between $180°$ and $360°$.

Reflexive Relation A relation having the property that each thing x is in the given relation to itself (x may be in the given relation to other things, as well). As an example, the relation "is as old as" between people is reflexive because "x is as old as x" is true of every person x; on the other hand the relation "is equal to the square of" between integers is not reflexive, because "n is equal to n^2" is not true of every integer n (it is true for the integers 0 and 1).

Regular Polygon   A polygon whose sides are all of equal length and whose angles are all congruent; it is studied in plane geometry. A regular polygon of three sides is an equilateral triangle, and of four sides is a square, for example.

The circle and regular polygon are closely related. A circle can be circumscribed about any regular polygon; its radius is the *long radius* of the regular polygon. A circle can also be inscribed in any regular polygon; its radius is the *short radius,* or *apothem,* of the regular polygon. The common center of the circumscribed and inscribed circles is the *center* of the regular polygon. A *central angle* of the regular polygon is one subtended at its center by a side of the polygon. Formulas for various angles associated with an n-sided regular polygon are the following: central angle, $360°/n$; interior angle, $[(n - 2)/n]180°$; exterior angle, $360°/n$. The formula

$$r = a \cos (180°/n)$$

is a relation between the long radius

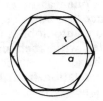

a and the short radius r. The length of a side is given by $2r \tan (180°/n)$ [also by, $2a \sin (180°/n)$]; the perimeter equals n times this. The area is one-half the perimeter times the short radius, or $nr^2 \tan (180°/n)$.

A circle is the limiting figure of a sequence of regular polygons inscribed in the circle, as the number of sides n grows without bound; the circle is also the limiting figure of the

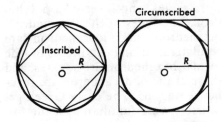

sequence of regular polygons circumscribed about the circle, as n grows without bound. This technique can be used to derive the length and area of the circle.

The **geometric construction** of regular polygons is a problem of considerable historical interest. Only certain regular polygons can be constructed by straight edge and compass; the seven-sided regular polygon is the one of fewest number of sides that cannot be so constructed.
Ref. [110].

Regular Polyhedron   A polyhedron whose faces are all congruent polygons and whose polyhedral angles are all congruent. An important theorem of space geometry is that there are only five regular polyhedra; they are the regular *tetrahedron* (4 faces), the regular *hexahedron,* or cube (6 faces), the regular *octahedron* (8 faces), the regular *dodecahedron* (12 faces), and the regular *icosahedron* (20 faces). This result can be established using Euler's theorem on polyhedrons, relating the number of ver-

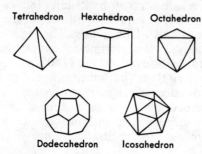

Tetrahedron   Hexahedron   Octahedron

Dodecahedron   Icosahedron

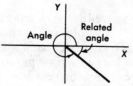

Angle   Related angle

tices, edges, and faces of a polyhedron. The faces of the tetrahedron,
octahedron, and icosahedron are
equilateral triangles, those of the
regular hexahedron are squares, and
those of the dodecahedron are regular pentagons. The early Greek geometers were familiar with the five
regular polyhedrons.

A sphere can be circumscribed
about a regular polyhedron; a sphere
can also be inscribed in the same
polyhedron; the common center is
the *center* of the polyhedron.. The
area of a regular polyhedron is expressible in terms of the length e of
an edge by the following formulas:
tetrahedron, $3e^2$; cube, $6e^2$; octahedron, $2\sqrt{3}e^2$; dodecahedron, $15e^2 \times$
cot 36° (or 20.65 e^2, approximately);
icosahedron, $5\sqrt{3}\, e^2$. Formulas also
exist for the volume; these formulas
are simplest for the tetrahedron,
cube, and octahedron and give the
values $(\sqrt{2}/12)e^3$, e^3, and $(\sqrt{2}/3)e^3$,
respectively.

Ref. [28,110].

Regular Prism   A right **prism** whose
bases are regular polygons.

Regular Pyramid   A **pyramid** whose
base is a regular polygon and whose
altitude passes through the center of
the base.

Related Angle   Of any angle of rotation of the positive x-axis, the

acute angle between the terminal
side and the x-axis. For example, the
related angle of 300° is 60°, and of
−150° is 30°. The value of a trigonometric function of any angle is
equal to the same function of the related angle, apart from algebraic
sign; for example,

$$\sin 300° = -\sin 60°,$$
$$\tan(-150°) = \tan 30°.$$

See **Reduction formulas of trigonometry**.

Relation   A *relation in a set* is a correspondence from members of the
set to members of the same set. For
example, "y is an offspring of x" expresses a relation between people
(that is, in the set of people); it associates with an individual x, any
individual y who is his child. Similarly, "y is a divisor of x" expresses
a relation in the set of natural numbers; it associates with a natural
number x, any natural number y
which divides x (for example, it associates with the value 6 any of the
values 1, 2, 3, or 6).

More generally a *relation from a
set A to a set B* is synonymous with
a correspondence from A to B; it associates with any member x of A, no
member, one member, or several
members of B. A *functional relation,*
or *function,* is one for which each x
has at most one y associated with it.
The sentence "y owns x" expresses a
relation from automobiles to people;
it associates with each car x, the
owner y. The sentence "y contains x"
expresses a relation from lines x in
space, to planes y, for example.

The following are examples of relations in mathematics denoted by

special symbols: *equality,* " $=$ "; *is less than,* " $<$ "; *is congruent to,* " $\cong$." A general relation may be denoted by a letter, say R. Then $y\,Rx$ means that y is in the relation R to x; the special symbols listed provide the examples, $y = x$, $y < x$, $\triangle ABC \cong \triangle EFG$. A distinction must be made between the notation for a relation and that for a binary operation—a relational expression, such as "$a < b$," or "$a\,R\,b$," is a sentence, and is either true or false of particular things a and b; an expression such as "$a + b$," or "$a * b$," on the other hand, stands for a thing or number ($+$ and $*$ being binary *operations*) and cannot be said to be true or false of particular things.

A relation can be described as a set of ordered pairs; (x, y) is a member of the set if and only if y is in the given relation to x; that is, a relation singles out a certain subset of pairs from the rectangular array of all possible pairs. This is illustrated in the figure for the relation "y is a divisor of x" in the set of numbers 1, 2, 3, 4, 5, 6 [a check ($\checkmark$) in a box means that the number y at the head of the column is in the given relation to the number x at the left of the row]. A similar way to visualize a relation is as a graph; in this case the

y is a divisor of x

point (x, y) belongs to the graph in case y is in the given relation to x (see **Graph of inequality**).

Certain general properties of relations occur in the study of relations.

A relation R is *reflexive* in case xRx for every x, that is, every element is in the given relation to itself (examples are equality and divisibility of integers); a relation is *symmetric* in case yRx implies xRy (examples are parallelism and congruence); a relation is *transitive* in case xRy and yRz implies xRz (examples are similarity and "is not greater than"). A relation having all three of these properties is an **equivalence relation**. The relations which serve to "order" sets are important types of relations (see **Ordered set**).

Relations may be combined or modified to produce other relations, as in the **composition of relations** and **inverse relations**. The study of these and other fundamental aspects of relations belongs to the field of logic. Symbolic methods are important in this study, and lead to an algebra of relations, much as the symbolic treatment of propositions leads to an algebra of propositions.

Ref. [89, 134].

Relative Error See **Error**.

Relative Frequency See **Frequency** (statistics).

Relative Maximum (Minimum) See **Function of real variable**.

Relatively Prime Two integers (polynomials) are relatively prime in case they have no common factors other than ± 1 (other than constants). See **Factor of integer, Factor of polynomial**.

Remainder See **Division of whole numbers, Division of polynomials**.

Remainder Theorem The following proposition of the theory of equations: when a polynomial $p(x)$ is divided by $x - a$, the remainder equals the value of $p(x)$ at $x = a$, that is, $p(a)$. For example, when $x^3 - 3x +$

5 is divided by $x - 2$, the remainder is $2^3 - 3 \cdot 2 + 5$, or 7. The theorem permits the useful conclusion that a polynomial $p(x)$ has $x - a$ as a factor just in case the equation $p(x) = 0$ has a as a root—this is the *factor theorem* of algebra. See **Division of polynomials**.

Repeated Root See **Multiple root** (syn.).

Repeated Trials See **Probability in repeated trials**.

Repeating Decimal (Syn.: Circulating decimal, Periodic decimal, Recurring decimal) A decimal number with an unending number of digits following the decimal point whose digits eventually repeat a fixed pattern; for example, the decimal 53.065183183183 $\cdots$ is a repeating decimal (repeating pattern 183). When a fraction is divided out by long division, it presents itself as a terminating or a repeating decimal. Conversely, any repeating decimal is equal to a fraction. See **Decimal number system**, **Geometric series**.

Ref. [16, 60].

Resultant of Vectors The sum of two **vectors**.

Rhombus A parallelogram in which all four sides are equal.

Rhumb Line See **Loxodromic spiral** (syn.).

Riemannian Geometry See **Non-Euclidean geometry**.

Right Angle An angle of 90°.

Right Circular Cone or Cylinder A *right circular cone* is a cone with a circular base such that the line from the vertex to the center of the base is perpendicular to the base. A *right circular cylinder* is a cylinder with circular bases such that the line between

the centers of its two bases is perpendicular to the bases.

Right Parallelepiped or Prism A **parallelepiped** or **prism** whose lateral edges are perpendicular to the bases.

Right Section Of a **cylinder** or **prism**, the intersection with a plane

which is perpendicular to the elements or lateral edges of the solid.

Right Spherical Triangle A **spherical triangle** having a right angle. Unlike a plane right triangle, such a triangle may have two (even three) right angles, in which case it is *birectangular* (*trirectangular*).

Right Triangle A plane triangle having a right angle. The side opposite the right angle is the *hypotenuse;* the other two sides are the *legs,* or

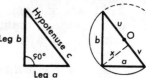

arms, of the right triangle. The celebrated *theorem of Pythagoras* states that $a^2 + b^2 = c^2$, where a, b are the lengths of the legs and c is the length of the hypotenuse. Two of the many properties of the right triangle are the following: **(1)** any right triangle can be inscribed in a semicircle; **(2)** the perpendicular segment from the vertex of the right angle to the hypotenuse is the mean proportional between the two legs, and also between the two segments into which it divides the hypotenuse.

Rigid Motion Of a *plane,* any transformation of the plane into itself which is a *translation,* a *rotation,* or a combination of any number of successive application of these. A translation moves each point in the same direction by the same amount. A rotation has a single fixed point O; it rotates each point of the plane around O in the same sense by the same angular amount. Any rigid motion of the plane can be realized by a single translation followed by a single rotation (or vice versa). An *isometry* of the plane is a one-to-one transformation of the plane into itself which leaves the distance between any two points unchanged; that is, if the points P and Q are carried into the points P' and Q', respectively, then the distances $P'Q'$ and PQ are equal. A rigid motion can also be defined as an isometry which does not change the *orientation* of a pair of coordinate axes, that is, does not change the sense of rotation of the positive half of the x-axis into the positive half of the y-axis. An example of an isometry which is not a rigid motion (according to this definition) is a *reflection in a line;* this reverses the orientation of axes. Every isometry of the plane is a rigid motion, a reflection, or a combination of these. Under a rigid motion, a

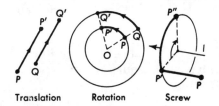

Translation   Rotation   Screw

plane figure, such as a triangle, is carried into its image figure without being lifted out of the plane; under other isometries, the figure requires lifting and putting back in the plane (with its "orientation" reversed). See **Congruent figures in plane**.

Similar definitions apply to transformation of *space.* A translation slides each point in the same direction by the same amount; a rotation has a fixed line l, and each point P is rotated around l in the same sense by the same amount (in the plane through P which is perpendicular to l); finally, the other rigid motions are combinations of these. An example of a combination is a *screw motion,* that is, a translation in a direction of a line l, followed by a rotation about l. An isometry of space is defined as before as a transformation that preserves distance. A rigid motion can be defined as an isometry which does not reverse the *orientation* of coordinate axes x, y, z (where orientation means right-handed or left-handed). A *reflection in a plane* is a type of isometry which is not a rigid motion. Every isometry of space is a rigid motion, a reflection, or a combination of these. Under an isometry which is not a rigid motion, a solid such as a tetrahedron, cannot be carried into coincidence with its image by a continuous physical motion in space; it can under a rigid motion. See **Congruent figures in space**.

Ring A mathematical system described as follows. It is a set of entities (called "numbers") subject to two binary operations (called "addition" and "multiplication") and satisfying the following *axioms of the ring:* (1) under the operation of addition, the set is a commutative **group**; (2) the set is closed under the operation of multiplication, and this operation is associative; (3) addition and multiplication are related by the distributive laws,

$$a \cdot (b + c) = a \cdot b + a \cdot c,$$

233

$(b + c) \cdot a = b \cdot a + c \cdot a.$

A *commutative* ring is one in which multiplication is commutative. See **Integral Domain**.

This general description is an abstraction of various examples of rings. The most familiar is the set of integers (under ordinary addition and multiplication). Other examples are: **(1)** the set of all polynomials in a variable x; **(2)** finite arithmetic modulo m; **(3)** the algebra of matrices. Of these examples, all are commutative rings except the last. The ring and *field* are allied concepts of twentieth century higher algebra. The difference between the two is this: the field is a system closed under the four fundamental operations of addition, subtraction, multiplication, and (nonzero) division; the ring is a more general system that need not be closed under division. For example, the integers and the polynomials are not closed under division.

Ref. [134].

Roman Numerals The ancient number system of the Roman empire. These numerals involve a mixture of ten and five as base values. The numerals I, X, C, and M stand for 1, 10, 100, and 1,000, respectively, and V, L, and D stand for 5, 50, and 500, respectively; any whole number is represented by an appropriate combination of these symbols. The following principle is used in forming combinations: an individual numeral *preceding* one of higher value signifies a decrease in the amount of the higher, while one *following* a numeral of the same or higher value signifies an increase in the latter; for example, VII = 7, IX = 9, XXVI = 26, MCMLXI = 1961 (the first rule is applied first to a numeral, such as C in the example). Roman numerals are inconvenient for representing large numbers, but more, they are awkward for carrying out arithmetical operations; the decimal number system was a significant advance over the Roman system.

Root of Complex Number A *square root* $\sqrt{a + bi}$ of a complex number $a + bi$ is a solution z of the equation $z^2 = a + bi$; in general, an nth *root* is a solution z of $z^n = a + bi$. Every nonzero complex number has two square roots; these are given by $\pm \sqrt{r} [\cos (\theta/2) + i \sin (\theta/2)]$, in terms of the polar form $r(\cos \theta + i \sin \theta)$ of the complex number. For example, the polar form of the complex unit i itself is $\cos 90° + i \sin 90°$; hence, the two square roots of i are $\pm(\cos 45° + i \sin 45°)$ or $\pm(\sqrt{2}/2) \times (1 + i)$. In general, a non-zero complex number has n distinct n^{th} roots; one way to compute them is to multiply the particular root $\sqrt[n]{r}[\cos (\theta/n) + i \sin (\theta/n)]$ by each of the n **roots of unity**. Ref. [28].

Root of Equation Of an equation in one variable, any number which converts the equation to a true statement when it is substituted for the variable. The root is said to *satisfy* the equation; the variable is called the *unknown*. For example, the equation $2x - 1 = 0$ has $\frac{1}{2}$ as a root; substituting $\frac{1}{2}$ for the unknown x converts the equation to the true statement $2 \cdot \frac{1}{2} - 1 = 0$. See **Roots of polynomial equation, Solution of equation**.

Root of Number A *square root* of a real number b is a solution (real number) of the equation $x^2 = b$; a *cube root* is a solution of $x^3 = b$; ...; an nth *root* is a solution of $x^n = b$. These roots are denoted by $\sqrt{b}$, $\sqrt[3]{b}$,

..., $\sqrt[n]{b}$, respectively, the *index*, or *order,* being 2, 3, . . . , n. By definition, $(\sqrt{b})^2 = b$, $(\sqrt[3]{b})^3 = b$, . . . , $(\sqrt[n]{b})^n = b$.

Any (real) number has one root of odd order; for example $\sqrt[3]{8} = 2$, $\sqrt[3]{-27} = -3$. A positive number has two numerically equal roots of even order; a negative number has no (real) root of even order. For example, $\sqrt{9}$ is 3 or -3, and $\sqrt{-4}$ is not a real number. When there are two roots, the positive root is called the **principal root**. The equations $\sqrt{a^2} = a$, $\sqrt[3]{a^3} = a$, . . . hold when a is positive and the radical denotes the principal root. When the real number b is not an nth power of a rational number, then $\sqrt[n]{b}$ is an irrational number.

The special cases of no, one, or two roots disappear when complex numbers are allowed as roots; then, every (nonzero) real number has exactly n roots of order n. For example, the two square roots of -1 are i and $-i$, and the three cube roots of 8 are $2, -1 + \sqrt{3}\,i$, and $-1 - \sqrt{3}\,i$.

Root extraction is the operation of computing a root. There is a relatively simple procedure for computing a square root; the procedure for cube roots is more involved. Root extraction of any index is conveniently carried out through **computation by logarithms**. See **Radical**, **Roots of unity**.

Roots of Polynomial Equation
Roots of an equation $p(x) = 0$, with $p(x)$ a polynomial; usually, the coefficients are understood to be rational numbers.

The general *linear equation* $ax + b = 0$ can be solved as $x = -b/a$. The general *quadratic equation* $ax^2 + bx + c = 0$ can be solved by the quadratic formula. The general *cubic*

equation and *quartic* equation can also be solved by explicit algebraic formulas, although these formulas become progressively more involved. However, there is no explicit algebraic formula for the solution of the general *quintic* (fifth degree) equation, or higher; a proof of this difficult proposition was found in the first half of the nineteenth century. This problem was important in the development of modern higher algebra.

With no general formula available, various special techniques exist for attempting to find roots. The factor theorem is of use; if one root r can be found, then $x - r$ can be factored out of the polynomial and the degree of the equation reduced. Another useful fact is that if a polynomial $p(x)$ changes sign between the value a and b of x, then $p(x) = 0$ must have at least one root between a and b. Descrates' rule of signs is helpful. Various numerical methods have been developed for approximating roots; *Horner's method* is a standard one.

The theory of equations is concerned with the general study of the roots of polynomials. Central to this theory is the **fundamental theorem of algebra**; this assures that a polynomial equation of degree n has n roots, real or complex (allowing for multiple roots). (This "existence" theorem does not contradict the earlier assertion that there is no explicit algebraic formula for obtaining the roots.) When the coefficients of the polynomial are real, the complex roots come in conjugate pairs $a \pm bi$. Relations connecting the coefficients and roots of an equation are important in the theory of equations. For example, the coefficients of the quadratic $x^2 + a_1x + a_2 = 0$ are related to its roots r_1, r_2 by the formula $r_1 + r_2 = $

$-a_1$, and $r_1 \cdot r_2 = a_2$. The analogous relations for the cubic $x^3 + a_1x^2 + a_2x + a_3 = 0$ with roots r_1, r_2, r_3 are $r_1 + r_2 + r_3 = -a_1$, $r_1r_2 + r_1r_3 + r_2r_3 = a_2$, $r_1r_2r_3 = -a_3$. These are examples of general formulas relating the roots $r_1, r_2, \ldots, r_n$ and the coefficients of the equation of

$$x^2 + a_1x^{n-1} + a_2x^{n-2} + \cdots + a_n = 0,$$

treated in the theory of equations.
Ref. [80, 120, 132].

Roots of Unity The solutions of $x^n = 1$, allowing complex numbers as solutions. The two square roots of 1 are 1 and -1; they are the *square roots* of unity. The three *cube roots* of unity are 1, cos 120° + i sin 120°, cos 240° + i sin 240°; these are the same as 1, $-\frac{1}{2} + (\sqrt{3}/2)i$, $-\frac{1}{2} - (\sqrt{3}/2)i$. In general, unity has *n roots of order n*; these are

1,
cos (360°/n) + i sin (360°/n),
cos (2 · 360°/n) + i sin (2 · 360°/n),

.

.

.

cos [($n - 1$) 360°/n]
$\qquad$ + i sin [($n - 1$) 360°/n];

they are represented in the Argand diagram as equally spaced points on the unit circle with center at the origin.

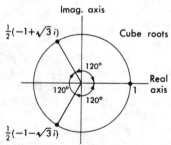

$\frac{1}{2}(-1+\sqrt{3}\,i)$ Cube roots

120°

120° Real axis

120° 1

$\frac{1}{2}(-1-\sqrt{3}\,i)$

To obtain the n complex n^{th} roots of any positive number b, multiply the ordinary positive n^{th} root of b by each of the n roots of unity. For ex-ample, to obtain the three cube roots of 8, multiply 2 by each of the cube roots of unity; the result is 2, $-1 + \sqrt{3}\,i$, $-1 - \sqrt{3}\,i$. When b is negative, say $-a$, the roots are obtained as i times the roots of the positive number a. For example, the square roots of -9 are $3i$ times the square roots of unity; this gives $3i$ and $-3i$. See **Root of complex number**.
Ref. [28].

Rotation See **Rigid motion**

Rotation of Coordinates See **Transformation of coordinates**

Rounding Off A procedure for modifying a decimal number to compensate for dropping the digits after a certain place. The usual rule is the following: **(1)** when the dropped digits begin with 4, make no change in the retained digits; **(2)** when the dropped digits begin with 5, increase the last retained digit by 1. An exception occurs when the dropped digits consist of 5 followed only by zeros; in this case it is common to round off to an even digit. For example, rounding off 2.7163 to three decimal places gives 2.176, and to two decimal places gives 2.72; also, rounding off 4.17500 to two places gives 4.18 but rounding off 3.5650 gives 3.56.

Rounding off produces a *round off error* in the retained number. This error can increase with successive arithmetical operations and rounding off. For example, consider the product (1.254)(10.14); this equals 12.71556 exactly, or 12.7 rounded off to three digits. Now in three digit computation the given factors would first be rounded off to 1.25 and 1.01, which are correct in their last places; their product 12.625, would be rounded off to 12.6; this result is incorrect in its last place. When a long series of arithmetic computations is carried out, the accumulation of round off errors may cause a serious error in the final result. This problem is especially important with modern digital computers where thousands of arithmetic operations are performed in one second and where the number of digits that are retained in a number may be fixed. Special means are required to control these errors.

Ref. [80].

Routine   Of a computer, a series of coded instructions intended to solve a given problem or achieve a certain result automatically; it is stored in the computer in advance of the computation. A *subroutine* is a portion of a larger routine which is typically repeated in cycles and produces intermediate results needed in the larger routine.

Rule of Detachment   See **Inference**.

Rule of Inference or Proof   See **Inference**.

Rule of Species   See **Species**.

Rule of Three   For a proportion, the assertion that the product of the means equals the product of the extremes. This rule was known in Hindu mathematics of the first millenium, and was popular in Europe in the middle ages.

Ruled Surface   A surface on which it is possible to draw a family of lines which completely cover the surface; such a surface is generated by a line moving in space. The cone and cylinder are ruled surfaces. A *doubly ruled surface* is one that contains two distinct families of lines, each covering the surface. A hyperboloid of one sheet is a doubly ruled surface; so is the hyperbolic paraboloid.

Russell's Paradox   See **Paradox**.

S

Saddle Point of Surface   Informally, a point at which the surface is shaped like a saddle; the hyperbolic paraboloid provides an example (see **Paraboloid**). Technically, a saddle point of a surface $z = f(x, y)$ is a point where both partial derivatives of $f(x, y)$ vanish, but which is neither a relative maximum nor relative minimum point.

Satisfy   Any *solution* of an equation or inequality is said to satisfy the equation or inequality. For example, the number 2 satisfies the equation $x^2 - 3x + 2 = 0$, and the pair of numbers 1, -3 satisfies the inequality $4x + y > 0$. In general, suppose a condition on members of a set A is given; then any member of A for which the condition holds is said to satisfy the condition. For example, within the set of polygons, the triangles satisfy the condition of being inscribable in a circle (so do some other polygons).   See **Property**.

Scalar   Usually, a real number, particularly in operations with **vectors**.

Scale   On a line, a displayed arrangement of real numbers in their natural order. In a *uniform scale,* the length of the segment from the point marked with the number a to the point marked b (with b greater than a) is the difference $b - a$; see **Linear Coordinates**. In a *logarithmic scale,* the length of the segment is $\log b - \log a$; see **Logarithmic coordinates**. In general, a scale constructed according to a function $f(x)$ is one such that $f(b) - f(a)$ is the length of the segment from a to b. Various scales are used in special types of graphs and in **nomographs**. The *decimal scale* (*binary scale*) is the set of markings of the uniform scale determined by successive division of intervals into tenths (halves); the term is also used to denote the **decimal number system (binary number system)** itself.

Scalene Triangle A **triangle** no two sides of which are equal.

Scientific Notation The expression of any finite decimal number as a decimal number between 1 and 10 multiplied by a power of 10. For example, 523.7 and .00170 are written in scientific notation as 5.237×10^2 and 1.70×10^{-3}, respectively; also, the number 8,000, regarded as having two significant digits, is written 8.0×10^3. In scientific notation, all digits that appear are taken to be *significant*. Similar notation applies to the binary number system, or a number system with any base. See **Approximate number**.

Secant Function One of the **trigonometric functions**; abbreviated "sec." It is the reciprocal of the cosine function, i.e., $\sec A = 1/\cos A$; it is a periodic function of period 360°, or 2π radians. The *secant curve*

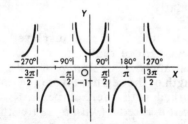

is the graph of $y = \sec x$, with x denoting radian measure.

Secant Line Of a curve, a line which intersects the curve but is not tangent to it; a *chord* is the portion of a secant line joining two points of the curve.

Second of Angle A 360ᵗʰ part of a degree of angle.

Secondary Parts of Triangle Parts of a triangle such as altitude, medians, exterior angles, etc., as against the *principal parts* which are the sides and (interior) angles.

Section of Solid A **plane section** of a solid. A *right section* of a cylinder or prism is a section perpendicular to the elements or edges of the solid. A *meridian section* of a surface of revolution is a section containing the axis of revolution. See **Trace of surface**.

Sector of Circle A region of the plane bounded by two radii of a circle and one of the arcs intercepted by the radii. The smaller (larger) of

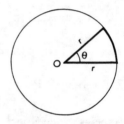

the two arcs is the *minor arc* (*major arc*). Let θ be the radian measure of the central angle, and r be the length of the radius; then the length of the intercepted arc is $r\,\theta$, and the area of the sector is $(\frac{1}{2})r^2\theta$. For example, a sector with central angle 60°, or $\pi/6$ radians, in a circle of radius 3 has length of arc $\frac{1}{2}\pi$ and area $\frac{1}{2}(3)^2(\frac{1}{6}\pi)$, or $\frac{3}{4}\pi$.

Sector, Spherical See **Spherical sector**.

Segment Of a *line* or *curve* the portion between two of its points. As a two-dimensional region, a segment is the plane region bounded by a portion of a plane curve and the chord joining its endpoints. See **Parabolic segment**.

Segment of Circle A region of the plane bounded by a chord of a circle and the arc cut off by the chord. A chord of a circle cuts off a minor arc (the smaller arc) and a major arc (the larger arc); corresponding to these are the *minor segment* and *major segment*. Let θ be the radian measure of the central angle subtended by the

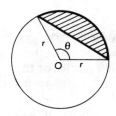

segment and r be the length of the radius, then its area is $\frac{1}{2}r^2(\theta - \sin\theta)$. For example, if $r = 3$ and $\theta = 90°$ ($\frac{1}{2}\pi$ radians), then the area is

$$\tfrac{1}{2}(3)^2(\tfrac{1}{2}\pi - 1) = \tfrac{9}{4}(\pi - 2).$$

Segment, Spherical See **Spherical segment**.

Semi-Axis A line segment (or its length) which is half of an axis of an ellipse, hyperbola, ellipsoid, etc. (one endpoint being at the center).

Semicircle Half of a circle (usually including the diameter joining the endpoints).

Semilogarithmic graph A plane graph using a uniform scale on one axis and **logarithmic coordinates** on the other.

Sense of Inequality The inequalities $a < b$ and $c < d$ have the *same* sense, as do $a > b$ and $d > c$. The inequalities $a < b$ and $c > d$ have *opposite* senses. See **Inequality relation**.

Sequence Numbers (or other entities) arranged in correspondence with whole numbers in their natural order 1, 2, 3, ... If the correspondence terminates at a finite number N, it is a *finite* sequence; if it is unending, it is an *infinite* sequence, or, simply, a *sequence*. (Put briefly, a sequence is a function from the natural numbers to a set of numbers, or other things.) A geometric progression is an example of a sequence; if it has a last term it is a finite sequence; if it continues without end, as in $1/2, 1/4, 1/8, \ldots 1/2^n \ldots$, it is an infinite sequence.

The notation "$A_1, A_2, A_3, \ldots$" is used to designate a sequence; the three dots, $\ldots$, indicate the continuation of the sequence. The individual elements A_1, A_2, and so on, are the *terms* of the sequence; the term in the nth place, or *general term*, is A_n. The rule for constructing the terms of a particular sequence can sometimes be understood from the early terms, or it can be expressed by formula. For example, the rule for the sequence $1/(1 \cdot 2), 1/(2 \cdot 3), 1/(3 \cdot 4), \ldots$ is clear by display; the formula for the general term is $A_n = 1/[n(n + 1)]$. The terms of a sequence need not be distinct; an example is 1, 1, 1, 0, 1, 0, 1, $\ldots$ where the rule of formation is to take $A_n = 1$ if n is a prime (or 1), and take $A_n = 0$ otherwise.

A sequence is *increasing* (*decreasing*) if each term is greater (less) than or equal to the preceding term, that is, $A_n \geq A_{n-1}$ ($A_n \leq A_{n-1}$). A sequence which is either increasing or decreasing is *monotonic*. A sequence is *bounded* if all its terms are numerically less than a fixed constant (see **Bound**). The sequence $-1, \frac{1}{2}, -\frac{1}{3}, \frac{1}{4}$, $\ldots$ (general term $(-1)^n/n$), is a bounded sequence which is not monotonic; the sequence $1^1, 2^2, 3^3$,

4^4, . . . is an unbounded, monotonic increasing sequence.

A sequence which has a finite **limit** is a *convergent sequence;* otherwise it is a *divergent sequence.* An unending decimal number is an example of a convergence sequence. For example, consider the fraction $\frac{25}{33}$ and its decimal representation .757575 . . ., the latter stands for the convergent sequence, .7, .75, .757, .7575, . . . (whose limit is $\frac{25}{33}$). A fundamental principle

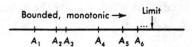

Bounded, monotonic → Limit
A_1 $A_2 A_3$ A_4 A_5 A_6

of the calculus is that a *bounded, monotonic sequence is convergent.* See **Cauchy condition.**

Sequential Analysis In statistics, a method of drawing conclusions in which the number of observations is not fixed in advance. Following each observation, a decision is made as to whether to terminate the experiment or to make another observation; this decision is based on all the observations to date, and on certain criteria applied to them. For example, in determining whether to accept or reject a given hypothesis H about a population, after each sample (observation) a criterion is applied for **(1)** accepting H, **(2)** rejecting H, or **(3)** taking another sample. The criteria may vary from one type of sequential analysis to another. An important advantage of this method is that it often requires fewer observations than methods specifying a fixed number of observations in advance.

Series An expression denoting the sum of the terms of a sequence. The series is *finite* in case the sequence is finite (as in the sum $1 + 3 + 5 + 7 + 9$ of the sequence, 1, 3, 5, 7, 9). It is

an *infinite series,* or simply *series,* in case the sequence is infinite [as in the (unending) geometric series $1 + \frac{1}{2} + \frac{1}{4} + \frac{1}{8} + \cdots$]. The notation "$a_1 + a_2 + a_3 + \cdots$" is used for a series; the dots indicate the continuation of the expression. The terms of the sequence, a_1, a_2, etc., are also the *terms* of the series; the nth term, or *general term,* is a_n. Another notation for a series is

$$\sum_{n=1}^{\infty} a_n,$$

the Greek letter Σ ("sigma") indicating summation. A series is generally specified by a rule for the formation of the terms; for example, the series $1 + 1/2^2 + 1/3^2 + 1/4^2 + \cdots$ is specified by the formula $a_n = 1/n^2$ for the general term.

An infinite series is only a symbolic expression, since the sum of an infinite number of terms has no meaning as an arithmetic or algebraic expression. Failure to recognize this and applying the ordinary rules of algebra to infinite series, can lead to logical errors. The following fallacy involving the series

$$1 - 1 + 1 - 1 + 1 - 1 + \cdots$$

(alternating 1's and -1's) is an illustration: grouping the terms as

$$(1 - 1) + (1 - 1) + (1 - 1) + \cdots$$

gives $0 + 0 + 0 + \cdots$, or 0; grouping the terms as

$$1 - (1 - 1) - (1 - 1) - (1 - 1) - \cdots$$

gives $1 - 0 - 0 - 0 - 0 - \cdots$, or 1; hence $0 = 1$.

A series is given precise meaning through the notion of a **limit,** in the following manner. With $a_1 + a_2 + a_3 + \cdots$, associate the sequence S_1, S_2, S_3, . . . of (finite) *partial sums* defined by $S_1 = a_1$, $S_2 = a_1 + a_2$, $S_3 = a_1 + a_2 + a_3$, . . . ; now when this sequence has a limit L, the series is said to be *convergent* and to have the *sum* L; thus is expressed by the equation $a_1 + a_2 + a_3 + \cdots = L$. Otherwise, the series is *divergent*. An example of a convergent series is the geometric series

$$1 + 1/2 + 1/2^2 + \cdots + 1/2^{n-1} + \cdots;$$

the partial sum S_n of the first n terms is $[1 - (1/2)^n]/[1 - 1/2]$; since this has the limit $1/(1 - 1/2)$, or 2 (as n increases without bound), the geometric series has the sum 2. Another example is the factorial series

$$1 + 1/1 + 1/(1 \cdot 2) + 1/(1 \cdot 2 \cdot 3) \\ + \cdots + 1/n! + \cdots$$

(its sum is e, the base of natural algorithms); the harmonic series

$$1 + 1/2 + 1/3 + \cdots + 1/n + \cdots$$

is an example of a divergent series. See **Absolutely convergent, Conditionally convergent**.

The *theory of infinite series* is the systematic study of series. Among questions considered are conditions for convergence (see **Ratio test**) and rules for the manipulation of series (for example, it is allowable to "add" convergent series term-by-term). Important types of series for representing functions are **power series** and **trigonometric series**.

Ref. [28, 41, 140, 148].

Set (Syn.: Class) A collection of things. It is a primitive, or undefined, concept of the general theory of sets.

The individual objects of a set are the *elements*, or *members*, of the set; an element is said to *belong to* the set. For example, any point of a line (considered as a set of points) belongs to the line; also, the number 5 belongs to the set of prime numbers, and George Washington belongs to the set of presidents of the United States. The Greek letter ε ("epsilon") is used to denote membership; the sentence "$x \varepsilon A$" stands for "x belongs to the set A." A *finite* (*infinite*) set is one with a finite (infinite) number of members. The example of presidents is a finite set; the set of prime numbers is an infinite set. An infinite set is *countable*, or *denumerable*, in case its members can be put into one-to-one correspondence with the natural numbers 1, 2, 3, . . . ; an example is the set of odd numbers 1, 3, 5, 7, ... The set of real numbers is a *nondenumerable* set. See **Cardinal number**.

One way to specify a set is to display its members, as in

$$\{0, 1, 2, 3, 4, 5, 6, 7, 8, 9\}$$

and $\{5, 10, 15, \ldots \}$. For a small finite set, this can be done completely; for a large finite set or an infinite set a partial listing can be used if the early members make clear what all the members are. A general method for specifying a set is to lay down an unambiguous test for individual membership; this may be done by giving a *property* which its elements must possess. For example, the set $\{5, 10, 15, \ldots \}$ is the set of natural numbers x with the property that x is a multiple of 5; also, in describing a set as the set of prime numbers the property of being prime is used as the defining characteristic.

Sets are subject to operations and relations such as *union, intersection, inclusion,* etc.; the **algebra of sets** is that part of the general theory of sets which studies these. The study of the **ordered set** treats the set from the point of view of the arrangement or ordering of its elements. The concept of a *set* is a basic and unifying one for all of mathematics. Logical studies of the foundations of mathematics show that from this concept, other basic concepts, such as *function, relation, operation,* and *number,* can be constructed.

Ref. [71, 89, 94, 142, 149].

Set of Ordered Pairs   A set whose members are ordered pairs. For example, the set $\{(a, b), (a, c), (b, c)\}$ has as its members the (ordered) pairs (a, b), (a, c), and (b, c). Sets of pairs arise naturally, for example, in the study of equations in two variables—such an equation determines the set of pairs which satisfy the equation, and the graph of the equation is a geometric representation of this set. For example, $x^2 + y^2 = 4$ specifies a set of ordered pairs (x, y) among which are found $(0, 2)$, $(1, \sqrt{3})$, and $(2, 0)$; the graph is the set of points (ordered pairs) making up the circle with center at the origin and radius 2. Similarly, any statement in two (free) variables determines a set of pairs; examples are "$x + 3y < 5$," and "the integer y is a divisor of the integer x." A **function** or a **relation** can be regarded as a set of ordered pairs.

Sexagesimal System   A system of numerical notation or measure which is based upon the number sixty. An example is the scheme of dividing a degree of angle into 60 minutes, and a minute of angle into 60 seconds. The familiar system of measuring time makes use of sexagesimal subdivision. The sexagesimal system was used in ancient Babylonia.

Sheaf of Planes   See **Bundle of planes** (syn.).

Short Arc (Syn.: Minor arc)   Of a circle, the shorter of the two arcs cut off by a chord, segment, or sector; the longer arc is the *major arc.*

Sieve of Eratosthenes   The following procedure for finding all the *prime numbers* up to a given integer N. Write down the integers from 2 to N; from 2, discard those integers in every second position; from the next remaining integer 3, discard those in every third position (keeping the integers in their original positions); from the next remaining integer 5, discard those in every fifth position; continue this until the next remaining integer p is greater than $\sqrt{N}$ (the integer p is retained); at this stage, the remaining integers are all the primes up to N. This method goes back to ancient Greek arithmetic.

Sign of Aggregation   See **Parentheses**.

Sign of Fraction   See **Fraction**.

Sign of Trigonometric Function   See **Trigonometric functions**.

Signed Numbers   Positive numbers and negative numbers. Two numbers, both positive or both negative, are of the *same sign;* two numbers, one positive and one negative, are of *opposite sign.* The number zero is neither positive or negative.

Significant Digit (Syn.: Significant figure)   In a decimal number, those digits which are relevant to its value as an **approximate number**.

Signs, Law of   See **Law of signs**.

Similar (geometry)   Informally, two geometric figures are similar in case each is a magnification or reduction of the other; this relation expresses the ordinary notion of "sameness of shape." (For similarity of special figures see **Conic, Polygon, Polyhedron**, etc.) A general definition of similarity of figures A and B in the plane or in space, is this: A is similar to B in case either can be brought into coincidence with the other by a *transformation of similitude* followed by a rigid motion [see **Transformation** (geometry)]. This relation is denoted by "$A \sim B$" (introduced by Leibniz). Areas and volumes of similar figures are proportional to the second and third powers, respectively, of the ratio of correspondng lengths.

Similar Decimals   In the decimal number system, numbers such as 5.106 and 11.583 with the same number of decimal places to the right of the decimal point. Two decimals can be made similar by adjoining zeros; for example, 62.8 and 7.096 become similar when written as 62.800 and 7.096. This is helpful in adding decimals.

Similar Fractions   Fractions with a **common denominator**.

Similar Terms   (Syn.: Like terms) Terms with the same literal factors, such as $3x^3$ and $-5x^3$, or $4ay^2$ and ay^2. In the addition of algebraic expressions, similar terms can be combined by combining their coefficients; for example,

$$3ax^2 + 6ax - 2ax^2 = ax^2 + 6ax.$$

Simple Closed Curve   A closed curve which does not intersect itself, such as a circle or ellipse.

Simple Fraction   In arithmetic (algebra) a **fraction** whose numerator and denominator are integers (polynomials).

Simple Root   See **Multiple root**.

Simplex   A 0-*simplex* is a point, a 1-*simplex* is a line segment, a 2-*simplex* is a triangle and its interior, and a 3-*simplex* is a tetrahedron and its in-

terior, etc. The *n-simplex* is the most elementary geometric figure lying in a space of n dimensions (and not lying in a space of lower dimension); for example, the triangle is the simplest figure in the (two-dimensional) plane. This terminology is used in topology where simplices are used as the building blocks for more complex configurations.

Simplex Method   See **Mathematical programming**.

Simplified   In a general way, a simplified algebraic expression is one that has been reduced as far as possible to a desired form.   See **Fraction**, **Radical**.

Simply Connected   See **Connected set**.

Simpson's Rule   In integral calculus, a method for approximating a definite integral by replacing short arcs of a curve by arcs of parabolas. More specifically, for an integral $\int_a^b f(x)dx$ over the interval from a to b, the interval is divided into an even number n of equal subintervals of length $h = (b - a)/n$ by points of division.

$$x_0 = a, x_1, x_2, \ldots, x_n = b;$$

the corresponding functional values are

$$y_0 = f(x_0), y_1 = f(x_1), \ldots, y_n = f(y_n).$$

Simpson's rule then leads to the following aproximation formula for the integral:

$$\tfrac{1}{3}h[(y_0 + y_n) + 4(y_1 + y_3 + \cdots + y_{n-1}) + 2(y_2 + y_4 + \cdots + y_{n-2})].$$

See **Trapezoid rule**.

Simulation   A general method of studying the behavior of a real system or phenomenon; the method usually involves the following features: **(1)** devising a *model*, or set of mathematical and logical relations, which represents the essential features of the system; **(2)** carrying out step-by-step computations with these relations which imitate the manner in which the real system might perform in real time. Typically, the real system is subject to chance elements, and this leads to the inclusion of probabilistic characteristics in the model. In systems of complexity, a high-speed digital computer may be programmed to carry out the sequence of computations (also, a simulation may involve both a computer and persons imitating certain human functions in a system). An important advantage of simulation is that the system can be studied under a wide variety of conditions which might be expensive or impossible to apply directly to the real system. Simulation is an important tool for a great variety of problems, particularly where ordinary mathematical solution is not possible, or where intangibles of human judgment are involved; it is widely used in **operations research**. Examples include **(1)** the functioning of a business firm, **(2)** the diffusion of neutrons in a nuclear reactor, and **(3)** the problem-solving behavior of a human being. See **Machine intelligence (computer)**, **Monte Carlo method**.

Simultaneous Equations (Syn.: System of equations) In algebra, two or more equations involving two or more unknowns, for which values of the unknowns are sought that are common solutions of the several equations. For example, $2x + 5y = -4$ and $x - 3y = 9$ are simultaneous equations in the two unknowns x and y; the values $3, -2$ for x, y comprise a solution, since they satisfy both equations (see figure). In general, one equation represents a single condition on unknowns; simultaneous equations represent a conjunction of conditions, which are to be satisfied "simultaneously." In algebra, techniques are studied for finding solutions of simultaneous equations.

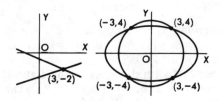

Geometrically, solutions of simultaneous equations are the points of intersection of the graphs of the several equations; these points make up the *graph* of the simultaneous equations (real number, not complex number, solutions being understood). In the above example, the point $(3, -2)$ is the point of intersection of the two (linear) graphs. The solutions of the simultaneous equations $x^2 + y^2 = 25$ (circle) and $x^2/36 + 3x^2/64 = 1$ (ellipse) are the four points of intersection $(3, 4)$, $(-3, 4)$, $(-3, -4)$ and $(3, -4)$ (see figure). Simultaneous equations may have no, one, or more solutions. If there is at least one solution, they are *consistent equations,* otherwise *inconsistent*. When the number of equations is the same as the number of unknowns there are, typically, a finite number of solutions; for example, two equations in two unknowns give the points of intersection of two curves in the plane, and three equations in three unknowns of three surfaces in space. *Simultaneous linear equations* arise frequently; methods of solutions are available by **Cramer's rule** and by

elimination of variables (also, see **Homogeneous linear equation**).

The number of equations and unknowns need not be the same—two equations in three variables typically represent the curve of intersection in space of the graphs (surfaces) of the

individual equations. For example, the simultaneous equations $x^2 + y^2 + z^2 = 9$ (sphere) and $x - y = 0$ (plane) intersect in a circle in space.

Ref. [75, 80, 120].

Simultaneous Inequalities (Syn.: System of inequalities)   In algebra, two or more inequalities, involving two or more variables, for which solutions common to the several inequalities are required. If they are *consistent* (have at least one common solution), the number of solutions is usually infinite, making up some region of points which is the *graph* of the inequalities. For a single inequality in two variables, the graph is a portion of the plane; for simultaneous inequalities in two variables, the graph

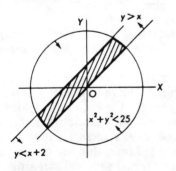

of solutions is the common part of the graphs of the several inequalities. For example, the graph of the three simultaneous inequalities $x^2 + y^2 <$ 25, $y > x$, $y < x + 2$ is that portion of the interior of the circle with center at the origin and radius 5 that lies between the parallel lines $y = x$ and $y = x + 2$ (see figure). Similar considerations apply to space in the case of simultaneous equations in three variables.

Simultaneous linear inequalities arise often. For several linear inequalities in two variables, the graph is a *convex set* bounded by lines. In three variables, the graph is a convex region in space bounded by planes. The interior of a polygon or polyhedron is described algebraically as a system of linear inequalities; these sets occur in **mathematical programming**.

Sine Function   One of the **trigonometric functions**; abbreviated "sin." Let A be an angle of rotation of the positive x-axis, terminating in the point (x, y); then sin A is defined as the ratio y/r, r being the distance of (x, y) from the origin. The sine is a periodic function of period $360°$, or

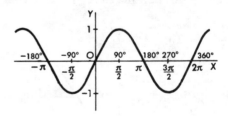

2π radians. The *sine curve* is the graph of $y = \sin x$, with x denoting radian measure.

Single-valued Function   Same as **function**, in contrast to "many-valued function."

Skew Lines   Two lines in space which do not lie in a single plane. Skew lines do not intersect, but they are not parallel lines (parallel lines lie

245

in common plane, by definition).

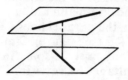

Among all the line segments joining points of skew lines, the shortest is the (unique) segment perpendicular to both lines; its length is the *distance* between the skew lines.

Slant Height   See **Cone, Pyramid**.

Slide Rule   A mechanical device for approximate calculation using the principle of the logarithm; it consists of scales of *logarithmic coordinates* arranged so as to be able to slide relative to one another.

Ref. [4].

Slope   The slope of a *line* is the ratio

$$\frac{y_2 - y_1}{x_2 - x_1}$$

where (x_1, y_1) and (x_2, y_2) are any two distinct points on the line (and the line is not parallel to the y-axis). This

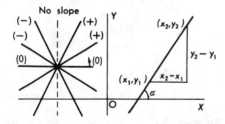

equals tan α, where α is the *angle of inclination,* or *slope angle* (that is, the positive angle from the positive x-axis to the line). The slope can be interpreted as the change in the y-coordinate for a unit increase in the x-coordinate, as a point moves from left to right along the line. A horizontal line (parallel to the x-axis) has slope 0; a vertical line (parallel to the

y-axis) has no slope defined for it. As the horizontal line rotates counterclockwise about a fixed point on it (see figure), its slope increases, and the slope grows without bound as the line approaches the vertical position. On the other side of the vertical position its slope is negative; the slope has a large negative value near the vertical position, and returns to 0 through negative values as the line rotates on to the horizontal position.

When a line in the plane is given as a linear equation in x and y, its slope m is equal to the coefficient of x in the *slope-intercept form* $y = mx + b$ of the equation. Distinct lines are parallel in case their slopes are equal, perpendicular in case the product of their slopes is -1. The slope of a *plane curve* at a point P is the slope of the tangent line at P; the slope of a curve $y = f(x)$ is given by the **derivative of the function** $f(x)$.

Slope-Intercept Equation of Line   In analytic geometry, the form $y = mx + b$ for the equation of a line in the plane, where m is the slope and $(0, b)$ is the y-intercept.

Small Circle of Sphere   See **Circle on sphere**.

Solid (Syn.: Geometric solid)   In solid geometry, a *closed surface* in space. (Sometimes "solid" is taken to mean the surface together with its interior.) The *measure* of a solid usually means the volume of its interior. Two solids are sometimes said to be *equal* (or *equivalent*) if they have the same volume; this use of "equality" differs from its logical meaning.   See particular solids such as **Cone, Prism, Regular polyhedron**, etc.

Solid Angle   A surface in space consisting of all half-lines having a common initial point (the *vertex*), and passing through a closed curve or polygon (hence, a nappe of a conical surface). For example, a polyhedral angle is a solid angle. The solid angle *subtended at a point O* by a portion of a surface is the solid angle of all half-lines from O passing through the boundary of the portion. The notion of a solid angle in space generalizes the notion of an angle in the plane.

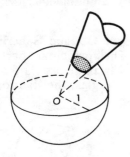

The *measure of a solid angle* is the area it intercepts on a sphere of radius 1 (when its vertex is at the center); this is taken as the number of *steradians* in the angle, one steradian being a solid angle which intercepts a unit area on the unit sphere. A sphere of radius 1 has a total surface area 4π, so that this is the largest measure a solid angle can have. A trihedral angle whose edges are mutually perpendicular measures $\pi/2$ steradians, for example. Steradian measure in space is the analog of radian measure in the plane.

Solid Geometry   The study of elementary geometric figures such as planes, polyhedrons, spheres, etc., in ordinary three-dimensional space; solid geometry, like plane geometry, was studied by the ancient Greek mathematicians. *Solid analytic geometry* is solid geometry treated by algebraic means through the use of

a coordinate system in space. See **Geometry**.
  Ref. [147].

Solid of Revolution   See **Surface of revolution**.

Solution of Equation (Syn.: Root of equation)   For an equation in *one variable* a value of the variable, or unknown, which satisfies the equation. ("Solution" also means a method for finding these values.) When the equation is in the form $f(x) = 0$, its solutions are called the *zeros* of the function $f(x)$; in this case the (real number) solutions can be interpreted as the points where the graph of $y = f(x)$ intersects the x-axis. De-

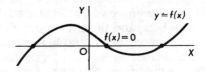

termining solutions of equations is a central problem, and various methods to accomplish this are studied in elementary and advanced mathematics; in practical applications, it is usually necessary to resort to methods of approximation. See **Fractional equation, Quadratic equation and formula, Rationalization of equation, Roots of polynomial equation**.
  The following two principles are useful in solving equations: **(1)** an equation of the form $F \cdot G = 0$ holds just in case either $F = 0$ or $G = 0$; **(2)** an equation of the form $F/G = 0$ holds just in case $F = 0$ (but $G \neq 0$). The first principle is the basis of solution by factoring. For example, to solve $x^3 + 5x = 2x^2$, write it as $x^3 - 2x^2 + 5x = 0$, then as $x(x^2 - 2x + 5) = 0$; it follows that $x = 0$ or $x^2 - 2x + 5 = 0$; hence one root is 0, and the problem is reduced to solving a quadratic. Again, to solve

247

$(3x - 2)/(x - 1) + 3 = 0$, write it as $[3x - 2 + 3(x - 1)]/(x - 1) = 0$ or $(6x - 5)/(x - 1) = 0$; from **(2)** it follows that $6x - 5 = 0$, or $x = \frac{5}{6}$; hence $\frac{5}{6}$ is a solution (since the denominator is not zero at this value of x).

Some algebraic procedures for solving an equation can lead to a **redundant equation** having extraneous roots, or to a **defective equation** lacking some roots. These procedures are still useful, provided they are applied with caution.

A solution of an *equation in two variables* is a pair of numbers which satisfy the equation; the collection of all real number solutions make up a graph in the plane. A solution of an *equation in three variables* is a triple of numbers, and the collection of solutions make up a graph in space. **Simultaneous equations** involve finding the common solutions of several equations in several unknowns.

Solution of Inequality For an inequality in *one variable,* a value of the variable for which the inequality holds (also, a method for finding these values). Usually, the set of all solutions is an infinite set of (real) numbers. An example is the linear inequality $2x - 3 < 1$; to solve it, write it as $2x < 4$; convert it to $x < 2$; hence, the solutions are all numbers less than 2. Any linear inequality in one variable can be solved in a like manner.

A solution of an *inequality in two variables* is a pair of numbers which satisfy the inequality [for example, $x^2 + y^2 < 9$ has solutions $(1, 2)$, $(-2, -2)$, etc.]. The *graph* of an inequality in two variables is the set of all points in the plane satisfying the inequality (for example, the graph of the last inequality is the interior of the circle

with center at the origin and radius

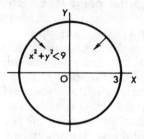

3). See **Linear inequality, Quadratic inequality, Simultaneous inequalities**.

Solution of Oblique Spherical Triangle The principal parts of a spherical triangle are its three sides and three angles; the solution of the

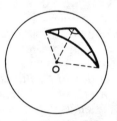

triangle consists in finding the measures of the principal parts when only a sufficient number are given to determine them all. This problem is studied in spherical trigonometry.

The following data determine spherical triangles: **(1)** two sides and the included angle; **(2)** two angles and the included side; **(3)** three sides; **(4)** three angles; **(5)** two sides and the angle opposite one of them; **(6)** two angles and the side opposite one of them. Case **(4)** is peculiar to the spherical triangle; it does not apply to the plane triangle. Another difference between the plane and sphere is that the sum of the angles of a spherical triangle is not the same for all triangles; all that can be said is that the sum is between 180° and 540°. As with plane triangles, certain ambiguous cases can occur in solving the spherical triangle; cases **(5)** and **(6)** fall in this group.

A useful theorem of solid geometry relates the parts of a spherical triangle to its *polar triangle;* it states that the angle (side) of a spherical triangle equals the supplement of the side (angle) opposite to it in the polar triangle. This means that solving one triangle also solves the other; that is, if the parts of one triangle are found, then the parts of the other are known. For example, if the data for a triangle are its three angles, then the data for the polar triangle are its three sides, and this problem may be solved instead. (For the definition of polar triangle, see **Pole of circle of sphere.**)

Spherical triangles are solved using trigonometric functions and various relations among the six parts of the triangle derived in spherical trigonometry. Case **(1)** can be solved by the **law of cosines** of spherical trigonometry, or by this and the **half-angle formulas** for a spherical triangle. Case **(2)** can be solved by using the polar triangle to reduce it to case **(1)**, and then solving this case; it can be solved directly by the law of cosines, or by this and the **half-side formulas** of spherical trigonometry. Cases **(1)** and **(2)** can also be solved conveniently by **Napier's analogies.** Case **(3)** can be solved by the half-angle formulas. Case **(4)** can be solved by the half-side formulas. Cases **(3)** and **(4)** can replace each other by use of polar triangles. Cases **(5)** and **(6)** can be solved by first using the **law of sines** of spherical trigonometry to obtain another part, and then applying Napier's analogies for the remaining two parts. A useful check on the derived parts for any of the cases is the law of sines.

The first systematic treatment of

this problem was given by Vieta in the latter half of the sixteenth century.

Solution of Right Spherical Triangle
The determination of the measures of the principal parts of a right spherical triangle when only a sufficient number are given to determine them all. In general, a right spherical triangle is determined when any two parts are given, other than the right angle. This statement applies even when the two parts are angles, in contrast to the plane right triangle.

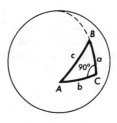

The solution can be carried out by the use of the following ten formulas relating the sides and angles of a right spherical triangle; they follow the pattern of **Napier's rules of circular parts.**

$$\sin a = \sin c \sin A \qquad \sin b = \sin c \sin B$$
$$\sin a = \tan b \cot B \qquad \sin b = \tan a \cot A$$
$$\cos A = \sin B \cos a \qquad \cos B = \sin A \cos b$$
$$\cos A = \tan b \cot c \qquad \cos B = \tan a \cot c$$
$$\cos c = \cot A \cot B \qquad \cos c = \cos a \cos b$$

Here A, B, C are the angles, with C the right angle, and a, b, c are the respective opposite sides. By these formulas any unknown part may be expressed in terms of known parts, and this permits the solution of any right triangle. The formulas are used with the rule of **species**, which helps specify the quadrant of a part when only a trigonometric function of the part is known.

249

Solution of Triangle in Plane The principal parts of a plane triangle are the three sides and the three angles; the solution of a triangle consists in finding the measures of these parts when only a sufficient number are given to determine them all. Triangles are solved by means of trigonometric functions, and methods of solution are developed in the study of plane trigonometry. The numerical work can be considerably reduced by logarithmic computation, and for this purpose tables of logarithms and of logarithms of trigonometric functions are widely used.

A *right triangle* has one angle equal to 90°, so that only five parts are required for the complete solution. Data which determine a right

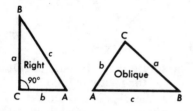

triangle are any two of these five parts, except both angles. The solution is carried out by using the definition of the trigonometric functions of acute angles as a ratio of two sides of a right triangle; this enables any unknown part to be related to known parts.

For an *oblique triangle,* six parts are required for a complete solution. The following data determine a plane triangle: (1) two angles and the included side; (2) two sides and the included angles; (3) three sides; (4) two sides and the angle opposite one of them. (The last is the *ambiguous case,* in which two triangles are usually determined, instead of one.) Oblique triangles are solved by the use

of various relations among the parts of a triangle derived in plane trigonometry. Case (1) is solved by using the fact that the sum of the angles is 180° to determine the third angle, and then applying the **law of sines** to find the unknown sides. Case (2) can be solved by the **law of cosines**; using this law, the side opposite the given angle is determined first, and then another angle is determined by the law of sines. An alternative method (preferred for logarithmic computation) is to use the **law of tangents**: suppose the given sides and angle are a, b, and C; then $(A + B)$ equals $180° - C$, and the law of tangents will yield $A - B$ from the given data; from $A + B$ and $A - B$, the angles A and B are determined; then the last side can be obtained by the law of sines. Case (3) is solved by the use of the **half-angle formulas**, which allows each angle to be determined separately by means of the three given sides. Case (4) is solved by the use of the law of sines again. In this ambiguous case, the two possible solutions emerge when determining an angle whose sine is given; there are two possible angles (which are supplementary), and these distinguish the two cases.

The first systematic treatment of this problem was given by Vieta in the second half of the sixteenth century.

Space In elementary geometry, ordinary three-dimensional space; in general, a collection of entities, called points, having geometric-like properties. More specifically, the line is a *one-dimensional space* (or one-space), the plane a *two-dimensional space* (or two-space), and ordinary space is a *three-dimensional space* (or three-space). The points of these spaces are represented in a coordinate system respectively, by single real numbers x, pairs of numbers (x, y), and triples of numbers (x, y, z). Points of spaces of higher dimension are represented by four numbers, five numbers, and so on; the set of n-tuples $(x_1, x_2, \ldots x_n)$ specify points in an *n-dimensional space,* a notion that evolved in the nineteenth century. Any one of these collections of points can be treated as a *Euclidean geometry,* or *Euclidean space;* the principal property of such a geometry is that the distance between points is the ordinary one; for example, in three-space the distance d between (x, y, z) and (a, b, c) is given by the formula

$$d = [(x - a)^2 + (y - b)^2 + (z - c)^2]^{1/2};$$

a similar formula applies in four-space, or higher dimensional space. These collections of points can also be treated as *non-Euclidean geometries,* or *spaces;* in such a space the Euclidean parallel postulate does not hold, and **distance** may have any one of various meanings. A famous example is the four-dimensional space of relativity theory.

Geometric configurations in the plane include one-dimensional figures such as lines and curves, as well as two-dimensional figures such as the interior of a polygon or a circle. Configurations in three-space include curves (one-dimensional), planes and surfaces (two-dimensional), and interiors of solids (three-dimensional). A space of n dimensions includes these as well as higher-dimensional "hypersurfaces," up to dimension n; these configurations are referred to in geometric terms but they are studied by algebraic means.

A space can be *infinite-dimensional;* this is the case with **Hilbert space,** which generalizes vectors with n components to vectors with a denumerable infinity of components. Classes of functions, such as all continuous functions of a real variable, also make up an infinite dimensional space. In very general spaces, it is not even necessary that there be defined a notion of distance between points; this occurs in *topology,* for example.

Ref. [52, 66, 73, 100].

Space Curve A curve in three-dimensional space. A *twisted curve* is a space curve which does not lie in a plane. A helix on a cylinder is an example of a twisted curve; on the other hand, a great circle on a sphere is not a twisted curve, since it lies on a plane through the center of the sphere.

Space Coordinates Any of several methods for locating points in three-dimensional space by means of triples of numbers. See **Cartesian coordinates in space, Cylindrical coordinates, Spherical coordinates.**

Species In a spherical triangle, two angles (or sides) are of the *same* species if they are both between 0° and 90° or both between 90° and 180°, and of *different* species if one is between 0° and 90°, while the other is between 90° and 180°. The *rule of species,* or *law of quadrants,* states the following for a spherical right triangle (let C be a right angle and let a, b, c be the sides opposite the vertices A, B, C). **(1)** angle A and side a are of the same species, and so are B and b; **(2)** if side c is less than 90°, then a and b are of the same species; **(3)** if side c is greater than 90°, then a and b are of different species. These relations are helpful in the solution of the right spherical triangle to de-

251

cide how to choose among the alternative roots of a trigonometric equation.

Sphere   In solid geometry, a closed surface in space consisting of all points at a given distance (the *radius*) from a fixed point O (the *center*); it is a principal object of study in solid geometry. (The term "sphere" sometimes means the surface together with its interior.) A unit sphere is a sphere of radius one. A *diameter* is a line segment (or its length) joining two points of the sphere and passing through the center. A sphere of radius r has area $4\pi r^2$ and volume $\frac{4}{3}\pi r^3$.

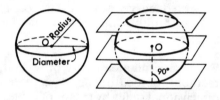

A plane in space which touches a sphere in one point is tangent to the sphere; in this case, the radius from the center to the point of contact is perpendicular to the plane. Otherwise, a plane either has no points in common with the sphere, or intersects it in a circle; if the intersecting plane passes through the center this circle is a *great circle;* otherwise it is a *small circle*. In either case, the diameter perpendicular to the plane is called the *axis* of the circle, and the two endpoints on the sphere are the *poles* of the circle; the axis passes through the center of the circle. A *meridian* of a sphere is any great circle passing through a given pole. A sphere is determined by four points in space which do not lie in one plane (a circle, by analogy, is determined by three points in a plane which are not on a straight line); for example,

a unique sphere can be circumscribed about a tetrahedron.   See **Circumscribed sphere, Inscribed sphere.**

Exactly one great circle can be drawn through two given points on a sphere; the shorter arc between the two points is the *geodesic* between them; its length is the *spherical distance* between the points (it is the shortest of all possible arcs, circular or otherwise, that can be drawn on the sphere between two points). In a rectangular coordinate system, the *equation of a sphere* with center at the origin and radius r is $x^2 + y^2 + z^2 = r^2$. If the center is at (a, b, c) instead, the equation is

$$(x - a)^2 + (y - b)^2 + (z - c)^2 = r^2.$$

Among the many interesting properties of the sphere is the following *isoperimetric property:* it has maximum volume among all closed surfaces with the same value of area. Another is that geometry on the sphere can be interpreted as a non-Euclidean geometry of the so-called "elliptic" type.

Spherical Angle   A figure on a sphere consisting of two arcs of great circles with a common endpoint, called the *vertex* of the angle; the arcs are the *sides*. For example, a spheri-

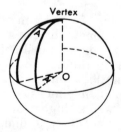

cal triangle contains three spherical angles. The *degree measure A* of a spherical angle is that of the arc it cuts off on the great circle whose pole is the vertex of the spherical angle.

Spherical Cone A **spherical sector** generated by rotating a minor sector of a circle through a complete revolution in space about a diameter passing through the sector.

Spherical Coordinates (Syn.: Polar coordinates in space) A coordinate system in space which locates a point P by means of its distance from a fixed point O (the *pole*) and two angles which describe the orientation of the segment OP. The coordinate system is fixed by two perpendicular half lines with common initial point O; one of these is the *polar axis,* and the plane containing the two is the *initial meridian plane.* Then the *spherical coordinates* of a point P are (r, θ, φ), where r is the length of OP (*radius vector* to P), θ the angle from the initial meridian plane to the plane through the polar axis and OP (the *longitude* of P), and φ the angle from the polar axis to OP (the *colatitude* of P). The spherical coordinate system

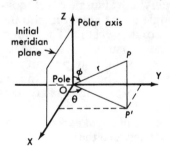

is usually aligned with a rectangular coordinate system in which the pole is at the origin, the polar axis coincides with the positive z-axis, and the initial meridian plane coincides with the xz-plane. In this case, θ is the angle from the positive x-axis to the *projection OP'* of OP on the xy-plane.

The radius vector r can have any nonnegative value. When r is held

constant at r_0 (while θ varies from 0° to 360° and φ from 0° to 180°), the point P generates a sphere of radius r_0 with center at O; this accounts for the name "spherical" coordinates.

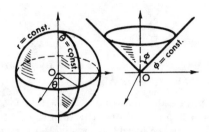

When θ is held constant at θ_0 (while r and φ vary) P describes the half plane which makes a dihedral angle of θ_0 with the initial meridian plane. When φ is held constant at φ_0 (while r and θ vary) P describes a conical surface (one nappe) whose elements make an angle φ_0 with the polar axis. For a sphere with center at the pole, a *meridian* is a great circle of intersection with a plane θ = constant, while a *circle of latitude* is a circle of intersection with a cone φ = constant. The *latitude* of a point P is the angle from the projection OP' to OP.

The *equations of transformation* expressing the rectangular coordinates (x, y, z) of a point in terms of its spherical coordinates are:

$$x = r \sin \varphi \cos \theta$$
$$y = r \sin \varphi \sin \theta$$
$$z = r \cos \varphi$$

Spherical Degree A unit of spherical area taken as $\frac{1}{720}$ of the surface of a sphere; the birectangular triangle whose third angle is one (ordinary) degree, measures one spherical degree. A hemisphere contains 360 spherical degrees, a sphere 720 spherical degrees. A birectangular triangle whose third angle is D (ordinary) degrees has a measure of D

253

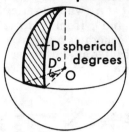

spherical degrees; its area in square units is $D\pi r^2/180$.

Spherical Distance Between two points on a sphere, the length of the shorter arc of the great circle joining the two points. See **Geodesic**.

Spherical Excess Of a *spherical triangle,* the difference between the sum of the degree measures of its angle and 180°. Since the sum is between 180° and 540°, the spherical excess E is between 0° and 360°. The formula for the area A of a spherical triangle is $A = (E/720)4\pi r^2$, or $A = E\pi r^2 \div 180$. The spherical excess of a *spherical polygon* is the difference between the sum of its angles and $(n - 2)\,180°$ (the latter is a minimum value for the sum). The area of a spherical polygon also equals $E\pi r^2/180$.

Spherical Helix See **Loxodromic spiral** (syn.).

Spherical Polygon A closed path on a sphere of connected (great circle) arcs $AB, BC, \ldots, PQ, QA$, which does not cut across itself (the arcs are generally required to be minor arcs, that is, no more than 180°). The successive points $A, B, C, \ldots, P, Q$ are the *vertices,* the connecting arcs are the *sides,* and the (interior) spherical angles at the vertices are the *angles,* of the polygon. A *diagonal* is an arc of a great circle joining two nonadjacent vertices (a spherical polygon can be subdivided into spherical triangles by means of

diagonals). The polygon is *convex* if it lies entirely in one of the two hemispheres determined by a great circle through any side (such a polygon does not "cut into itself" and its sides are necessarily restricted to arcs of no more than 180°). In solid geometry, "spherical polygon" usually means a convex spherical polygon.

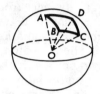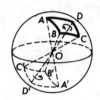

A spherical polygon determines a *central polyhedral angle* made up of all rays from the center of the sphere through the sides of the polygon. A face angle of the polyhedral angle corresponds to a side of the polygon, and the degree measure of the side equals the degree measure of the face angle; similarly, a dihedral angle of the polyhedral angle corresponds to an angle of the polygon, and the two have equal measure. The sum of the degree measures of the sides of a (convex) spherical polygon is less than 360°. The sum of the degree measures of its angles is greater than $(n-2)180°$ (n is the number of sides); its *spherical excess E* is the difference between the sum and $(n-2)\times 180°$. Its area is $E\pi r^2/180$.

To define *congruence* of spherical polygons, consider two polygons whose successive vertices are paired off so that corresponding sides and corresponding angles equal. Now if the rotational arrangement of the vertices of one polygon is the same as that of the vertices of the other (viewed from the center of the sphere), then the spherical polygons are *directly congruent* (or, simply, *congruent*); otherwise they are *oppo-sitely congruent* (or *symmetric*). Congruent spherical polygons are ones that can be brought into coincidence by a rigid motion; symmetric ones are those that can be only after one is reflected in a plane through the center of the sphere (see figure).

Spherical Pyramid The closed surface in space determined by a spherical polygon and its interior (the *base*) and the lateral surface made up of all radii from the center of the sphere to the sides of the polygon (hence, the lateral surface is the portion of a central polyhedral angle cut off by a sphere). The volume of a spherical pyramid equals $E\pi r^3/540$, where E is the spherical excess of the base.

Spherical Sector A closed surface of revolution generated by a plane sector of a circle rotated through a complete revolution about a diameter of the circle. There are two types, depending upon whether the diameter does or does not pass through the plane sector—in the first case, the arc of the plane sector generates a *zone of one base* and in the second base, a

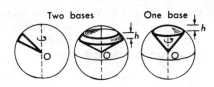

Two bases   One base

zone of two bases; the zone is the *base* of the spherical sector. In either case, the volume of the spherical sector equals $\frac{2}{3}\pi r^2 h$, where r is the radius of the sphere and h is the altitude of the zone.

Spherical Segment A *spherical segment of two bases* is a closed surface in space determined by two parallel planes cutting a sphere; it consists of two circular plane portions (the

bases) cut off by the planes, and a portion of the sphere between them

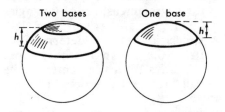

Two bases   One base

(the *zone*). The *altitude h* is the distance between the parallel planes. If one of the two planes is tangent to the sphere, they determine a *spherical segment of one base* (this is the surface generated when a segment of a circle is revolved about the diameter perpendicular to the chord). The volume V is given by the formula $V = \frac{1}{6}\pi h(3r_1^2 + 3r_2^2 + h^2)$ where r_1, r_2 are the radii of the bases (if there is only one base, one of these is zero).

Spherical Triangle A spherical polygon of three sides (each side being less than 180° of arc). The terms *acute, oblique, obtuse, right, scalene, isosceles, equilateral, equiangular* are used for spherical triangles as for plane triangles. However, a spherical triangle can have the sum of its angles any value between 180° and 540°, and there are *birectangular* spherical triangles (two right angles) and *trirectangular* spherical triangles (three right angles). A *quadrantal*

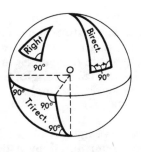

spherical triangle is one with a side

255

equal to a quarter of a great circle. The *spherical excess E* of a spherical triangle is the difference of the sum of the degree measures of its angles and 180°; the area equals $E\pi r^2/180$. A spherical triangle determines a central trihedral angle whose edges are the rays from the center of the sphere through the vertices of the triangle.

Suppose two spherical triangles have their respective vertices matched so that corresponding sides are equal and corresponding angles are equal. If the rotational arrangement of the vertices of one triangle is the same as that of the other (as viewed from the center of the sphere), then the triangles are *directly congruent* (or, simply, *congruent*); otherwise they are *oppositely congruent* (or *symmetric*). Conditions under which two spherical triangles are (directly or indirectly) congruent are the following: **(1)** two sides and included angle of one equal to two sides and included angle of the other; **(2)** two angles and the included side of one equal to two sides and the included angle of the other; **(3)** three sides of one equal to three sides of the other; **(4)** three angles of one equal to three angles of the other. See **Polar triangle, Solution of oblique spherical triangle, Solution of right spherical triangle.**

Spherical Trigonometry The study of spherical triangles, particularly methods for the solution of such triangles. The historical development of this subject is closely connected with astronomy. See **Solution of oblique spherical triangle, Solution of right spherical triangle.**

Ref. [128].

Spherical Wedge A closed surface in space determined by a dihedral angle whose edge passes through the

center of a sphere together with the

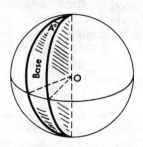

portion of the sphere it intersects (the *base*); the spherical portion is a lune. $A\pi r^3/270$ equals the volume of a wedge; A is the degree measure of the dihedral angle and r is the radius of the sphere.

Spheroid See **Ellipsoid of revolution** (syn.).

Spiral In a general way, a curve on a plane or surface which winds about a fixed point. A plane curve of this type is often represented by an equation in polar coordinates (r, θ), where the winding effect is described as θ rotates about the pole O through successive multiples of 360°.

The following plane spirals are of interest. The *spiral of Archimedes* has the polar equation $r = a\theta$, where a is a positive constant; it is the path of a point which moves outward along a

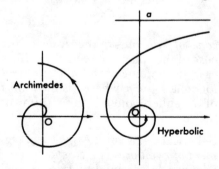

ray at a uniform speed as the ray rotates about the pole at a constant angular speed. The *hyperbolic,* or *reciprocal, spiral* has the polar equation $r\theta = a$; as θ increases through successive revolutions, the spiral winds about the origin, coming closer and closer to it as a limiting position; as θ decreases toward 0, the spiral approaches the line parallel to (and a units above) the polar axis as an asymptote. The *logarithmic spiral* has the polar equation $\log r = a\theta$; it is also called an *equiangular spiral* because for any point on it, the angle between the tangent line and the line to the origin is always the same (it is related to the conical **helix**). With a positive, as θ turns clockwise the curve winds closer and closer to the

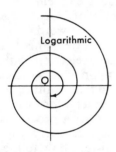

Logarithmic

origin; as θ turns counterclockwise, the spiral winds farther and farther from the origin. The *parabolic spiral,* or *Fermat's spiral,* is one with a polar equation $r^2 = a\theta$. See **Lituus, Loxodromic spiral**.

The spiral of Archimedes provides constructions for squaring the circle, and trisecting or n-secting an angle (but not by ruler and compass alone, as these problem are generally understood).

Square In *plane geometry,* a rectangle with all sides equal. The *unit square* has sides of length 1. A square with side a has perimeter $4a$ and area a^2.

In *algebra,* a square is an expres-

sion raised to the second power; a *perfect square* is an integer (polynomial) which is a second power of another integer (polynomial), such as 5^2, or $(2x + 3)^2$. See **Perfect power**.

Square Root Of a given expression A, an expression which multiplied by itself equals A; it is denoted by $\sqrt{A}$. For example, $\sqrt{4} = 2$, $\sqrt{0} = 0$, $\sqrt{9x^2y^4} = 3xy^2$. If b is a positive integer, then $\sqrt{b}$ is an irrational number, unless b is a perfect square. See **Radical, Root of number**.

Squaring the Circle (Syn.: Quadrature of circle) The following ancient problem of **geometric construction**: to construct a square whose area is equal to that of a given circle

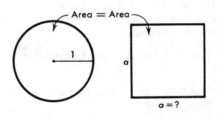

Area = Area

1

a

$a = ?$

(using only straight edge and compass). The problem has a long history; however, it was not until the latter half of the nineteenth century that a conclusive proof was given that the construction is impossible. A solution would require the construction of the number $\sqrt{\pi}$; the impossibility of this follows upon showing that π is a transcendental (that is, nonalgebraic) number. Ref. [6, 16].

Standard Deviation In statistics, a certain measure of the "dispersion" of a set of values about the mean value. First, consider N *numerical observations* a_1, a_2, a_3, . . . , a_N whose mean value is m; then the standard deviation is

$[\frac{1}{N} \{(a_1 - m)^2 + (a_2 - m)^2$

$+ \cdots + (a_N - m)^2\}]^{1/2};$

this is the square root of the mean value of the squares $(a_1 - m)^2$, $(a_2 - m)^2$, etc. Next, consider a *discrete random variable* which takes the values $x_1, x_2, x_3, \ldots$ with probabilities $p_1, p_2, p_3, \ldots$, respectively; the standard deviation is

$[p_1(x_1 - m)^2 + p_2(x_2 - m)^2$

$+ p_3(x_3 - m)^2 + \cdots]^{1/2}$

(where m is the expected value). Finally, consider a *continuous random variable* with frequency function $p(x)$; the standard deviation is the square root of the integral of $(x - m)^2 p(x)$ over the values of the random variable, with m again the expected value. The *variance,* in every case, is the second power of the standard deviation.

Standard Form See **Ellipse, Hyperbola, Polynomial**, etc.

Standard Position of Angle The position of a plane angle with the vertex at the origin and the initial side along the positive x-axis.

Stationary Point Of a *curve* $y = f(x)$, a point at which the derivative of $f(x)$ vanishes (it includes relative maximum and minimum points, and horizontal inflection points); of a *surface* $z = f(x, y)$, a point at which the two partial derivatives of $f(x, y)$ simultaneously vanish (it includes relative maximum and minimum points, and saddle points).

Stationary Process See **Stochastic process**.

Statistics (mathematical) The application of probability theory to problems in the analysis of data, and related questions; it is sometimes described as "decision-making under uncertainty." Statistics is concerned, for example, with the design of experiments and the acceptance or rejection of hypotheses on the basis of sampled data. It is used in various fields, such as biology, physics, psychology, etc.

Ref. [14, 45, 77, 151].

Steradian A unit of measurement for the **solid angle**.

Stochastic Process (Syn.: Random process) A chance process or phenomenon described by "states" at different times and having the following general characteristic: future states depend upon the history of states up to the present, as well as upon chance elements. An example is the chain of words uttered by a speaker—the nth word may be viewed as the nth "state"; this will depend upon chance selection by the speaker and also upon what words he has uttered up to that point (grammatical structure enters, for instance, in the second factor). A process is a **Markoff process** in case its future depends upon its history only to the extent of what the present state is, and not how it was reached. A process is often called *discrete* if the states occur in ordered steps 1, 2, 3, etc., and *continuous* if the states occur continuously in time.

A process is *stationary,* loosely speaking, in case it has the following feature: its long run statistical properties are not changed when the starting point is advanced to any point of the original process; that is, a stationary process is "homogeneous" with respect to time. A stationary process is *ergodic,* loosely speaking, in case the following holds: the statistical properties of an (indefinitely) long sequence of states running through time are the same as those of a sequence of states at a fixed point in time for (indefinitely) many repetitions of the total process. Precise statements of the stationary and ergodic properties call for advanced technical definitions.

Stochastic Variable   See **Random variable** (syn.).

Storage Unit   Of an automatic **digital computer**, a principal internal component for storing information in coded form; a less preferred term is *memory unit.* Physically, it consists of an array of many similar elements, each capable of being in either of two contrasting states, such as absence or presence of electrical charge, or one of two directions of magnetization. The elements are grouped into *registers,* or *storage locations;* each register is identified by an *address.* A *word* is a string of symbols which may occupy a single register; a word generally represents one item of information, such as a number or an instruction. In the course of a computation, words are copied into a storage register, held there, and removed later; the storage is *erasable,* that is, the same register can be occupied by different words at different times during the computation. One measure of the capacity of a computer is the number of words it can hold internally; for example, a 32,000 word machine is one that can hold 32,000 words (of a given length).

In addition to its *internal storage,* a computer has available *secondary,* or *auxiliary, storage;* these are units which are not integral parts of the computer but are linked to it and controlled by it (here, the time required to get information in and out of the computer is greater). Still further removed from the computer is

its *external storage;* in this case, the information is separate from the computer but is in a form which can be accepted by the computer through an input device. Examples of internal storage units are magnetic cores and cathode rays; examples of devices used for secondary storage are magnetic tapes and magnetic drums; magnetic tapes are also used for external storage, as are punched cards.

Stored-Program   Computer   See **Computer**.

Straight Angle   An angle of 180°

Straight Line   See **Line** (syn.).

Strategy   See **Theory of games**.

Subset   One set A is a subset of another set B in case every member of A is a member of B; this relation is written "$A \subset B$." The set A is a *proper subset* of B, if A is a subset of B and $A \neq B$. For example, the set of integers is a (proper) subset of the set of rational numbers.   See **Algebra of sets**.

Substitution   See **Inference, Elimination of variables**.

Subtend   In the *plane,* an arc or line segment with endpoints A and B subtends the plane angle at a point P

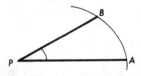

whose sides are the half-lines from P through A and B. For example, an arc or chord of a circle subtends a central angle at the center of a circle, and a side of a triangle subtends the opposite angle at a vertex of the triangle. In *space,* a portion of a surface, or plane, subtends the solid an-

259

gle at a point P which is made up of all half-lines from P through the boundary of the portion.

Subtraction Subtraction of numbers is one of the four fundamental operations of arithmetic; it can be defined as follows, as the inverse operation of addition: the *difference* $a - b$ is the number x satisfying the equation $b + x = a$. For example, $3 - 8$ is -5 because $8 + (-5) = 3$; also, $a - 0 = a$, because $0 + a = a$. In the difference $a - b$, a is the minuend and b is the subtrahend; $a - b$ is occasionally called the *remainder* of a and b. The notation "$a - b$" was introduced about 1500.

In elementary arithmetic, the operation of subtracting the whole number n from a larger whole number m is thought of, informally, as "taking n things away from m things." However, when m is less than n, this operation is not performable in the set of whole numbers. The extension of the **number** concept to integers (positive, negative, zero) resolves this difficulty; for example, $5 - 8 = -3$. This extension to integers leads to *algebraic subtraction,* or the subtraction of signed numbers. The following *law of signs* is used in this connection:

(1) $x - (-y) = x + y$;
(2) $(-x) - y = -(x + y)$;
(3) $(-x) - (-y) = y - x$.

For example, $3 - (-5) = 3 + 5$, or 8, and $(-3) - 7 = -(3 + 7)$, or -10; and $-4 - (-8) = 8 - 4$, or 4.

Subtraction Formulas (trigonometry) See **Addition formulas** (trigonometry).

Subtrahend See **Subtraction**.

Successive Approximations See **Approximation**.

Successive Trials See **Probability in repeated trials**.

Sufficient Condition One **condition** P is sufficient for another Q in case whenever P holds, so must Q; that is, P implies Q.

Sum The result of **addition**; the sum of a and b is denoted by $a + b$.

Sum of Like Powers An algebraic expression of the form $x^n + y^n$. When n is odd, the following factoring formulas hold.

$$x^3 + y^3 = (x + y)(x^2 - xy + y^2)$$
$$x^5 + y^5 =$$
$$(x + y)(x^4 - x^3y + x^2y^2 - xy^3 + y^4)$$
$$\vdots$$

In general, the sum of like odd powers of x and y has the factor $(x + y)$. When n is even, the expression cannot be factored in ordinary algebra. See **Difference of like powers**.

Sum of Perfect Powers of Integers The following formulas hold for the sum of the squares and cubes of the first n positive integers;

$$1^2 + 2^2 + \cdots + n^2 = \frac{n(n + 1)(2n + 1)}{6}$$

$$1^3 + 2^3 + \cdots + n^3 = \frac{n^2(n + 1)^2}{4}$$

In general, the sum of the pth powers of the numbers 1 through n equals a polynomial in n of degree $p + 1$. A more advanced result is *Lagrange's theorem* of the theory of numbers: this asserts that every positive integer is the sum of four perfect squares (for example, $45 = 0^2 + 2^2 + 4^2 + 5^2$).

Sum of Series See **Series**.

Sum of Sets See **Union of sets** (syn.).

Sum of Vectors The result of the addition of vectors.

Summation Sign   The Greek letter Σ ("sigma"), used to denote a sum of terms as follows:

$$\sum_{i=1}^{5} a_i$$

stands for $a_1 + a_2 + a_3 + a_4 + a_5$,

$$\sum_{i=1}^{n} a_i$$

for $a_1 + a_2 + \cdots + a_n$ (with n terms), and

$$\sum_{i=1}^{\infty} a_i$$

for the infinite **series** $a_1 + a_2 + a_3 + \cdots$.

Summit Angle (Syn.: Vertex angle) Of an isosceles triangle, the angle formed by the two equal sides.

Superposition   The action (or result) of bringing one geometric figure into coincidence with another. The following statement is sometimes referred to as the *axiom of superposition:* A figure may be moved without changing its size or shape. This may be interpreted as the statement that the properties of a figure of Euclidean geometry do not change when the figure is subjected to a rigid motion; its relationship to superposition is that any figure can be superposed on a **congruent figure** by a rigid motion.

Supplemental Chords   Of a circle, two chords which join a point on the

circle to the endpoints of a diameter; supplemental chords form a right angle.

Supplementary Angles   Two angles whose sum is 180°; each angle, then,

is the *supplement* of the other.

Surd   An irrational number which is a root of a positive integer or fraction as, for example, $\sqrt{\tfrac{2}{3}}$ and $\sqrt[3]{5}$. The term "surd" is also used for a sum involving such terms, as in the "binomial surds" $1 + \sqrt{3}$ and $\sqrt{3} - \sqrt[3]{2}$. See **Conjugate radicals**.

Surface   Informally, a continuous two-dimensional portion of space; it is a *closed surface,* or *solid,* when it is the complete boundary of a finite, three-dimensional portion of space. The *area* of a surface is a measure of its two-dimensional "extent"; the *volume* of a closed surface is the volume of its three-dimensional interior.

In elementary solid geometry, a study is made of such surfaces as planes, spheres, polyhedrons, cones, and cylinders. In solid analytic geometry, a surface is represented by an equation in rectangular space coordinates x, y, z; for example, a plane is given as (the graph of) a linear equation $ax + by + cz + d = 0$. A systematic study is made of the *quadric surfaces,* which are the graphs of second degree equations in x, y, z; these include the paraboloid, hyperboloid, and ellipsoid. In the calculus, the study of a function $f(x, y)$ of two variables is connected with the study of the surface which is the graph of $z = f(x, y)$ (for example, see **Tangent plane to surface**).

Some types of surfaces that occur in the general study of surfaces are the following. The *plane* or a portion of a plane is the simplest type. An *elementary surface* is one put together of planar portions (such as a polyhedron); this type of surface is useful in the analysis of a *curved surface,* which is one that contains no planar portion (such as a sphere). A *surface of revolution* is one generated

261

by rotating a curve through a com-

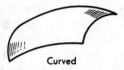

Curved

plete revolution about a fixed line (a torus is an example); a *developable surface* is one that can be rolled out on a plane without distortion (a cone is an example). A *ruled surface* is a surface which can be constructed as a family of straight lines; an example is the hyperbolic paraboloid. The latter is also a *doubly ruled surface,* that is, a surface which contains two distinct families of straight lines.

The general theory of surfaces is an advanced and important part of modern mathematics. One concept is the *curvature* of a surface; another is the *geodesic,* or curve of shortest length, on a surface. A surface which has the least area of all surfaces which share its boundary falls in the class of *minimal surfaces.* If the boundary is a plane curve, then the minimal surface is simply the plane surface enclosed by the curve; the problem becomes difficult and interesting when the bounding curve is "twisted," that is, does not lie in a plane. A minimal surface can be realized physically as a soap film; if a wire, in the shape of a closed space curve, is dipped in a soap solution and carefully removed, the film surface adhering to the wire is the minimal surface with the given boundary. This problem belongs to the **calculus of variations**, which deals with various properties of surfaces.
Ref. [54].

Surface of Revolution The surface generated by rotating a plane figure through a complete revolution in space about a line in the plane of the

figure; the line is the *axis of revolution*. A closed surface of revolution

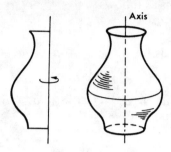

Axis

is called a *solid of revolution*. For example, a cone of revolution is generated by rotating a right triangle about one of its legs; an ellipsoid of revolution by rotating an ellipse about one of its axes. A section of a surface of revolution by a plane perpendicular to the axis is always a circle; a section by a plane containing the axis is called a *meridian section*.

The methods of the integral calculus can be used to obtain the volume and area of a solid of revolution in terms of the rotated plane figure; if the curve $y = f(x)$ between $x = a$ and $x = b$ is rotated about the x-axis, then the surface area A and the volume V are given by

$$A = \int_a^b 2\pi f(x) \sqrt{1 + (df/dx)^2}\, dx$$

and

$$V = \int_a^b \pi [f(x)]^2 dx.$$

See **Theorem of Pappus.**

Syllogism A logical *inference* involving a *major* and *minor premise,* and a *conclusion,* which follows from these premises. A classical example is the following inference. Major premise, "All men are mortal"; minor premise, "Socrates is a man"; conclusion, "Socrates is mortal."

Traditional logic dealt principally with syllogisms; today, this is a minor part of logic.   Ref. [59].

Symbol   Symbols are the letters and marks out of which mathematical expressions, formulas, and so on, are built. They are used in a great variety of ways. Symbols may stand for individual members of a set; for example, 5 and x for numbers, and P and Q for points. They may stand for operations which combine or act on things to give things; for example, "$+$" for addition and "$\sqrt{}$" for root extraction. They may stand for relations between things; for example, "$=$" for equality and "$\cong$" for congruence. Some symbols stand for functions; for example, *log* and *sin.*

An important distinction is that between a symbol which is a *constant* and one which is a *variable;* the constant names a particular entity, the variable, as such, does not. For example, in the case of numbers, "5" is a constant and "x" is (usually) a variable. The logical use of symbols depends upon whether they are constants or variables; for example, substitution is generally made for a variable, not for a constant. The appendix contains a list of some commonly used mathematical symbols.

Symbolic Logic   Modern **logic**, so-called because of its extensive use of mathematical symbolism.

Symmetric Equation   In two variables x and y, an equation which is equivalent to itself on interchanging x and y. For example, $x^2 + y^2 = 4$ is a symmetric equation, as is the equation $xy = 4$; but $x^2 + 2y^2 = 4$ is not, nor is the equation $x^2 + y = 4$. The *graph* of a symmetric equation is (geometrically) symmetric with respect

to the 45° line $y = x$.   See **Symmetry in plane**.

Symmetric Relation   A **relation** with the following property: if one thing is in the given relation to another, then the second is necessarily in the given relation to the first; examples of symmetric relation are **(1)** congruence of plane triangles, and **(2)** the relation "*a* is a sibling of *b*," among persons. A relation fails to be symmetric if there is at least one instance where the condition fails; an example is the relation "*a* likes *b*" (if *a* likes *b*, it does not follow that *b* likes *a*).   See **Asymmetric relation**.

Symmetric Solids   See **Congruent figures in space**.

Symmetric Spherical Figures   See **Spherical polygon, Spherical triangle**.

Symmetry in Plane   Two points P and P' in a plane are *symmetric with respect to a line l* (*with respect to a point Q*) in case P and P' correspond under **reflection in the line** l **(reflection in the point** Q **)**. More generally, a plane figure F is symmetric with respect to the line l (the point Q) in case F contains with each of its points P, the point P' symmetric to

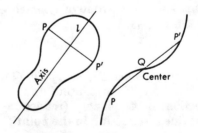

P; that is, F goes into itself under reflection in l (in Q). In this case, l is an *axis of symmetry* (Q is a *center of symmetry*). For example, a circle is symmetric with respect to any diameter, and an isosceles triangle is symmetric with respect to the altitude to its base. When a figure is symmetric with respect to each of two perpendicular lines, then it is symmetric with respect to their point of intersection; an example is an ellipse, which is symmetric with respect to each of its axes, and consequently with respect to its center. Symmetry with respect to a line (point) is called *axial* (*central*) *symmetry*.

When a plane curve C is given by an equation in rectangular coordinates x, y, the following *tests for symmetry* are available: **(1)** C is symmetric with respect to the x-axis (y-axis) in case replacing y by $-y$ (x by $-x$) produces an equivalent equation; **(2)** C is symmetric with respect to the origin in case replacing x by $-x$ and y by $-y$ produces an equivalent equation. These tests applied to the equation $x^2 + y^2 = r^2$ of a circle with center at the origin and radius r verify that it has all three symmetries. They also show that the graphs of $y = x^2$ and $y = \cos x$ are symmetric with respect to y-axis, and that the graph of $xy = k$ is symmetric with respect to the origin (but not either axis). A graph is symmetric with respect to the 45° degree line, $y = x$, in case its equation is a **symmetric equation**. See **Group of symmetries**.
Ref. [66, 83, 119].

Symmetry in Space   Two points P and P' in space are *symmetric with respect to a plane P (line l, point Q)* in case P and P' correspond under **reflection in the plane** p (**reflection in the line** l, **reflection in the point** Q). A figure S in space is symmetric with respect to a plane (line, point) in case S contains with every point P on it, the point P' symmetric to P; that is, S goes into itself under reflection in p (in l, in Q). In this case, the plane is a *plane of symmetry* (the line an *axis*

of symmetry,* the point a *center of symmetry*). A sphere is symmetric with respect to any plane through the center, a right circular cylinder is symmetric with respect to the line joining the centers of its bases, and an ellipsoid is symmetric with respect to its center. Any surface of revolution is symmetric with respect to its axis of revolution, and also symmetric with respect to any plane containing this axis.

When a surface is given by an equation in rectangular coordinates x, y, and z, there are available direct *tests for symmetry* with respect to the coordinate planes, the coordinate axes, and the origin. For instance, the xy-plane is a plane of symmetry if replacing z by $-z$ produces an equivalent equation; thus, the graph of $x + y = z^2$ is symmetrical with respect to the xy-plane. Also, the origin is a center of symmetry if replacing x, y, z by $-x$, $-y$, $-z$, respectively, produces an equivalent equation; for example, the plane $x + y + z = 0$ is symmetric with respect to the origin.
Ref. [66, 83, 119].

Synthetic   See **Analytic, Proof.**

Synthetic Division   Of polynomials, an abbreviated method for division when the divisor is a first degree polynomial $x - a$.

System   See **Coordinate system, Mathematical system, Number system.**

System of Equations or Inequalities See **Simultaneous equations, Simultaneous inequalities.**

T

Table of Function   A listing of numerical values of a function in correspondence with ordered values of the argument, or independent variable. The argument values are usually equally spaced, and the corresponding functional values are typically approximate numbers correct to a certain number of decimal places. To simplify interpolation for intermediate values, auxiliary lists of *proportional parts* of tabular differences are commonly provided (see **Linear interpolation**). Familiar tables are those for the common logarithm, the trigonometric functions, and the logarithms of trigonometric functions. These appear in the Appendix D of this book; they are widely used in computations, including the solution of triangles.

Many functions are available in tabulated form. Techniques for computing tables of transcendental functions are based on representation of the functions in an infinite series or in some similar form that is convenient for numerical evaluation.

Ref. [22].

Tabular Difference   The difference between successive entries in a table of a function; used for interpolation. See **Increment**.

Tangent Circles, Curves   Two *circles* are tangent at a point *P*, if *P* is the one point they have in common. If one circle is inside the other, they are *internally* tangent; otherwise they are

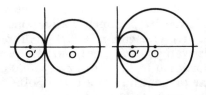

externally tangent. In either case, the line through the two centers (the *line of centers*) passes through the point of tangency *P*; the perpendicular at

P to this line is a common tangent line to the two circles.

More generally, two *curves* are tangent at a common point *P* in case they have the same tangent line at *P*. See **Tangent line to curve**.

Tangent Cone   A tangent cone of a sphere is a conical surface whose elements are all tangent to the sphere;

the points of tangency trace out a circle on the cone. For a cone, if the base is also tangent to the sphere then the cone is a **circumscribed cone**.

Tangent Function   One of the **trigonometric functions**; abbreviated "tan." Let *A* be the angle of rotation of the positive *x*-axis into the point (x, y); then tan *A* is defined as the

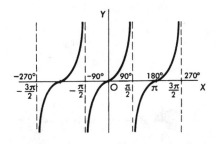

ratio y/x. The tangent is a periodic function of period 180°, or π radians. The *tangent curve* is the graph of the equation $y = \tan x$, with *x* denoting radian measure.

Tangent Line to Conic   Consider a conic represented in the general form

$ax^2 + 2bxy + cy^2 + 2dx + 2ey + f = 0$; let (x_0, y_0) be a point on the conic. Then the equation of the tangent line at this point is given by

$$ax_0x + b(xy_0 + x_0y) + cy_0y$$
$$+ d(x + x_0) + e(y + y_0) + f = 0,$$

where x, y is any point on the tangent line. For example, consider the ellipse $(x^2/8) + (y^2/18) = 1$; here $a = \frac{1}{8}, c = \frac{1}{18}, f = -1$, and the other coefficients are 0. The tangent line at $(2, 3)$, according to the formula, is $(2x/8) + (3y/18) - 1 = 0$, or $3x + 2y = 12$.

Tangent Line to Curve Let P be a given point on a *plane curve C*. Informally, the tangent line to the curve at P is the line which just "contacts" C at P, rather than "cutting across" at P (at least when the curve does not reverse its direction of bending at P). A more precise definition is this: Let P have coordinates (a, b), and let Q be another point on C with coordinates (x, y). Consider the (secant) line l through P and Q. Let Q approach P; as it does, the line l will, in general, change position (rotating about P).

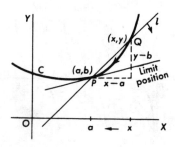

The *tangent line at P* is taken as the line in the limiting position of l as Q moves along C into coincidence with P (providing there is a limiting position). Point P is the *point of tangency,* or *contact,* of the tangent line. The slope of a secant line l is $(y - b) \div$

$(x - a)$; this will have a limit, say m, as Q approaches P (provided the tangent line at P is not vertical), and this will be the *slope* of the tangent line itself. Hence, the *equation of the tangent line* at P is $y - b = m(x - a)$, (x, y) here denoting any point on the tangent line.

For a plane curve given as the graph of $y = f(x)$, the slope m equals the **derivative of the function** $f(x)$, evaluated for $x = a$; when the curve is given in the form $F(x, y) = 0$, the derivative can be found by **implicit differentiation**. Consider a curve C given by parametric equations $x = f(t), y = g(t)$; let α be the angle of inclination of the tangent line to C. Then the derivatives dx/dt and dy/dt, that is, $df(t)/dt$ and $dg(t)/dt$, are proportional to $\cos \alpha$ and $\sin \alpha$, respectively; in this case the derivative dy/dx (and hence the slope, $\tan \alpha$, of the tangent line) is given by

$$m = \frac{dy}{dx} = \frac{dy}{dt} \div \frac{dx}{dt}.$$

When the parameter t is taken as arc length s, then

$$\frac{dx}{ds} = \cos \alpha, \quad \frac{dy}{ds} = \sin \alpha.$$

(Here the tangent line is taken as a line directed in accordance with increasing s.)

For a *space curve,* the tangent line is also defined as the limiting position of secant lines. When the curve is given by parametric equations $x = f(t), y = g(t), z = h(t)$, the three derivatives of $f(t), g(t), h(t)$ are proportional to the *direction cosines* of the tangent line at a given point of the curve; that is,

$$\frac{dx}{dt} = k \cos \alpha,$$
$$\frac{dy}{dt} = k \cos \beta,$$

$$\frac{dz}{dt} = k \cos \gamma,$$

where α, β, γ are the direction angles of the tangent line. When the parameter t is taken as arc length s, the constant of proportionality k has the value 1 (for the directed tangent).

Tangent Plane to Surface   Let P be a given point on a surface S. Informally, the tangent plane to S at P is the plane which just "contacts" the surface at P, instead of "cutting across" the surface at P (at least when the surface has a concave shape near P). For example, if S is a

Tangent plane

sphere, then the tangent plane is the plane through P which is perpendicular to the radius to P; if S is a cone or cylinder, the tangent plane touches the surface S along an element of S (called the element of contact). In general, the tangent plane at a point P of a surface S can be described in terms of the *normal*, or perpendicular, to S at P: the tangent plane is the plane through P which is perpendicular to the normal. If a, b, c are the direction numbers of the normal, and P has coordinates (x_0, y_0, z_0), then the *equation of the tangent plane* is

$$a(x - x_0) + b(y - y_0) + c(z - z_0) = 0.$$

When the surface is described by an equation $z = f(x, y)$, or by $F(x, y, z) = 0$, the direction numbers of the normal are given by the **partial derivatives of the function** $f(x, y)$ or $F(x, y, z)$; also, see **Normal to surface**.

Taylor's Theorem

Taylor's Series   See **Taylor's theorem**.

Taylor's Theorem (Syn.: Taylor's formula)   A basic theorem of the calculus which relates a general function $f(x)$ to a certain approximating polynomial function. More precisely, let a be a fixed value of x, and let $f(a), f'(a), f''(a), \ldots, f^{(n)}(a)$ be the successive derivatives of $f(x)$ evaluated at a; then *Taylor's formula* represents $f(x)$ as follows.

$$f(x) = f(a) + f'(a)(x - a)$$
$$+ f''(a)\frac{(x - a)^2}{2!} + \cdots$$
$$+ f^{(n)}(a)\frac{(x - a)^n}{n!} + R_n;$$

here, R_n is the *remainder* and is given by

$$R_n = \frac{(x - a)^{(n+1)}}{(n + 1)!} f^{(n+1)}(X),$$

where X is some number between a and x. For $n = 0, 1$, and 2, Taylor's formula reads, respectively,

$$f(x) = f(a) + f'(X)(x - a)$$
$$f(x) = f(a) + f'(a)(x - a)$$
$$+ f''(X)\frac{(x - a)^2}{2!}$$

$$f(x) = f(a) + f'(a)(x - a)$$
$$+ f''(a)\frac{(x - a)^2}{2!} + f'''(X)\frac{(x - a)^3}{3!}.$$

(The first equation is the *mean value theorem of differential calculus*.) Taylor's formula is intended to represent $f(x)$ in a neighborhood of a, that is, for values of x in an interval containing a; the polynomial on the right side, with the remainder disregarded, is often a useful approximation to $f(x)$ when x is sufficiently near a. Taylor's formula can be proved under the assumption, for instance, that $f(x)$ has continuous derivatives up to and including the $(n + 1)^{st}$ order in a closed interval about a.

(Taylor discovered the formua early in the eighteenth century, but it was not satisfactorily proved until the nineteenth century, when the calculus was put on a rigorous basis.) The remainder R_n has several alternative forms. The formula is often used with $a = 0$; in this case,

$$f(x) = f(0) + f'(0)x + f''(0)\frac{x^2}{2!} + \cdots$$
$$+ f^{(n)}(0)\frac{x^n}{n!} + R_n.$$

Taylor's theorem provides a means of expanding a function in an (infinite) power series; allowing n to approach infinity gives *Taylor's series* expansion of $f(x)$. When $a = 0$, this specializes to the *Maclaurin series*

$$f(x) = f(0) + f'(0)\frac{x}{1!} + f''(0)\frac{x^2}{2!}$$
$$+ f'''(0)\frac{x^3}{3!} + \cdots.$$

This formula yields convergent power series expansions for many important functions. For example, let $f(x) = \sin x$; then $f'(x) = \cos x$, $f''(x) = -\sin x$, $f'''(x) = -\cos x$, $f^{(4)}(x) = \sin x$, etc.; hence $f(0) = 0$, $f'(0) = 1$, $f''(0) = 0$, $f'''(0) = -1$, $f^{(4)}(0) = 0$, etc.; this leads to

$$\sin x = x - \frac{x^3}{3!} + \frac{x^5}{5!} - \frac{x^7}{7!} + \cdots,$$

which can be shown to be valid for all x.

Taylor's theorem can be generalized to functions of two or more variables; in the case of, say, two variables the function is expanded in the neighborhood of a point (a, b) in terms of powers and products of $(x - a)$ and $(y - b)$, and the coefficients are various partial derivatives of the function evaluated at (a, b).

Term See **Algebraic expression, Polynomial, Proportion, Sequence, Series**.

Terminating Decimal A decimal number with a finite number of digits. See **Decimal number system.**

Ternary Number System A system of notation for numbers, like the decimal system, that uses the method of place values, but with the base 3 instead of 10; this system is built on three digits, 0, 1, and 2. In this notation, the string of digits 1021 stands for $1 \cdot 3^3 + 0 \cdot 3^2 + 2 \cdot 3 + 1 \cdot 1$, which equals 34 in the decimal system; also 2.12 stands for $2 \cdot 1 + 1 \cdot 1/3 + 2 \cdot 1/3^2$ which equals $2\frac{3}{9}$, or $2.555 \ldots$, in the decimal system.

Tetrahedral Angle A polyhedral angle with four faces.

Tetrahedron (Syn.: Triangular pyramid) A polyhedron with four faces; it is determined by four points in space (the *vertices*) not in a plane. It is the polyhedron with the fewest number of faces possible; in solid geometry it is analogous to the triangle in plane geometry (for example, just as any plane polygon can be subdivided into triangles, so can any polyhedron be subdivided into tetrahedrons). As with any pyramid, the volume of the tetrahedron is $\frac{1}{3}$ the altitude times the area of the base. A

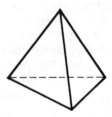

sphere can be circumscribed about any tetrahedron (this is another way of saying that four points in space determine a sphere). A sphere can also be inscribed in any tetrahedron. A *regular* tetrahedron is a regular polyhedron with four faces; these faces are congruent equilateral triangles. For a regular tetrahedron, the circumscribed and inscribed sphere are concentric; the common center is the common point of intersection of the four altitudes of the tetrahedron, and it is three-fourths the way along the altitude from any vertex. See **Circumscribed sphere, Inscribed sphere.**

Theorem Of a mathematical theory, a proved proposition. In such a theory, the proved propositions are derived one after the other; each has available for its proof the assumptions (axioms) of the theory and all previously proved propositions. Generally, only proved propositions which are regarded as principal results or worthy of particular attention are specifically singled out as theorems. A proved proposition which is an immediate consequence of a theorem is often designated as a *corollary of the theorem;* a *lemma* is a proved proposition which is preliminary to the proof of a theorem. The *converse* of a theorem is a statement in which the hypothesis and conclusion of the theorem are reversed, or at least partially reversed (the converse may or may not itself be a theorem). Various important theorems of mathematics have acquired specific names, such as the binomial theorem, the theorem of Pythagoras, and so on. Research in mathematics involves the discovery and proof of theorems that help to answer unsettled questions. See **Deductive theory, Existence theorem.**

Theorem of Pappus Commonly, a certain formula for the area and volume of a surface of revolution obtained by revolving a closed plane figure R through 360° in space about a line in its plane which does not pass

through the figure. The theorem uses the point C which is the *centroid* of R

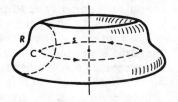

and the length s of the circular path generated by revolving C. It asserts that i) the area is the perimeter of R times s, and ii) the volume is the area of R times s. [It is named after the mathematician Pappus of Alexandria (about A.D. 300).] The theorem gives a simple formula for the area and volume of the torus, for example.

Theorem of Pythagoras (Syn.: Pythagorean theorem) The following famous theorem of geometry (attributed to Pythagoras in the sixth century B.C.): the sides of a right triangle satisfy the relation $c^2 = a^2 + b^2$, where c is the length of the hypotenuse, and a, b that of the other sides. Geometrically, it means that the area of the square built on the

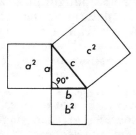

hypotenuse equals the sum of the areas of the squares built on the two legs. This theorem is a cornerstone of geometry. Another form of the theorem is that the square (second power) of the diagonal of a rectangle equals the sum of the squares of the sides. In this form the theorem

269

generalizes to three-dimensional space as follows: the square of the diagonal of a rectangular parallelepiped equals the sum of the squares of three mutually perpendicular edges. The *converse* of the theorem of Pythagoras also holds: if a triangle with three sides a, b, c satisfies the relation $c^2 = a^2 + b^2$, then it is a right triangle, and c is the hypotenuse.

Theory of Equations The general study of the solution of polynomial equations. Usually, the polynomials considered are those with rational numbers as coefficients.

Ref. [120].

Theory of Games A mathematical theory of competitive games in which each participant has only partial control and each wishes to determine the best method of playing under these circumstances. Major credit for the invention of the theory is generally given to John von Neumann; it has been applied, for example, to economics and military strategy.

A game is thought of as a set of rules that determine the course of play. A participant in a game is called a *player;* this may be an individual, a nation, or any decision-making unit. The game proceeds as a series of *moves,* or single steps, by the players; the (set of rules of the) game specifies at each stage what moves are allowed each player. A move may be either a *personal move* or a *chance move;* in the first case, the player is free to choose from any one of a set of alternatives; in the second, the alternative is selected by a chance, or random, device (such as the roll of dice). A *play* of the game is one complete performance from beginning to end; it results in a *pay-off* for each player (which may be a gain or a loss).

A fundamental notion is that of a *pure strategy,* or simply *strategy,* of a player; this is a plan, or set of instructions, selected by the player which specifies every personal move of the player under every conceivable circumstance during a play. With a strategy selected, a player removes all choice on his part. In general, various (pure) strategies are available to each player; in a game which has no chance moves, such as checkers (assuming a given player (color of checker) always moves first), the selection of a particular strategy by each player determines a unique play and outcome of the game. In repeated plays, a player may resort to a *mixed strategy*—this is specified by assigning a numerical probability to each of his possible pure strategies; in advance of any given play of the game, he chooses a pure strategy by random selection according to these probabilities. For example, suppose only two pure strategies S_1 and S_2 are available, and the mixed strategy is adopted of probability $\frac{1}{2}$ for each strategy; then a choice could be made before each play by a toss of a coin. (In this case of two pure strategies, a mixed strategy is specified by fixing a number p between 0 and 1 and playing S_1 with probability p and S_2 with probability $1 - p$.)

The theory of best play is concerned with the determination of best strategies; it is most completely developed for games of two opposing interests. Suppose there are two players, and each has a finite number of pure strategies. Let each choice of pure strategies by the two players result in some pay-off w, denoting the amount paid to player 1 by player 2; $-w$ represents the amount paid to player 2 by player 1 (thus, negative *w* means payment to player 2 by player 1). This is a *finite, two-person, zero-sum game.* Every such game has a so-called *value;* this is a number *v* with the following property. There is a mixed (or pure) strategy for player 1 which guarantees him, in the long run, an expected pay-off of at least *v* (regardless of the strategy of player 2), and there is a mixed strategy for player 2 which guarantees him an expected pay-off of no more than *v* (regardless of the strategy of player 1). For each player, such a strategy is called an *optimal strategy*—if both players use optimal strategies, then each will realize an expected pay-off of *v;* furthermore, neither can be *sure* of doing better by another method of play. The optimal strategies are described by the *minimax principle;* that is, player 2 plays so as to minimize his maximum losses, and player 1 plays so as to maximize his minimum winnings (this is a "safe" principle which assumes that the opponent plays in the best possible way). The *fundamental theorem* of the theory of games is the preceding statement that the minimax strategies for both players (that is, "minimax" for player 2 and "maximin" for player 1) will realize a common expected pay-off for the two players.

The preceding results can be extended to games with an infinite, or continuous, range of pure strategies; this arises, for example, in a situation of pursuit and evasion (as with a fighter aircraft and a bomber). Less complete is the theory of *n*-person games, where players can form coalitions for their mutual benefit.

Ref. [50, 75, 150].

Theory of Numbers The study of the properties of the integers, espe-

cially as it concerns factoring, divisibility, prime numbers, the representation of natural numbers in certain algebraic forms, and related subjects. [In the theory of numbers, "number" means "integer"; it is not the general study of all numbers (real, complex, etc.).] The history of the theory of numbers is a long and famous one in mathematics. One of the early important contributions was the work of Diophantus of ancient Alexandria in what is known today as *Diophantine analysis.* Modern theory of numbers began with the work of Fermat in the first half of the seventeenth century. The field was significantly advanced by Gauss at the beginning of the nineteenth century, particularly with his concept of *congruent integers.* The intellectual appeal of number theory has been and continues to be irresistible to the greatest mathematicians; one of the reasons is the simplicity with which many of its most difficult problems can be stated. To this day, some of its early conjectures are unsettled; these include the **Goldbach conjecture, Fermat's last theorem**, and the problem of twin primes (see **Prime number**). The study of the **Mersenne number, Fermat number,** and **perfect numbers**, belong to number theory. The **prime number theorem** and Lagrange's theorem (see **Sum of perfect powers of integers**) are well-known theorems; an important recent result concerns **transcendental** numbers. These are some of the more easily described topics of the theory.

Ref. [11, 23, 57, 59, 94, 106].

Three Dimensional See **Dimension, Space**.

Topology A branch of modern **geometry** which studies the properties of figures that depend only upon how a figure is "held together," and not upon its size or shape, for instance. Topology has been described as "rubber-sheet" geometry; it is concerned with what is not lost in a geometric object when it is pulled, bent, stretched, or otherwise distorted, without tearing it or causing the loss of identity of its points. For example, whether or not a closed curve in space is knotted is a topological property of the curve in space; the fact that a simple closed curve in the plane divides the plane into two separately connected parts, the inside and outside, is a topologi-

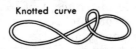

Knotted curve

cal property (see **Interior of closed curve**); so is the fact that a region in the plane or in space has a boundary. The dimension of a figure is a topological property of the figure.

Technically, a topological property, or "invariant," is defined as follows. A *topological transformation* between a figure (set of points) A and a figure B is a correspondence such that: (1) it matches each point of A with a single point of B, and each point of B with a single point of A; (2) it is *continuous,* as a function from A to B, and as a function from B to A. When such a transformation exists, the figures A and B are said to be *topologically equivalent;* a *topological property* of A, then, is any property which it shares with all figures topologically equivalent to it.

The sphere and cube (or any polyhedron) are topologically equivalent; the torus (doughnut) is topologically different from these. A topological

property of a closed surface in space is its *genus;* this is the number of "holes" in the surface (it is also the largest number of closed cuts that the surface can suffer without separating into two distinct pieces). For example, the sphere has genus 0 (no holes, and one cut will separate it); the

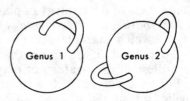

Genus 1   Genus 2

torus has genus 1 (one hole, and two cuts will separate it). A torus is topologically equivalent to a sphere with one handle; a sphere with k handles has genus k (the figure shows the cases $k = 1$ and 2).

Topology is an important and relatively recent field of mathematics; examples of individual topics that arose before its modern development are the **four-color problem**, the **Königsberg bridge problem**, and the **Möbius strip**. The study of knots and networks in topology is related to problems of electrostatics and chemical combinations. The systematic treatment of topology began with the work of Poincaré at the beginning of the twentieth century; this sprang out of questions of celestial mechanics, particularly the so-called "three body problem."

Ref. [27, 52, 145].

Torus (Syn.: Anchor ring) The doughnut-like surface of revolution generated by rotating a circle through 360° in space about a line in its plane but not passing through the circle. The area equals $4\pi^2 Rr$, and the volume $2\pi^2 Rr^2$, where r is the radius of the rotated circle and R is the distance from its center to the axis of

revolution; these formulas are im-

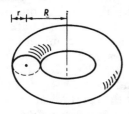

mediate consequences of the *theorem of Pappus.*

Trace of Surface The intersection of a surface in space with a coordinate plane; the traces help to visualize the surface in space. Suppose

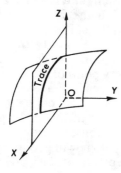

the surface is the graph of an equation in x, y, z; then the trace in the xy-plane is the graph (in this plane) of the equation in x, y obtained by setting z equal to 0; similarly, setting y equal to 0, gives the equation of the trace in the xz-plane, and setting $x = 0$ gives the yz-trace. For example, the linear equation $3x - 2y + z - 4 = 0$ represents a plane; $z = 0$ gives the line $3x - 2y - 4 = 0$, which is the trace of the plane on the xy-plane; $y = 0$ gives the line $3x + z - 4 = 0$, the trace on the xz-plane. Also, the trace of the sphere $x^2 + y^2 + z^2 = r^2$ in the xy-plane is the circle $x^2 + y^2 = r^2$. See **Plane section.**

Transcendental Nonalgebraic, that is, not expressible by algebraic oper-

ations. A *transcendental number* is a real number which is not an algebraic number; examples are π, e, and $2^{\sqrt{3}}$. A function of a real variable which is not an algebraic function is a *transcendental function;* its graph is a *transcendental curve.* The functions $\log x$, e^x, $\sin x$, $\cos x$ are examples of so-called *elementary transcendental functions.* A *transcendental equation* is an equation containing a transcendental function involving the variable.

A difficult proposition of the theory of numbers that defied proof for a long time was that an irrational power of a rational number (not 0 or 1), such as $2^{\sqrt{3}}$, is transcendental; a proof was finally discovered in 1934. Ref. [28, 29, 132].

Transfinite Number An infinite **ordinal number** or an infinite **cardinal number.** The familiar operations of the arithmetic of finite cardinal numbers (whole numbers) can be extended to an arithmetic of transfinite cardinal numbers. This has some features of ordinary arithmetic but it also has some strikingly different properties; among these are the formulas $m = m + 1$, $m + m = m$, $m \cdot m = m$, which hold for any infinite cardinal number m. Ref. [44, 73, 149].

Transformation In general, any **correspondence**. Also, often, conversion of a given expression, equation, etc. to another form, equivalent to the given one. For example, the equation $(x - 2)^2 = x + 4$ can be "transformed" to $x^2 - 5x = 0$.

Transformation (geometry) A transformation of the *plane* into itself is a correspondence which carries each point P in the plane into some point P' of the plane. Examples are *trans-*

lations and *rotations* of the plane (see **Rigid motion**); these transformations arise in the study of congruence of plane figures. The *transformation of similitude* arises in the study of similar figures; using rectangular coordinates in the plane, it is defined as follows: it carries a point P with coordinates (x, y) into the point P' with coordinates (x', y') given by equations $x' = kx$, $y' = ky$ (k being a constant called the *ratio of similitude*). This transformation moves P into P' along the ray from O through P so that the ratio of the distance OP' to OP is k. More generally, for any points P, Q carried into P', Q' respectively, the ratio of $P'Q'$ to PQ is k. When k is positive and less

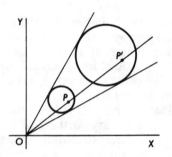

than 1, this "shrinks" the plane; when k is greater than 1, this "stretches" the plane. This transformation carries any plane figure into a similar figure [see **Similar** (geometry)].

A transformation of ordinary *space* (or *n*-dimensional space) into itself is likewise a correspondence carrying each point P into some point P'. Examples are again translations and rotations, which are connected with congruence of figures. The transformation of similitude is given by the analogous equations $x' = kx$, $y' = ky$, $z' = kz$; again, this multiplies distances in space by the factor k.

A *linear transformation* of the plane or space is a more general type of transformation than one of similitude; here each coordinate of P' is given as a linear combination of the coordinates of P (such a combination has the form $ax + by$ in the plane, and $ax + by + cz$ in space). It includes the rotation of axes, for example (see **Transformation of coordinates**).

The idea of a transformation of a space is a unifying one in geometry. A *group of transformations* is a collection of transformations with the following features: **(1)** the successive application of two yields another in the collection; and **(2)** each transformation T in the collection has another S in the collection such that T followed by S yields the identity transformation (that is, the one that leaves every point of the space fixed). This is a **group** in the technical sense of the term. (The collection of all translations in the plane is a group of transformations, for example.) Now one point of view in geometry is that a given geometry is the study of those properties of figures that remain unchanged under a particular group of transformations; this was developed in the latter half of the nineteenth century by F. Klein and others. For example, Euclidean geometry is the study of "invariance" under the group of *rigid motions*, plane **projective geometry** of invariance under the group of *central projections*, and **topology** of invariance under the group of *topological transformations*.

Transformation of Coordinates When two coordinate systems are imposed on the plane (or on space), then each point P has two pairs (or triples) of coordinates. The correspondence between these is called a transformation of coordinates; it is expressed by *equations*, or *formulas*, *of transformation* in which the individual coordinates of one set of coordinates for P are given in terms of the other set of coordinates for P.

A *translation of axes*, or *coordinates*, is a transformation between two rectangular coordinate systems in which the origins O and O' are at different locations, but the corresponding axes are parallel and have the same direction (see figure). The *equations of translation* in the plane are $x = x' + h, y = y' + h$ where (x, y), (x', y') are the coordinates of a point P in the two systems, and (h, k) are the coordinates of the origin O' of the (x', y')-system in terms of the (x, y)-system. A common reason for translating axes is to simplify the equation of a curve. As an example, consider the following translation in the plane: $x = x' + 2, y = y' - 3$. The origin of the "new" system (x', y') is $(2, -3)$, relative to the "old" system (x, y). If P is the particular point with old coordinates $(3, -2)$, then the new coordinates of P are

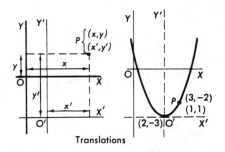

Translations

obtained by replacing (x, y) by $(3, -2)$ in the equations of transformation; this gives $(1, 1)$. Now let C be the curve with the equation $x^2 - 4x - y + 1 = 0$ in the old coordinates. The equation of C in the new coordinates is obtained by substitution for

x and y; this gives

$$(x' + 2)^2 - 4(x' + 2) - (y' - 3) + 1 = 0,$$

or the simplified equation $(x')^2 = y'$ (see figure). (The problem of discovering a transformation which will simplify a given graph is studied in analytic geometry.) A *rotation of axes*, or *coordinates*, in the plane is a transformation in which the axes X, Y of one rectangular system are rotated about the origin O through an angle θ to locate the axes X', Y' of

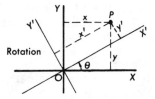

Rotation

the second coordinate system. The formulas, or *equations of rotation* are $x = x' \cos \theta - y' \sin \theta, y = x' \sin \theta + y' \cos \theta$. For example if $\theta = 90°$, these become $x = -y', y = x'$.

In *space*, the translation formulas are $x = x' + h, y = y' + k, z = z' + l$; here (h, k, l) are the coordinates of the origin of the (x', y', z') system as a point in the (x, y, z) system. A rotation of axes in space is a transformation in which rectangular axes X, Y, Z are rotated about a given line through the origin to locate the axes X', Y', Z' of the second system. The equations of rotation have the form

$$x = l_1 x' + l_2 y' + l_3 z',$$
$$y = m_1 x' + m_2 y' + m_3 z',$$
$$z = n_1 x' + n_2 y' + n_3 z';$$

here (l_1, m_1, n_1) are the direction cosines of X' relative to the first system, and (l_2, m_2, n_2) and (l_3, m_3, n_3) those of Y' and Z', respectively, relative to that system.

275

Transformations of coordinates also occur between coordinate systems of different types; for the equations of transformation between rectangular systems and others, see **Cylindrical coordinates, Polar coordinates in plane, Spherical coordinates.**

Transitive Relation   **A relation** with the following property: if *a* is in the given relation to *b* and *b* in the given relation to *c*, then *a* is in the given relation to *c*. For example, the relation "*m* is an exact divisor of *n*" between whole numbers is transitive; the relation "*a* loves *b*" between people is not transitive.

Translation of Coordinates   See **Transformation of coordinates**.

Transposition   In algebra, to *transpose a term* of an equation (inequality) is to move it from one side to the other, changing its sign in the process. This procedure yields an equation (inequality) equivalent to the given one, according to the rule that the same number can be subtracted from both sides of an equation (inequality). For example, $x^2 = 2x - 3$ is equivalent to $x^2 - 2x + 3 = 0$, obtained by transposing $2x$ and -3 to the left side.

As a *permutation,* a transposition is an interchange of two of the places in a given arrangement.

Transversal   In geometry, a line intersecting two or more lines. When a transversal intersects two lines, it forms eight angles, as shown in the figure. The angles 1, 2, 7, 8 are *exterior angles,* the angles 3, 4, 5, 6 are *interior angles.* Angles 3 and 6 are a pair of *alternate-interior angles,* as are angles 4 and 5. Angles 1 and 8 are a pair of *alternate-exterior angles,* as are angles 2 and 7. Angles 1 and 5

are a pair of *corresponding angles*, as

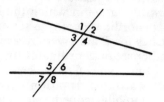

are angles 3 and 7, angles 2 and 6, and angles 4 and 8.

The following conditions for parallelism are useful in plane geometry: **(1)** equality of a pair of alternate-interior angles; **(2)** equality of a pair of corresponding angles; **(3)** a pair of interior angles on the same side of the transversal being supplementary.

Transverse Axis   See **Hyperbola, Hyperboloid**.

Trapezium   A **quadrilateral** in which neither pair of opposite sides is parallel.

Trapezoid   A **quadrilateral** which has exactly one pair of parallel sides (sometimes, the parallelogram, with both pairs of sides parallel, is included). The *bases* of the trapezoid

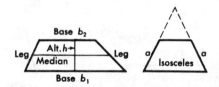

are the parallel sides, sometimes distinguished as the *upper* base and the *lower* base; the *legs* are the nonparallel sides. If the legs are equal in length, the trapezoid is *isosceles.* An *altitude* is a perpendicular line segment (or its length) between the lines of the bases. The *median* is the line segment joining the midpoints of the legs; it is parallel to the bases and has length equal to the average, $\frac{1}{2}(b_1 +$

b_2), of the lengths b_1, b_2 of the bases. The area of a trapezoid equals $\frac{1}{2}h(b_1 + b_2)$, that is, the altitude times the length of the median. A line intersecting two sides of a triangle and parallel to the third side cuts off a trapezoid; when the triangle is isosceles and the third side is the base, the trapezoid is *isosceles*.

Trapezoid Rule (Syn.: Trapezoid formula)   In integral calculus, a method for approximating a definite integral by estimating the area under a curve as a sum of trapezoids. More specifically, the integral $\int_a^b f(x)dx$ is approximated as follows:

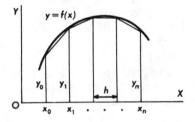

divide the interval from a to b into n equal subintervals of length $h = (a - b)/n$ by the points of division

$$x_0 = a, x_1, x_2, \ldots, x_n = b;$$

the graph of $y = f(x)$ is correspondingly divided at the successive functional values

$$y_0 = f(x_0), y_1 = f(x_1), \ldots, y_n = f(x_n).$$

Form trapezoids by joining the succesive points of division on the curve; adding the areas of the trapezoids gives the desired approximation formula

$$h[\tfrac{1}{2}(y_0 + y_n) + y_1 + y_2 + \cdots + y_{n-1}]$$

See **Simpson's rule**.

Triangle   A polygon of three sides; it consists of three points not on a line (the *vertices*) and the three line segments (the *sides*) joining pairs of vertices. An *angle*, or *interior angle*,

is an angle formed by two sides at a vertex (and lying inside the triangle, near the vertex). The triangle is a fundamental figure of geometry; it is the polygon with the fewest possible number of sides, and any polygon can be subdivided into triangles.

The *base* of a triangle is any side so designated. An *altitude* is a perpendicular line segment (or its length) from a vertex to the opposite

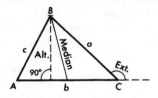

side (possibly extended); a *median* is a line segment from a vertex to the midpoint of the opposite side. An *exterior angle* is an angle at a vertex formed by one side and the extension of the adjacent side. In the figure, a and b are *adjacent* sides; angle A (or vertex A) and side a are *opposite;* sides a and b *include* angle C, and angles A and B *include* side c. The sum of the (interior) angles of any triangle is $180°$.

One way of classifying triangles is by angle: a triangle is **(1)** *acute* if all

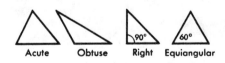

its angles are less than $90°$; **(2)** *obtuse* if one angle is greater than $90°$; **(3)** *oblique* if no angle is $90°$; **(4)** *right* if one angle is $90°$; and **(5)** *equiangular* if all angles are equal (and hence, $60°$). Another way to classify triangles is by side: a triangle is **(1)** *scalene* if all sides are unequal; **(2)** *isosceles* if at least two sides are equal; and **(3)** *equilateral* if all sides are equal. A tri-

277

angle has two equal sides if and only if it has two equal angles; a triangle is equilateral if and only if it is equiangular.

A circle can be circumscribed about any triangle; the center of a *circumscribed circle* is the *circumcenter* of the triangle, and it is the common point of intersection of the three perpendicular bisectors of the sides. A circle can be inscribed in any triangle; the center of the *inscribed circle* is the *incenter* of the triangle, and it is the common point of intersection of the three angle bisectors of the triangle. The three altitudes of a triangle also meet in a common point, called the *orthocenter* of the triangle. The three medians also meet in a common point, called the *centroid* of the triangle. It is an interesting fact about a triangle that the circumcenter, orthocenter, and centroid lie on a line.

Two triangles are *congruent* in case the vertices of one can be paired with the vertices of the other so that corresponding angles are equal and corresponding sides are equal (in this case, each can be made to coincide with the other by a rigid motion in space). Two triangles are *similar* in

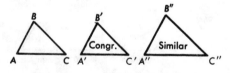

case corresponding angles are equal and corresponding sides are proportional (in this case, each is congruent to a blown-up or shrunk version of the other). See **Transformation** (geometry). Conditions for two triangles to be congruent are the following: **(1)** two sides and the included angle of one equal to the corresponding parts of the other; **(2)** corresponding parts of the other; **(2)**

two angles and the included side of one equal to corresponding parts of the other; **(3)** three sides of one equal to three sides of the other. Conditions for two triangles to be similar are the following: **(1)** two angles of one equal to two angles of the other; **(2)** an angle of one equal to an angle of the other, and the included sides proportional to those of the other; **(3)** three sides of one proportional to three sides of the other. Congruent triangles have all corresponding secondary parts equal—altitudes, medians, etc. Similar ones have such corresponding secondary parts proportional to corresponding sides; they have areas proportional to the squares of corresponding sides.

The area A of a triangle equals $\frac{1}{2}bh$, where b is the length of the base and h is the altitude to the base. The area can also be expressed in terms of the lengths of the sides a, b, c by Hero's formula:

$$A = \sqrt{s(s - a)(s - b)(s - c)};$$

here, s equals half the perimeter, that is, $\frac{1}{2}(a + b + c)$. The radius of the circumscribed circle equals $abc/4A$, and the radius of the inscribed circle equals A/s.

The problem of the **solution of the triangle in the plane** is that of determining the measure of all its angles and sides when just enough data is given to determine the triangle (up to congruence); such data is described above. The methods of plane trigonometry are used in the solution.

Triangle Inequality The property that any side of a triangle has a length less than the sum of the lengths of the other two sides. It can also be expressed as follows: for any three points P, Q, R, the distance PR is not greater than $PQ + QR$; in this form it applies to more general spaces than Euclidean geometry (see **Metric space**).

Triangle, Spherical   See **Spherical triangle**.

Triangular Number   Any of the numbers 1, 3, 6, 10, . . . , the general or, n^{th}, number being given by

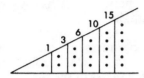

$n(n + 1)/2$. The nth triangular number is the sum of the arithmetic series $1 + 2 + 3 + \cdots + n$. The reason for the name "triangular" is that these numbers give the number of dots in successive triangular arrays, as shown in the figure. These numbers were considered by the Pythagoras school in ancient Greece; other "figurate" numbers, associated with the number of dots in other geometric arrays (square numbers, pentagonal numbers, and so on), were considered, as well.

Trigonometric Equation, Expression, Curve   A *trigonometric equation* or *expression* is one containing a trigonometric function involving a variable: $\cos 2x = 2 \sin x$ is a trigonometric equation, and $\sin^2 x + \tan x$ is a trigonometric expression. The *trigonometric curves* include the graphs of trigonometric functions; they also include the graphs of additive combinations of trigonometric functions, such as $\sin 2x + 2 \cos x$.

Trigonometric Form of Complex Number   See **Polar form of complex number** (syn.).

Trigonometric Functions (Syn.: Circular functions; Trigonometric ratios)   Ordinarily, the six functions *sine, cosine, tangent, cotangent, secant,* and *cosecant;* abbreviated *sin, cos, tan, cot* (or *ctn*), *sec,* and *csc.* The trigonometric functions of an *acute angle* can be defined as *trigonometric ratios*, which are ratios of sides of a right triangle. Let A be an acute angle of the right triangle ABC, as shown in the figure (next page); then

$$\sin A = \frac{a}{c} = \frac{\text{side opposite}}{\text{hypotenuse}}$$

$$\cos A = \frac{b}{c} = \frac{\text{side adjacent}}{\text{hypotenuse}}$$

$$\tan A = \frac{a}{b} = \frac{\text{side opposite}}{\text{side adjacent}}$$

$$\cot A = \frac{b}{a} = \frac{1}{\tan A} = \frac{\text{side adjacent}}{\text{side opposite}}$$

$$\sec A = \frac{c}{b} = \frac{1}{\cos A} = \frac{\text{hypotenuse}}{\text{side adjacent}}$$

$$\csc A = \frac{c}{a} = \frac{1}{\sin A} = \frac{\text{hypotenuse}}{\text{side opposite}}.$$

Some particular values of trigonometric functions are the following:

$$\sin 30° = \cos 60° = \frac{1}{2}$$

$$\cos 30° = \sin 60° = \frac{\sqrt{3}}{2}$$

$$\tan 30° = \cot 60° = \frac{\sqrt{3}}{3}$$

$$\cot 30° = \tan 60° = \sqrt{3}$$

$$\sin 45° = \cos 45° = \frac{\sqrt{2}}{2}$$

$$\tan 45° = \cot 45° = 1.$$

The functions *sin* and *cos* are *cofunctions;* so are *tan* and *cot,* and *sec* and *csc.* A trigonometric function of an angle equals the cofunction of the complementary angle, that is, $\sin A = \cos (90° - A)$, $\cot A = \tan (90° - A)$, etc. Tables of trigonometric functions make use of this property

Trigonometric Functions

to reduce their length by one-half (see Appendix D).

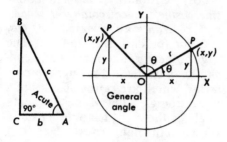

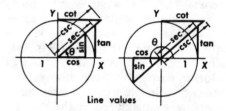

Signs of Functions

Quadrant	sin csc	cos sec	tan cot
I	+	+	+
II	+	−	−
III	−	−	+
IV	−	+	−

The trigonometric functions are not restricted to acute angles. Consider the *general angle,* or *directed angle,* θ (counterclockwise rotation if θ is positive, clockwise rotation if θ is negative). Suppose θ is in standard position relative to a rectangular coordinate system, with initial side along the positive x-axis. Let P, any point on the terminal side, have coordinates (x, y) and distance r from the origin. Then, by definition

$$\sin \theta = \frac{y}{r}, \quad \cos \theta = \frac{x}{r}$$

$$\tan \theta = \frac{y}{x}, \quad \cot \theta = \frac{x}{y}$$

$$\csc \theta = \frac{r}{y}, \quad \sec \theta = \frac{r}{x}.$$

These definitions depend only upon the final position of the terminal side, not the rotation that led to it; hence, the functions are periodic, repeating their values every 360 degrees. The distance r is always taken as positive, but the coordinates x and y may be positive or negative. The algebraic sign of a trigonometric function depends upon the *quadrant of the angle* θ, that is, the quadrant of the terminal side. All the functions are positive in the first quadrant; the table shows the algebraic signs in the various quadrants. The value of a trigonometric function of any angle can be reduced to that of an acute angle

by the **reduction formulas of trigonometry**; for this reason, a table of trigonometric values is restricted to acute angles.

The functions can also be represented by line segments associated with the unit circle; the figure shows these *line values* of the functions for θ

Line values

in the first and third quadrants. The variation of its line value, as θ goes through a complete revolution, exhibits the history of a 360° cycle of a trigonometric function.

Many relations hold among the trigonometric functions, as expressed by the **trigonometric identities**. The **addition formulas** express a function of a sum or difference of angles in terms of functions of the individual angles; the **double angle formulas** are special cases of these. The **half-angle formulas** express a function of half an angle in terms of functions of the angle itself. The **product formulas of trigonometry** express products of sines and cosines as sums of these functions. One of the many uses of trigonometric functions is the solution of triangles; for that purpose special relationships are developed in trigonometry among functions of the parts of triangles. An example is the **law of sines**; there are many others. See **Solution of oblique spherical triangle, Solution of right spherical triangle, Solution of triangle in plane**.

When a trigonometric function is considered simply as a *function of a real variable,* apart from its direct relation to angles and triangles, it is common to write sin x, cos x, tan x, etc., where x is a real number (radian measure of an angle). This is done, for example, in the consideration of *trigonometric curves,* which are the graphs of the trigonometric functions. For these graphs, see **Cosecant function, Cosine function, Cotangent function, Secant function, Sine function, Tangent function**; also, see **Power series** for the representation of the sine and cosine functions in power series. Each trigonometric function has an **inverse trigonometric function**. For example, the inverse sine of a number x is defined as the number (angle measure) whose sine equals x. The *coversine, exsecant, haversine,* and *versine* are other trigonometric functions, little used today.
Ref. [2, 128].

Trigonometric Identity An identity in trigonometric functions. The *fundamental identities* of trigonometry include the following:

$$\csc \theta = \frac{1}{\sin \theta}, \qquad \sec \theta = \frac{1}{\cos \theta},$$
$$\cot \theta = \frac{1}{\tan \theta}, \qquad \tan \theta = \frac{\sin \theta}{\cos \theta},$$
$$\sin^2\theta + \cos^2\theta = 1,$$
$$\tan^2\theta + 1 = \sec^2\theta,$$
$$1 + \cos^2\theta = \csc^2\theta.$$

(The last three are also called *Pythagorean identities*). The equations hold for all values of θ for which the func-

tions are defined. These are only a few of many trigonometric identities which are useful for various purposes. See **Trigonometric functions**.

Trigonometric Series An infinite series made up of terms in sine and cosine functions and used in the general study of the **periodic function**; it has the form

$$\frac{a_0}{2} + (a_1 \cos x + b_1 \sin x)$$
$$+ (a_2 \cos 2x + b_2 \sin 2x)$$
$$+ (a_3 \cos 3x + b_3 \sin 3x) + \cdots,$$

where the coefficients a_0, a_1, b_1, a_2, b_2, etc., are constants. The most important trigonometric series arise in representing given periodic functions. Let $f(x)$ be a periodic function of period 2π; in this case, the coefficients are given by the formulas

$$a_0 = \frac{1}{\pi}\int_{-\pi}^{\pi} f(x)dx, \quad a_n = \frac{1}{\pi}\int_{-\pi}^{\pi} f(x)\cos nx\, dx$$

$$b_n' = \frac{1}{\pi}\int_{-\pi}^{\pi} f(x)\sin nx\, dx.$$

These are called the *Fourier coefficients* of $f(x)$ and the associated series its *Fourier series.* The Fourier series of $f(x)$ is its "harmonic analysis" in terms of simple "harmonic components" (namely, the individual terms in cos kx and sin kx). The Fourier series is widely used in applied mathematics (the above formulas are readily modified to apply to functions of any period).

Under general assumptions, the Fourier series will converge to the value of the function; for instance, if $f(x)$ is continuous and has a derivative everywhere, then the Fourier series will converge to $f(x)$ for every x. In addition, Fourier series can represent discontinuous functions of certain types; for instance, if a function has a "jump" at $x = c$, the series

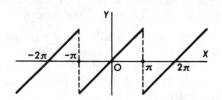

will typically converge to the average of the values approached by $f(x)$ on either side of c. As an example, consider the following function; let $f(x) = x$ inside the interval from $-\pi$ to π, and let $f(x)$ repeat this pattern between all odd multiples of π (see figure). This function has a jump of 2π at π, and at all odd multiples of π. Computing the Fourier coefficients leads to the Fourier series

$$f(x) = 2[\sin x - \frac{\sin 2x}{2} + \frac{\sin 3x}{3} - \frac{\sin 4x}{4} + \cdots].$$

The series converges to $f(x)$ at every point of continuity of $f(x)$; it converges to the average value 0 at each point of discontinuity.
Ref. [34].

Trigonometry (Syn.: Plane trigonometry)   The study of the trigonometric functions and various applications of these functions, including the solution of triangles in the plane. *Spherical trigonometry,* among other things, applies these functions to the solution of spherical triangles. Trigonometry was well established in Europe by the sixteenth century. Ref. [64, 128, 140].

Trigonometry, Spherical   See **Spherical trigonometry**.

Trihedral   The "framework" in space made up of three half-lines, not in a plane, issuing from a common point O. If the lines are perpendicular in pairs then the trihedral is

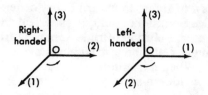

trirectangular; for example, the positive axes of a system of rectangular coordinates in space form a trirectangular trihedral. A trihedral is *oriented* when its rays are labeled (1), (2), (3) in some order. There are two types of orientation, *right handed* and *left handed;* in the first, the rays (1), (2), (3) can be fitted by the middle finger, thumb, and forefinger of the right hand, respectively; in the second, this is true for the left hand. Another description is this: if a right-handed screw is pointed in the direction (3), then it will advance when it is rotated from (1) to (2), if the orientation is right handed; otherwise it will retreat. The orientation of a trihedral does not change when it is subjected to a *rigid motion;* it does when it is reflected in a plane.

Trihedral Angle   A polyhedral angle with three faces. (A *trihedral angle* differs from a *trihedral* in that the latter consists of only the three edges of the trihedral angle.) The trihedral angle is the simplest polyhedral angle, having the minimum number of edges and of faces. An *isosceles trihedral angle* is one which has two equal face angles. A trihedral angle is *rectangular, birectangular,* or *trirectangular* according to whether it has one right dihedral angle, two right dihedral angles, or three right dihedral angles. The trihedral angle is oriented according to the orientation of the trihedral composed of its edges. The trihedral angle is closely associated with the spherical triangle. If a sphere is described whose center is at its vertex, then the trihedral angle intercepts a spherical triangle on the sphere. Conversely, every spherical triangle determines a corresponding *central trihedral angle.*

Consider two trihedral angles in which the edges (1), (2), (3) of one are matched with the edges (1′), (2′), (3′) of the other so that corresponding face angles are equal and corresponding dihedral angles are equal. Then the trihedral angles are *directly congruent* (or, simply, *congruent*) if the orientations (1), (2), (3) and (1′), (2′), (3′) are the same; if the orientations are opposite, then the trihedral angles are *oppositely congruent* (or *symmetric*).   See **Congruent figures in space**.

Trinomial   A polynomial of three terms; in one variable, it has the form $Ax^2 + Bx + C$. The following formulas for factoring trinomials are useful.

$$x^2 + 2ax + a^2 = (x + a)^2,$$
$$x^2 - 2ax + a^2 = (x - a)^2,$$
$$x^2 + (a + b)x + ab = (x + a)(x + b).$$

The left members of the first and second equations are *perfect trinomial squares;* they are recognized by the fact that the middle term is twice the product of the square roots of the other terms; the last is recognized by the fact that the coefficient of x is the sum of the factors of the last term. For example,

$$x^2 - 6x + 9 = x^2 - 2(3 \cdot x) + 3^2$$
$$= (x - 3)^2,$$
$$x^2 + 13x + 12 = x^2 + (1 + 12)x + 1 \cdot 12$$
$$= (x + 1)(x + 12).$$

See **Completing the square**.

Triple   See **Ordered pair, triple, n-tuple**.

Trirectangular   Having three right angles. For example, a spherical triangle is trirectangular if its angles are all right angles, and a trihedral angle is trirectangular if its dihedral angles are all right angles.

Trisection   Division into three equal parts. The trisection of an *angle* is the famous problem of antiquity that calls for a *geometric construction* using only a compass and an unmarked straight edge; the construction is known to be impossible. In spite of the fact that a rigorous proof of the impossibility has been available for over 100 years, amateur mathematicians continue to propose "solutions" to the problem. Trisection is possible by various means if the limitation on the nature of the construction is removed; for example it can be accomplished with a compass and a ruler marked with two points. It can also be solved with the **spiral** of Archimedes.

Ref. [6, 16, 38].

Trochoid   A plane curve which is the following generalization of the *cycloid:* it is the curve traced by a fixed point on a radius (or radius extended) of a circle as the circle rolls

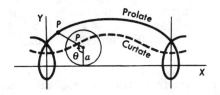

along a line. Let a equal the radius of the rolling circle and b equal the distance of the fixed point from the center. If b is greater than a, then the trochoid is a *prolate cycloid;* if b is less than a, it is a *curtate cycloid;* if $b = a$, it is a cycloid. In all cases the parametric equations of the curve

283

are $x = a\theta - b\sin\theta$, $y = a - b\cos\theta$, where θ is the angle shown in the figure (measured in radians).

Truncated A truncated solid is a solid cut off a given solid by two non-parallel planes. See **Cone, Frustrum, Pyramid**.

Turning Point Of a plane graph, a point (a, b) near which the graph is increasing (decreasing) for x less than a, but decreasing (increasing) for x greater than a; for the graph of $y = f(x)$, such a point is necessarily a (relative) maximum or minimum point of the function f.

Twin Primes See **Prime pair** (syn.).

Twisted Curve A space curve which does not lie in a plane.

Two-Dimensional See **Dimension, Space**.

U

U **Unbounded** See **Bound**.

Unconditional Inequality (Syn.: Absolute inequality) An inequality containing variables which is true for all values of the variables; otherwise it is a *conditional inequality*. For example, replacement of both variables by constants in $x^2 + y^2 + 1 > 0$, or in $x + y > 0$ produces a statement, true or false; in the first case all replacements yield true statements, so that the inequality is unconditional; in the second, replacement of "x" by "-1" and "y" by "0" produces a false statement, so that the inequality is conditional.

Undefined Term (Syn.: Primitive term) Of a mathematical system or **deductive theory**, the assumed terms which, for purposes of proof, are assigned no properties other than those

stated in the axioms (or deduced from the axioms).

Undetermined Coefficients The method of undetermined coefficients for polynomials refers to any procedure for finding required polynomials by treating their coefficients as unknowns, then solving the relations which these unknowns must satisfy. To illustrate the principle, consider the problem of factoring $x^2 - 2x - 3$; first write it as $(x + a)(x + b)$, with undetermined coefficients a and b. Since

$$(x + a)(x + b) = x^2 + (a + b)x + ab,$$

and the right side is to equal $x^2 - 2x - 3$, the following relations must hold; $a + b = -2$ and $ab = -3$. Solving for a and b gives $a = -3$, $b = 1$, hence $(x - 3)(x + 1)$ is the factored form of $x^2 - 2x - 3$. Undetermined coefficients are commonly used, for example, in decomposing a rational function into a sum of *partial fractions*. The method is also extended to include, for instance, problems requiring finding the coefficients of a power series.

Uniform Scale See **Linear coordinates**.

Union of Sets (Syn.: Sum of sets) Of two sets, A and B, the smallest set which contains both; its members are those of A and B collected together; it is denoted by "$A \cup B$" (see **Algebra of sets**). For example, the union of the sets $\{0, 2, 4, 6\}$ and $\{1, 2, 3, 4, 5\}$ is $\{0, 1, 2, 3, 4, 5, 6\}$; also the union of the set of real numbers between 2 and 4 with the set of real numbers between 3 and 5, is the set of real numbers between 2 and 5.

Unique An entity is unique in a given set, relative to given conditions, in case it is the only member of the set satisfying the conditions; these conditions are said to *determine* the element. For example, consider the condition that the square of a number equal 4; in the set of positive numbers, this determines the unique number 2; in the set of all numbers the condition is met by both 2 and -2, so that it does not determine a unique number.

Unique Factorization Theorem (Syn.: Fundamental theorem of arithmetic) In arithmetic, the proposition that every integer greater than 1 can be written as a product of positive prime integers in one and only one way, apart from the arrangement of the factors. For example, 12 equals $2 \cdot 2 \cdot 3$ (or $2 \cdot 3 \cdot 2$, or $3 \cdot 2 \cdot 2$). This theorem shows the basic nature of the prime numbers in arithmetic; it was derived by Euclid in his Elements. A similar theorem applies to the factorization of a *polynomial* in terms of irreducible polynomials. See **Factor of polynomial**. Ref. [137].

Unit The unit *number* is the number 1. A unit *length* is a line segment of length 1. A unit *square* (*cube*) is one with all dimensions equal to 1; it has unit area (volume). A unit *circle* (*sphere*) is one of radius 1. A unit *vector* is a vector of length 1. The unit circle and unit sphere are used for the measurement of plane angles and solid angles. See **Measure**.

Unit Fraction A fraction of the form $1/n$, with n a whole number.

Universal Quantifier The **quantifier** "for every x"; often abbreviated "$(\forall x)$" or "(x)."

Universe The set of all admissible things. See **Algebra of sets**.

Unknown Of a conditional equation, a variable whose values are solutions of the equation.

Upper Bound See **Bound**.

V

Valid A *valid statement* is one that is true, or provable. A *logically valid statement* is one that is true because of its sentence form alone, not its meaning. See **Algebra of propositions**, **Quantifier**.

Value When a variable stands in place of constants, then any one of these constants represents a *value of the variable*. For example, if n stands for any integer in $3n + 1$, then 2 is a value of n, but $\frac{2}{3}$ is not (it is, if n stands for any real number). A *value of the unknown x* of an equation is any solution of the equation; that is, a value of the variable x which satisfies the equation [for example, 3 is a value of the unknown x in the equation $(x - 3)(x - 2) = 0$]. A *value of an expression* designating a number, such as $x^2 + 2$, is a number obtained by replacing x by a value of x; for example, 11 is the value of the last expression when x is 3. To find the value of an expression is to *evaluate* it.

Vanish To equal zero; for example, $x - 2$ vanishes when x equals 2.

Variable A symbol used to stand for any one of a set of numbers, points, or other entities; the set is called the *range* of the variable, and any member of the set is called a *value* of the variable. This is in contrast to a *constant* which stands for a particular thing; thus, a value of a variable is a constant, and a variable stands in place of constants. For example, in algebra, symbols such as "x," "y," "a," "b," etc., are used as variables, while some constants are

285

"2," "$\frac{1}{2}$," etc. Also, in geometry "P," "Q" are used as variables designating points. Such descriptions as "integral variable," "rational variable," "real variable" mean variables whose ranges are the set of all integers, rational numbers, real numbers, respectively. See **Symbol**.

Variables are essential to mathematical language, and they are used in a variety of ways. In an expression or sentence, such as "$x^2 - 3x + 1$" or "$x + y$ is greater than $x - y$," the variable can serve as a blank, holding a place for constants; replacement of the variable "x" in the first by any constant produces another constant, while replacement of both "x" and "y" in the second produces a specific statement, true or false (in replacement, equal constants are substituted at different occurrences of the same variable). Variables are used to state general mathematical **formulas**; they serve as unknowns in the solution of conditional equations; they are used to describe a family of graphs or functions (where they are called **parameters**, or arbitrary constants). Variables occur in describing a function, as in "$f(x) = 2x^2 + 1$." The role of the variable as a cross-reference symbol is studied in logic, as in expressing the sentence "he told him he was to go" unambiguously in the form "x told y that y was to go"; the theory of the propositional **quantifier** is concerned with this aspect.

Ref. [81, 115, 148].

Variable, Dependent and Independent
When a *function* is described as a correspondence from values of one variable to values of a second, the first is called the *independent variable,* and the second the *dependent variable.*

286

Variable, Random See **Random variable**.

Variance The second power of the **standard deviation**.

Variation An equation relating values of one variable to those of others. Certain simple types of variations are given particular names. An equation of the form $y = kx$ is a *direct variation* of y with x; y is said to *vary directly* as x, or to be *directly proportional* to x. An equation of the form $y = k/x$ (same as $xy = k$) is an *inverse variation* of y with x; y is said to *vary inversely* as x, or to be *inversely proportional* to x. An equation $z = kxy$ is a *joint variation* of z with x and y (this is also a direct variation of z with xy). A *combined variation* is any equation with one variable set equal to an expression in several others; for example, $z = kx^2/y$ is a combined variation of z with x and y (z varies directly with x^2 and inversely with y). See **Proportionality**.

Vector An entity representable by a directed line segment, and subject to certain operations and relations (described below). It may be interpreted as a physical quantity, such as velocity, force, or displacement, which has both magnitude and direction; it is also representable as a set of numbers (an ordered pair in the plane, and an ordered triple in space; see below). Two directed segments with the same direction and

length are understood to represent the same vector; hence, any vector can be identified with a directed segment having its initial point at the origin O of a rectangular coordinate system. A *unit vector* is one of length 1; the *zero vector* (length 0) is represented by a point. Vectors are *orthogonal* if they lie along perpendicular lines.

In the *algebra of vectors,* which treats vectors symbolically, certain operations on vectors occur. The *negative* of a vector **V**, denoted by −**V**, is the vector **V** with its direction

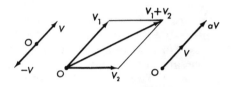

reversed. The *addition* of vectors is defined by the following *parallelogram law:* the *sum* of two vectors, $V_1 + V_2$ is the directed diagonal of the parallelogram whose sides are the given vectors. (This definition corresponds to the way that vectorial physical entities combine.) Addition is also called *composition,* and the sum called the *resultant* of the vectors. The sum of **V** and its negative, −**V**, is the zero vector; the sum of **V** and the zero vector is **V**. When two vectors V_1 and V_2 lie on a line, then addition corresponds to ordinary (algebraic) addition of numbers. The length, or *absolute value,* of a vector **V** is sometimes denoted by $|V|$; it satisfies the *triangle inequality* $|V_1 + V_2| \leq |V_1| + |V_2|$ (a side of a triangle is less than the sum of the other two).

In the algebra of vectors, a real number is called a *scalar. Scalar multiplication* of a number a and a vector **V**, which has the effect of expanding, shrinking, or reversing **V**, is defined as follows: the scalar product

a**V** is the vector **(1)** whose length is the numerical value of a times the length of **V**, and **(2)** whose direction is that of **V** or −**V**, according to whether a is positive or negative (for example, −2**V** has twice the length of **V** and is directed opposite to **V**). The *inner product,* or scalar product, of two vectors, denoted by $V_1 \cdot V_2$, is the following scalar: the product of the length of one vector times the length of the projection of the other on it; it equals $l_1 l_2 \cos \theta$, with θ the angle between the vectors and l_1, l_2 their lengths. When $V_1 \cdot V_2 = 0$, the vectors V_1 and V_2 are orthogonal.

A basic notion is the representation of a vector as a linear combination of other vectors. Let V_1 and V_2 be two fixed vectors in a plane; then a vector of the form $aV_1 + bV_2$ is called a *linear combination* of V_1 and V_2. If V_1 and V_2 are *linearly independent,* that is, do not lie along a common line (when sharing initial points), then every vector in the plane is a linear combination of them, and V_1, V_2 is a *basis* for the plane vectors. (If V_1 and V_2 lie along a line, their linear combinations lie along that line.) If V_1 and V_2 are also orthogonal, then they are an *orthogonal basis;* if they are orthogonal and of unit length they are an *orthonormal basis.* A convenient orthonormal basis consists of the unit vectors E_1,

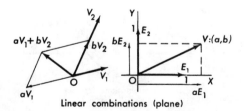

Linear combinations (plane)

E_2 along the positive axes of a rectangular coordinate system. In this case, in the expression of a vector **V** as a linear combination $a\mathbf{E}_1 + b\mathbf{E}_2$, the coefficients a and b are the coordinates (a, b) of the terminal point of $\mathbf{V}$. The vectors $a\mathbf{E}_1$ and $b\mathbf{E}_2$ are the *components* of $\mathbf{V}$ along the x-axis and y-axis, respectively.

When plane vectors $\mathbf{V}$ are represented in this way by coordinates (a, b), the various operations among vectors take the form of ordinary algebraic operations on these coordinates. More precisely, let $\mathbf{V}_1$ and $\mathbf{V}_2$ be the vectors (a_1, b_1) and (a_2, b_2); then $-\mathbf{V}_1$ is the vector $(-a_1, -b_1)$, the sum $\mathbf{V}_1 + \mathbf{V}_2$ is the vector $(a_1 + a_2, b_1 + b_2)$, and the inner product $\mathbf{V}_1 \cdot \mathbf{V}_2$ is the number $a_1 a_2 + b_1 b_2$; also the product of a with (a_1, b_1) is the vector $(a a_1, a b_1)$. (The designation of a plane vector by (a, b) can also be thought of as identifying it as a complex number $a + bi$; addition of complex numbers, for example, then corresponds to vector addition.)

The preceding notions extend to vectors in space. There, three vectors $\mathbf{V}_1$, $\mathbf{V}_2$, $\mathbf{V}_3$ which are not in a common plane are said to be linearly independent; they make up a basis for vectors—every vector is a linear combination $a\mathbf{V}_1 + b\mathbf{V}_2 + c\mathbf{V}_3$ of the three. This combination is pictured as the diagonal of the parallelepiped whose sides are $a\mathbf{V}_1$, $b\mathbf{V}_2$, and $c\mathbf{V}_3$.

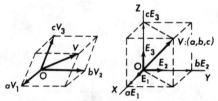

Linear combinations (space)

If the vectors $\mathbf{V}_1$, $\mathbf{V}_2$, $\mathbf{V}_3$ are orthogonal in pairs, they make up an orthogonal basis; if they are also unit vectors, they comprise an ortho-

normal basis. The unit vectors $\mathbf{E}_1$, $\mathbf{E}_2$, $\mathbf{E}_3$ along the positive axes of a rectangular coordinate system in space provide a convenient orthonormal basis. When $\mathbf{V}$ is written as a linear combination $a\mathbf{E}_1 + b\mathbf{E}_2 + c\mathbf{E}_3$, the number triple (a, b, c) is the terminal point of $\mathbf{V}$. The vectors $a\mathbf{E}_1$, $b\mathbf{E}_2$, $c\mathbf{E}_3$ are the components of $\mathbf{V}$ along the coordinate axes. Again, representing the vector by its coordinate triple (a, b, c) translates operations on vectors into ordinary algebra, just as with plane vectors.

Vectors in *spaces of higher dimension* are most conveniently represented directly in terms of coordinates. For example, vectors in four-space are quadruples of numbers (a, b, c, d). The length of a vector is $\sqrt{a^2 + b^2 + c^2 + d^2}$; the sum of two vectors (a_1, b_1, c_1, d_1) and (a_2, b_2, c_2, d_2) is $(a_1 + a_2, b_1 + b_2, c_1 + c_2, d_1 + d_2)$, and the inner product is $a_1 a_2 + b_1 b_2 + c_1 c_2 + d_1 d_2$. Two vectors are orthogonal if their inner product is 0. The four unit vectors $(1, 0, 0, 0)$, $(0, 1, 0, 0)$, $(0, 0, 1, 0)$, $(0, 0, 0, 1)$ comprise an orthogonal basis; every vector can be expressed as a linear combination of these. The set of plane vectors, space vectors, or n-dimensional vectors are finite dimensional **vector spaces** (or *linear vector spaces*); such spaces, introduced in the middle of the nineteenth century, are of importance in pure and applied mathematics. A generalization to an infinite number of dimensions is provided by **Hilbert space**.

Ref. [26, 75, 89, 127].

Vector Space (Syn.: Linear vector space) As a mathematical system, the following generalization of vectors in the plane or in space. Let A be a set of elements in which a *binary operation* is defined, say $U +$

V, for any two members U and V of A; suppose further that a *scalar product* aV of any real number a and any member V of the set is defined (yielding a member U of the given set). Then A is a (real) vector space under these operations in case the following axioms are satisfied: **(1)** A is a commutative **group** under " $+$ "; **(2)** the *distributive laws* $a(U + V) = aU + aV$, and $(a + b)V = aV + bV$ hold; **(3)** *the associative law* $(ab)V = a(bV)$ holds; and **(4)** $1 \cdot V = V$. See **Vector**.

Vectorial Angle   See **Polar coordinates in plane**.

Velocity   The study of nonuniform motion is a major application of the differential calculus, closely associated with the invention of the calculus. In *rectilinear motion* (that is motion along a line), the position of a particle at time t is given by its location $x(t)$ on a linear scale; the (instantaneous) velocity at any time t is then the derivative $dx(t)/dt$ (which is positive or negative according to whether the motion is to the right or left, on a usual linear scale). In the case of *plane curvilinear motion* (that is, motion along a plane curve) the position of a particle at time t can be specified by its rectangular coordinates $x(t)$, $y(t)$; the instantaneous velocity is then represented by a *vector,* or directed line segment, which is tangent to the curve. It is described by two components v_x and v_y, the velocities along the x-direction and y-direction, respectively; these components are given as derivatives by the formulas

$$v_z = \frac{dx(t)}{dt}, \quad v_y = \frac{dy(t)}{dt}.$$

The *speed* of motion is the length of the vector, or $\sqrt{v_z^2 + v_y^2}$. If the po-

sition of the particle is specified by the arc-length distance $s(t)$ from a fixed point on the curve, then the speed equals the numerical value of $ds(t)/dt$. Similar descriptions apply to motion in space.   See **Acceleration**.

Venn Diagram   A schematic device for representing relations and operations in the **algebra of sets**.
Ref. [44, 115].

Versine Function (Syn.: Versed sine function)   A **trigonometric function** defined as $1 - \cos A$, and written "vers A"; rarely used.

Vertex   See particular figures such as **Ellipse, Polygon, Polyhedron**, etc.

Vertex Angle   In an **isosceles** triangle, the angle formed by the equal sides.

Vertical   In the plane (space), parallel to the second (third) axis of a rectangular coordinate system.

Vertical Angles (Syn.: Opposite angles)   For *plane angles,* two angles with a common vertex in which the sides of one are the extensions of those of the other. Two intersecting

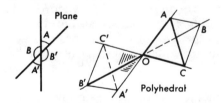

lines form two pairs of vertical angles (A, A' and B, B' in the figure). Vertical angles are equal [this is one of the earliest theorems in the history of mathematics (Thales, sixth century B.C.)]. For *polyhedral angles* in space, angles with a common vertex in which the edges of one are the extensions of the edges of the other

289

(*OABC* and *OA'B'C'* in the figure). Opposite angles are symmetric, or oppositely congruent, polyhedral angles; they have equal measure as solid angles.

Vinculum   See **Parentheses**.

Volume   A numerical measure expressing three-dimensional extent in space. A geometric cube of side 1 has volume 1, or *unit* volume; the volume of any portion of space can be thought of as the number of such units it contains [this is not necessarily a whole number, or even a rational number (fraction)]. By the volume of a closed surface or polyhedron is meant the volume of its interior. The volume of a rectangular solid is the product of its three dimensions; this can be used as the basis for defining the volume of other figures. The volume of a tetrahedron turns out to have the value of $\frac{1}{3}$ the area of the base times the altitude; any polyhedron can be divided into tetrahedrons, and its volume is then given as the sum of the volumes of the tetrahedrons. The volume of a curved *closed surface*, such as a sphere, can be gotten at by the volume of an inscribed polyhedron; the volume of the closed surface is taken as the *limit* of the volumes of an infinite sequence of inscribed polyhedrons, which approach the curved surface as their limiting figure. This method leads, for example, to the well-known formula $4\pi r^3/3$ for the volume of a sphere. A useful fact is that volumes of similar figures are in the ratio of the third powers of corresponding lengths (for example, if the radius of a sphere is doubled, the volume is multiplied by the factor 8). General formulas for the volumes of solids are derived in the calculus. See **Double integral, Surface of revolution** (Archimedes in the third century B.C. was able to compute volumes of special solids in the spirit of modern calculus by the early Greek "method of exhaustions"). See **Cone, Cylinder**, etc., for volumes of particular figures. Also, see **Cavalieri's theorem, Isoperimetric, Theorem of Pappus**.

Vulgar Fraction (Syn.: Common fraction)   A fraction which is a ratio of whole numbers, such as $\frac{2}{3}$ or $\frac{8}{5}$.

W

Wallis' Product   See **Pi, π**.

Wedge   See **Spherical wedge**.

Well-ordered Set   See **Ordered set**.

Whole Number   Any one of the **natural numbers**, 1, 2, 3, ...

Word   In a **digital computer**, the string of symbols which may occupy one storage location; it is transported and, typically, processed by the computer as one item. A word can represent different kinds of information; for example, it may be interpreted by the control unit as a coded instruction and by the arithmetic unit as numerical information.

X

X-Axis, Y-Axis, Z-Axis   The *x*-axis and *y*-axis (and *z*-axis) are the first and second (and third) axes, respectively, of a system of **Cartesian coordinates in the plane (space)**.

X-Coordinate, Y-Coordinate, Z-Coordinate   The coordinates along the *x*-, *y*-, *z*-axes, respectively.

X-Intercept, Y-Intercept, Z-Intercept See **Intercept**.

Z

Zeno's Paradox See **Paradox**.

Zero In arithmetic, the number denoted by "0"; it is the "identity element" of addition, that is, $x + 0 = 0 + x = x$, for any number x. It satisfies the following equations: $x - 0 = x, 0 - x = -x, 0 \cdot x = 0$. In the case of division, $0 \div x = 0$, provided $x \neq 0$; but *division* by zero is not an allowable arithmetical operation. However, the indeterminant form $0 \div 0$ can sometimes assume a value in the sense of a limit.

Zero may be thought of as the cardinal number of the empty set (set with no members). Also, the symbol "0" is used to denote the empty set itself in the algebra of sets.

Zero Exponent The expression x^0, with **exponent** 0, has the value 1 (provided $x \neq 0$).

Zero of Function A value of the argument, or independent variable, for which the corresponding value of the function is zero; hence, for a given function $f(x)$, a solution of the equation $f(x) = 0$.

Zone In solid geometry, a surface which is the portion of a sphere included between two parallel planes meeting the sphere. If one of the planes is tangent to the sphere, it is a *zone of one base;* if both planes intersect the sphere, it is a *zone of two bases.* A circle in which either plane intersects the sphere is a *base* of the zone. The *altitude* is a perpendicular line segment (or its length h) between the parallel planes. The area of a

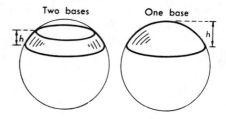

Two bases   One base

zone equals $2\pi rh$, where r is the radius of the sphere (this is the same as the length of a great circle times the altitude). The solid made up of a zone and the planar surfaces of its bases is a *spherical segment.*

Zermelo's Axiom See **Axiom of choice** (syn.).

291

APPENDIX A
LIST OF REFERENCES·

1. Albers, D. J. and Alexanderson, G. I. (eds), *Mathematical People: Profiles and Interviews*, Birkhauser, Boston, 1985.

2. Allendoerfer, C. B., and Oakley, C. O., *Principles of Mathematics*, 3rd ed., McGraw-Hill, New York, 1969.

3. Angel, A. A. and Porter, S. R., *A Survey of Mathematics with Applications*, 2nd ed., Addison-Wesley, Reading, Mass., 1985.

4. Arnold, J. N., *The Slide Rule-Principles and Applications*, Prentice-Hall, New York, 1954.

5. Ashby, W. R., *An Introduction to Cybernetics*, Barnes and Noble, New York, 1984.

6. Ball, W. W. and Coxeter, H. S. M., *Mathematical Recreations and Essays*, 13th ed., Dover, New York, 1987.

7. Barnette, D., *Map Coloring, Polyhedra and the Four-Color Problem*, Dolciani Mathematical Expositions, Mathematical Association of America, Wash., D.C., 1983.

8. Beck, A., Bleicher, M. N. and Crowe, D. W., *Excursions Into Mathematics*, Worth Publishers, New York, 1969.

9. Beckman, P., *A History of π (pi)*, 5th ed., Golem Press, Boulder, Colo., 1982.

10. Bell, E. T., *Men of Mathematics*, Dover, New York, 1937.

11. Bell, E. T., *Mathematics, Queen and Servant of Science*, McGraw-Hill, New York, 1951.

12. Benson, W. H. and Jacoby, O., *The New Recreations with Magic Squares*, Dover, New York, 1976.

13. Bezuszka, S., et al., *Perfect Numbers*, Boston College, Chestnut Hill, Mass., 1980.

14. Blackwell, D., *Basic Statistics*, McGraw-Hill, New York, 1969.

15. Bockner, S., *The Role of Mathematics in the Rise of Science*, Princeton University Press, Princeton, New Jersey, 1981.

16. Bold, B., *Famous Problems of Mathematics. A History of Constructions with Straight Edge and Compasses*, Van Nostrand, New York, 1969.

17. Boyer, C. B., *A History of Mathematics*, Princeton University Press, Princeton, New Jersey, 1985.

18. Brook, D. E., *Elementary Algebra for Today*, Prentice-Hall, Englewood Cliffs, New Jersey, 1985.

293

19. Brookshear, J. G., *Computer Science: An Overview*, Benjamin/Cummings, New York, 1985.

20. Budden, F. J., *The Fascination of Groups*, Cambridge University Press, New York, 1972.

21. Bunch, B. H., *Mathematical Fallacies and Paradoxes*, Van Nostrand, New York, 1982.

22. Burington, R. S., *Handbook of Mathematical Tables and Formulas*, 5th ed., McGraw-Hill, New York, 1973.

23. Burton, D. M., *Elementary Number Theory*, Allyn and Bacon, Boston, Mass., 1980.

24. Burton, D. M., *The History of Mathematics. An Introduction*, Allyn and Bacon, Boston, Mass., 1985.

25. Campbell, D. M. and Higgings, J. C. (eds.), *Mathematics: People Problems Results*, Wadsworth, Belmont, Calif., 1984, 3 vols.

26. Campbell, H. G., *An Introduction to Matrices, Vectors, and Linear Programming*, Appleton-Century-Crofts, New York, 1965.

27. Chinn, W. G., and Steenrod, N. E., *First Concepts of Topology*, Random House, New York, 1966.

28. Courant, R., and Robbins, H., *What is Mathematics*, Oxford University Press, New York, 1961.

29. Dantzig, T., *Number, the Language of Science*, 4th edit., Free Press, New York, 1967.

30. Dauben, J. W., *Georg Cantor: His Mathematics and Philosophy of the Infinite*, Harvard University Press, Cambridge, Mass., 1979.

31. David, F. N., *Games, God and Gambling*, Hafner, New York, 1962.

32. Davis, P. J., *The Mathematics of Matrices*, Blaisdell, New York, 1965.

33. Davis, P. J., *The Lore of Large Numbers*, New Mathematical Library, Mathematical Association of America, Wash., D.C., 1975.

34. Davis, P. J., and Hersh, R., *The Mathematical Experience*, Birkhäuser, Boston, 1980.

35. Davis, W. S., *Business Data Processing*, Addison-Wesley, Reading, Mass., 1978.

36. Deitel, H. M. and B., *Computers and Data Processing*, Academic Press, New York, 1985.

37. Dorf, R. C., *Introduction to Computers and Computer Science*, Boyd and Fraser, San Francisco, 1972.

38. Dudley, U., *A Budget of Trisections*, Springer-Verlag, New York, 1987.

39. Edwards, C. H., *The Historical Development of the Calculus*, Springer-Verlag, New York, 1979.

40. Eves, H., *An Introduction to the History of Mathematics*, 5th ed., Saunders, Philadelphia, 1983.

41. Eves, H., *Great Moments in Mathematics (After 1650)*, Dolciani Mathematical Expositions, Mathematical Association of America, Wash., D.C., 1983.

42. Eves, H., and Newsom, C. V., *An Introduction to the Foundations and Fundamental Concepts of Mathematics*, rev. ed., Holt, Rinehart and Winston, New York, 1965.

43. Flegg, G., *Numbers: Their History and Meaning*, Schocken, New York, 1983.

44. Freund, J. E., *A Modern Introduction to Mathematics*, Prentice-Hall, Englewood Cliffs, N.J., 1956.

45. Freund, J. E., *Modern Elementary Statistics*, 5th ed., Prentice-Hall, Englewood Cliffs, New Jersey, 1979.

46. Fults, J. L., *Magic Squares*, Open Court, LaSalle, Ill., 1974.

47. Gamow, G., *One, Two, Three—Infinity*, Bantam Books, New York, 1971.

48. Gans, D., *An Introduction to Non-Euclidean Geometry*, Academic Press, New York, 1973.

49. George, F. H., *The Foundations of Cybernetics*, Gordon and Breach, New York, 1977.

50. Glicksman, A. M., *An Introduction to Linear Programming and the Theory of Games*, Wiley, New York, 1963.

51. Goldman, S., *Information Theory*, Dover, New York, 1968.

52. Gray, J., *Ideas of Space: Euclidean, Non-Euclidean, and Relatavistic*, Clarendon Press, New York, 1979.

53. Greenberg, M. J., *Euclidean and Non-Euclidean Geometry*, W. H. Freeman, San Francisco, 1974.

54. Griffiths, H. B., *Surfaces*, 2nd ed., Cambridge University Press, New York, 1981.

55. Grossman, I., and Magnus, W., *Groups and Their Graphs*, New Mathematical Library, Mathematical Association of America, Wash., D.C., 1964.

56. Guillen, Michael, *Bridges to Infinity: The Human Side of Mathematics*, Houghton Mifflin, Boston, Mass., 1983.

57. Guy, R. E., *Unsolved Problems in Number Theory*, Springer-Verlag, New York, 1981.

58. Hall, A. R., *Philosophers at War: The Quarrel Between Newton and Leibniz*, Cambridge University Press, New York, 1980.

59. Hall, T., *Carl Friedrich Gauss*, MIT Press, Cambridge, Mass., 1970.

60. Hamming, R. W., *Computers and Society*, McGraw-Hill, New York, 1972.

61. Havel, D., *The Spirit of Computing*, Addison-Wesley, Reading, Mass., 1987.

62. Heims, S. J., *John Von Neumann and Norbert Wiener*, MIT Press, Cambridge, Mass., 1982.

63. Hillier, F. S., and Lieberman, G. J., *Operations Research*, 2nd ed., Holden-Day, San Francisco, 1974.

64. Hogben, L., *Mathematics for the Million*, 4th ed., Norton, New York, 1968.

65. Hoggatt, V. E., *Fibonacci and Lucas Numbers*, Houghton Mifflin, Boston, 1969.

66. Holden, A., *Shapes, Space, and Symmetry*, Columbia University Press, New York, 1971.

67. Ifrah, G., *From One to Zero: A Universal History of Numbers*, Viking, New York, 1985.

68. Infeld, L., *Whom the Gods Love: The Story of Evariste Galois*, NCTM, Reston, Va., 1978.

69. Jacobs, H. W., *Mathematics: A Human Endeavor*, 2nd ed., W. H. Freeman, San Francisco, 1982.

70. Johnson, L. H., *Nomography and Empirical Equations*, Wiley, New York, 1966.

71. Johnson, P. E., *A History of Set Theory*, Prindle, Weber and Schmidt, Boston, 1972.

72. Jones, D. S., *Elementary Information Theory*, Oxford University Press, New York, 1979.

73. Kasner, E. and Newman, J., *Mathematics and the Imagination*, Simon and Schuster, New York, 1967.

74. Kazarinoff, N. D., *Geometric Inequalities*, New Mathematical Library, Mathematical Association of America, Wash, D.C., 1961.

75. Kemeny, J. G., Snell, J. L., and Thompson, G. R., *Introduction to Finite Mathematics*, 3rd ed., Prentice-Hall, Englewood Cliffs, New Jersey, 1974.

76. Kennedy, H. C., *Peano: Life and Works of Giuseppe Peano*, Reidel Publ., Co., Boston, 1980.

77. Kimble, G. A., *How to Use (and Misuse) Statistics*, Prentice-Hall, Englewood Cliffs, New Jersey, 1978.

78. Kline, M. (ed.), *Mathematics: An Introduction to Its Spirit and Use*, W. H. Freeman, San Francisco, 1979.

79. Kramer, E. E., *The Nature and Growth of Modern Mathematics*, Princeton University Press, Princeton, New Jersey, 1982.

80. Kunz, K. S., *Numerical Analysis*, McGraw-Hill, New York, 1957.

81. Levi, H., *Elements of Algebra*, 4th ed., Chelsea Publishing Co., New York, 1961.

82. Linn, C. F., *The Golden Mean: Mathematics and the Fine Arts*, Doubleday, Garden City, New York, 1974.

83. Lockwood, E. H., and MacMillan, R. H., *Geometric Symmetry*, Cambridge University Press, New York, 1978.

84. Loweke, G. P., *The Lore of Prime Numbers*, Vantage Press, New York, 1982.

85. Mahoney, M. S., *The Mathematical Career of Pierre de Fermat*, Princeton University Press, Princeton, New Jersey, 1973.

86. Maistrov, L. E., *Probability Theory: A Historical Sketch*, Academic Press, New York, 1974.

87. Maly, K. and Hanson, A. R., *Fundamentals of the Computing Sciences*, Prentice-Hall, Englewood Cliffs, New Jersey, 1978.

88. Maor, E., *To Infinity and Beyond: A Cultural History of the Infinite*, Birkhäuser, Boston, 1987.

89. May, K. O., *Elements of Modern Mathematics*, Addison-Wesley, Reading, Mass., 1962.

90. McCloskey, J. F., and Trefethen, F. N. (eds.), *Operations Research for Management*, The Johns-Hopkins Press, Baltimore, 1956.

91. McCorduck, P., *Machines Who Think*, W. H. Freeman, San Francisco, 1979.

92. McCracken, D. D., *Digital Computer Programming*, Wiley, New York, 1957.

93. McHale, D., *George Boole: His Life and Work*, Boole Press, Dublin, 1985.

94. Meserve, B. E. and Sobel, M. A., *Contemporary Mathematics*, 3rd ed., Prentice-Hall, Englewood Cliffs, New Jersey, 1981.

95. Meyer, B., *An Introduction to Axiomatic Systems*, Prindle, Webster and Schmidt, Boston, 1974.

96. Miller, N., *Limits, The Concept and Its Role in Mathematics*, Blaisdell, New York, 1964.

97. Montaga, A. and Snyder, S. S., *Man and the Computer*, Auerbach Publishers, Philadelphia, 1972.

98. Moon, G., *The Abacus: Its History; its design, its possibilities in the modern world*, Gordon and Breach, New York, 1971.

99. Moore, G. H., *Zermelo's Axiom of Choice: Its Origins, Development, and Influence*, Springer-Verlag, New York, 1982.

100. Newman, J. R., (ed.), *The World of Mathematics*, Simon and Schuster, New York, 1956-60, 4 vols.

101. Newsom, C. V., *Mathematical Discourses: The Heart of Mathematical Science*, Prentice-Hall, Englewood Cliffs, New Jersey, 1963.

102. Niven, I., *Mathematics of Choice*, New Mathematical Library, Mathematical Association of America, Wash., D.C., 1965.

103. Northrop, E. P., *Riddles in Mathematics, A Book of Paradoxes*, Krieger, New York, 1975.

104. Nosal, M., *Basic Probability and Applications*, Saunders, Philadelphia, Penn., 1977.

105. O'Beirne, T. H., *Puzzles and Paradoxes*, Dover, New York, 1984.

106. Ore, O., *Invitation to Number Theory*, New Mathematical Library, Mathematical Association of America, Wash., D.C., 1967.

107. Otto, E., *Nomography*, Pergamon, New York, 1963.

108. Pachel, E., *The Mathematics of Games and Gambling*, New Mathematical Library, Mathematical Association of America, Wash. D.C., 1981.

109. Paulos, J. A., *Mathematics and Humor*, University of Chicago Press, Chicago, Illinois, 1980.

110. Pearce, P. and S., *Polyhedra Primer*, D. Van Nostrand, New York, 1978.

111. Pedoe, D., *Circles, A Mathematical View*, Dover, New York, 1979.

112. Phillips, D. T., Ravindran, A. and Solberg, J. J., *Operations Research: Principles and Practice*, Wiley, New York, 1976.

113. Pierce, J. R., *An Introduction to Information Theory*, 2nd ed., Dover, New York, 1980.

114. Quine, W. V., *The Ways of Paradox and Other Essays*, rev. ed., Harvard University Press, Cambridge, Mass., 1976.

115. Quine, W. V., *Methods of Logic*, 4th ed., Harvard University Press, Cambridge, Mass., 1982.

116. Reid, C., *Hilbert*, Springer-Verlag, New York, 1970.

117. Resnikoff, H. L., and Wells, R. O., *Mathematics in Civilization*, Dover, New York, 1984.

118. Richardson, T., *A Guide to Metrics*, Prakken Publ., Ann Arbor, Michigan, 1978.

119. Rosen, J., *Symmetry Discovered: Concepts and Applications in Nature and Science*, Cambridge University Press, New York, 1975.

120. Rosenbach, J. B., and Whitman, E. A., *College Algebra*, 4th ed., Ginn, Boston, 1958.

121. Rucker, B., *Infinity and the Mind*, Birkhäuser, Boston, 1982.

122. Rucker, R., *The 4th Dimension: Toward a Geometry of Higher Reality*, Houghton Mifflin, Boston, Mass., 1984.

123. Russell, B., *The Autobiography of Bertrand Russell*, Little, Brown, Boston, 1967.

124. Saaty, T. L. and Kainen, P. C., *The Four-Color Problem: Assault and Conquest*, McGraw, New York, 1977.

125. Savage, J. E., Magidson, S., and Stein, A. M., *The Mystical Machine: Issues and Ideas in Computing*, Addison-Wesley, Reading, Mass., 1986.

126. Sawyer, W. W., *Introducing Mathematics*, 4 vols., Penguin Books, New York, 1964-70.

127. Schwartz, J. T., *Introduction to Matrices and Vectors*, McGraw-Hill, New York, 1961.

128. Seymour, F. E. and Smith, P. J., *Plane and Spherical Trigonometry*, Macmillan, New York, 1946.

129. Smart, J. R., *Metric Math: The Modernized Metric System (SI)*, Brooks/Cole, Monterey, California, 1974.

130. Smythe, W. R., and Johnson, L. A., *Introduction to Linear Programming with Applications*, Prentice-Hall, Englewood Cliffs, New Jersey, 1966.

131. Solow, D., *How to Read and Do Proofs: An Introduction to Mathematical Thought Process*, Wiley, New York, 1982.

132. Sondheimer, E., and Rogerson, A., *Number and Infinity: A Historical Account of Mathematical Concepts*, Cambridge University Press, New York, 1981.

133. Sowa, J. F., *Conceptual Structures: Information Processing in Mind and Machine*, Addison-Wesley, Reading, Mass., 1984.

134. Stabler, E. R., *An Introduction to Mathematical Thought*, Addison-Wesley, Reading, Mass., 1959.

135. Steen, L. A. (ed.), *Mathematics Today, Twelve Informal Essays*, Springer-Verlag, New York, 1978.

136. Steen, L. A. (ed.), *Mathematics Tomorrow*, Springer-Verlag, New York, 1981.

137. Stein, K., *Mathematics. The Man-Made Universe*, 3rd ed., W. H. Freeman, San Francisco, 1976.

138. Stewart, I., *Concepts of Modern Mathematics*, Penguin, New York, 1975.

139. Stewart, I., *The Problems of Mathematics*, Oxford University Press, New York, 1987.

140. Titchmarsh, E. C., *Mathematics for the General Reader*, Dover, New York, 1981.

141. Trappl, R. (ed.), *Cybernetics: Theory and Applications*, Hemisphere Publishing Corp., Washington, 1983.

142. Vilenkin, N. Ya., *Stories About Sets*, Academic Press, New York, 1968.

143. Wang, Hao, *Popular Lectures on Mathematical Logic*, Van Nostrand Reinhold, New York, 1981.

144. Weaver, W., *Lady Luck: The Theory of Probability*, Dover, New York, 1982.

145. Weeks, J. R., *The Shape of Space*, Pure and Applied Mathematics, Vol. 96. Dekker, New York, 1985.

146. Weizenbaum, J., *Computer Power and Human Reason: From Judgment to Calculation*, W. H. Freeman, San Francisco, 1976.

147. Welchons, A. M., and Krichenberger, W. R., *New Solid Geometry*, Ginn and Co., New York, 1955.

148. Whitehead, A. N., *An Introduction to Mathematics*, Oxford University Press, New York, 1958.

149. Wilder, R. L., *Introduction to the Foundations of Mathematics*, 2nd ed., Wiley, New York, 1965.

150. Williams, J. D., *The Compleat Strategist*, (rev. ed.), McGraw-Hill, New York, 1966.

151. Wonnacott, T. H., and R. J., *Introductory Statistics for Business and Economics*, 3rd ed., Wiley, New York, 1984.

152. Young, J. F., *Information Theory*, Wiley, New York, 1971.

153. Zippin, L., *Uses of Infinity*, New Mathematical Library, Mathematical Association of America, Wash., D.C., 1962.

APPENDIX B

FAMOUS MATHEMATICIANS*

ABEL, NIELS HENRIK (1802–29) Norwegian. Algebraic functions, solution of fifth-degree equation. Pioneer in rigorous standards of modern mathematics.

APPOLLONIUS (about 230 B.C.) Greek. Geometry, astronomy. Developed comprehensive theory of conics in classic treatise *Conic Sections.*

ARCHIMEDES (287–212 B.C.) Greek. Geometry, areas and volumes by "method of exhaustions," astronomy, mechanics, and hydrostatics. Greatest scientist of antiquity; anticipated spirit of modern mathematics.

BERNOULLIS Swiss family, including JAMES, or JAKOB (1654–1705), JOHN (1667–1748), and DANIEL (1700–82). Analytic geometry and calculus, calculus of variations, probability, mathematical physics. Pioneers in development of the calculus.

BOLYAI, JOHANN (1802–60) Hungarian. An originator of non-Euclidean geometry.

BOOLE, GEORGE (1815–64) English. Symbolic logic. Initiated modern logic in treatise, *Laws of Thought.*

BROUWER, L. E. J. (1882–1966) Dutch. Foundations of mathematics, topology. Leader of school of intuitionism.

CANTOR, GEORG (1845–1918) German. Creator of theory of infinite sets and transfinite numbers, shaping modern foundations of mathematics. Pioneer in theory of irrational numbers.

CAUCHY, AUGUSTIN LOUIS (1789–1857) French. Analysis, functions of complex variable, theory of groups, other fields. Initiator of rigorous methods in the calculus; unusually prolific.

CAYLEY, ARTHUR (1821–95) English. Theory of matrices, geometry of *n*-dimensional space, higher algebra. Productive in various fields of mathematics.

DEDEKIND, RICHARD (1831–1916) German. Continuity and irrational numbers, modern theory of algebraic numbers.

DESCARTES, RENÉ (1596–1650) French. Invented and developed analytic geometry in classic work, the *Method,* marking start of modern mathematics. Philosopher.

EUCLID (about 300 B.C.) Greek. Systematized Greek mathematics as a deductive system in famous thirteen books of *Elements*; profoundly influenced mathematical and scientific thought.

EUDOXUS (about 370 B.C.) Greek. Invented early theory of irrational numbers; created the "method of exhaustions," anticipating the calculus.

EULER, LEONHARD (1707–83) Swiss. Calculus, calculus of variations, theory of numbers, applied mathematics. Pioneer in development of calculus; remarkably prolific in all mathematics.

FERMAT, PIERRE (1601–65) French. Father of modern theory of numbers. Originator in analytic ge-

---

* See E. T. Bell, *Men of Mathematics,* Simon and Schuster, New York, 1937.

ometry, differential calculus, and probability.

FOURIER, JOSEPH (1768–1830) French. Mathematical physics. His treatise *Mathematical Theory of Heat* opened new fields of mathematics and physics.

GALOIS, ÉVARISTE (1811–32) French. Brief work in theory of algebraic equations shaped modern higher algebra.

GAUSS, CARL FRIEDRICH (1777–1855) German. Theory of surfaces, functions of complex variable, non-Euclidean geometry, mathematical physics, other fields. Wrote profound work, *Arithmetical Researches*, in theory of numbers. Astronomer. Ranks with Archimedes and Newton as scientific genius.

HAMILTON, WM. ROWAN (1805–65) Irish. Pioneer in optics, mathematical physics. Invented theory of quaternions (generalization of complex numbers).

HERMITE, CHARLES (1822–1901) French. Theory of numbers, general equation of fifth degree, transcendental numbers.

HILBERT, DAVID (1862–1943) German. Creator of Twentieth-century mathematics and logic. Works include classic *Foundations of Geometry*. Leader of school of axiomatics in logical foundations.

JACOBI, CARL G. J. (1804–51) German. Theory of numbers, algebraic functions, mathematical physics. Founder of theory of determinants.

KLEIN, FELIX (1849–1925) German. Developed unified theory of geometry. Influential teacher.

KRONECKER, LEOPOLD (1823–91) German. Modern higher algebra; father of intuitionism in foundations of mathematics.

LAGRANGE, JOSEPH LOUIS (1736–1813) French. Analysis, theory of numbers, celestial mechanics, other fields. His masterpiece, *Analytical Mechanics,* unified dynamics. Greatest mathematician of eighteenth century.

LAPLACE, PIERRE SIMON (1749–1827) French. Mathematical astronomy and probability. Monumental *Celestial Mechanics* expounded comprehensive theory of the solar system.

LEGENDRE, ADRIEN MARIE (1752–1833) French. Theory of numbers and analysis. Published influential revision of Euclid's *Elements.*

LEIBNIZ, GOTTFRIED WILHELM (1646–1716) German. Inventor of the calculus (with Newton), and its modern notation. Anticipated modern symbolic logic. Highly original in many fields of knowledge.

LOBACHEVSKY, NICOLAI I. (1793–1856) Russian. Pioneer in non-Euclidean geometry.

NEUMANN, JOHN VON (1903–57) Hungarian and American. Foundations of mathematics, analysis, abstract mathematics, mathematical physics. Creator of theory of games; pioneer in computing machines and theory of automata.

NEWTON, ISAAC (1642–1727) English. Created the calculus (with Leibniz), providing the impetus for modern mathematics. Created modern physics in masterpiece *Principia* (or "Mathematical principles of natural philosophy"). One of the greatest scientific geniuses of all time.

PASCAL, BLAISE (1623–62) French. Projective geometry and probability.

POINCARÉ, JULES HENRI (1854–1912) French. Creator of twentieth-century mathematics; analysis, topology, mathematical physics, other fields. Works include treatise *New Methods of Celestial Mechanics* and writings on the scientific method.

PONCELET, JEAN VICTOR (1788–1867) French. Originator of projective geometry.

PYTHAGORAS (about 540 B.C.) Greek. Founder of Greek mathematics. Philosopher and mystic.

RIEMANN, BERNHARD (1826–1866) German. Highly original research, greatly affecting modern analysis, geometry, and mathematical physics. Wrote classic *On the Hypotheses Which Form the Foundation of Geometry*.

RUSSEL, BERTRAND A. W. (1872–1970) English. Logical foundations of mathematics. Influential treatise *Principia mathematica* (with A. N. WHITEHEAD). Philosopher.

SYLVESTER, JAMES JOSEPH (1814–97) English. Modern higher algebra and theory of numbers.

VIETA, FRANCOIS (1540–1603) French. Early work in algebra and trigonometry. Inventor of modern notation of algebra.

WEIERSTRASS, KARL (1815–97) German. Analysis and power series, calculus of variations, continuity and irrational numbers, other areas. Leader of modern rigor; influential teacher.

WIENER, NORBERT (1894–1964) American. Analysis, applied mathematics. Creator of cybernetics. Pioneer in theory of automata.

APPENDIX C

MATHEMATICAL SYMBOLS

Arithmetic, Algebra

SYMBOL	DEFINITION	SYMBOL	DEFINITION
$= (\neq)$	equals (does not equal)	a^{-n}	reciprocal, $\dfrac{1}{a^n}$
$\equiv$	is identical with	$a^{m/n}$	nth root of a^m
$+$	positive; plus	$\|a\|$	absolute value of a
$-$	negative; minus	G.C.D., g.c.d.	greatest common divisor
$\pm$	plus or minus		
$a + b$	addition	L.C.D., l.c.d.	least common divisor
$a - b$	subtraction		
$ab, a \cdot b, a \times b$	multiplication	L.C.M., l.c.m.	least common multiple
$a \div b$	division		
$\dfrac{a}{b}, a/b$	division; fraction	%	per cent
		$f(a)$	value of function f at a
$a{:}b$	ratio of a to b		
$> (<)$	is greater (less) than	$\log, \log_{10}$	common logarithm (base 10)
$\geqq, \geq (\leqq, \leq)$	is greater (less) than or equal to	$\log_e, \ln$	natural logarithm (base e)
$a < b < c$	a is less than b and b is less than c	$\log_b$	logarithm (base b)
		antilog	antilogarithm
a^2	product $a \cdot a$	colog	cologarithm
a^n	product $a \cdot a \cdots a$ of n factors a	$n!, \lfloor n$	n factorial = product $1 \cdot 2 \cdots n$
$\sqrt{a}, a^{1/2}$	square root of a	e	base of natural logarithms
$\sqrt[n]{a}, a^{1/n}$	nth root of a		
a^0	unity, 1	i	imaginary unit $\sqrt{-1}$
a^{-1}	reciprocal, $\dfrac{1}{a}$		

Geometry, Trigonometry, Analytic Geometry

SYMBOL	DEFINITION	SYMBOL	DEFINITION
$\angle$ ($\measuredangle$)	angle (angles)	tan	tangent function
$\triangle$ ($\triangle$)	triangle (triangles)	cot, ctn	cotangent function
$\square$ ($\square$)	parallelogram (parallelograms)	sec	secant function
		csc	cosecant function
$\square$ ($\square$)	square (squares)	$\sin^{-1}$, arc sin	inverse sine function
$\bigcirc$ ($\odot$)	circle (circles)		
$p \parallel q$	p is parallel to q	$\cos^{-1}$, arc cos	inverse cosine function
$\parallel$ ($\parallel_s$)	parallel (parallels)		
$p \perp q$	p is perpendicular to q	$\tan^{-1}$, arc tan	inverse tangent function
$\perp$ ($\perp_s$)	perpendicular (perpendiculars)	$\cot^{-1}$, arc cot	inverse cotangent function
$\cong, \equiv$	is congruent to	$\sec^{-1}$, arc sec	inverse secant function
$\sim$	is similar to		
s.a.s. (s.s.s.)	side, angle, side (side, side, side)	$\csc^{-1}$, arc csc	inverse cosecant function
$\therefore$	therefore	O	origin of coordinate system
Q.E.D.	which was to be proved	X	axis of abscissas
PQ	line segment between P and Q	Y	axis of ordinates
		(x, y)	rectangular coordinates in plane
$\overrightarrow{PQ}$	vector, or directed line segment from P to Q	(x, y, z)	rectangular coordinates in space
		(r, θ), (ρ, θ)	polar coordinates in plane
$\overarc{PQ}$	arc between P and Q	(r, θ, φ), (ρ, θ, φ)	spherical coordinates in space
π	ratio of circumference to diameter of circle	(r, θ, z)	cylindrical coordinates in space
$A°$	A degrees of angle	m	slope of line in plane
A' (A'')	A minutes (seconds) of angle	l, m, n	direction numbers in space
$\doteq$	is measured by	$\cos \alpha$, $\cos \beta$, $\cos \gamma$	direction cosines in space
sin	sine function		
cos	cosine function		

Calculus

SYMBOL	DEFINITION
$\sum\limits_{i=1}^{n} a_i$	sum $a_1 + a_2 + \cdots + a_n$
$\{a_n\}, (a_n)$	infinite sequence $a_1, a_2, a_3, \ldots$
$\sum\limits_{i=1}^{\infty} a_i$	infinite series $a_1 + a_2 + a_3 + \cdots$; sum of series
$\lim\limits_{n\to\infty} a_n$	limit of a_n as n approaches infinity
$\lim\limits_{x=a} f(x), \lim\limits_{x\to a} f(x)$	limit of $f(x)$ at $x = a$
$\triangle x, dx$	increment of independent variable x
$\triangle f(x)$	increment $f(x + \triangle x) - f(x)$ of function $f(x)$
$\dfrac{df(x)}{dx}, D_x f(x), f'(x)$	derivative of $f(x)$
$df(x)$	differential of $f(x) = f'(x)dx$
$\int f(x)dx$	indefinite integral of $f(x)$
$\int_a^b f(x)dx$	definite integral of $f(x)$ from a to b
$F(x)]_a^b$	difference $F(b) - F(a)$
$\dfrac{d^2 f(x)}{dx^2}, D_x^2 f(x), f''(x)$	second derivative of $f(x)$
$\dfrac{d^n f(x)}{dx^n}, D_x^{(n)} f(x), f^{(n)}(x)$	n^{th} derivative of $f(x)$
$\dfrac{\partial f(x, y)}{\partial x}, D_x f(x,y), f_x(x,y)$	partial derivative of $f(x, y)$ with respect to x
$f^{-1}(x)$	inverse function of $f(x)$
$\dfrac{\partial^2 f(x, y)}{\partial y \partial x}, f_{yx}(x, y)$	second partial derivative of $f(x, y)$ with respect to x and then y

Logic, Set Theory

SYMBOL	DEFINITION
$\sim P, \bar{P}$	not P
$P \wedge Q, P \cdot Q$	P and Q
$P \vee Q$	P or Q
$P \rightarrow Q, P \supset Q$	if P then Q
$P \leftrightarrow Q, P \equiv Q$	P if and only if Q
$a \, \varepsilon \, A$	a is a member of set A
$a \, R \, b$	a is in the relation R to b
$A = B$	set A is identical with set B
$A \subset B$	set A is included in set B
$A \supset B$	set A contains set B
$A \cap B, A \cdot B$	intersection (product) of sets A and B
$A \cup B, A + B$	union (sum) of sets A and B
$CA, A', \bar{A}$	complement of set A
$\Lambda, 0, \phi$	null set
$V, 1$	universe
$(x), (Vx), A_x$	for every x
$(\exists x), (Ex), E_x$	for some x; there exists an x such that
$\aleph_0$	aleph null $=$ cardinal number of positive integers
c	cardinal number of real numbers
ω	first ordinal number greater than the positive integers

Greek Alphabet

LOWER CASE	CAPITAL	NAME
α	A	alpha
β	B	beta
γ	Γ	gamma
δ	Δ	delta
ε	E	epsilon
ζ	Z	zeta
η	H	eta
θ	Θ	theta
ι	I	iota
κ	K	kappa
λ	Λ	lambda
μ	M	mu
ν	N	nu
ξ	Ξ	xi
ο	O	omicron
π	Π	pi
ρ	P	rho
σ	Σ	sigma
τ	T	tau
υ	Υ	upsilon
φ	Φ	phi
χ	X	chi
ψ	Ψ	psi
ω	Ω	omega

APPENDIX D
TABLES
Table 1—Powers and Roots

n	n^2	n^3	$\sqrt{n}$	$\sqrt[3]{n}$	n	n^2	n^3	$\sqrt{n}$	$\sqrt[3]{n}$
1	1	1	1.000	1.000	51	2 601	132 651	7.141	3.708
2	4	8	1.414	1.260	52	2 704	140 608	7.211	3.733
3	9	27	1.732	1.442	53	2 809	148 877	7.280	3.756
4	16	64	2.000	1.587	54	2 916	157 464	7.348	3.780
5	25	125	2.236	1.710	55	3 025	166 375	7.416	3.803
6	36	216	2.449	1.817	56	3 136	175 616	7.483	3.826
7	49	343	2.646	1.913	57	3 249	185 193	7.550	3.849
8	64	512	2.828	2.000	58	3 364	195 112	7.616	3.871
9	81	729	3.000	2.080	59	3 481	205 379	7.681	3.893
10	100	1 000	3.162	2.154	60	3 600	216 000	7.746	3.915
11	121	1 331	3.317	2.224	61	3 721	226 981	7.810	3.936
12	144	1 728	3.464	2.289	62	3 844	238 328	7.874	3.958
13	169	2 197	3.606	2.351	63	3 969	250 047	7.937	3.979
14	196	2 744	3.742	2.410	64	4 096	262 144	8.000	4.000
15	225	3 375	3.873	2.466	65	4 225	274 625	8.062	4.021
16	256	4 096	4.000	2.520	66	4 356	287 496	8.124	4.041
17	289	4 913	4.123	2.571	67	4 489	300 763	8.185	4.062
18	324	5 832	4.243	2.621	68	4 624	314 432	8.246	4.082
19	361	6 859	4.359	2.668	69	4 761	328 509	8.307	4.102
20	400	8 000	4.472	2.714	70	4 900	343 000	8.367	4.121
21	441	9 261	4.583	2.759	71	5 041	357 911	8.426	4.141
22	484	10 648	4.690	2.802	72	5 184	373 248	8.485	4.160
23	529	12 167	4.796	2.844	73	5 329	389 017	8.544	4.179
24	576	13 824	4.899	2.884	74	5 476	405 224	8.602	4.198
25	625	15 625	5.000	2.924	75	5 625	421 875	8.660	4.217
26	676	17 576	5.099	2.962	76	5 776	438 976	8.718	4.236
27	729	19 683	5.196	3.000	77	5 929	456 533	8.775	4.254
28	784	21 952	5.292	3.037	78	6 084	474 552	8.832	4.273
29	841	24 389	5.385	3.072	79	6 241	493 039	8.888	4.291
30	900	27 000	5.477	3.107	80	6 400	512 000	8.944	4.309
31	961	29 791	5.568	3.141	81	6 561	531 441	9.000	4.327
32	1 024	32 768	5.657	3.175	82	6 724	551 368	9.055	4.344
33	1 089	35 937	5.745	3.208	83	6 889	571 787	9.110	4.362
34	1 156	39 304	5.831	3.240	84	7 056	592 704	9.165	4.380
35	1 225	42 875	5.916	3.271	85	7 225	614 125	9.220	4.397
36	1 296	46 656	6.000	3.302	86	7 396	636 056	9.274	4.414
37	1 369	50 653	6.083	3.332	87	7 569	658 503	9.327	4.431
38	1 444	54 872	6.164	3.362	88	7 744	681 472	9.381	4.448
39	1 521	59 319	6.245	3.391	89	7 921	704 969	9.434	4.465
40	1 600	64 000	6.325	3.420	90	8 100	729 000	9.487	4.481
41	1 681	68 921	6.403	3.448	91	8 281	753 571	9.539	4.498
42	1 764	74 088	6.481	3.476	92	8 464	778 688	9.592	4.514
43	1 849	79 507	6.557	3.503	93	8 649	804 357	9.644	4.531
44	1 936	85 184	6.633	3.530	94	8 836	830 584	9.695	4.547
45	2 025	91 125	6.708	3.557	95	9 025	857 375	9.747	4.563
46	2 116	97 336	6.782	3.583	96	9 216	884 736	9.798	4.579
47	2 209	103 823	6.856	3.609	97	9 409	912 673	9.849	4.595
48	2 304	110 592	6.928	3.634	98	9 604	941 192	9.899	4.610
49	2 401	117 649	7.000	3.659	99	9 801	970 299	9.950	4.626
50	2 500	125 000	7.071	3.684	100	10 000	1 000 000	10.000	4.642

Table 1 from N. J. Lennes, J. W. Maucker, and John J. Kinsella, *A Second Course in Algebra* (New York: Macmillan, 1957).

Table 2—Common Logarithms of Numbers*

N	0	1	2	3	4	5	6	7	8	9
10	0000	0043	0086	0128	0170	0212	0253	0294	0334	0374
11	0414	0453	0492	0531	0569	0607	0645	0682	0719	0755
12	0792	0828	0864	0899	0934	0969	1004	1038	1072	1106
13	1139	1173	1206	1239	1271	1303	1335	1367	1399	1430
14	1461	1492	1523	1553	1584	1614	1644	1673	1703	1732
15	1761	1790	1818	1847	1875	1903	1931	1959	1987	2014
16	2041	2068	2095	2122	2148	2175	2201	2227	2253	2279
17	2304	2330	2355	2380	2405	2430	2455	2480	2504	2529
18	2553	2577	2601	2625	2648	2672	2695	2718	2742	2765
19	2788	2810	2833	2856	2878	2900	2923	2945	2967	2989
20	3010	3032	3054	3075	3096	3118	3139	3160	3181	3201
21	3222	3243	3263	3284	3304	3324	3345	3365	3385	3404
22	3424	3444	3464	3483	3502	3522	3541	3560	3579	3598
23	3617	3636	3655	3674	3692	3711	3729	3747	3766	3784
24	3802	3820	3838	3856	3874	3892	3909	3927	3945	3962
25	3979	3997	4014	4031	4048	4065	4082	4099	4116	4133
26	4150	4166	4183	4200	4216	4232	4249	4265	4281	4298
27	4314	4330	4346	4362	4378	4393	4409	4425	4440	4456
28	4472	4487	4502	4518	4533	4548	4564	4579	4594	4609
29	4624	4639	4654	4669	4683	4698	4713	4728	4742	4757
30	4771	4786	4800	4814	4829	4843	4857	4871	4886	4900
31	4914	4928	4942	4955	4969	4983	4997	5011	5024	5038
32	5051	5065	5079	5092	5105	5119	5132	5145	5159	5172
33	5185	5198	5211	5224	5237	5250	5263	5276	5289	5302
34	5315	5328	5340	5353	5366	5378	5391	5403	5416	5428
35	5441	5453	5465	5478	5490	5502	5514	5527	5539	5551
36	5563	5575	5587	5599	5611	5623	5635	5647	5658	5670
37	5682	5694	5705	5717	5729	5740	5752	5763	5775	5786
38	5798	5809	5821	5832	5843	5855	5866	5877	5888	5899
39	5911	5922	5933	5944	5955	5966	5977	5988	5999	6010
40	6021	6031	6042	6053	6064	6075	6085	6096	6107	6117
41	6128	6138	6149	6160	6170	6180	6191	6201	6212	6222
42	6232	6243	6253	6263	6274	6284	6294	6304	6314	6325
43	6335	6345	6355	6365	6375	6385	6395	6405	6415	6425
44	6435	6444	6454	6464	6474	6484	6493	6503	6513	6522
45	6532	6542	6551	6561	6571	6580	6590	6599	6609	6618
46	6628	6637	6646	6656	6665	6675	6684	6693	6702	6712
47	6721	6730	6739	6749	6758	6767	6776	6785	6794	6803
48	6812	6821	6830	6839	6848	6857	6866	6875	6884	6893
49	6902	6911	6920	6928	6937	6946	6955	6964	6972	6981
50	6990	6998	7007	7016	7024	7033	7042	7050	7059	7067
51	7076	7084	7093	7101	7110	7118	7126	7135	7143	7152
52	7160	7168	7177	7185	7193	7202	7210	7218	7226	7235
53	7243	7251	7259	7267	7275	7284	7292	7300	7308	7316
54	7324	7332	7340	7348	7356	7364	7372	7380	7388	7396

* Logarithm to the base 10; to obtain natural logarithm (base *e*) multiply by 2.30258 (=log$_e$10)

Table 2—Common Logarithms of Numbers, cont.

N	0	1	2	3	4	5	6	7	8	9
55	7404	7412	7419	7427	7435	7443	7451	7459	7466	7474
56	7482	7490	7497	7505	7513	7520	7528	7536	7543	7551
57	7559	7566	7574	7582	7589	7597	7604	7612	7619	7627
58	7634	7642	7649	7657	7664	7672	7679	7686	7694	7701
59	7709	7716	7723	7731	7738	7745	7752	7760	7767	7774
60	7782	7789	7796	7803	7810	7818	7825	7832	7839	7846
61	7853	7860	7868	7875	7882	7889	7896	7903	7910	7917
62	7924	7931	7938	7945	7952	7959	7966	7973	7980	7987
63	7993	8000	8007	8014	8021	8028	8035	8041	8048	8055
64	8062	8069	8075	8082	8089	8096	8102	8109	8116	8122
65	8129	8136	8142	8149	8156	8162	8169	8176	8182	8189
66	8195	8202	8209	8215	8222	8228	8235	8241	8248	8254
67	8261	8267	8274	8280	8287	8293	8299	8306	8312	8319
68	8325	8331	8338	8344	8351	8357	8363	8370	8376	8382
69	8388	8395	8401	8407	8414	8420	8426	8432	8439	8445
70	8451	8457	8463	8470	8476	8482	8488	8494	8500	8506
71	8513	8519	8525	8531	8537	8543	8549	8555	8561	8567
72	8573	8579	8585	8591	8597	8603	8609	8615	8621	8627
73	8633	8639	8645	8651	8657	8663	8669	8675	8681	8686
74	8692	8698	8704	8710	8716	8722	8727	8733	8739	8745
75	8751	8756	8762	8768	8774	8779	8785	8791	8797	8802
76	8808	8814	8820	8825	8831	8837	8842	8848	8854	8859
77	8865	8871	8876	8882	8887	8893	8899	8904	8910	8915
78	8921	8927	8932	8938	8943	8949	8954	8960	8965	8971
79	8976	8982	8987	8993	8998	9004	9009	9015	9020	9025
80	9031	9036	9042	9047	9053	9058	9063	9069	9074	9079
81	9085	9090	9096	9101	9106	9112	9117	9122	9128	9133
82	9138	9143	9149	9154	9159	9165	9170	9175	9180	9186
83	9191	9196	9201	9206	9212	9217	9222	9227	9232	9238
84	9243	9248	9253	9258	9263	9269	9274	9279	9284	9289
85	9294	9299	9304	9309	9315	9320	9325	9330	9335	9340
86	9345	9350	9355	9360	9365	9370	9375	9380	9385	9390
87	9395	9400	9405	9410	9415	9420	9425	9430	9435	9440
88	9445	9450	9455	9460	9465	9469	9474	9479	9484	9489
89	9494	9499	9504	9509	9513	9518	9523	9528	9533	9538
90	9542	9547	9552	9557	9562	9566	9571	9576	9581	9586
91	9590	9595	9600	9605	9609	9614	9619	9624	9628	9633
92	9638	9643	9647	9652	9657	9661	9666	9671	9675	9680
93	9685	9689	9694	9699	9703	9708	9713	9717	9722	9727
94	9731	9736	9741	9745	9750	9754	9759	9763	9768	9773
95	9777	9782	9786	9791	9795	9800	9805	9809	9814	9818
96	9823	9827	9832	9836	9841	9845	9850	9854	9859	9863
97	9868	9872	9877	9881	9886	9890	9894	9899	9903	9908
98	9912	9917	9921	9926	9930	9934	9939	9943	9948	9952
99	9956	9961	9965	9969	9974	9978	9983	9987	9991	9996

Table 3—Four Place Trigonometric Functions

[Characteristics of Logarithms omitted—determine by the usual rule from the value]

RADIANS	DEGREES	SINE Value	SINE Log₁₀	TANGENT Value	TANGENT Log₁₀	COTANGENT Value	COTANGENT Log₁₀	COSINE Value	COSINE Log₁₀		
.0000	0° 00'	.0000	——	.0000	——			1.0000	.0000	90° 00'	1.5708
.0029	10	.0029	.4637	.0029	.4637	343.77	.5363	1.0000	.0000	50	1.5679
.0058	20	.0058	.7648	.0058	.7648	171.89	.2352	1.0000	.0000	40	1.5650
.0087	30	.0087	.9408	.0087	.9409	114.59	.0591	1.0000	.0000	30	1.5621
.0116	40	.0116	.0658	.0116	.0658	85.940	.9342	.9999	.0000	20	1.5592
.0145	50	.0145	.1627	.0145	.1627	68.750	.8373	.9999	.0000	10	1.5563
.0175	1° 00'	.0175	.2419	.0175	.2419	57.290	.7581	.9998	.9999	89° 00'	1.5533
.0204	10	.0204	.3088	.0204	.3089	49.104	.6911	.9998	.9999	50	1.5504
.0233	20	.0233	.3668	.0233	.3669	42.964	.6331	.9997	.9999	40	1.5475
.0262	30	.0262	.4179	.0262	.4181	38.188	.5819	.9997	.9999	30	1.5446
.0291	40	.0291	.4637	.0291	.4638	34.368	.5362	.9996	.9998	20	1.5417
.0320	50	.0320	.5050	.0320	.5053	31.242	.4947	.9995	.9998	10	1.5388
.0349	2° 00'	.0349	.5428	.0349	.5431	28.636	.4569	.9994	.9997	88° 00'	1.5359
.0378	10	.0378	.5776	.0378	.5779	26.432	.4221	.9993	.9997	50	1.5330
.0407	20	.0407	.6097	.0407	.6101	24.542	.3899	.9992	.9996	40	1.5301
.0436	30	.0436	.6397	.0437	.6401	22.904	.3599	.9990	.9996	30	1.5272
.0465	40	.0465	.6677	.0466	.6682	21.470	.3318	.9989	.9995	20	1.5243
.0495	50	.0494	.6940	.0495	.6945	20.206	.3055	.9988	.9995	10	1.5213
.0524	3° 00'	.0523	.7188	.0524	.7194	19.081	.2806	.9986	.9994	87° 00'	1.5184
.0553	10	.0552	.7423	.0553	.7429	18.075	.2571	.9985	.9993	50	1.5155
.0582	20	.0581	.7645	.0582	.7652	17.169	.2348	.9983	.9993	40	1.5126
.0611	30	.0610	.7857	.0612	.7865	16.350	.2135	.9981	.9992	30	1.5097
.0640	40	.0640	.8059	.0641	.8067	15.605	.1933	.9980	.9991	20	1.5068
.0669	50	.0669	.8251	.0670	.8261	14.924	.1739	.9978	.9990	10	1.5039
.0698	4° 00'	.0698	.8436	.0699	.8446	14.301	.1554	.9976	.9989	86° 00'	1.5010
.0727	10	.0727	.8613	.0729	.8624	13.727	.1376	.9974	.9989	50	1.4981
.0756	20	.0756	.8783	.0758	.8795	13.197	.1205	.9971	.9988	40	1.4952
.0785	30	.0785	.8946	.0787	.8960	12.706	.1040	.9969	.9987	30	1.4923
.0814	40	.0814	.9104	.0816	.9118	12.251	.0882	.9967	.9986	20	1.4893
.0844	50	.0843	.9256	.0846	.9272	11.826	.0728	.9964	.9985	10	1.4864
.0873	5° 00'	.0872	.9403	.0875	.9420	11.430	.0580	.9962	.9983	85° 00'	1.4835
.0902	10	.0901	.9545	.0904	.9563	11.059	.0437	.9959	.9982	50	1.4806
.0931	20	.0929	.9682	.0934	.9701	10.712	.0299	.9957	.9981	40	1.4777
.0960	30	.0958	.9816	.0963	.9836	10.385	.0164	.9954	.9980	30	1.4748
.0989	40	.0987	.9945	.0992	.9966	10.078	.0034	.9951	.9979	20	1.4719
.1018	50	.1016	.0070	.1022	.0093	9.7882	.9907	.9948	.9977	10	1.4690
.1047	6° 00'	.1045	.0192	.1051	.0216	9.5144	.9784	.9945	.9976	84° 00'	1.4661
.1076	10	.1074	.0311	.1080	.0336	9.2553	.9664	.9942	.9975	50	1.4632
.1105	20	.1103	.0426	.1110	.0453	9.0098	.9547	.9939	.9973	40	1.4603
.1134	30	.1132	.0539	.1139	.0567	8.7769	.9433	.9936	.9972	30	1.4573
.1164	40	.1161	.0648	.1169	.0678	8.5555	.9322	.9932	.9971	20	1.4544
.1193	50	.1190	.0755	.1198	.0786	8.3450	.9214	.9929	.9969	10	1.4515
.1222	7° 00'	.1219	.0859	.1228	.0891	8.1443	.9109	.9925	.9968	83° 00'	1.4486
.1251	10	.1248	.0961	.1257	.0995	7.9530	.9005	.9922	.9966	50	1.4457
.1280	20	.1276	.1060	.1287	.1096	7.7704	.8904	.9918	.9964	40	1.4428
.1309	30	.1305	.1157	.1317	.1194	7.5958	.8806	.9914	.9963	30	1.4399
.1338	40	.1334	.1252	.1346	.1291	7.4287	.8709	.9911	.9961	20	1.4370
.1367	50	.1363	.1345	.1376	.1385	7.2687	.8615	.9907	.9959	10	1.4341
.1396	8° 00'	.1392	.1436	.1405	.1478	7.1154	.8522	.9903	.9958	82° 00'	1.4312
.1425	10	.1421	.1525	.1435	.1569	6.9682	.8431	.9899	.9956	50	1.4283
.1454	20	.1449	.1612	.1465	.1658	6.8269	.8342	.9894	.9954	40	1.4254
.1484	30	.1478	.1697	.1495	.1745	6.6912	.8255	.9890	.9952	30	1.4224
.1513	40	.1507	.1781	.1524	.1831	6.5606	.8169	.9886	.9950	20	1.4195
.1542	50	.1536	.1863	.1554	.1915	6.4348	.8085	.9881	.9948	10	1.4166
.1571	9° 00'	.1564	.1943	.1584	.1997	6.3138	.8003	.9877	.9946	81° 00'	1.4137
		Value Log₁₀ COSINE		Value Log₁₀ COTANGENT		Value Log₁₀ TANGENT		Value Log₁₀ SINE		DEGREES	RADIANS

Table 3—Four Place Trigonometric Functions, cont.

[Characteristics of Logarithms omitted—determine by the usual rule from the value]

Radians	Degrees	Sine Value	Sine Log₁₀	Tangent Value	Tangent Log₁₀	Cotangent Value	Cotangent Log₁₀	Cosine Value	Cosine Log₁₀		
.1571	9° 00′	.1564	.1943	.1584	.1997	6.3138	.8003	.9877	.9946	81° 00′	1.4137
.1600	10	.1593	.2022	.1614	.2078	6.1970	.7922	.9872	.9944	50	1.4108
.1629	20	.1622	.2100	.1644	.2158	6.0844	.7842	.9868	.9942	40	1.4079
.1658	30	.1650	.2176	.1673	.2236	5.9758	.7764	.9863	.9940	30	1.4050
.1687	40	.1679	.2251	.1703	.2313	5.8708	.7687	.9858	.9938	20	1.4021
.1716	50	.1708	.2324	.1733	.2389	5.7694	.7611	.9853	.9936	10	1.3992
.1745	10° 00′	.1736	.2397	.1763	.2463	5.6713	.7537	.9848	.9934	80° 00′	1.3963
.1774	10	.1765	.2468	.1793	.2536	5.5764	.7464	.9843	.9931	50	1.3934
.1804	20	.1794	.2538	.1823	.2609	5.4845	.7391	.9838	.9929	40	1.3904
.1833	30	.1822	.2606	.1853	.2680	5.3955	.7320	.9833	.9927	30	1.3875
.1862	40	.1851	.2674	.1883	.2750	5.3093	.7250	.9827	.9924	20	1.3846
.1891	50	.1880	.2740	.1914	.2819	5.2257	.7181	.9822	.9922	10	1.3817
.1920	11° 00′	.1908	.2806	.1944	.2887	5.1446	.7113	.9816	.9919	79° 00′	1.3788
.1949	10	.1937	.2870	.1974	.2953	5.0658	.7047	.9811	.9917	50	1.3759
.1978	20	.1965	.2934	.2004	.3020	4.9894	.6980	.9805	.9914	40	1.3730
.2007	30	.1994	.2997	.2035	.3085	4.9152	.6915	.9799	.9912	30	1.3701
.2036	40	.2022	.3058	.2065	.3149	4.8430	.6851	.9793	.9909	20	1.3672
.2065	50	.2051	.3119	.2095	.3212	4.7729	.6788	.9787	.9907	10	1.3643
.2094	12° 00′	.2079	.3179	.2126	.3275	4.7046	.6725	.9781	.9904	78° 00′	1.3614
.2123	10	.2108	.3238	.2156	.3336	4.6382	.6664	.9775	.9901	50	1.3584
.2153	20	.2136	.3296	.2186	.3397	4.5736	.6603	.9769	.9899	40	1.3555
.2182	30	.2164	.3353	.2217	.3458	4.5107	.6542	.9763	.9896	30	1.3526
.2211	40	.2193	.3410	.2247	.3517	4.4494	.6483	.9757	.9893	20	1.3497
.2240	50	.2221	.3466	.2278	.3576	4.3897	.6424	.9750	.9890	10	1.3468
.2269	13° 00′	.2250	.3521	.2309	.3634	4.3315	.6366	.9744	.9887	77° 00′	1.3439
.2298	10	.2278	.3575	.2339	.3691	4.2747	.6309	.9737	.9884	50	1.3410
.2327	20	.2306	.3629	.2370	.3748	4.2193	.6252	.9730	.9881	40	1.3381
.2356	30	.2334	.3682	.2401	.3804	4.1653	.6196	.9724	.9878	30	1.3352
.2385	40	.2363	.3734	.2432	.3859	4.1126	.6141	.9717	.9875	20	1.3323
.2414	50	.2391	.3786	.2462	.3914	4.0611	.6086	.9710	.9872	10	1.3294
.2443	14° 00′	.2419	.3837	.2493	.3968	4.0108	.6032	.9703	.9869	76° 00′	1.3265
.2473	10	.2447	.3887	.2524	.4021	3.9617	.5979	.9696	.9866	50	1.3235
.2502	20	.2476	.3937	.2555	.4074	3.9136	.5926	.9689	.9863	40	1.3206
.2531	30	.2504	.3986	.2586	.4127	3.8667	.5873	.9681	.9859	30	1.3177
.2560	40	.2532	.4035	.2617	.4178	3.8208	.5822	.9674	.9856	20	1.3148
.2589	50	.2560	.4083	.2648	.4230	3.7760	.5770	.9667	.9853	10	1.3119
.2618	15° 00′	.2588	.4130	.2679	.4281	3.7321	.5719	.9659	.9849	75° 00′	1.3090
.2647	10	.2616	.4177	.2711	.4331	3.6891	.5669	.9652	.9846	50	1.3061
.2676	20	.2644	.4223	.2742	.4381	3.6470	.5619	.9644	.9843	40	1.3032
.2705	30	.2672	.4269	.2773	.4430	3.6059	.5570	.9636	.9839	30	1.3003
.2734	40	.2700	.4314	.2805	.4479	3.5656	.5521	.9628	.9836	20	1.2974
.2763	50	.2728	.4359	.2836	.4527	3.5261	.5473	.9621	.9832	10	1.2945
.2793	16° 00′	.2756	.4403	.2867	.4575	3.4874	.5425	.9613	.9828	74° 00′	1.2915
.2822	10	.2784	.4447	.2899	.4622	3.4495	.5378	.9605	.9825	50	1.2886
.2851	20	.2812	.4491	.2931	.4669	3.4124	.5331	.9596	.9821	40	1.2857
.2880	30	.2840	.4533	.2962	.4716	3.3759	.5284	.9588	.9817	30	1.2828
.2909	40	.2868	.4576	.2994	.4762	3.3402	.5238	.9580	.9814	20	1.2799
.2938	50	.2896	.4618	.3026	.4808	3.3052	.5192	.9572	.9810	10	1.2770
.2967	17° 00′	.2924	.4659	.3057	.4853	3.2709	.5147	.9563	.9806	73° 00′	1.2741
.2996	10	.2952	.4700	.3089	.4898	3.2371	.5102	.9555	.9802	50	1.2712
.3025	20	.2979	.4741	.3121	.4943	3.2041	.5057	.9546	.9798	40	1.2683
.3054	30	.3007	.4781	.3153	.4987	3.1716	.5013	.9537	.9794	30	1.2654
.3083	40	.3035	.4821	.3185	.5031	3.1397	.4969	.9528	.9790	20	1.2625
.3113	50	.3062	.4861	.3217	.5075	3.1084	.4925	.9520	.9786	10	1.2595
.3142	18° 00′	.3090	.4900	.3249	.5118	3.0777	.4882	.9511	.9782	72° 00′	1.2566
		Value Cosine	Log₁₀	Value Cotangent	Log₁₀	Value Tangent	Log₁₀	Value Sine	Log₁₀	Degrees	Radians

313

Table 3—Four Place Trigonometric Functions, cont.

[Characteristics of Logarithms omitted—determine by the usual rule from the value]

Radians	Degrees	Sine Value	Sine Log₁₀	Tangent Value	Tangent Log₁₀	Cotangent Value	Cotangent Log₁₀	Cosine Value	Cosine Log₁₀		
.3142	18° 00′	.3090	.4900	.3249	.5118	3.0777	.4882	.9511	.9782	72° 00′	1.2566
.3171	10	.3118	.4939	.3281	.5161	3.0475	.4839	.9502	.9778	50	1.2537
.3200	20	.3145	.4977	.3314	.5203	3.0178	.4797	.9492	.9774	40	1.2508
.3229	30	.3173	.5015	.3346	.5245	2.9887	.4755	.9483	.9770	30	1.2479
.3258	40	.3201	.5052	.3378	.5287	2.9600	.4713	.9474	.9765	20	1.2450
.3287	50	.3228	.5090	.3411	.5329	2.9319	.4671	.9465	.9761	10	1.2421
.3316	19° 00′	.3256	.5126	.3443	.5370	2.9042	.4630	.9455	.9757	71° 00′	1.2392
.3345	10	.3283	.5163	.3476	.5411	2.8770	.4589	.9446	.9752	50	1.2363
.3374	20	.3311	.5199	.3508	.5451	2.8502	.4549	.9436	.9748	40	1.2334
.3403	30	.3338	.5235	.3541	.5491	2.8239	.4509	.9426	.9743	30	1.2305
.3432	40	.3365	.5270	.3574	.5531	2.7980	.4469	.9417	.9739	20	1.2275
.3462	50	.3393	.5306	.3607	.5571	2.7725	.4429	.9407	.9734	10	1.2246
.3491	20° 00′	.3420	.5341	.3640	.5611	2.7475	.4389	.9397	.9730	70° 00′	1.2217
.3520	10	.3448	.5375	.3673	.5650	2.7228	.4350	.9387	.9725	50	1.2188
.3549	20	.3475	.5409	.3706	.5689	2.6985	.4311	.9377	.9721	40	1.2159
.3578	30	.3502	.5443	.3739	.5727	2.6746	.4273	.9367	.9716	30	1.2130
.3607	40	.3529	.5477	.3772	.5766	2.6511	.4234	.9356	.9711	20	1.2101
.3636	50	.3557	.5510	.3805	.5804	2.6279	.4196	.9346	.9706	10	1.2072
.3665	21° 00′	.3584	.5543	.3839	.5842	2.6051	.4158	.9336	.9702	69° 00′	1.2043
.3694	10	.3611	.5576	.3872	.5879	2.5826	.4121	.9325	.9697	50	1.2014
.3723	20	.3638	.5609	.3906	.5917	2.5605	.4083	.9315	.9692	40	1.1985
.3752	30	.3665	.5641	.3939	.5954	2.5386	.4046	.9304	.9687	30	1.1956
.3782	40	.3692	.5673	.3973	.5991	2.5172	.4009	.9293	.9682	20	1.1926
.3811	50	.3719	.5704	.4006	.6028	2.4960	.3972	.9283	.9677	10	1.1897
.3840	22° 00′	.3746	.5736	.4040	.6064	2.4751	.3936	.9272	.9672	68° 00′	1.1868
.3869	10	.3773	.5767	.4074	.6100	2.4545	.3900	.9261	.9667	50	1.1839
.3898	20	.3800	.5798	.4108	.6136	2.4342	.3864	.9250	.9661	40	1.1810
.3927	30	.3827	.5828	.4142	.6172	2.4142	.3828	.9239	.9656	30	1.1781
.3956	40	.3854	.5859	.4176	.6208	2.3945	.3792	.9228	.9651	20	1.1752
.3985	50	.3881	.5889	.4210	.6243	2.3750	.3757	.9216	.9646	10	1.1723
.4014	23° 00′	.3907	.5919	.4245	.6279	2.3559	.3721	.9205	.9640	67° 00′	1.1694
.4043	10	.3934	.5948	.4279	.6314	2.3369	.3686	.9194	.9635	50	1.1665
.4072	20	.3961	.5978	.4314	.6348	2.3183	.3652	.9182	.9629	40	1.1636
.4102	30	.3987	.6007	.4348	.6383	2.2998	.3617	.9171	.9624	30	1.1606
.4131	40	.4014	.6036	.4383	.6417	2.2817	.3583	.9159	.9618	20	1.1577
.4160	50	.4041	.6065	.4417	.6452	2.2637	.3548	.9147	.9613	10	1.1548
.4189	24° 00′	.4067	.6093	.4452	.6486	2.2460	.3514	.9135	.9607	66° 00′	1.1519
.4218	10	.4094	.6121	.4487	.6520	2.2286	.3480	.9124	.9602	50	1.1490
.4247	20	.4120	.6149	.4522	.6553	2.2113	.3447	.9112	.9596	40	1.1461
.4276	30	.4147	.6177	.4557	.6587	2.1943	.3413	.9100	.9590	30	1.1432
.4305	40	.4173	.6205	.4592	.6620	2.1775	.3380	.9088	.9584	20	1.1403
.4334	50	.4200	.6232	.4628	.6654	2.1609	.3346	.9075	.9579	10	1.1374
.4363	25° 00′	.4226	.6259	.4663	.6687	2.1445	.3313	.9063	.9573	65° 00′	1.1345
.4392	10	.4253	.6286	.4699	.6720	2.1283	.3280	.9051	.9567	50	1.1316
.4422	20	.4279	.6313	.4734	.6752	2.1123	.3248	.9038	.9561	40	1.1286
.4451	30	.4305	.6340	.4770	.6785	2.0965	.3215	.9026	.9555	30	1.1257
.4480	40	.4331	.6366	.4806	.6817	2.0809	.3183	.9013	.9549	20	1.1228
.4509	50	.4358	.6392	.4841	.6850	2.0655	.3150	.9001	.9543	10	1.1199
.4538	26° 00′	.4384	.6418	.4877	.6882	2.0503	.3118	.8988	.9537	64° 00′	1.1170
.4567	10	.4410	.6444	.4913	.6914	2.0353	.3086	.8975	.9530	50	1.1141
.4596	20	.4436	.6470	.4950	.6946	2.0204	.3054	.8962	.9524	40	1.1112
.4625	30	.4462	.6495	.4986	.6977	2.0057	.3023	.8949	.9518	30	1.1083
.4654	40	.4488	.6521	.5022	.7009	1.9912	.2991	.8936	.9512	20	1.1054
.4683	50	.4514	.6546	.5059	.7040	1.9768	.2960	.8923	.9505	10	1.1025
.4712	27° 00′	.4540	.6570	.5095	.7072	1.9626	.2928	.8910	.9499	63° 00′	1.0996
		Value Log₁₀ Cosine		Value Log₁₀ Cotangent		Value Log₁₀ Tangent		Value Log₁₀ Sine		Degrees	Radians

Table 3—Four Place Trigonometric Functions, cont.

[Characteristics of Logarithms omitted—determine by the usual rule from the value]

Radians	Degrees	Sine Value	Log₁₀	Tangent Value	Log₁₀	Cotangent Value	Log₁₀	Cosine Value	Log₁₀		
.4712	27° 00′	.4540	.6570	.5095	.7072	1.9626	.2928	.8910	.9499	63° 00′	1.0996
.4741	10	.4566	.6595	.5132	.7103	1.9486	.2897	.8897	.9492	50	1.0966
.4771	20	.4592	.6620	.5169	.7134	1.9347	.2866	.8884	.9486	40	1.0937
.4800	30	.4617	.6644	.5206	.7165	1.9210	.2835	.8870	.9479	30	1.0908
.4829	40	.4643	.6668	.5243	.7196	1.9074	.2804	.8857	.9473	20	1.0879
.4858	50	.4669	.6692	.5280	.7226	1.8940	.2774	.8843	.9466	10	1.0850
.4887	28° 00′	.4695	.6716	.5317	.7257	1.8807	.2743	.8829	.9459	62° 00′	1.0821
.4916	10	.4720	.6740	.5354	.7287	1.8676	.2713	.8816	.9453	50	1.0792
.4945	20	.4746	.6763	.5392	.7317	1.8546	.2683	.8802	.9446	40	1.0763
.4974	30	.4772	.6787	.5430	.7348	1.8418	.2652	.8788	.9439	30	1.0734
.5003	40	.4797	.6810	.5467	.7378	1.8291	.2622	.8774	.9432	20	1.0705
.5032	50	.4823	.6833	.5505	.7408	1.8165	.2592	.8760	.9425	10	1.0676
.5061	29° 00′	.4848	.6856	.5543	.7438	1.8040	.2562	.8746	.9418	61° 00′	1.0647
.5091	10	.4874	.6878	.5581	.7467	1.7917	.2533	.8732	.9411	50	1.0617
.5120	20	.4899	.6901	.5619	.7497	1.7796	.2503	.8718	.9404	40	1.0588
.5149	30	.4924	.6923	.5658	.7526	1.7675	.2474	.8704	.9397	30	1.0559
.5178	40	.4950	.6946	.5696	.7556	1.7556	.2444	.8689	.9390	20	1.0530
.5207	50	.4975	.6968	.5735	.7585	1.7437	.2415	.8675	.9383	10	1.0501
.5236	30° 00′	.5000	.6990	.5774	.7614	1.7321	.2386	.8660	.9375	60° 00′	1.0472
.5265	10	.5025	.7012	.5812	.7644	1.7205	.2356	.8646	.9368	50	1.0443
.5294	20	.5050	.7033	.5851	.7673	1.7090	.2327	.8631	.9361	40	1.0414
.5323	30	.5075	.7055	.5890	.7701	1.6977	.2299	.8616	.9353	30	1.0385
.5352	40	.5100	.7076	.5930	.7730	1.6864	.2270	.8601	.9346	20	1.0356
.5381	50	.5125	.7097	.5969	.7759	1.6753	.2241	.8587	.9338	10	1.0327
.5411	31° 00′	.5150	.7118	.6009	.7788	1.6643	.2212	.8572	.9331	59° 00′	1.0297
.5440	10	.5175	.7139	.6048	.7816	1.6534	.2184	.8557	.9323	50	1.0268
.5469	20	.5200	.7160	.6088	.7845	1.6426	.2155	.8542	.9315	40	1.0239
.5498	30	.5225	.7181	.6128	.7873	1.6319	.2127	.8526	.9308	30	1.0210
.5527	40	.5250	.7201	.6168	.7902	1.6212	.2098	.8511	.9300	20	1.0181
.5556	50	.5275	.7222	.6208	.7930	1.6107	.2070	.8496	.9292	10	1.0152
.5585	32° 00′	.5299	.7242	.6249	.7958	1.6003	.2042	.8480	.9284	58° 00′	1.0123
.5614	10	.5324	.7262	.6289	.7986	1.5900	.2014	.8465	.9276	50	1.0094
.5643	20	.5348	.7282	.6330	.8014	1.5798	.1986	.8450	.9268	40	1.0065
.5672	30	.5373	.7302	.6371	.8042	1.5697	.1958	.8434	.9260	30	1.0036
.5701	40	.5398	.7322	.6412	.8070	1.5597	.1930	.8418	.9252	20	1.0007
.5730	50	.5422	.7342	.6453	.8097	1.5497	.1903	.8403	.9244	10	.9977
.5760	33° 00′	.5446	.7361	.6494	.8125	1.5399	.1875	.8387	.9236	57° 00′	.9948
.5789	10	.5471	.7380	.6536	.8153	1.5301	.1847	.8371	.9228	50	.9919
.5818	20	.5495	.7400	.6577	.8180	1.5204	.1820	.8355	.9219	40	.9890
.5847	30	.5519	.7419	.6619	.8208	1.5108	.1792	.8339	.9211	30	.9861
.5876	40	.5544	.7438	.6661	.8235	1.5013	.1765	.8323	.9203	20	.9832
.5905	50	.5568	.7457	.6703	.8263	1.4919	.1737	.8307	.9194	10	.9803
.5934	34° 00′	.5592	.7476	.6745	.8290	1.4826	.1710	.8290	.9186	56° 00′	.9774
.5963	10	.5616	.7494	.6787	.8317	1.4733	.1683	.8274	.9177	50	.9745
.5992	20	.5640	.7513	.6830	.8344	1.4641	.1656	.8258	.9169	40	.9716
.6021	30	.5664	.7531	.6873	.8371	1.4550	.1629	.8241	.9160	30	.9687
.6050	40	.5688	.7550	.6916	.8398	1.4460	.1602	.8225	.9151	20	.9657
.6080	50	.5712	.7568	.6959	.8425	1.4370	.1575	.8208	.9142	10	.9628
.6109	35° 00′	.5736	.7586	.7002	.8452	1.4281	.1548	.8192	.9134	55° 00′	.9599
.6138	10	.5760	.7604	.7046	.8479	1.4193	.1521	.8175	.9125	50	.9570
.6167	20	.5783	.7622	.7089	.8506	1.4106	.1494	.8158	.9116	40	.9541
.6196	30	.5807	.7640	.7133	.8533	1.4019	.1467	.8141	.9107	30	.9512
.6225	40	.5831	.7657	.7177	.8559	1.3934	.1441	.8124	.9098	20	.9483
.6254	50	.5854	.7675	.7221	.8586	1.3848	.1414	.8107	.9089	10	.9454
.6283	36° 00′	.5878	.7692	.7265	.8613	1.3764	.1387	.8090	.9080	54° 00′	.9425
		Value	Log₁₀ Cosine	Value	Log₁₀ Cotangent	Value	Log₁₀ Tangent	Value	Log₁₀ Sine	Degrees	Radians

Table 3—Four Place Trigonometric Functions, cont.

[Characteristics of Logarithms omitted—determine by the usual rule from the value]

Radians	Degrees	Sine Value	Sine Log₁₀	Tangent Value	Tangent Log₁₀	Cotangent Value	Cotangent Log₁₀	Cosine Value	Cosine Log₁₀		
.6283	36° 00′	.5878	.7692	.7265	.8613	1.3764	.1387	.8090	.9080	54° 00′	.9425
.6312	10	.5901	.7710	.7310	.8639	1.3680	.1361	.8073	.9070	50	.9396
.6341	20	.5925	.7727	.7355	.8666	1.3597	.1334	.8056	.9061	40	.9367
.6370	30	.5948	.7744	.7400	.8692	1.3514	.1308	.8039	.9052	30	.9338
.6400	40	.5972	.7761	.7445	.8718	1.3432	.1282	.8021	.9042	20	.9308
.6429	50	.5995	.7778	.7490	.8745	1.3351	.1255	.8004	.9033	10	.9279
.6458	37° 00′	.6018	.7795	.7536	.8771	1.3270	.1229	.7986	.9023	53° 00′	.9250
.6487	10	.6041	.7811	.7581	.8797	1.3190	.1203	.7969	.9014	50	.9221
.6516	20	.6065	.7828	.7627	.8824	1.3111	.1176	.7951	.9004	40	.9192
.6545	30	.6088	.7844	.7673	.8850	1.3032	.1150	.7934	.8995	30	.9163
.6574	40	.6111	.7861	.7720	.8876	1.2954	.1124	.7916	.8985	20	.9134
.6603	50	.6134	.7877	.7766	.8902	1.2876	.1098	.7898	.8975	10	.9105
.6632	38° 00′	.6157	.7893	.7813	.8928	1.2799	.1072	.7880	.8965	52° 00′	.9076
.6661	10	.6180	.7910	.7860	.8954	1.2723	.1046	.7862	.8955	50	.9047
.6690	20	.6202	.7926	.7907	.8980	1.2647	.1020	.7844	.8945	40	.9018
.6720	30	.6225	.7941	.7954	.9006	1.2572	.0994	.7826	.8935	30	.8988
.6749	40	.6248	.7957	.8002	.9032	1.2497	.0968	.7808	.8925	20	.8959
.6778	50	.6271	.7973	.8050	.9058	1.2423	.0942	.7790	.8915	10	.8930
.6807	39° 00′	.6293	.7989	.8098	.9084	1.2349	.0916	.7771	.8905	51° 00′	.8901
.6836	10	.6316	.8004	.8146	.9110	1.2276	.0890	.7753	.8895	50	.8872
.6865	20	.6338	.8020	.8195	.9135	1.2203	.0865	.7735	.8884	40	.8843
.6894	30	.6361	.8035	.8243	.9161	1.2131	.0839	.7716	.8874	30	.8814
.6923	40	.6383	.8050	.8292	.9187	1.2059	.0813	.7698	.8864	20	.8785
.6952	50	.6406	.8066	.8342	.9212	1.1988	.0788	.7679	.8853	10	.8756
.6981	40° 00′	.6428	.8081	.8391	.9238	1.1918	.0762	.7660	.8843	50° 00′	.8727
.7010	10	.6450	.8096	.8441	.9264	1.1847	.0736	.7642	.8832	50	.8698
.7039	20	.6472	.8111	.8491	.9289	1.1778	.0711	.7623	.8821	40	.8668
.7069	30	.6494	.8125	.8541	.9315	1.1708	.0685	.7604	.8810	30	.8639
.7098	40	.6517	.8140	.8591	.9341	1.1640	.0659	.7585	.8800	20	.8610
.7127	50	.6539	.8155	.8642	.9366	1.1571	.0634	.7566	.8789	10	.8581
.7156	41° 00′	.6561	.8169	.8693	.9392	1.1504	.0608	.7547	.8778	49° 00′	.8552
.7185	10	.6583	.8184	.8744	.9417	1.1436	.0583	.7528	.8767	50	.8523
.7214	20	.6604	.8198	.8796	.9443	1.1369	.0557	.7509	.8756	40	.8494
.7243	30	.6626	.8213	.8847	.9468	1.1303	.0532	.7490	.8745	30	.8465
.7272	40	.6648	.8227	.8899	.9494	1.1237	.0506	.7470	.8733	20	.8436
.7301	50	.6670	.8241	.8952	.9519	1.1171	.0481	.7451	.8722	10	.8407
.7330	42° 00′	.6691	.8255	.9004	.9544	1.1106	.0456	.7431	.8711	48° 00′	.8378
.7359	10	.6713	.8269	.9057	.9570	1.1041	.0430	.7412	.8699	50	.8348
.7389	20	.6734	.8283	.9110	.9595	1.0977	.0405	.7392	.8688	40	.8319
.7418	30	.6756	.8297	.9163	.9621	1.0913	.0379	.7373	.8676	30	.8290
.7447	40	.6777	.8311	.9217	.9646	1.0850	.0354	.7353	.8665	20	.8261
.7476	50	.6799	.8324	.9271	.9671	1.0786	.0329	.7333	.8653	10	.8232
.7505	43° 00′	.6820	.8338	.9325	.9697	1.0724	.0303	.7314	.8641	47° 00′	.8203
.7534	10	.6841	.8351	.9380	.9722	1.0661	.0278	.7294	.8629	50	.8174
.7563	20	.6862	.8365	.9435	.9747	1.0599	.0253	.7274	.8618	40	.8145
.7592	30	.6884	.8378	.9490	.9772	1.0538	.0228	.7254	.8606	30	.8116
.7621	40	.6905	.8391	.9545	.9798	1.0477	.0202	.7234	.8594	20	.8087
.7650	50	.6926	.8405	.9601	.9823	1.0416	.0177	.7214	.8582	10	.8058
.7679	44° 00′	.6947	.8418	.9657	.9848	1.0355	.0152	.7193	.8569	46° 00′	.8029
.7709	10	.6967	.8431	.9713	.9874	1.0295	.0126	.7173	.8557	50	.7999
.7738	20	.6988	.8444	.9770	.9899	1.0235	.0101	.7153	.8545	40	.7970
.7767	30	.7009	.8457	.9827	.9924	1.0176	.0076	.7133	.8532	30	.7941
.7796	40	.7030	.8469	.9884	.9949	1.0117	.0051	.7112	.8520	20	.7912
.7825	50	.7050	.8482	.9942	.9975	1.0058	.0025	.7092	.8507	10	.7883
.7854	45° 00′	.7071	.8495	1.0000	.0000	1.0000	.0000	.7071	.8495	45° 00′	.7854
		Value Cosine	Log₁₀	Value Cotangent	Log₁₀	Value Tangent	Log₁₀	Value Sine	Log₁₀	Degrees	Radians

Table 4—Important Constants

$$1° = 0.0174 \quad 5329 \text{ radians}$$
$$1' = 0.0002 \quad 9089 \text{ radians}$$
$$1'' = 0.0000 \quad 0485 \text{ radians}$$
$$1 \text{ radian} = 57°.29578$$
$$= 57° \, 17' \, 45''$$
$$\pi = 3.1415 \quad 9265$$
$$\log_{10}\pi = 0.4971 \quad 4987$$
$$e = 2.7182 \quad 8183$$
$$\log_{10}e = 0.4342 \quad 9448$$
$$\log_e 10 = \frac{1}{\log_{10}e} = 2.3025 \quad 8509$$